THE MEMOIRS OF FRAY SERVANDO TERESA DE MIER

THE MEMOIRS OF FRAY SERVANDO TERESA DE MIER

FRAY SERVANDO TERESA DE MIER

Translated from the Spanish by
HELEN LANE

EDITED AND WITH AN INTRODUCTION BY
SUSANA ROTKER

New York   Oxford
Oxford University Press
1998

Oxford University Press

Oxford New York

Athens Auckland Bangkok Bogotá Buenos Aires Calcutta
Cape Town Chennai Dar es Salaam Delhi Florence Hong Kong Istanbul
Karachi Kuala Lumpur Madrid Melbourne Mexico City Mumbai
Nairobi Paris São Paulo Singapore Taipei Tokyo Toronto Warsaw

and associated companies in

Berlin Ibadan

Copyright © 1998 by Oxford University Press, Inc.

Published by Oxford University Press, Inc.
198 Madison Avenue, New York, New York 10016

Oxford is a registered trademark of Oxford University Press, Inc.

Library of Congress Cataloging-in-Publication Data
Mier Noriega y Guerra, José Servando Teresa de, 1763–1827.
[Memorias. English]
The memoirs of Fray Servando Teresa de Mier / Fray Servando Teresa
de Mier ; edited and with an introduction by Susana Rotker ;
translated from the Spanish by Helen Lane.
p. cm. — (Library of Latin America)
Includes bibliographical references
ISBN 0-19-510673-3
ISBN 0-19-510674-1 (pbk.)
1. Mier Noriega y Guerra, José Servando Teresa de, 1763–1827.
2. Mexico—History—19th century.   3. Statesmen—Mexico—Biography.
4. Dominicans—Mexico—Biography.   5. Historians—Mexico—Biography.
I. Rotker, Susana, 1954– .   II. Lane, Helen.   III. Title.
IV. Series
F1232.M6778313   1998
972'.02'092—dc21   [B]   97-40671

1 3 5 7 9 8 6 4 2

Printed in the United States of America
on acid-free paper

Contents

Series Editors'
General Introduction

The Library of Latin America series makes available in translation major nineteenth-century authors whose work has been neglected in the English-speaking world. The titles for the translations from the Spanish and Portuguese were suggested by an editorial committee that included Jean Franco (general editor responsible for works in Spanish), Richard Graham (series editor responsible for works in Portuguese), Tulio Halperín Donghi (at the University of California, Berkeley), Iván Jaksić (at the University of Notre Dame), Naomi Lindstrom (at the University of Texas at Austin), Francine Masiello (at the University of California, Berkeley), and Eduardo Lozano of the Library at the University of Pittsburgh. The late Antonio Cornejo Polar of the University of California, Berkeley, was also one of the founding members of the committee. The translations have been funded thanks to the generosity of the Lampadia Foundation and the Andrew W. Mellon Foundation.

During the period of national formation between 1810 and into the early years of the twentieth century, the new nations of Latin America fashioned their identities, drew up constitutions, engaged in bitter struggles over territory, and debated questions of education, government, ethnicity, and culture. This was a unique period unlike the process of nation formation in Europe and one which should be more familiar than it is to students of comparative politics, history, and literature.

The image of the nation was envisioned by the lettered classes—a minority in countries in which indigenous, mestizo, black, or mulatto peasants and slaves predominated—although there were also alternative nationalisms at the grassroots level. The cultural elite were well educated in European thought and letters, but as statesmen, journalists, poets, and academics, they confronted the problem of the racial and linguistic heterogeneity of the continent and the difficulties of integrating the population into a modern nation-state. Some of the writers whose works will be translated in the Library of Latin America series played leading roles in politics. Fray Servando Teresa de Mier, a friar who translated Rousseau's *The Social Contract* and was one of the most colorful characters of the independence period, was faced with imprisonment and expulsion from Mexico for his heterodox beliefs; on his return, after independence, he was elected to the congress. Domingo Faustino Sarmiento, exiled from his native Argentina under the presidency of Rosas, wrote *Facundo: Civilización y barbarie,* a stinging denunciation of that government. He returned after Rosas' overthrow and was elected president in 1868. Andrés Bello was born in Venezuela, lived in London where he published poetry during the independence period, settled in Chile where he founded the University, wrote his grammar of the Spanish language, and drew up the country's legal code.

These post-independence intelligentsia were not simply dreaming castles in the air, but vitally contributed to the founding of nations and the shaping of culture. The advantage of hindsight may make us aware of problems they themselves did not foresee, but this should not affect our assessment of their truly astonishing energies and achievements. It is still surprising that the writing of Andrés Bello, who contributed fundamental works to so many different fields, has never been translated into English. Although there is a recent translation of Sarmiento's celebrated *Facundo,* there is no translation of his memoirs, *Recuerdos de provincia (Provincial Recollections).* The predominance of memoirs in the Library of Latin America series is no accident—many of these offer entertaining insights into a vast and complex continent.

Nor have we neglected the novel. The series includes new translations of the outstanding Brazilian writer Joaquim Maria Machado de Assis' work, including *Dom Casmurro* and *The Posthumous Memoirs of Brás Cubas.* There is no reason why other novels and writers who are not so well known outside Latin America—the Peruvian novelist Clorinda Matto de Turner's *Aves sin nido,* Nataniel Aguirre's *Juan de la Rosa,* José de Alencar's *Iracema,* Juana Manuela Gorriti's short stories—should not be read with as much interest as the political novels of Anthony Trollope.

A series on nineteenth-century Latin America cannot, however, be limited to literary genres such as the novel, the poem, and the short story. The literature of independent Latin America was eclectic and strongly influenced by the periodical press newly liberated from scrutiny by colonial authorities and the Inquisition. Newspapers were miscellanies of fiction, essays, poems, and translations from all manner of European writing. The novels written on the eve of Mexican Independence by José Joaquín Fernández de Lizardi included disquisitions on secular education and law, and denunciations of the evils of gaming and idleness. Other works, such as a well-known poem by Andrés Bello, "Ode to Tropical Agriculture," and novels such as *Amalia* by José Mármol and the Bolivian Nataniel Aguirre's *Juan de la Rosa*, were openly partisan. By the end of the century, sophisticated scholars were beginning to address the history of their countries, as did João Capistrano de Abreu in his *Capítulos de história colonial*.

It is often in memoirs such as those by Fray Servando Teresa de Mier or Sarmiento that we find the descriptions of everyday life that in Europe were incorporated into the realist novel. Latin American literature at this time was seen largely as a pedagogical tool, a "light" alternative to speeches, sermons, and philosophical tracts—though, in fact, especially in the early part of the century, even the readership for novels was quite small because of the high rate of illiteracy. Nevertheless, the vigorous orally transmitted culture of the gaucho and the urban underclasses became the linguistic repertoire of some of the most interesting nineteenth-century writers—most notably José Hernández, author of the "gauchesque" poem "Martín Fierro," which enjoyed an unparalleled popularity. But for many writers the task was not to appropriate popular language but to civilize, and their literary works were strongly influenced by the high style of political oratory.

The editorial committee has not attempted to limit its selection to the better-known writers such as Machado de Assis; it has also selected many works that have never appeared in translation or writers whose work has not been translated recently. The series now makes these works available to the English-speaking public.

Because of the preferences of funding organizations, the series initially focuses on writing from Brazil, the Southern Cone, the Andean region, and Mexico. Each of our editions will have an introduction that places the work in its appropriate context and includes explanatory notes.

We owe special thanks to Robert Glynn of the Lampadia Foundation, whose initiative gave the project a jump start, and to Richard Ekman of

Note on the Author

Fray Servando Teresa de Mier y Noriega (Mexico, 1763–1827) is, beyond a doubt, the most revealing and most polemical figure of his time because of his bold, innovative ideas, his lucidity, his corrosive humor. Mier confronted the difficult challenge of being a thinker able to link two eras, overcoming the colonial mentality in order to play an active role in movements for emancipation. Respected for his historical essays and his commitment to republicanism, going so far as to dare to propose that Creole theology concerning the Virgin of Guadalupe be revised (as a means of making the thought of his compatriots more autonomous), fray Mier was persecuted by the Inquisition for nearly thirty years and by the end of his life was regarded as one of the founding fathers of Mexico. His *Memoirs* constitute an extraordinary document: written in prison, they tell the story of his adventures as an exile and an eyewitness to the Europe of Napoleon Bonaparte. Unlike the aristocratic scientist who writes on his travels in the New World and its "savages," Mier—engaging in dialogue with Humboldt, De Pauw, Buffon—reverses the terms in which we are accustomed to thinking of the relations between central countries and the periphery: it is the Europeans who are the "barbarians" whose daily manners and mores are portrayed. A fugitive from the law and a learned scholar, a heretic and a megalomaniac, Mier continues to inflame the imagination of today's readers and writers.

Chronology of the Author

1763   Servando Teresa de Mier y Noriega is born on October 18 in
        Monterrey (Mexico), a city in what was then called the New
        Kingdom of León of New Spain. One of the principal figures
        of Mexican independence, José María Morelos, will be born
        three years later. Servando's father and mother are Joaquín
        Mier y Noriega and Antonia Guerra; he spends his childhood
        and early school years in Monterrey. He receives his bachelor's
        degree from the Dominican College of Mexico City.

1779   Mier enters the Dominican order, in Mexico City.

1780   Mier receives the degree of doctor of theology from the Col-
        lege of Porta Coeli. He returns to the Monastery of Santo
        Domingo, where he is a reader in philosophy.

1792   Mier obtains an official permit to preach.

1794   On November 8, Mier delivers the funeral sermon in honor of
        Hernán Cortés. On December 12, he preaches his famous ser-
        mon in the Collegiate Church of Guadalupe, offering a new
        version of the appearance of the Virgin of Guadalupe in Mex-
        ico. The following day an ecclesiastical trial is brought against
        him, he is kept in detention in the Monastery of Santo
        Domingo, and his permit to preach is revoked.

1795   Archbishop Alonso Núñez de Haro y Peralta issues an edict sentencing Mier to ten years' imprisonment in the monastery at Las Caldas (Santander, Spain), following the verdict against him handed down by Canons Uribe and Omaña. In addition to the prison sentence, his punishment includes the suspension in perpetuity of his right to teach, to preach from the pulpit and to act as confessor. In March he is imprisoned for a little more than two months in the Castle of San Juan de Ulúa, and then put aboard the frigate *La Nueva Empresa* and taken to Cádiz, Spain. He finally arrives in Las Caldas toward the end of the year; he escapes, is captured and is again imprisoned.

1797   Mier spends the year as a prisoner in the Monastery of San Pablo, Burgos, where he writes his *Letters to Dr. Juan Bautista Muñoz (Cartas al Dr. Juan Bantista Muñoz sobre la tradición guadalupana de México)*, a chronicler of the Indies, tracing in detail for him the Mexican tradition of the Virgin of Our Lady of Guadalupe. He asks to be transferred to Cádiz. En route to Cádiz, Mier retires to the monastery of San Francisco in Madrid, to draft his defense and bring his case to the attention of the Council of the Indies, petitioning it to examine Haro's edict.

1800   The Academy of History finds against Haro and in favor of Mier. He is sent to a monastery in Salamanca, but he eludes the authorities and flees to Madrid. They find him in Burgos, and he is sent once again to the monastery of San Francisco; he escapes, and this time he crosses the border into France disguised as a French priest.

1801   Mier lives in lodgings in Bayonne and Bordeaux. He goes to Paris with the Count of Gijón; in that city, with Simón Rodríguez, who uses the alias Samuel Robinson and was the teacher of Simón Bolívar, he founds a school for the teaching of Spanish. He cotranslates with Rodríguez Chateaubriand's *Atala*. He writes a dissertation against Count Constantine de Volney—a Girondin, rationalist and historian—which earns him the protection of the grand vicar of Paris and an appointment as head of the parish of Saint-Thomas.

1802   Mier journeys to Rome to seek secularization and authorization to hold curacies, benefices and prebends. He attempts to return to Spain in the entourage of Princess Isabel, who is about to marry Ferdinand, Prince of Asturias, but he arrives too late to accompany her. He remains in Naples for several months and then returns to Rome.

1803   Mier is granted permanent secularization. He journeys to Florence, Siena, Genoa, Barcelona, Zaragoza and Madrid, where he is again arrested.

1804   Mier is sent to the jail of Los Toribios, in Seville. He escapes through the window, is again apprehended and is kept in shackles; he falls ill and manages to make his escape.

1805   From Cádiz Mier crosses the border into Portugal and chances to witness the battle of Trafalgar. He secures a post as secretary of the Spanish consul in Lisbon.

1808   Mier aids Spaniards imprisoned by order of General Andoche Junot, the commander of the Bonapartist occupation forces in Portugal and the north of Spain. In recognition of his work in their behalf, the Spaniards name him their chaplain; Mier journeys to Catalonia to join the battalion of volunteers from Valencia. Charles IV and Ferdinand VII have abdicated the throne of Spain and been succeeded by Napoleon's brother, Joseph Bonaparte.

1809   Mier is taken prisoner by the French. They transfer him to Zaragoza and he escapes. The Central Junta of Aranjuez recommends him for a canonry in Mexico in recognition of his patriotic labors, but the Spanish rebels are defeated by the Bonapartist forces and the junta is dissolved.

1810   Mier is sent to Cádiz by his battalion of volunteers.

1811   The regency plans to give Mier the bishop's miter in the cathedral of Mexico City, but there are no vacant bishoprics and therefore he is offered instead half an annual prebend. Mier refuses it and goes to London. There he meets José María Blanco White, the exiled Spanish journalist and advocate of relative independence for America; he begins an important correspondence with him. He publishes his *Carta de un Americano al Español (Letter from an American to El Español)*.

1812   Mier continues his epistolary polemic with Blanco White on the subject of independence. He publishes his *Segunda carta de un americano al español (Second Letter from an American to El Español)*. He is already decidedly opposed to any sort of ongoing political or economic relation with Spain, defending absolute independence and arguing for an America for Americans.

1813   Mier publishes, under the pseudonym José Guerra, his *Historia de la revolución de Nueva España*, which he has been working on since before his arrival in London. In it he makes an impassioned declaration in favor of American independence and provides for his English readers an explanation of this cause, denouncing the despotism of the Inquisitors and of the Spanish monarchy. He is still undecided as to whether a monarchical system of government or a republic is preferable, and mistrusts the example of the United States, being greatly influenced by his admiration for England. In the *Historia* he maintains that America already has a constitution, based on the centuries-old Magna Carta and laid down in the Laws of the Indies.

1814   Mier journeys to Paris, where he is made a member of the Institute National of France. He meets the man who is to be the great conservative historian of Mexico, Lucas Alamán.

1815   Mier returns to London, disappointed by the outcome of events in Spain and France: Ferdinand VII, restored to the throne, has rejected the liberal constitution promulgated by the Legislative Assembly of Cádiz; Bonaparte has returned to Paris. He meets the insurgent Francisco Javier Mina; the English court grants him a pension to enable him to travel to the United States.

1816   In Liverpool Mier boards the frigate *Caledonia*, along with other volunteers headed by Mina. They reach Virginia and from there go on to Baltimore.

1817   Mier leaves for Mexico with Mina's expedition from the island of San Luis, in Galveston Bay. He reaches Soto de la Marina, where a fort is being constructed that will soon fall into the hands of the royalist brigadier general Joaquín Arredondo. At the time of his arrival, the fort had been dismantled because Mina had left with most of the combatants; Mier is taken prisoner, has all of his books confiscated and is sent to Mexico. En route, kept in shackles, he falls off his horse and fractures his arm; once again he is placed in an Inquisition prison. And once more he is put on trial.

1818   While in prison Mier writes his *Apología y Relación de lo sucedido en Europa hasta octubre de 1805 (Apologia and An Account of What Happened in Europe up to October 1805).*

1820   Mier testifies in his own defense before the Inquisitors' Tribunal, which, after reviewing all his supporting documents, declares the case closed. As it is already common knowledge that the Holy Office is to be abolished in June and Mier is, in effect, a political prisoner, he is transferred to the Royal Prison, in Veracruz, and finally (for the second time) to the Castle of San Juan de Ulúa. There he writes his *Manifiesto apologético (Apologetic Manifesto), Carta de despedida a los mexicanos (Farewell Letter to the Mexican People), Cuestión política: ¿iqPuede ser libre la Nueva España? (Political Question: Can New Spain Be Free?)* and *Idea de la constitución (Idea of the Constitution).* Though still in prison, he manages to remain in contact with the rebels fighting for independence.

1821 The authorities put Mier aboard a ship to Cuba, with Spain as his final destination. In Havana he escapes from the hospital where he is being treated. He is captured and imprisoned in the fortress known as La Cabaña, (The Cabin), from which he manages to make yet another break. He takes passage on the frigate *Robert Fulton,* headed for the United States. In Philadelphia he writes and publishes his *Memoria política-instructiva (Instructive-Political Memorandum)* in favor of a republican government in Mexico and against the Iguala Plan, which, though it provides for absolute independence, proposes that Ferdinand VII be made emperor. He now totally distrusts England, which he calls a secret enemy, and proposes an alliance with the United States, which he identifies with anti-monarchism. In August the viceroy O'Donojú and Agustín de Iturbide sign the Treaties of Córdoba, which incorporate a declaration of absolute independence and provide for a moderate monarchical government. The province of the New Kingdom of León elects Mier as deputy to the Mexican Constituent Congress. He decided to return to his native land and journeys to Veracruz.

1822 The commander of the Castle of San Juan de Ulúa, faithful to the royalist forces, arrests Mier once again. While imprisoned Mier writes *Exposición de la persecución que he padecido desde el 14 de junio de 1817 hasta el presente de 1822 (Account of the Persecution I Have Suffered from June 14, 1817, to Date in 1822).* The Constituent Congress demands that he be released from prison. On May 21 he is freed: it is the day on which Agustín Iturbide is proclaimed emperor of Mexico; the new emperor receives Mier personally in Tlalpan. Mier becomes a member of the Congress and begins his anti-Iturbide activities. Toward the middle of the year he is incarcerated once more, this time for being a republican, in the Monastery of Santo Domingo.

1823 Mier makes his escape, is arrested and is sent to the Royal Prison and then to the prison of the Inquisition, an institution that has been abolished. Two infantry regiments in Mexico stage an uprising against Iturbide and free Mier and other incarcerated deputies. The First Constituent Congress is dissolved. As a deputy, Mier takes an active part in the Second Constituent Congress: in one of its sessions he delivers his speech "on prophecies," attacking the adoption of a federal system of government. He warns that imitating the United States is not the right course to follow. Because of this speech he is attacked as a centralist, but his party loses the battle and in the parliamentary session of December 16 he votes in favor of a popular, representative and federal republic.

1824 Mier's name appears among those of the signers of the new Constitutive Act of Federation, which will be superseded by the Federal Constitution of the United States of Mexico. He receives by decree an annual pension of three thousand pesos, and President Guadalupe Victoria gives him living quarters in the Palacio Nacional.

1825 Mier publishes his *Discurso sobre la encíclica del Papa León XII (Discourse on the Encyclical Issued by Pope Leo XII)*.

1827 José Miguel Ramos Arizpe administers the viaticum to Mier in the presence of the president of the Republic and a great many others. It should be pointed out to those who accuse Mier of being a centralist that Ramos Arizpe—the very person who, as minister of Ecclesiastical Affairs, will later decree the secularization of land holdings in upper and lower California, his aim being to wrest control of them from Spanish priests—was one of the principal leaders of federalism. On December 3, Servando Teresa de Mier y Noriega dies in his quarters in the Palacio Nacional, a few months after his sixty-fourth birthday. Vice President Nicolás Bravo is the ranking government official at his interment, in the Monastery of Santo Domingo.

1842 Mier's body is exhumed and preserved in the ossuary of the monastery.

1861   Mier's mummy is sold to don Bernabé de la Barra, owner of a circus, purportedly with the intent of exhibiting it in Brussels and Buenos Aires.

1882   Mier's mummy is said to have been exhibited in Brussels as that of a victim of the Inquisition. The whereabouts of these remains is not known.

Note on the Text

Fray Servando Teresa de Mier's Memoirs consist of texts of various provenance: depending on the edition, texts have been included, either in whole or in part, from the *Apología del Doctor Mier (Apology of Dr. Mier)*, the *Relación de lo que sucedió en Europa al Doctor Don Servando Teresa de Mier después que fue transladado allá por resultas de lo actuado contra él en México, desde julio de 1795 hasta octubre de 1805 (Account of What Happened in Europe to Dr. don Servando Teresa de Mier After He Was Transferred There as a Result of the Proceedings against Him in Mexico, from July 1795 to October 1805)*, the *Manifiesto apologético (Apologetic Manifesto)*, the *Exposición de la persecución que ha padecido desde el 14 de junio de 1817 hasta el presente de 1822 al Doctor Servando Teresa de Mier Noriega Guerra (Account of the persecution suffered by Doctor Servando Teresa de Mier Noriega Guerra from June 14, 1817 to date in 1822)*. For the present edition, the first in English, the area of the *Memoirs* most likely to interest the general reader has been chosen: the extraordinary tale of what the Europe of Napoleon Bonaparte was like, told from the point of view of a Mexican priest persecuted by the Inquisition, until his return to Mexico as a participant in the struggle for independence.

The introduction is an attempt to fill in the historical context and explain in detail certain facts of enormous significance to which these memoirs allude, such as the reasons for which Mier spent nearly thirty years as a fugitive and his troubled relations with the Spanish monarchy.

With regard to his travels in the Peninsula, abundant use has been made of quotations form the original sources. A chronology of the author and explanatory notes have been included, as well as a select bibliography of "further readings."

For the translation, the text of the *Memorias* established by Antonio Castro Leal has been employed, with adaptation, however, of the chapter numbers (Mexico City: Porrúa, 1946; 2 vols.; a new edition was published in 1988), based in turn on the new edition of the *Biografía del benemérito mexicano D. Servando Teresa de Mier Noriega y Guerra* by José Eleuterio Gonzàlez [1876] (Monterrey: Tipografía del Gobierno, 1895). There are other versions: Manuel Payno, ed. *Vida, aventuras, escritos y viajes del Dr. Servando Teresa de Mier* (Mexico City: Imprenta Abadiano, 1856); Alfonso Reyes, ed., *Memorias de fray Servando Teresa de Mier* (Madrid: Ediciones América, Colección Ayacucho, c. 1917); Alessio Robles, ed., *El pensamiento del padre Mier* (Mexico City: Biblioteca Enciclopédica Popular, 1944); Edmundo O'Gorman, ed., *Escritos y memorias* (Mexico City: UNAM, 1945); Oscar Rodríguez Ortiz, ed., *Memorias* (Caracas: Ayacucho, 1988).

Editor's Introduction

The *Memoirs* of fray Servando Teresa de Mier, a Mexican friar persecuted by the Inquisition and a direct witness of Napoleonic Europe, extend to the reader an invitation hard to resist: to look at history upside
down and, therefore, to look at it from the proper perspective. With
fray Servando, Europeans cease to read the America invented by their
own colonizing culture, and Americans in turn cease once and for all to
compare their reality with a model that they imagine to be superior and
begin to think of themselves as they really are.

The adventures of a priest who spends thirty years escaping, time
and time again, from the prisons of the Holy Office by means of won-
drously clever tricks and who turns out to be one of the founding fathers of Mexico are extravagant enough in and of themselves. But the
impression the *Memoirs* leave of a world upside down results not from
the exoticism of Mier's biography but from his hilarious, clear-sighted
accounts of his years spent as a fugitive in Europe, which subvert the
image of the world recorded in the travel literature of the era. People
who are products of the Age of Enlightenment are still heatedly arguing about the "good savage" of the American continent when this supposed "savage" (a Creole born in the New World) presents, in his
encounter with the Spanish Empire, a portrait of manners and morals
that is a far cry from the "civilized" *esprit des nations* that Empire is en-
deavoring to impose in its colonies.

In the *Memoirs,* for example, the ones who are Others, observed from the more or less anthropological angle that the accounts of imperial travelers are inclined to adopt, are the Europeans. A completely marginal figure, born in New Spain, a fugitive and in the bargain a friar—a status held in little esteem at the time of the French Revolution—adopts, in Europe, the attitude of the traveler with an amateur scientists's bent who is seeking to explain local peculiarities to his Mexican compatriots. The strange creatures whose rites are described are not aborigines but Frenchmen, with their ventriloquists, galvanizers and resuscitators of the dead (43–4);[1] Italy is "the country of treachery and chicanery, of poison; the country of murder and robbery," where the women wander about bare naked at home because of the heat (50, 51). According to Mier's testimony, the Napoleonic wars have spread death and poverty throughout Europe: by comparison, imperial splendors are irrelevant.

In this era of ocean voyages, of rediscovery of the world, fray Servando takes the reverse route: he looks upon Europe as though it were the Other; he is (if the metaphor were possible) the Humboldt who draws up the inventory of an arrogant, and in many senses decadent, continent. Fray Servando is not the dazzled American who comes to know the marvels of an imperial civilization whose codes he will hasten to imitate the moment he returns home; he is the first learned Creole to acquire a familiarity with the Iberian Peninsula, and he is the first colonized observer to reveal the weaknesses and shortcomings of the colonizer.

Despite his situation as a person enjoying no prestige or advantage, his tone is never that of a subordinate. Thus, if a film were to be made today about the departure of this Mexican for Europe contemporaneous with that of Humboldt for America, the result would be pathetically comic by virtue of the disproportion between the two men. The dates coincide: the German traveler Friedrich Wilhelm Karl Heinrich Alexander von Humboldt—Baron von Humboldt, to be precise—secures the backing of the government of Spain for a visit to its colonies in America, which will result in his century's great naturalist testimonial, *Voyage de Humboldt et Bonpland aux régions équinoxiales du nouveau continent, fait en 1799–1804 (Voyage of Humboldt and Bonpland to the Equinoctial Regions of the New Continent, 1799–1804),* in twenty-three volumes, so influential an example of how to study the nature of the New World that it will be the Rosetta stone even for the key works subsequently written by Charles Darwin. The Mexican friar, on the other hand, will

bring with him no large inheritance received from a noble mother nor illustrious scientists of the stature of the Frenchman Aimé Bonpland: his
epic is that of a runaway prisoner without a penny in his pocket, far from
the scientific sphere, detested by the Spanish colonial authorities, abandoned by one and all ("even those who appeared to be my kinfolk were
ashamed of being seen as such," he says, "even though in all America
there was no one whose nobility outranked mine" [M 114])[2] and whose
only company in prison was ordinarily that of rats. Proud and fond of ex-
aggeration as was his habit, he describes his plight in Las Caldas:[3] "[The
rats] were so numerous and so big, that they ate my hat, and I had to
sleep armed with a stick so that they wouldn't eat me alive." (M 229).

So Far From God

Fray Servando Teresa de Mier is not in Europe in the position of the sa-
vant who pontificates, classifies and orders with the discerning eye of
the discoverer: he is there almost as an erudite adventurer in a cassock
whom chance has brought to the heart of the Empire in the Napoleonic
era. Dazzled, clear-sighted and sarcastic, he tells his compatriots of New
Spain the truth "to open their eyes." (M 243)

Toward Spain, the heart of the Empire, he is particularly implacable.
Which model should be the one that the Mexican colony ought to imitate, which one ought to be respected as the cradle of power? He says,
for example, that the soil is extraordinarily barren in the Iberian Peninsula, and "when it produces a crop it is because of the use of manure; in
Madrid the human variety is sold in sacks that are worth their weight in
gold." To cap it all, he adds that "in Catalonia they go about making manure inside their very own houses, keeping the inner courtyard flooded
almost all the time, and throwing out into it all the slops and excrement,
which keep the house permanently perfumed." (115) He then speaks of
the poverty: "There are no factories or industrial enterprises in Spain, or
any workers for them. Almost everyone, men and women alike, wear
garments of coarse wool and rough-woven cloth; their footwear is hemp
sandals, and their blouses are made of cloth woven from flax."(115)[4]

Is this the scatological image of an empire to which they must bow
down and pay tribute and which they must allow to occupy all government posts? What is above (culture) and what is below (the humiliated
manifestations of the body) are inverted in the imagery of the dominant
culture, since the central power is in the habit of representing the social

periphery in scatological terms and not the reverse.[5] It is the logic of the grotesque, but applied to a geography that ordinarily does not embody it. Fray Servando Teresa de Mier is not writing from the submissive status of the colonial subject: he speaks with the voice of a nation that at the time is very rich, and with that voice he denounces the ignorance of the mother country with regard to its colonies. Hence he writes:

> In Madrid, when I said that I was from Mexico [they answered]: "How rich that king of yours must be, seeing as how such a lot of silver comes from there!" In a royal office in Madrid that I happened to go into, when I stated that I was an American they were amazed. "But you aren't black," they said to me. "A countryman of yours came by just now," the friars at the monastery of San Francisco in Madrid said to me, and when I asked how they knew that, they answered that he was black. In the Cortes the deputy from Cádiz, a Philippine priest, asked whether we Americans were white and professed the Catholic religion. In certain hamlets, hearing that I was from America, they asked after Señor X or Y; you must know him, they said to me, because in such-and-such a year he went to the Indies. As though the Indies were the size of a small village. When I arrived in Las Caldas, the mountain folk "came to see the Indian. . . ." (60)

His main objective is to explain "the practice of our government" (he is referring to Spain) and open the eyes of his "countrymen, so that they place no trust whatsoever in their being able to attain justice." (M 243)[6] The account shows in detail the corruption of the system, "because the power there is more absolute, the court and the tribunals more venal, the number of people in dire need, of wicked men and of schemers greater." The ignorance of what is really happening in the New World is such that utterly nonsensical orders are issued. Fray Servando cites the ridiculous case of an edict to take all termites on the island of Santo Domingo prisoner for "having destroyed the records of court proceedings that His Majesty was requesting."

The inhabitants of the New World have no idea of the degree to which the Empire lacks knowledge of them and disregards them. Because, as he says in the *Memoirs:* "Since the Conquest there has been an apothegm on the lips of the mandarins of America: 'God is far above, the king in Madrid and I here' " (M 208), a saying, to be sure, very much like the lament of contemporary Mexico: "So far from God and so close to the United States." Unlike his compatriots, Mier has had the opportunity (though forced upon him) to come to know the heart of the Empire: "I did not know that the real kings of Spain are the *covachuelos,* and the ministers know nothing except what the latter tell them and want them to know." The *covachuelos,* minor bureaucrats of the Council of the Indies, are the ones who really manipulate and bring about, in their own interest, decisions that affect the New World. Any and all complaints are addressed to them and live or die in their hands. "I then learned that the *covachuelos* bring up whatever petitions they please, the minister signs as if they were of no interest to him, and they are the real kings of Spain and of the Indies." Concerning these functionaries, he explains: "One gains access to these posts, as to all those of the Monarchy, through money, women, ties of kinship, recommendations or intrigues; merit is an accessory, useful only if accompanied by these aids. Some are ignorant, others very clever; some honest Christian men; others, scoundrels and even atheists. In general they are vice-ridden, corrupt, well supplied with concubines, and burdened with debts, because the salaries are very meager." The *covachuelo* drafts and submits, if he so pleases, reports to the ministers, who, with the same scant interest, submits them to the king:

> The minister reads to the king the *covachuelo's* little marginal annotation on each memorandum. The king asks each of them how the matter should be resolved; the minister answers by reading the resolution noted down by the *covachuelo,* and the king scribbles a little signature. After five minutes Charles IV used to say: "Enough," and with this word whatever is in the diplomatic pouch is taken care of, in accordance with the opinion of the *covachuelos,* to whom power over all things is handed over from the Royal Country Estate so that they may dispatch orders. They then put whatever words they please in the king's mouth, without the king knowing what is happening in his own palace, nor the minister in the kingdom. (M 245)

The description naturally does not fall on deaf ears when it is read in the colonies. The sovereign's indifference toward the New World is a grave matter: "When, then, we rack our brains pondering the terms of a royal order in order to discern His Majesty's intention, it is that of a *covachuelo* who is a rascal or a madman." If there is anyone who is still laboring under any illusion to the contrary, to the Empire New Spain is nothing more than a means to continue to enrich itself, but, in accordance with this image, not even important enough for the king or his ministers to take the trouble to devote their time to it.

In point of fact, even though Spain from the first conferred the status of provinces on its new dominions (a political status that incorporated them as extensions of the territory of the mother country and not merely a commercial formula), neither the king nor the most illustrious names in the Empire were capable of evaluating the consequences of the Conquest. Hence, while America saw itself as an active part of the Empire from the very beginning, Spain continued to elaborate epic poems to the glory of its soldiers in Italy and Africa, and the extraordinary material offered by the adventure of its own men in the Indies was long looked upon with scorn or ignored. It is understandable that, at the dawn of the nineteenth century, Servando Teresa de Mier should want to share with his compatriots his indignation at the bureaucracy of which he had been a witness and a victim: the Creoles should feel the weight of that disdain.[7]

More of a Savage than You

Another of the extraordinary contributions of these *Memoirs* lies in the fact that Mier is the one who best expresses the tension inherent in the formation of the center/periphery dichotomy, that is to say Europe/Latin America in this era. In the rhetoric of accounts of journeys abroad, "barbarian" or "savage" is the basic word applied to the peoples encountered. The *Memoirs* attribute this barbarism to the conquistador, a conclusion that, seen from our contemporary point of view, is almost comic. An example: "Everyone journeys like a barbarian through a land of barbarians, trembling at the highwaymen who sally forth to rob travelers, and a carriage is escorted only by troupes of beggars and children, clamoring for alms at the top of their lungs." (46) And also: "Spaniards perpetually ape the dress and the customs of other Europeans." (41–2)

In all likelihood the debates of the period did not allow people of that time—immersed as they were in the epistemological system of the end of the eighteenth century—to appreciate the true import of that gaze that totally reverses colonial values, at least in the terms center/periphery employed at that time.[8] It must be remembered that this was the era of the denigration of the American continent. The attacks by Buffon, de Pauw, Raynal and Robertson as well as the idealization of the good savage in the manner of Rousseau were in fashion. According to the theories in vogue, the inhabitants of America were weak, inferior and degraded; in fact, similar arguments were used by the Legislative Assembly of Cádiz to enact a law that would limit the parliamentary representation of Mexicans, on the grounds that "of its six million inhabitants, ten [million] were Indians, two halfbreeds, and a half of the million whites incapable of exercising their political rights."[9]

It is worth recalling that as Jean-Jacques Rousseau was dreaming of the lost happiness of aborigines, Georges-Louis Leclerc, Count of Buffon, was maintaining in his *Histoire naturelle, générale et particulière (A Natural History, General and Particular,* 1748–1804) that American degradation had gone so far that the New World man suffered from sexual frigidity, and his passivity in the face of nature put him on the same level as animals. In his "Of National Characters" (1748, revised in 1754), David Hume assured his readers, for instance, that "[t]here never was a civilized nation of any other complexion than white, nor even any individual eminent either in action or speculation."[10] Another abbot, Corneille de Pauw—whom fray Servando cites several times as "Paw"—claimed in his *Recherches philosophiques sur les Américains, ou Mémoires intéressants pour servir à l'histoire de l'espèce humaine (Philosophical Research on Americans, or Memoirs of Interest for a History of the Human Species, 1768),* at the very height of the Encyclopedist movement, that an American is not an immature animal or a child, but a degenerate.

Of all the great European thinkers of the era, Johann Gottfried von Herder was one of the few pluralists for whom no culture was inferior to another; each one, rather ought to be considered from the perspective of its own particular value and its own particular truth, and in his *Ideen zur Philosophie der Geschichte der Menschheit (Ideas on the History of Mankind,* 1784–91) proposed a revision of the theory of history. Another, whom Mier cites in his *Memoirs,* was Gian Rinaldo Carli, the author of *Lettere americane* (1776), a panegyric to the Incas, who places no credence in the accusations of American inferiority, even though in his case there was already evident a tendency to rehabilitate indigenous societies of the distant past and forget the situation of the contemporary Indian (a forgetfulness that has been traditional among Latin American governments themselves down to the present). Other readings that would have enabled the Mexican friar to think of the New World in a more positive light were Thomas Jefferson's *Notes on Virginia* (1782)—the first printed defense of North America—and Thomas Paine's *Rights of Man* (1791).

The intense and influential debate regarding the New World followed Aristotle's old idea that in the tropics conditions were less favorable to life;[11] the thinkers of the Enlightenment exaggerated their arguments on the grounds that rational law is universal, and it went without saying that what they meant by "universal" was "in their own image and likeness." This battle to determine who is more rational, or rather, who is truly civilized, reflects a fight for geopolitical power between the European metropolises. Abbot Guillaume–Thomas Raynal, in his *Histoire philosophique et politique des établissements et du commerce des Européens dans les deux Indes* (*Philosophical and Political History of the Settlements and of the Commerce of Europeans in the Two Indies,* 1770) is a direct attack on Spain: his book contains a condemnation of the cruelty of the colonizers and a denunciation of the immense sufferings of the indigenous peoples. Diderot takes up this line of argument by accusing the Spanish conquest of America of engendering ignorance, fanatical missionary zeal, abuses. It is not only the colonized world, then, that is deemed inferior, but also very obdurate colonizers (Spain): the battle is for the possession of the world. Voltaire, Jean-François Marmontel and William Robertson, a Scot, with his *History of America,* contribute to these attacks.[12]

The attacks on Spain are linked to the "black legend" of the Conquest, spread by another Dominican, fray Bartolomé de Las Casas, through his *Brevísima relación de la destrucción de las Indias (A Very Brief Account of the Destruction of the Indies).* Fray Servando is regarded as the direct heir of the tradition of Las Casas, by virtue of his attack on Spanish abuses.[13]

The cultural framework of *Mier's Memoirs* is complex. One factor is the self-interested inferiorization of the New World, another the attacks against Spain (also inferiorized, and furthermore, accused of excessive cruelty), and yet another the official (and positive) versions that the Empire itself offered with regard to the Conquest of America. Among these versions, wherein the Creoles found it hard to recognize themselves completely, is the classic summa of the Conquest composed by fray Juan de Torquemada, *De los veintiún libros espirituales de la Monarquía Indiana (Concerning the Twenty-one Spiritual Books of the Monarchy of the Indies,* 1615)—which Mier cites several times—and Antonio de Solís's *Historia de la Conquista de México (History of the Conquest of Mexico,* 1684), which went through some twenty editions during the eighteenth century. "[A]longside this official, traditional, propagandistic vision, as reassuring to the general public as a fairy tale, written for the most part by members of religious orders, there existed another vision of America, that of the lay bureaucrats of the State" (Ross, 221): that of José Campillo in *Lo que hay de más en España para que sea lo que debe ser y no lo que es o Nuevo sistema de gobierno económico para la América (What There Is an Excess of and a Lack of in Spain for It to Be What It Ought to Be and Not What It Is or New System of Economic Government for America),* that of Bernardo Ward in his *Proyecto económico (Economic Plan)* or that of the Count of Campomanes in *Reflexiones sobre el comercio español a Indias (Reflections on Spanish Commerce in the Indies)*, all works that had been recently published, in Servando Teresa de Mier's early years. These books present a vision of "America as a problem." To counter the attacks of Enlightenment writers against the abuses of Spanish rule in America, Abbot Nuix's *Reflexiones imparciales* and Juan de Escóiquiz's *México conquistado*—pious defenses based on the pretext of evangelization, a pretext that Mier was to try to discredit—were published. Also toward the end of the eighteenth century, José Cadalso, in his *Cartas marruecas (Moroccan Letters)*, accuses those European countries that traffic in slaves "and with the profits from this trade print books full of elegant invective, high-flown insults and eloquent slander against Hernán Cortés for what he did." (cited in Tietz, 230)[14]

A campaign of disinformation is pursued on both sides, as is ambition. In the name of reason the Encyclopedists flaunted ridiculous prejudices concerning realities that they really knew nothing about; the Spanish answered with arguments about a world that they too knew nothing about, as is noted again and again in Mier's *Memoirs*. Affairs in the New World were in such chaos that when the king ordered that a refutation of Robertson and Raynal be drafted, it was discovered that "the documentation required to do so was not accessible, but rather was scattered more or less throughout the whole of Spain. By direct order of the king, Juan Bautista Muñoz was assigned the difficult task of gathering these documents together and of writing in accordance with modern criteria his history of the New World (*Historia del Nuevo Mundo*)— which goes only as far as 1500 and went to press in 1793." (Tietz, 233) Moreover, the founding of the famous Archives of the Indies in Seville does not date, as anyone who does not know otherwise might believe, to the period of the Discovery or the beginning of the Conquest, but only to the time at the end of the eighteenth century when Muñoz began the search for documents in order to write the history that the king had commissioned.

The writings of the period cannot be readily understood without taking these debates into account. They are the background that Antonello Gerbi called "the New World dispute" in an extraordinary book on the subject.[15] The Americans knew (and absorbed) the inferiorization of which they were the object since they read the Encyclopedists, despite the censorship of books imposed by the Inquisition and the authorities of the viceroyalties. Hence it is almost a cliché (and also a simplification) to attribute the intellectual bases of the movement for independence in America in large part to these readings concerning the repositioning of secular power and the weakening of that of the Church, social contracts and magna cartas, equal rights and the free self-determination of man.[16]

Fray Servando read the work of Benito Jerónimo Feijoo y Montenegro, a member of the Benedictine order and no doubt the intellectual pillar that supported the Spanish version of the Enlightenment (its bases: recovering the sense of usefulness to society, fostering knowledge of the natural sciences, education, law, medicine and philology, while at the same time preserving the Catholic faith); he was also familiar with the texts of Buffon, Montesquieu, Rousseau, Marmontel, Raynal, and Robertson. Once he reached Europe, Mier kept company with Jesuits in exile, Francisco Javier Clavijero, the Abbot Grégoire and Alexander von Humboldt, whom he cites several times in his *Memoirs* and tries to persuade of the truth of his own ideas about the evangelization of America. Mier assures his reader that "Baron von Humboldt also told me in Paris: 'I believed that it [the evangelization of America before the arrival of the Spaniards] was an invention of the friars, and said as much in my statistics, but after I saw your curious essay I see that this is not so." (35)

Concerning De Pauw, Mier wrote jokingly that "he said that America is a continent that has just emerged from the waters; consequently, all full of swamps and foul-smelling and deadly lakes," and that "from its rank ponds there has leapt forth a caste of frogs called Indians who managed to speak some sort of crude mumbo-jumbo and consequently they should be classified as members of a species halfway between men and orangutans." (cited by Gerbi, 396–8) In answer to these delirious ravings, "deserving of a cage," Mier writes: "it is impossible to describe the portrait painted of them with a pen dipped in the blood of cannibals, heaping upon America and its aborigines all the absurdities and insults that the Spaniards themselves passed on to Pauw." (cited by Gerbi, 396) Hence it is "also necessary to take a broom to all these many annoying beetles, squashing them on top of their own dung, and providing my countrymen with a little manual of exorcisms against such *antuerpias*."[17]

The stereotypes of Aztec barbarism and Creole ineptitude were already matters of argument between Spain and Mexico as early as two centuries before the Enlightenment. The first written response from Latin America was that of the Mexican Jesuit Francisco Javier Clavijero in his *Historia antigua de México* (*History of Ancient Mexico*, 1780–1), a refutation of the postulates of De Pauw, Robertson and Raynal. Clavijero says, for example: "Mexicans, in particular, are handsome, healthy, robust, and unaffected by many afflictions and sicknesses. No Mexican's breath ever smells bad" (Gerbi 255, quoted in his *Storia antica*, vol. 1, 118–23). More important still, in it he flaunts the argument that the Creoles will increasingly vaunt the fact that the Aztec Empire cannot be accused of barbarism but was, rather, a very advanced civilization. Mier, naturally, takes up the detail concerning a Mexican's sweet-smelling breath and accuses Europeans of having introduced into America such plants as garlic and onions "which make the breath reek."[18]

Analyzed in retrospect and in light of the complete change of direction that was to be taken by Latin American history toward the end of the nineteenth century, the defense of Jesuits such as Clavijero and even that of fray Mier were in all likelihood accorded a more or less ambiguous reception by Creole society. Such a defense meant that that society was being given the possibility of creating a thought that was autonomous and proud of itself, of emerging from its supposed inferiority, but at the same time, there is no gainsaying the fact that at bottom this Creole thought continued to have very strong ties to the imperial gaze, even long after the wars of independence.[19] In point of fact, the "gaze" that the power of the metropolitan center had trained on these countries in order to draw their portrait was eventually assimilated: even after their countries had become independent republics, Americans looked at themselves with borrowed eyes, with the same gaze to which the metropolitan centers of power had subjected them.[20] At a time when the nineteenth century was well under way, the rivers and the mountains ceased to be a part of what constituted nature and were transformed into trade routes or obstacles to trade; the value of human beings came to be determined by the measuring rod of European knowledge. Figures as central as Domingo F. Sarmiento or Andrés Bello spoke of Latin America in almost the same idiom as Chateaubriand or Hegel; that is to say, in the idiom of amazement or of usefulness. The nations of Latin America tried to model their identity on parameters of progress that owed less to their own realities than to the ideas of London, Paris and later on New York as well. They believed that they were putting distance between themselves and the Spanish Empire, that they were leaving behind their colonial or neocolonial status; but quite to the contrary, they were confirming it.[21] This is part and parcel of the dynamics of former colonies.

Although Mier's writings did not always have the effect he had hoped, Mier's texts are expert at turning arguments upside down, ripping traditions apart, discovering points of view that others had not thought of before or that had failed to be put to good use even a century later. There are any number of examples. As though to refute the accusations of cannibalism leveled against Spanish-American Indians, although he does not expressly refer to these charges, he says of the Italians at the time of the Republic:

> The hoi polloi, called *lazzaronis* [*sic*], are very talkative, a filthy rabble and so barbaric that . . . they took the decapitated corpse of each noble and carried it in front of his house, shouting for bread to be thrown to them to eat with it, and devoured the body. Human flesh was sold in the public square at a price of four *granos* (cuartos) for a strip four fingers wide. The only one they didn't eat was the bishop: they were greatly offended, rather, that the the king had hanged him, when secular nobles simply had their heads cut off. (M 68)

With this passage, the inversion of the question of who is the true savage is complete. Fray Servando's discursive maneuvers are a model of the strategies employed by the colonized to oppose imperial power (and, above all, the oppressive molds into which it forced knowledge), invaluable material for the development of a postcolonial theory for Latin America.[22] His humor is well-nigh prophetic: word games such as the one just cited, which dismantle the logic of Empire, give the impression of having been written two centuries later. There is another marvelous example, a jewel that demolishes, with humor and clear-sightedness, the logic of colonization:

> Discoverers! [used as a title signifying the right to rule over America that was put forward by the Spaniards], that is to say, you did not know that the greater part of the world existed: therefore on learning this, you are its masters. Hence, if the Indians had known sooner that Europe existed, were they *ipso facto* its masters? (*Historia*, vol. 14, 277)

From the Picaresque Victim of Persecution to the Birth of the Learned Man

Servando Teresa de Mier is a witness not only to two worlds but also to two eras. Hence it is difficult to pigeonhole him: he is neither a learned colonial scholar nor a Romantic writer; as a Dominican he is not an out-and-out product of the Enlightenment, nor does his life end with the Inquisition, but rather he lives on to see the coronation of the first Creole emperor. He is a transitional figure (as perhaps we contemporary readers are, trapped in the vacuum of the change of episteme created by a new millennium), a witness and a committed participant. The conflicts engendered by this transition are also part of the fascination that his work creates: like a boiling cauldron where no idea is yet a certainty, not even those that seem indispensable for the foundation of nations, so obvious and so interwoven with the image of the nation that they give the impression of having been present since the beginning of time. As seldom before or since in history, fray Servando's era looks intently backward, forward and sideways in time: searching in our origins, in our present and in our dreams for what we are as peoples, in our own eyes and in those of others. Though Servando was born at a time of great repression (at once cultural, political and religious), he was to live part of his adult life amid the effervescence of the insurgent and of the politician who, blotting out the past and beginning all over, can sit down to imagine (and negotiate) the Mexico that for the first time is independent, the country to come.

There have been a number of studies of the colonial era in Latin America and also of what happened after independence, but Mier's period, the period that throughout the continent is the mother and father of plans for founding a country, continues to attract the attention of scholars. We know, of course, that it is in those final years of the eighteenth century that the die was cast for the destiny of America, but there are figures in this period as gigantic as Francisco de Miranda, Simón Rodríguez, or Mier himself, who are remembered as protagonists of an exceptional history, but whose thought has not yet been exhausted or explored as deeply as it deserves.[23] In fact, we speak today of the supposed romance between Empress Catherine of Russia and the Venezuelan general Miranda or of how his name came to figure on the Arc de Triomphe in Paris; we speak today of the eccentricities of Rodríguez, Simón Bolívar's teacher, to whom the future liberator personally promises to bring about the independence of all America (the Oath of the Sacred Mountain), because of Rodríguez's faith in the ideas of Rousseau, because he wrote under other names, such as Samuel Robinson, or because he went so far as to strip naked in class to provide an anatomical demonstration. Their images in glowing colors as founding fathers endure on the one hand, as do the anecdotes about them on the other, but the core of their meaning escapes us.

In the same way, the *Account of What Happened in Europe to Dr. don Servando Teresa de Mier, After He Was Transferred There as a Result of the Proceedings against Him in Mexico from July 1795 to October 1805* was long read as the adventures of one of the most outlandish characters of the Latin American scene. The only remaining traces of fray Servando are the name of an avenue in Mexico, the fact that he was the coauthor with Simón Rodríguez of the first translation into Spanish of Chateaubriand's *Atala,* or that he and Rodríguez, both fugitives, penniless and with no regular means of livelihood, founded a school in France to teach spoken Spanish.[24] The echo of his adventures, above all that of his hilarious prison breaks, may also linger on, in large part thanks to the Cuban writer Reinaldo Arenas, who takes up, and invents, the life of Mier in his novel *El mundo alucinante* (*Hallucinations,* 1969), in which he describes him as "a man of a thousand dimensions, an innocent, a rogue, an adventurer, a hothead," an impudent fellow. In quick strokes, Arenas limns the image of the friar: "The man who traveled on foot all across Europe, experiencing unbelievable adventures, the one who suffered every sort of persecution, the tireless victim, on several occasions on the point of being burned at the stake, the habitual guest of the most dreaded prisons of America and of Europe (San Juan de Ulúa, La Cabaña, Los Toribios, etc.), the patriot and political rebel, the fighter. . . ."[25] The distinguished Mexican historian and essayist Alfonso Reyes also contributes to the construction of the myth of fray Servando: "He is as light and frail as a bird, and possesses that force of 'levitation' that the historians of miracles believe they find in saints. He makes use of the trick of disappearance with ghostlike mastery. His adventures are so extraordinary that at times they appear to be products of his imagination." But he is quick to add: "Father Mier might have been no more than an eccentric, had his sufferings and his faith in the fate of his nation not caused him to grow in stature."[26]

That reading of Mier was prompted in part by the latter's own *Memoirs,* which portray him as "the picturesque victim of persecution." (*Escritos,* x) Like all autobiographical accounts, the *Memoirs* tell the story of a fictitious I, created by the author himself.[27] Emir Rodríguez Monegal points out the influence on Mier of the picaresque tradition and of the model of Rousseau. "In the various autobiographical accounts he left, he was mainly concerned with setting the record of his life straight. But, like Rousseau or Casanova, he also wrote to fulfill a deeply narcissistic need: to leave behind a record of his dashing, brilliant, beautiful self," and there is no doubt that on occasion he goes to megalomaniacal extremes.[28]

Be that as it may, and to return to the problem of how to read Mier's life, it must be kept in mind that not only his writing but also all his movements as the first-person narrator tend to become myth, as do even certain events that supposedly occurred after his death in 1827. Antonio

Castro Leal recounts that the Monastery of Santo Domingo exhumed fray Servando's mummified corpse in 1842 and sold the mummy in 1861 to a certain don Bernabé de la Barra, who intended to exhibit it in Europe or America. According to this account, Mier's mummy, as great a wanderer as Mier was in life, ended up being exhibited at a fair in Brussels as a victim of the Inquisition. (M xii)

From a heretic to a father of his country, from a mummy in a sideshow to a character in a novel, the I that narrates, and either charms or exasperates, is of interest not so much because of the biographical facts in and of themselves (regardless of their fascination), but rather as evidence of the way in which the author conceived of his specific place and role in the societies in which he was active. As Kathleen Ross notes, there are two discourses in the *Memoirs*: one focuses on the self as subject, the other looks outward and describes the world, reflecting the revolutionary era. As Tulio Halperín Donghi also explains, the relevance of this sort of text is "the effort to pour a life-experience into a certain [social] mold, to make it fit a certain model whose characteristics are to be individualized."[29] Mier's account is also a sign of the "metamorphoses" that learned men undergo in this era of transition between colony and independence, hemmed in "by ideological limits and rigidly defined behavior." Halperín adds:

> The drama of the person who feels hemmed in within suffocating limits was lived out, with an intensity that took him to the verge of madness, by fray Servando Teresa de Mier. . . . The resounding failure of this attempt [to redefine a regeneration within the colonial framework], in all truth stillborn, and fray Servando's inability to come to terms with it, give rise to texts whose richness is owed at times to an extreme, exasperated lucidity, at times to the ravings of an obsessive imagination; in the sway of this twofold inspiration fray Servando records for us the march of a quarter of a century of reflections on the experience of the dissident learned man in an Ancien Régime in the throes of death. (55–6)

Mier himself expresses it differently: "Faced with a bishop whose habit it was to preach a sermon only once every twelve years at most, a brilliant American was unable to preach anything that did not entirely accord with the bishop's ideas without immediately provoking an attempt [on the latter's part] to trip him up in order to destroy him, as he did in my case. . . . " (M 181) It was not easy to be a learned man in this period of transition between the eighteenth century and the nineteenth, between the colony and independence, between being a Spaniard born in America or an American by right of birth, between that sort of

Catholic Enlightenment kept under close surveillance by the Inquisition that was typical of intellectual life in Mexico and the fervor of Romanticism and palingenesis. Edmundo O'Gorman, one of the great Mier specialists, describes him as a "champion of Independence" and furthermore as "punctilious with regard to his aristocratic lineage," ever loyal to his Catholic faith despite persecutions, so jealous of proper recognition of his academic degrees and of his prerogatives as the pope's domestic prelate that it pleased him to wear the dress of a bishop (which he was not). "Possessed of a way with words, mordant, erudite, intelligent and insolent, he unfailingly captured the attention of his listeners." O'Gorman criticizes the lack of unity of his works, the repetitions and inaccuracies, the exaggerated use of the first person; but he then immediately explains:

> Let them not be disdained for that reason. His body of work is admirable; the style is original and vigorous, and all his writings, enlivened by the impassioned personality of their author, are full of unerring flashes of insight and felicitous *trouvailles*. Father Mier is indispensable reading for anyone who aspires to acquire a profound knowledge of the origin, the antecedents and the solutions of that great historical turning point, the political Independence of the Spanish possessions in America; and even more indispensable for anyone who is interested in learning of the tidal wave of problems that greeted those incipient republics, as incipient as they were hallucinated.[30]

The levels of possible interpretation, the accretions of the imaginary are a product of the strategies of the text itself: Mier's heterological vocation and his comic irreverence are such that they corrupt the field of legibility. An illustrative case is that of Antonelli Gerbi, the extraordinary researcher, who loses his perspective and ends up labeling Mier a "poor and incoherent" spirit. Bold, peripatetic and megalomaniacal perhaps, and contradictory as well, but never poor in spirit. Jacques Lafaye recognizes the contradictions inherent in the I of the narrator, but at the same time he shows that, within the European millenarian atmosphere and the messianic cycle in which the war of independence in Mexico was fought, Mier's religious and political thought was coherent.

Perhaps the worst "accusation" that could be leveled against this complex figure, the one portrayed in the *Memoirs* and the one in real life, would be that he was so often in the wrong place, acting at the wrong time. Two events in his life will suffice as examples. The first: he was just beginning to be famous in Mexico when he delivered the public sermon that was to cause him so many problems with the Inquisition; the sermon was intended to strengthen Creole pride in the face of Spanish colonial power, but instead of holding fast to local traditions, Mier criticized them, thereby antagonizing both the imperial authorities and many Creoles. Another example: when the Inquisition was abolished and Mexican independence was declared, Mier could have ceased at last to be a marginal figure and a fugitive and instead enjoy the privileges of power and the recognition brought him by his appointment as a deputy to the Congress; he was nearly sixty years old (the reader must keep in mind what it meant to reach that age in that era and in view of the precarious conditions in which he had lived), but he had not learned, or else refused to learn, his lesson. On the day that Agustín de Iturbide was proclaimed emperor of Mexico, fray Servando was let out of the prison of San Juan de Ulúa (where he was incarcerated at the time, not on account of his enmity toward the Inquisition, which had now disappeared, but on account of his sympathies with the cause of independence) and the emperor received him personally in Tlalpan. Before three months were out, Iturbide himself issued orders to have him imprisoned for his anti-Iturbide activities: fray Servando was once again put under lock and key in the Monastery of Santo Domingo. This friar had a certain rather odd quirk of personality: he repeatedly went about things in such a way that he found himself a man persecuted, each time for a different reason. Only the last four years of his adult life were spent without a warrant out for his capture.

In the margin of the margin, while a prisoner, he writes this text from out of the space of memory, fifteen years after the events he recounts. The value of these memories (of this gaze), centered on his escape and his wanderings through Spain, England, Italy, France and Portugal, is exceptional: "Even though in my twenty-four years of persecution I have acquired the gift of painting monsters, my discourse will make it evident that I am merely copying the originals here," he writes implacably. (M 4)

In the *Memoirs,* past and present are conjoined in a single time and on a single map, where the "there" is not the primitive space of Africa or America, nor yet the touristic exotic place of travels to Jerusalem or the Mediterranean à la Chateaubriand. Past, present and the motion of otherness are represented through the gaze of a Creole American that has nothing to do with the inferiority supposedly suffered by the inhabitants of the New World. Quite the opposite is the case:

Furthermore [fray Servando repeatedly states with great pride], I am a nobleman and a gentleman, not only by virtue of my Mexican doctorate,

xl | Editor's Introduction

in accordance with the Law of the Indies, not only by virtue of my lineage, well-known to the most exalted nobility of Spain, inasmuch as the
dukes of Granada and Altamira belong to the same house as I, and that
of Mioño, to whom it is now related, its grandeur evident, but also because in America I am a descendant of the first conquistadors of the New
Kingdom of León, as is recorded in the examining magistrates' reports
presented to the Tribunal, already verified within the Order, and, consequently, in accordance with the terms of the Laws of the Indies, I am a
knight and gentleman of known noble ancestry with all the privileges and
rights appertaining to this title in the kingdoms of Spain. (M 101)

Proud of his supposed Creole-style nobility, he also assured his readers that he was a descendant of Cuauhtémoc and Montezuma on his
mother's side, "so that on various occasions he expressed the opinion
that if the Mexican empire were to be restored, he could claim the right
to occupy the throne."[31] How to read assertions of this sort at a time
when Europeans whiled away their time debating the question of the
inferiority of the zoological species and the races of the New World, or
waxing enthusiastic about the possibilities of that American space that,
they believed, was about to take shape *ex novo?* History would have
been quite different had Europe been willing to listen, instead of looking through self-interested spectacles at the map of the colonies.

This is the change of point of view, of literary genre, of cultural
framework. The reader is subjected to personal anecdotes only to be
obliged to go on almost without transition to social panoramas or theological reflections, attempting to weigh this information within the context of the era continually brought to mind by the text itself—it is
practically impossible to dissociate in this book the autobiographical element, social biography and political analysis. It is quite possible, rather,
to see the birth of the nineteenth century in the textual overlapping of
all these traditions of writing, as Halperín Donghi suggests. "Here the
intellectual is born—in a painful birth rife with conflict—of the colonial learned man."[32]

Sudden Scandal

José Servando de Santa Teresa de Mier Noriega y Guerra is born on
October 18, 1763, in the capital of what was then the Kingdom of New
León, into a family that had counted among its members a provincial
governor and a president of the Inquisition Tribunal.[33] At the age of

sixteen he enters the Dominican order, a decision that later on he regards as imprudent since he made it at too early an age and with insufficient knowledge. He earns a doctorate in theology and in 1792 receives his license to preach. He is an immediate success, and more and more frequently he is asked to give public sermons on important occasions. His success is as sudden as his fall will be resounding: "I shone so brilliantly in Mexico thanks to my talent, [knowledge of] literature and eloquence that, as with every outstanding American, I brought upon myself the envy and the hatred of Archbishop Haro." (*Manifiesto*) The year of his disgrace is 1794: on November 8 he preaches on the anniversary of the funeral honors paid the conquistador Hernán Cortés; his talent is greeted with such enthusiasm that he is requested to give the sermon on the day of the Virgin of Guadalupe. As Mier wrote: "some seventeen days before that of [the appearance of Our Lady of] Guadalupe, councilman Rodríguez asked me to deliver the sermon for the fiesta of the Sanctuary, and as a trained orator, and one who had already preached three times on that very image and been applauded, I soon found my subject. I was rehearsing my sermon, when Father Mateos, a Dominican, told me that an attorney had recounted to him such curious things about Our Lady of Guadalupe that he had held his attention the entire afternoon." (M 5)

The die is cast: it falls to him to give the main sermon in the Collegiate Church of Guadalupe on December 12, the feast day of the Virgin of Guadalupe, patron saint of Mexico. The viceroy, Archbishop Alonso Núñez de Haro y Peralta, the authorities and all important Creoles will be present; the young friar decides to surpass himself and deliver an unforgettable sermon, a Creole sermon. He goes to the house of the lawyer in question, a certain Licenciado Borunda, and there receives the idea that will serve as inspiration for his sermon. As he recalls it: "He told me: 'I think that the image of Our Lady of Guadalupe dates from the time of the preaching in this kingdom of Saint Thomas, whom the Indians called Quetzacohatl [*sic*].'" (M 5) The theory is a new version of the Guadalupan tradition according to which the Virgin appeared to the Indian Juan Diego, choosing colonial Mexico to receive her message and leaving her image imprinted on the Indian's cape as proof; declaring that the image is prior to the arrival of the Spaniards in America is tantamount to a denial of the justification for the Conquest: the evangelization of the New World. It creates an immediate scandal. "The clergymen attached to the diocese deliberately misled the Mexicans as to the glory that I had attained for them with my sermon; but it was they themselves [the clergymen] who were misled. And they said that it was a Creole conspiracy meant to rob the Spaniards of the glory of having brought us the Gospel." (M 96) Fray Servando Teresa de Mier is locked away in the monastery of Santo Domingo, and the retraction he makes is of no avail, nor is his later attempt to secure secularization. The Canons Uribe and Omaña condemn him; Archbishop Haro issues an edict decreeing that Mier be imprisoned in the monastery of Las Caldas (Santander, Spain) for ten years and deprives him in perpetuity of the right to deliver lectures and sermons or to hear confession. In disgrace and ill from fever, he is sent by ship to Cádiz, a journey that begins his odyssey of prison breaks and attempts to flee unceasing persecution by the Inquisition: nearly thirty years of defending himself against the injustice that has been done him.

To understand the dimensions of the scandal, it is necessary, first, to understand the situation in Mexico at the time, what the Virgin of Guadalupe represented, and within this framework, precisely what it was that Mier was proposing.

Mexico, Spain and the Church

For part of the colonial era the Spaniards enforced the prohibition against bringing a wife to the New World, a policy that produced a burgeoning racial mixture and great social inequalities. A person's social position was measured according to a multilevel scale that went from the humblest Indian to the Spanish noble, producing a degree of hostility between human groups that the wars of independence did not succeed in mitigating completely.[34] The *gachupines* (Spaniards born in the Peninsula) even discriminated against their own legitimate offspring, despite the fact that this progeny was 100 percent white: it sufficed to have been born in America to be looked upon as inferior, as though the climate and the atmosphere of the continent made these scions incapable of occupying public posts (this is one aspect of the inferiorization of the New World).[35] This constantly gave rise to obvious resentment between one group and another.

The royal preference for appointing peninsular Spaniards to fill public posts became even more deep-rooted in New Spain after 1763, when José Moñino y Redondo, count of Floridablanca, Charles III's prime minister in an effort to strengthen Spanish commerce against its competitors in Latin America broadened the colonial bureaucracy, and in an attempt to reduce corruption took steps to reduce the number of Creoles who held posts in it. As Raymond Carr has noted, the relative success of Charles III's reforms began to undermine the foundations of Empire, increasing considerably the resentment between castes.[36] The situation did not improve: in 1792, for instance, Archbishop Alonso Núñez de Haro—the same prelate who was to persecute fray Servando so relentlessly—ordered that Creoles be given only minor ecclesiastical posts. The Creoles began to prefer being called Americans rather than Spaniards. The enmity between Spaniards and Americans finds expression in cruel stereotypes: *gachupines* were regarded as ignorant misers, while Creoles were seen as well-educated spendthrifts.[37]

The situation in Spain was unstable: in 1795 the republican conspiracy led by Juan Picornell y Gomila was discovered, rumors of republican conspiracies proliferated in the north of the country, and many Spaniards shared the idea that their country was backward by comparison to the rest of Europe and ended up looking hopefully toward Napoleon Bonaparte. An uprising in 1808 forced Charles V to dismiss his minister Manuel de Godoy y Alvarez, Prince of Peace and of Basano, duke of Alcaudio y de Succa (royal favorite and twice prime minister) and abdicate in favor of his son, Ferdinand VII, the prince of Asturias. In Bayonne in April, Napoleon, who had already sent French troops to Spain, forced Ferdinand to abdicate in favor of Joseph Bonaparte, the emperor's brother. The Spanish monarchy never recovered. When the masses took to the streets of Madrid to welcome Ferdinand back in 1814, the republican foundations for the antimonarchical revolutions that followed, from 1820 to 1931, were already laid.

The Creoles had been petitioning for greater political autonomy for their town councils since the middle of the eighteenth century, and Pedro Pablo Abance de Bolee, known as the count of Aranda, one of the most prominent reformers in the government of Charles III, had suspected for some time that Spain had best replace the old notion of Empire and accept independent Bourbon throne what history would have been like had these ideas been came to nothing, the social tension continued to mount the wars of independence, there was also the French Revolution of the United States, and of particular importance, Spanish helplessness in the face of Napoleon's power and the country's inability to supply goods to the colonies. "With Great Britain the major maritime and commercial power as its enemy, the disadvantages of ties with Spain and the advantages of Independence became clear. . . . The successive defeats of the Spanish forces in the peninsula, the abdication of Ferdinand VII and the ultimate failure of the Central Junta left the Spaniards feeling rootless and lost. . . . It was not that the Americans rose against Spain; it was that Spain fell away from America." (Carr, 102–3)[38]

In Mexico, at the time when Bonaparte imprisoned Ferdinand VII, two out of every five inhabitants was an Indian, one out of every eight was a mestizo, and there were no more than seventy or eighty thousand *gachupines*. This meant that only one-seventieth of the total population occupied all of the administrative, ecclesiastical and military posts. Mestizos, even more discriminated against than the white Creoles, were able to find employment only as craftsmen, miners or household servants or in the low clergy. Indians were treated as contemptible foreigners; despite their having been exempted from paying tribute to the king, they were forbidden to own personal property and were made to live apart from others on barren land. Both deprivations and privileges were so extreme that poverty was widespread and the cities teemed with beggars. In accordance with the Laws of the Indies, every man able to work who was without a job was forced to choose between laboring on public works projects, entering military service or being sent to prison. "Of the 810,000 families in Mexico in 1799 Abad Queipo estimated that 540,000 were poor and, counting five to each family, there were at least 2,700,000 poor people in the viceroyalty." (Fischer, 52–3)

In 1812, the Creoles joined forces to lend their support to the imprisoned monarch and demand their right to self-government. The ideological evolution of the Creoles is reflected in fray Servando's thought: at first he advocates relative independence, in the manner of Blanco White, but over the years that follow he comes to realize that the system would be a farce and calls for the absolute emancipation of Mexico.[39]

The Creoles accused the Mexican *gachupines* of allying themselves with Bonaparte to ensure that Spain would surrender to the French. After 1810, during the uprising led by Miguel Hidalgo, they could give concrete expression to their longstanding resentment: the cry of "Death to the *gachupines!*" was heard everywhere. Hidalgo, a village priest with progressive ideas, led other priests in organizing a religious war to be waged by peasants, Indians and mestizos from Guanajuato, Guerrero, Jalisco and Michoacán, assuring them that the authorities of the viceroyalty were backing the French and the liberals. The rebel sectors held High Masses and Te Deums in the cathedrals of Valladolid and Guadalajara; following the execution of Hidalgo, another priest, José María Morelos, took over as head of the movement.

But all this happened later. At the time of Servando Teresa de Mier's birth, the division of castes was on the rise, as was the power of the Inquisition. The schools were controlled by the clergy, whose only interest was in education as a means of producing people who would serve the Church. Despite these controls, the University of Mexico offered a high level of education to the Creoles, and the eighteenth century, like the Spain of Charles III, saw a great intellectual flowering. The natural sciences prospered, the Botanical Garden was founded and Creole writers such as Francisco Javier Clavijero, Francisco Javier Alegre, Andrés Cavo and Mariano Veyta flourished. The bishop of Michoacán, Manuel Abad y Queipo, produced an outstanding body of work from the philosophical, political and economic points of view. It is very revealing of the situation in New Spain that all the important men of learning were members of the Catholic clergy, that the principal insurgents of the war of independence were warrior priests, that the entire emancipation movement took place beneath the banner of the Virgin of Guadalupe, and that even the declaration of Mexican independence is a document that unconditionally favored religion: in it Catholicism is proclaimed the sole national religion. It is no mere happenstance that a young man with as great an intellectual thirst as Servando Teresa de Mier decided to enter the Dominican order, thereby earning the opportunity to enter the university and obtain his doctorate in theology.

The Church was the most powerful institution in Mexico, not simply because there was only one religion but also because it had a monopoly on education and untold wealth that included buildings, loans, land holdings, urban constructions—all assets that once in the Church's possession could not be alienated by governmental authorities. The high clergy (archbishops, bishops, prelates of the episcopal court or heads of urban monasteries and convents), was made up of peninsular Spaniards with high salaries and control over the religious orders.[40] In the regular clergy were Creoles who could take holy orders, receive an education, hold certain Church posts and obtain a certain celebrity by virtue of their erudition, as in the case of Mier. This gave rise to problems, because, as the friar notes in his *Memoirs*, "[S]ince the Conquest it has been the constant policy of our Cabinet to keep out of America any of its sons who stands out and attracts the attention of his countrymen. If a pretext can be found, he is imprisoned as punishment." (M 279).

The tensions between the regular and the high clergy were similar to those between castes and between Creoles and *gachupines*. Mier writes in his *Apología:*

> Oh, bishops, bishops! You say that you are successors of the apostles, and would that you might ever have emulated their virtues, without any of you

setting before yourselves as your model the accursed apostle Judas Iscariot. The miter and the power that your incomes give you, which except for a modest sum subtracted from them for your subsistence, belong in strictest justice to the poor of each diocese, and ought not to accompany you beyond the grave save to serve you to enter a realm of sternest justice. (M 219)

In any event, the regular clergy had access to a solid education, giving rise to the paradox whereby Mexican priests were more cultivated than those of the same level as they in Spain—a paradox or a verification of the fact that fray Servando's vision of the world upside down, in which in the center/periphery relationship appears to be altered, is simply seeing the reality of the era by breaking through the discursive net that legitimized power over the colonies by maintaining, in order to justify itself, that they were inferior. Servando never ceases to be amazed at the ignorance of friars in Spain: "In Mexico City the royal preachers would barely pass for students practicing their rhetorical skills on Saturdays. They are idiots," he says, confessing that it nearly made him split his sides laughing to hear the sermon of a Basilian monk. The parishioners were equally ignorant, for on seeing him people said to him: "You are laughing because he preaches to your liking, isn't that so? He has a silver tongue." (156)

There was a third class of priests in Mexico, the so-called low clergy (which included many white Creoles and mestizos), with little education and a salary that was scarcely enough to live on. Despite the precariousness of their situation, the priests of this low clergy had a notable influence on the people and were in the habit of preaching faith in the Virgin of Guadalupe; their hatred of *gachupines* was such that four out of every five Creole priests collaborated with the insurgents, despite the censure of the Church. The viceroy had to proceed with caution when it was a matter of punishing the rebel priests, out of fear of the reaction of the people, who worshipfully regarded this group as sacred.

Given this social background, it is not too daring a thesis to maintain that the war of independence against Spain would have come about sooner or later in any case and that the instability of the monarchy of Ferdinand VII merely served as a handy excuse for precipitating events. The Order of Preachers or Dominicans that fray Servando entered was Thomist: it represented ultra-orthodoxy, faith as absolute reason; the elegant and cultivated Jesuits found themselves expelled from America (Mier met many of them during his European exile) and later from Portugal, France and Spain as well.

David Brading explains the formation of the ideology of Hispano-American independence in accordance with two versions: one of them focuses on the dismemberment of the Hispanic world because of the Napoleonic invasions, a turn of events that the Creole elite took advantage of to demand the power of the colonial bureaucracy for themselves, invoking the Spanish constitution itself. The other has it that the ideas of the rights of man and of the citizen that sustained the French Revolution and the North American Declaration of Independence inspired the Creoles to destroy the old monarchic order and ethnic hierarchies. This second version is the one most frequently recounted in Latin America, citing the republican example of Simón Bolívar; but, at least in the specific case of Mexico, the necessary transition in order to break with colonial structures was slower. In fact, once independence was consolidated, instead of leading to the creation of a republic, it resulted in the coronation of Agustín de Iturbide as emperor.

The Guadalupan Tradition

"Our America takes its stand in defense of the American rights violated by the peninsular Spaniards.[41] Our America takes its stand in defense of the universal rights of man and therefore of the American man, denied by monarchical despotism. But it also takes its stand in favor of the special interpretation of the history of our America created by American Spaniards. Integrating the most enlightened sectors of society, it is not surprising that history takes on the role of an affirmative ideological element of the American nation," Ricaurte Soler writes.[42]

Thus, at the end of the sixteenth century, Creoles began to recall with nostalgia the era of the Conquest, whose heroism and heritage was denied them. The most intellectual among them, usually men of the cloth, began to extol the Aztec Empire as the principal glory of their Mexican fatherland. This too was part of a global phenomenon, an epistemological change in the West: the more secular powers, the experts, devote themselves to the *esprit des nations* and to specific *national character*. Johann Gottfried von Herder the German philosopher and poet, expresses this idea in the sentence: "Each nation, harbors within it the center of its felicity, just as a sphere possesses a center of gravity." If the nation's center of gravity was to be found within itself, then it should give evidence of very specific characteristics, it should be distinguishable from other nations.[43]

Writing as a serious pursuit in Mexico begins with a theological problem: if the discovery of the Indies was, as Cortes's secretary, Francisco Lápez de Gomara maintained, "the greatest thing after the creation of the world, with the exception of the incarnation and death of the one in whom I believe," the fact, by its importance, ought in some way to be already recorded in the sacred texts.[44] At the beginning of the seventeenth century, the Dominican monk Gregorio García ponders the question of whether at the time of the apostles the Gospel might already have been preached in these lands and bases his conclusion on a general principle: if Jesus had sent the apostles to preach the Gospel throughout the world, it was not possible to object that the distance across the ocean was an obstacle, for Saint Augustine had already resolved the problem by pointing out that the apostles could have been transported to one part of the world or another on the wings of angels.

A literal interpretation of Scripture made it imperative that at least one of the apostles should have evangelized the Indians fifteen centuries before the Spaniards. The Augustinians, through fray Antonio de la Calancha, were firm proponents of evangelism at such an early date, maintaining that it would be an insult to God's merciful justice to think that since the coming of Jesus down to the arrival of the Spaniards He had left the Indians without the light of faith for so many centuries. The Franciscans were opposed, imposing the official thesis: the Indians had been kept in the dark for fifteen centuries in order that they might one day be chosen by the Lord, by a king and a people who had also been chosen. The providential right of the Spaniards appears as a divine grace, which promises the attainment of universal salvation through the intermediary of the Catholic Sovereigns.

Despite the Franciscan opposition, there was increasing devotion to a Creole virgin. Bishop Montúfar ordered an investigation and in 1555 founded the first basilica of Our Lady of Guadalupe. Nearly a century was to go by before the Guadalupan faith was formulated in writing. In 1648 the Mexican Miguel Sánchez, a university graduate, published *Imagen de la Virgen María Madre de Dios de Guadalupe, milagrosamente aparecida en México (An Image of the Virgin Mary, Mother of God, of Guadalupe, which Miraculously Appeared in Mexico)*, in which he explains the tradition: the Virgin Mary appeared in person at Tepeyac, near Mexico City, to the illiterate Indian Juan Diego; as proof she left the imprint of her image on the Indian's cape (a mantle woven of mezcal fibers). If the Virgin chose Mexico as God's domain, the role assigned the Spaniards by Providence in America was diminished, since the divine image preceded the Conquest. The conquistadors continued to appear as the right arm of God, but the leading role belonged to the "first among Creole women." The appearance of the Virgin conferred on Mexico a title of nobility: a nobility or grace that came not from the king but from God. The appearance of the Virgin Mary to the Indian Juan Diego signified that the Mother of God was the founder and the patron saint of the Mexican Church. This was a myth and a cult that kindled both religious devotion and patriotic sentiments (cf. Brading). It was imperative to find a new spiritual beginning: the more and more widespread cult of Guadalupe was also being identified with that of the god Quetzalcóatl, whom a number of priests had seen, beginning in the seventeenth century, as the incarnation of Saint Thomas the Apostle. From the theological point of view, the thesis is not far-fetched: Saint Gregory, in his *Acta Thomae,* had assured his readers that it fell to this apostle to preach in the regions *supra Gangem,* that is to say, to the east of India. With this religious idea of the world, it is not surprising that the Jesuits should discover signs of Saint Thomas's preaching of the Gospel in Brazil and Paraguay (they interpreted certain religious symbols as Christian ones), that Marco Polo should discover the place where the apostle was martyred on the outskirts of Madras, or that more than one eighteenth-century apologist should stress the Christian coincidences to be found in Chinese Confucianism. The list of those who supported the thesis that Saint Thomas and Quetzalcóatl were one includes illustrious seventeenth-century figures such as the priests Bernardino de Sahagún, Diego Durán and Juan de Tovar, and in the eighteenth century, Manuel Duarte and the well-known writer Carlos de Sigüenza y Góngora.[45]

None of these authors and none of the devoted followers of the Mexican Virgin (by 1747 all the dioceses of New Spain had acclaimed Our Lady of Guadalupe as their patron saint and all the provincial capitals had erected special altars, often located on the outskirts, in emulation of her appearance at Tepeyac) dared put forth the theory of the pre-evangelization of America. For more than two centuries, the cornerstone of the Spanish Conquest had been evangelization, and that is where the famous sermon of 1794 that was to cost fray Servando Teresa de Mier thirty years of persecution enters history. His sermon conjoins the two traditions, as he assures his listeners that the Virgin did not appear to the Indian Juan Diego but to Saint Thomas, thereby canceling out with a single stroke of his pen the justification for the Conquest of America. "I have said that this opinion is the one that most closely conforms to Sacred Scripture, because Jesus Christ, sending his apostles forth to preach the Gospel, commanded them: 'Go into the whole world and preach the Gospel to every creature under heaven; and be witnesses for me from Jerusalem and Judea to the ends of the earth.' Is it feasible that in an order so compelling, general and absolute half the globe had not been included?" (M 21) Moreover, Mier maintains that if the conquistadors had recognized the Mexican religion as being a variant or a transfiguration of Christianity, the Conquest would not have necessitated the shedding of a single drop of blood. Hence the Spaniards desecrated the very religion that they professed.

The sermon is known from three different copies or versions that Mier handed over to the censors. There is also a syncretic version. Mier's thesis differs from that of Sánchez on one basic point: the image of the Virgin of Guadalupe is the product of a meeting, which took place in Mexico, between the Virgin in person and Saint Thomas. Mier returns to this point in all his writings, but the sermon sums it up in four propositions or postulates that affirm: (1) the superiority of the Nahuatl language to others, (2) the evangelization of Mexico by Saint Thomas, (3) the great age of the image of the Virgin (it is seventeen hundred years old; therefore it is not contemporaneous with the Indian Juan Diego and 4) the biblical roots of the Mexican people. Rather than the prophetic reason that Miguel Sánchez attributes to it, Mier invents a historical reason, a sort of new lineage. Fray Servando cities dates and names, outlines conjectures and conclusions; the Virgin is the goddess Tonantzin, as she had been known by the Indians until "the Spaniards baptized her with a Saracen name, which has nothing in common with the sweet appellation of Mother of God." (M 98)

His ideas are judged to be heterodox, and rightly so. For what underlies them is not a discussion of temporal details and goes beyond even the movements of religious fusion/conversion that had been gradually forming in the New World to further the acceptance of Catholicism as the local faith. His ideas point to a political revolution: "I say this because certain people accused me of having tried to rob Spaniards of the glory of having brought the Gospel [to Mexico]. How could I have intended to rob them of a glory that is so clearly ours, since it was that of our fathers the conquistadors, or the first missionaries, whose apostolic succession is to be found among us?" (27–8)

Alonso Núñez de Haro y Peralta, named archbishop of Mexico in 1791, was to make of the persecution of Mier a personal cause. As has already been seen, he himself, a few years before, had decreed that restrictions be placed on important ecclesiastical posts, and it is evident that this time a Creole priest has gone beyond the limits of the tolerable. It matters little that the friar offers to make a public retraction and even promises "to compose and publish at my expense a work contrary to my sermon" (M 108); Haro is implacable. ("Haro," Mier writes, "liked only one thing about America, its hard pesos, to enrich his family." [M 180]) Mier is brought to trial in an ecclesiastical court, he is placed on trial for heresy by an Inquisition court, and he is sentenced to ten years' imprisonment "as a State criminal" in the monastery of Las Caldas. But before his first year as a prisoner is out, Mier cuts the lead bars of his cell and escapes through the window, leaving behind a letter in verse explaining why he has fled. He is immediately taken prisoner again and is sent to the Monastery of San Pablo (in Burgos); he manages to secure his transfer to Cádiz, and on the way there, petitions the Council of the Indies to review his case. Over the course of 1797 he writes a defense of his sermon to present to the council. In 1800 the Royal Academy of History rejects Haro's edict and renders an opinion in Mier's favor. Mistrustful that justice will be done him, Mier flees and is captured in Burgos, whence he will escape once again. He goes to Madrid, then to Valladolid and from there to France, beginning the stage of his life's travels covered by this edition of his *Memoirs*. In 1802 in Italy he formally requests his secularization; he returns to Madrid and is once again imprisoned; he is then sent to Los Toribios (in Seville), escaping once more through his cell window. The story repeats; he is arrested in Cádiz and again sent to Los Toribios, this time in irons, but eventually he escapes yet again. This time he manages to cross the border and enter Portugal, where this series of adventures recounted in his *Memoirs* comes to an end and his life begins to take on a more political orientation: first he opposes the Napoleonic occupation, then the viceregal authorities in Mexico, and finally, Iturbide's imperial dreams. He will then write such important texts as his *Historia de la revolución de Nueva España, Memoria político-instructiva*, his *Apología*, the *Memorias* and various open letters of political importance, but he will never disavow his sermon on the Virgin of Guadalupe, even though once it had been delivered, and in the face of the general scandal it aroused, he tried in vain to apologize for it.

On occasion Fray Servando contradicts himself in his defense, going so far as to admit that Borunda did not have the proofs he had promised for the Guadalupan sermon: "I confess that far from having found the indisputable proofs that the man had assured me he possessed, I discovered a fair number of absurdities characteristic of a man who was not versed in Theology, and even of any antiquarian and etymologist who begins with divinations, goes on to visions and ends up in fits of delirium. The man had read a great deal, conceived but was unable to give birth, and what he did give birth to he could not persuade me of, owing to his lack of other pertinent knowledge." (M 108) Despite this, Mier never failed to stand his ground with regard to his thesis. Even in a text as late as "Carta de despedida a los mexicanos escrita desde el Castillo de San Juan de Ulúa por el Doctor don Servando Teresa de Mier Noriega y Guerra" ("Letter of farewell to the Mexican people written from the Castle of San Juan de Ulúa by Dr. don Servando Teresa de Mier Noriega y Guerra," 1821), he emphasized not only his original thesis but also the biblical roots of Mexico, going so far as to use the country's very name: "Yes, Mexico with its soft *x,* as the Indians pronounce it, means: where Christ is or is adored, and *Mexicans* means the same thing as *Christians.*"[46] And he comes back to his accusation. "What was the religion of the Mexicans if not Christianity disordered by time . . . ? The Spaniards . . . brought ruin to the very religion that they professed, and adopted as their own images that which they were in the habit of burning because they were under different symbols."

One of Servando Teresa de Mier's mistakes was to oppose a faith that had already become deeply rooted in his compatriots—oppose in the sense of wanting to modify it in order to make it politically more extreme. If on the one hand it is true that the bases existed for supposing that the union of Guadalupe and Quetzalcóatl could be accepted, it is also true that, by eliminating the intercession of the Spaniards, it reduced by the same token the role of the Indian Juan Diego, with whom the popular masses could more easily identify than with the remote Saint Thomas. Mier's error lay in questioning a tradition that "had imperceptibly become another of the great symbols incarnating national aspirations." (*Ideario político,* xxvi)

But in reality the arguments were a pretext for dealing out exemplary punishment to a Creole priest who had tried to be too clever. Mier explains it well: "I shall speak out clearly: all this is nothing more than a comedy in two acts with an interlude. . . . The Europeans, who despite their not believing in the tradition of Guadalupe, shouted louder than the Creoles in order to destroy the false information regarding Saint Thomas's preaching, because they believe that it robs them of the glory of having brought the Gospel, and makes them the equal of the Indians in their own creation of the image of the Virgin of the Pillar. Unfortunately, a brilliant Creole struck precisely the right note." (M 146–7) And a few pages later he emphasizes: "Americans, idiots that we are, the Archbishop's Europeans made mock of us. . . . [O]ne of the reasons behind my persecution was that I secured equal favor [for the Virgins of Guadalupe and of Pillar] and made you their [the Europeans'] equals."[47] The image of Guadalupe and the tradition taken up by Miguel Sánchez (not Mier's thesis) were raised on high by Father Hidalgo and by the insurgents, and even today they continue to represent Mexicans' pride in their national identity.

Sinner or Prophet

Fray Servando's body of work includes the *Historia de la revolución de Nueva España* (1813), written under the pseudonym of José Guerra, a text that has been regarded as a precursor of the thought that lay behind the movement for independence. In it Mier maintained that America was not really a colony of Spain but its equal, as decreed in the early Laws of the Indies. This idea implied that the American peoples should be able to govern themselves independently; on many counts his arguments become confused with the defense of the Mexican aristocracy. Fray Servando was the spokesman for the protest against the "otherness" of the religious orders and against the decrees giving the Creole friars no access to prelacies and wealth; it was he who set down on paper the rancor against the monarchy and the Creole protests against being obliged to assume all of the expenses of the Church in New Spain. But this does not mean that Mier supported the principle of equality or the abolition of the caste system, subjects on which he shared the reserve of Creoles in general. (Lafaye, 195 et seq.)[48]

In the last analysis, despite the scandals, Mier was a legalist. As with most Creoles, espousal of revolution was a slow process in his case, becoming more and more pronounced as the driving force of historical events themselves increased. "I am a son of Spaniards," he writes in his *Manifiesto apologético*, "I detest them only insofar as they are oppressors." His original revolutionary act, in addition to the Guadalupan sermon and the attempt to diminish the importance of the evangelization of the New World, was to call for the application of a body of longstanding laws that formed, in his opinion, the real "American Constitution" within the framework of the Spanish monarchy. "I return to . . . the solemn and explicit pact that the Americans concluded with the sovereigns of Spain, which no other nation ever made more clearly; and its authentication is to be found in the very code of its laws. This is our magna carta." (*Histo-*

ria, vol. 14) In Philadelphia in 1821, he wrote his *Memoria político-instructiva*, in which he says: "America is ours, because our fathers won it if there was such a thing as a right to do so; because it came from our mothers, and because we were born there. This is the natural law of peoples in their respective regions. . . . God has separated us from Europe by an immense ocean, and our interests are different." He has turned profoundly republican: "God free us from emperors or kings. They keep none of their promises, and always end up becoming despots. All men are inclined to impose their will, without challenge. And there is nothing to which man is more accustomed." In the *Memoria político-instructiva*, he was also to pen the words that were the cause of the last of his imprisonments: "Iturbide! Renounce the new opinion [giving Mexico a king according to the Plan of Iguala]. . . . Support independence; but absolute independence, independence without a new master, republican independence."

Mier participated in the war against Napoleon Bonaparte; he carried on a correspondence with Blanco White (to whom he addressed two public documents, the first and second *Carta de un americano al Español* (1811 and 1812); he was elected a member of the Institut National de France (1814); he was a warrior who fought alongside Francisco Javier Mina in an attempt to liberate Mexico from the Spanish Empire (1817); he was a deputy.

The life and the work intermingle in this formidable thinker, one of the first to find the formula for imagining an autonomous America: the full observance of the Laws of the Indies, an idea that Simón Bolívar made good use of in his *Carta profética*. Mier also joined in the effort to recover a heroic past, exalting Montezuma and Cuauhtémoc as patriotic heroes, equating the morality of contemporary Spaniards with that of the conquistadors, thus following the best tradition of fray Bartolomé de Las Casas. Both were Dominican friars; that order—the Order of Preachers and also that of Inquisitors—tended to weigh and to denounce the excesses of the Conquest, whereas the Franciscans, for example, justified those excesses as a "necessary evil" for evangelization. This does not mean that, once condemned by the viceregal authorities, Mier received the support of the Dominicans—who were accused like all the rest of corruption—but rather that he subscribed to a critical tradition. Las Casas was the first to replace the providentialist legend (that is to say, Spain chosen as the savior of the New World) with the "black legend" of the Spanish Conquest; his denunciations were even invoked by Voltaire in the already cited Enlightenment attacks against Spain's colonial regime.[49]

With regard to the dispute concerning the New World, fray Bartolomé had left a much more favorable precedent in the sixteenth century. In his *De unico vocationis modo (On the Sole Way of Attracting All Peoples to the True Religion)* he maintained that all the nations of the earth possess a similar level of intelligence, and in his *Apologética historia sumaria de las Indias (Brief Apologetic History of the Indies)* he showed that the Old and the New World were equal if they were compared both as to their barbarism and to their level of civilization. (Brading, 45–50) But, as has already been explained, polemics during the eighteenth century were based on a "borrowed language," inherited from the language of science and its taxonomy, which gave the Encyclopedists an overall tone modeled on that of natural history that was imposed and/or superimposed upon the colonial subject, in the guise of a "creative act issuing forth a unique, totalizing, hegemonic form of truth."[50] What Mier did in his *Memoirs* was to displace this "borrowed language" and apply it in reverse: what is filthy and crude is not on the periphery but in the center—a weak center, with poverty-stricken people, prostitutes, dung in the houses, priests with concubines, and governed by corrupt petty bureaucrats. The description of space is, naturally, a scientist and legitimizing battle. It is therefore commonly asserted that both travel literature and maps were forms of the language of power and not of protest. The *Memoirs* serve as an invitation to a heterological rereading of these useful theories, because with marginalization and the periphery as their point of departure, Columbus's voyage is undertaken in reverse: discovering the Old World, so as to reinscribe it and rehierarchize it, because the "place on the map . . . is . . . also a place in history," and everything depends on how it is described.[51]

Fray Servando is, as I have already said, a traveler in reverse. Breasting the current of his era, he enabled his readers to reflect on reality in another way. The great Cuban writer of this century, José Lezama Lima, analyzing the greatness of this rebel priest and his historical projection, accuses him of turning out, in the long run, to be a conservative. "In Fray Servando, in that transition from the Baroque to Romanticism, we unexpectedly come across very American hidden surprises. He believes that he is breaking with tradition, when he is broadening its scope. Hence, when he believes that he is parting company with what is Hispanic, he finds it again in himself, ever on the rise. Reforming within the established order, not breaking the thread of what is Spanish but, rather, taking it up again, Fray Servando skims it off and makes it stronger, to the point of temerity. Catholicism leans on it and makes itself a throne."[52]

A polemical figure even two centuries later, fray Servando Teresa de Mier deserves to be read today while taking into account the context that in his own era people were unable to see because it was too close at hand. Whether he was a conservative or a heretic, his *Memoirs* should be contemplated within the framework of the Spanish colonial era and the Bonapartist invasions, within the framework of the discourses of Buffon and the Encyclopedists, within the framework of the newborn (and still faltering) emancipation of America. In order to moderate the condemnation of those who accept his ideological contributions or the marvel of the "upside-down gaze" that his writings bring to bear on Europe, yet reject his bold Guadalupan theses, one need only call to mind how difficult the status of a supporter of the movement for independence must have been in New Spain. After three centuries of domination, thinking of oneself as independent was a real feat, even more so if we take into account the fact that the majority of the tools in vogue for proclaiming freedom among men were tools that made Americans out to be inferior. It is not surprising that there was more than one error made or blind swipe dealt in the search for images that would call forth republican sentiments and action. To this overall picture there must be added a most peculiar sociocultural condition; unlike other latitudes in which the arrival of the nineteenth century meant the separation of the powers of Church and State, Mexican independence was not achieved beneath the banner of the rights of Americans: the war was begun with the image of the Virgin and the initial cry of "Long live religion!"

Fray Servando's life work lies between eras, between worlds: from the Enlightenment to Romanticism, from colonial status to independence, from America to Europe, from the Church to the Congress or the university. He was heretic, megalomaniac, rebel, character in a novel, and father of his country, a man perhaps sometimes misguided but also a visionary. The value of Mier's *Memoirs* lies in the fact that—as a space par excellence outside imperial power, within Mexico and abroad—it is writing underscored by a perpetually differentiating, disorderly, dissident gesture; the reader will find his upside-down gaze contagious.

—*Susana Rotker*

NOTES TO THE INTRODUCTION

1. The page numbers between parentheses refers to this edition.

2. Quotations from fray Mier's *Memorias (Memoirs)*, vol. 1, in the edition by Antonio Castro Leal, (Mexico City: Porrúa, 1946) will be indicated in the text by an "M" in parentheses, followed by the page number.

3. The monastery of Las Caldas, in the diocese of Santander (Spain), is the place to which Father Mier was sent from Mexico as punishment for his sermon on the Virgin of Guadalupe. He was sentenced to ten years' imprisonment there.

4. Mier was not the only traveler of his time who made frequent references to the body and to the vulgarity of European habits; cf. John Macdonald, *Memoirs of an Eighteenth-Century Footman* (London: Century, 1985) [1745–79]. Although Mier was the first Mexican to write about Spanish reality, there were a few other Americans who also criticized the social injustices and European urban poverty of that era, among them Simón Rodríguez; see *Inventamos o erramos*, ed. Dardo Cúneo (Caracas: Monte Avila, 2d ed., 1982).

5. See Peter Stallybras and Allon White, *The Politics & Poetics of Transgression* (Ithaca, N.Y.: Cornell University Press, 1986); M. M. Bakhtin, *Rabelais and His World,* trans. Hélène Iswolsky (Cambridge: MIT Press, 1968); Norbert Elias, *The History of Manners,* trans. Edmund Jephcott (New York: Pantheon, 1987).

6. Except when otherwise indicated, in order to avoid repetition all references in the text immediately following concerning *covachuelos* and Spain are taken from M 234–47.

7. In the prologue to *Historia de la conquista y población de la provincia de Venezuela* (Caracas: Ayacucho, 1992) by José de Oviedo y Baños, there is a wide-ranging reflection on the Spanish disdain toward the New World and its effect on literature: "[I]f imperial culture itself did not discover epic traits in the captains of overseas territories, from what locus of speech, from what desperate backwater of silence ought those men lost in the vastness of America, the heirs of contempt, whose voices rarely reached the threshold of the Court, to have constructed their first accounts?" Citation from the preliminary study by Tomás Eloy Martínez and S. Rotker, xiii.

8. Ernst Cassirer, *The Philosophy of the Enlightenment,* trans. Fritz C. A. Koelln and James P. Pettegrove (Princeton: Princeton University Press, 1951); Peter Gay, *The Enlightenment: An Interpretation,* 2 vols. (New York: Norton, 1969); Ulrich Im Hoff, *Europa de la Ilustración* (Madrid: Grijalbo, 1993); Mark Horkheimer and Theodor W. Adorno, *Dialéctica del iluminismo,* trans. H. A. Murena (Buenos Aires: Sur, 1994); Pierre Saint-Amand, *The Laws of Hostility: Politics, Violence, and the Enlightenment,* foreword by Chantal Mouffe, trans. Jennifer Curtis Gage (Minneapolis: University of Minnesota Press, 1996); H. M. Scott, ed., *Enlightened Absolutism: Reform and Reformers in Late Eighteenth-Century Europe* (Ann Arbor: University of Michigan Press, 1990). Of great interest: Arthur Preston Whitaker, *Latin America and the Enlightenment* (Ithaca: Cornell University Press, 1967).

9. Antonelli Gerbi, *La disputa del Nuevo Mundo: Historia de una polémica, 1750–1900,* trans. Antonio Alatorre (México: Fondo de Cultura Económica, 2d ed., corrected and expanded, 1982), 397.

10. Emmanuel Chukwudi Eze selects a series of basic texts for understanding of the subject. See *Race and the Enlightenment* (Cambridge: Blackwell, 1997), 33.

11. Aristotle defined the rationality of the human being by his ability to live in a society organized more or less along the lines of Athenian democracy. The Encyclopedists, seeing themselves as the embodiment of the Age of Reason itself, extended the concept by pairing the "cultivated" (now called the "civilized") against the barbarians. Aristotle's line of reasoning was to be used to support the opposite argument and rehabilitate America, since the architecture and the social complexity of the Aztecs, Mayas and Incas refuted the thesis of America as the locus of barbarism.

12. A large part of the information that follows, concerning the Spanish versions of the New World, including citations of texts, is taken from Manfred Tietz, "La visión de América y de la conquista en la España del siglo XVIII," in *El precio de la "invención" de América,* ed. Reyes Mate and Friedrich Niewöhner, (Barcelona: Anthropos, 1992) 219–34.

13. In his *Brevísima relación de la destrucción de las Indias* (1542), Bartolomé de Las Casas characterized the Spaniards as thieves, torturers and murderers of defenseless Indians, "with the result that after half a century of European colonization, some fifteen million Indians had disappeared from the face of the Earth." (Brading, 45) These memoirs of Las Casas were partially responsible for the abolition of the *encomienda* system in the New World.

14. See René Jara, "The Inscription of Creole Consciousness: Fray Servando Teresa de Mier," in *1492–1992: Re/Discovering Colonial Writing,* ed. René and Nicholas Spadaccini (Minneapolis: The Prisma Institute, 1989), 349–79.

15. Many other books deal with the same subject as Gerbi's. A useful one is the overview in Tzevan Todorov's *La conquista de América: El problema del otro,* trans. Flora Botton Burlá (Mexico City: Siglo XXI, 3d ed., 1991).

16. On the influence of the Enlightenment in Spain, see Richard Herr, *The Eighteenth-Century Revolution in Spain* (Princeton: Princeton University Press, 1958). On the eclectic Enlightenment in Latin America, see José Carlos Chiaramonte's excellent prologue to his *Pensamiento de la Ilustración: Economía y sociedad iberoamericanas en el siglo XVIII* (Caracas: Biblioteca Ayacucho, 1979). Chiaramonte says: "The fact that the intellectual movement of the nineteenth century is regarded as being the heir of revolutionary anti-metropolitan ideology led to a global condemnation of the colonial past and spared from this condemnation only those expressions that could be considered to be *antecedents* of independence, that is to say, primarily, enlightened manifestations dating from the late eighteenth century. The polemical attitude of Romanticism toward eighteenth-century rationalism, insofar as it had to do with Ibero-American expressions of the Enlightenment, was thus attenuated on certain planes. And consequently, the

influence of the Enlightenment endured for a much longer time and with un-usual vigor even at the height of the Romantic and positivist period, being safe-guarded by the continual eclecticism of local thought as well." (xii).

17. The *antuerpia* is a marine boar that was sighted in 1537, according to An-tonio Torquemada in his *Jardín de flores curiosas* (Salamanca, 1570), cited by Al-fonso Reyes, "De un autor censurado [Torquemada] en el *Quijote,*" *Obras completas,* vol. 6 (Mexico City: Fondo de Cultura Económica, 1957), 378.

18. Gerbi, quoted in footnote, 256. See also David Brading, *The First Amer-ica: The Spanish Monarchy, Creole Patriots and the Liberal State, 1492–1867* (Cam-bridge: Cambridge University Press, 1991); the quotations translated above are based on the edition in Spanish, *Orbe indiano: De la monarquía católica a la república criolla, 1492–1867,* trans. Juan José Utrilla (Mexico City: Fondo de Cul-tura Económica, 1994), 82–83.

19. In order to reflect on this problem in relation to countries of the Third World in their postcolonial status, or that of "post-colonies," see Partha Chatter-jee, *Nationalist Thought and the Colonial World: A Derivative Discourse* (Min-neapolis: University of Minnesota Press, 1986).

20. There is an excellent article on the way in which the colonized subject incor-porates the "borrowed language" (or the "imperial gaze") in order to represent itself: Iris M. Zavala's "Representing the Colonial Subject," in *1492–1992: Re/Discovering Colonial Writing,* 323–48. Another indispensable book is Mary Louise Pratt's *Imper-ial Eyes: Travel Writing and Transculturation* (New York: Routledge, 1992).

21. On the later development of ideas on emancipation in Latin America, see E. Bradford Burns, *The Poverty of Progress* (Berkeley: University of Califor-nia Press, 1980); also my prologue to *Ensayistas de nuestra América,* vol. 1 (Buenos Aires: Losada, 1994).

22. On postcolonial theory useful for this specific approach, see Homi K. Bhabha, "A Question of Survival: Nations and Psychic States," in *Psychoanalysis and Cultural Theory: Thresholds,* ed. James Donald (New York: St. Martin's Press, 1991), 89–103; "The Other Question: The Stereotype and Colonial Discourse," in *Screen twenty-four* (1983): 18–36; and *The Location of Culture* (London-New York: Routledge, 1994). Also Edward Said, *Culture and Imperialism* (New York: Alfred A. Knopf, 1993); Bill Ashcroft, Gareth Griffiths and Helen Tiffin, *The Empire Writes Back: Theory and Practice in Post-Colonial Literatures* (New York-London: Routledge, 1989); and Chris Tiffin and Alan Lawson, eds., *De-Scribing Empire: Post-Colonialism and Textuality* (New York-London: Routledge, 1994).

23. A number of excellent collections of documents endeavor to fill the vac-uum of materials concerning this period in Latin America in general, for in-stance the previously mentioned *Pensamiento de la ilustración: Economía y sociedad iberoamericanas en el siglo XVIII* by José Carlos Chiaramonte, and although it concentrates on a slightly later period, *Pensamiento político de la emancipación (1790–1825),* 2 vols., prologue by José Luis Romero, ed. J. L. Romero and Luis Alberto Romero (Caracas: Biblioteca Ayacucho, 1977).

24. The authorship of the translation is a matter of dispute. Servando maintains that it is his work and says that "it was printed under the name of Robinson, because this is a sacrifice demanded of poor authors by those who pay the
expenses of having their works printed." (20) This self-attribution would appear
to be an overstepping of the limits on his part: Simón Rodríguez was as poor as
he was and could scarcely have exploited him as a ghost writer in order to show
off talents not his own. The maneuver seems, rather, to have been an act of revenge for the concrete fact that all the labors of translation finally appeared under the name Samuel Robinson; all the evidence points to the fact that it was a
cotranslation.

25. *El mundo alucinante* has, among its merits, that of having popularized the
figure of the Mexican friar. It has also aided in making a myth of him: taking all
the liberties with history that fiction permits, Arenas casts his character Mier as
the protagonist of this sort of "formless, desperate poem, this galloping, torren-
tial lie, irreverent and grotesque, desolate and loving, this (it must have a name
of some sort) novel," as Arenas himself defines it at the end of the prologue that
he added to the Monte Avila edition of the novel (Caracas, 1980). This prologue
is entitled "Fray Servando, Indefatigable Victim." Arenas's novel about Mier has
produced in turn a great many interesting studies, for example: Perla Rozencvaig, *Reinaldo Arenas: Narrativa de transgresión* (Mexico City: Oasis, 1986); Julio
E. Hernández Miyares and Perla Rozencvaig, comps. *Reinaldo Arenas: Alucina-
ciones, fantasía y realidad* (Illinois: Scott, Forsman, 1990); Francisco Soto,
Reinaldo Arenas: The Pentagonia (Gainesville: University Press of Florida, 1994);
Alicia Borinsky, "Re-escribir y escribir: Arenas, Menard, Borges, Cervantes,
Fray Servando" in *Revista Ilberoamericana* (julio-diciembre 1975): 605–16.

26. Alfonso Reyes, "Fray Servando Teresa de Mier," in *Visión de Anáhuac y
otros ensayos* (Mexico City: Fondo de Cultura Económica, 1983), 33.

27. The mania for speaking at such length about oneself was not an exception in this period. Another distinguished traveler, a European, from a wealthy
family and with access to official circles, was Viscount François-Auguste-René
Chateaubriand. As is true of fray Servando, his major preoccupation was to talk
about himself, to create himself as a fictional character (*Mémoires d'outre-tombe*,
the writing of which Chateaubriand began in 1810).

28. Emir Rodríguez Monegal, ed., *The Borzoi Anthology of Latin American
Literature*, vol. 1 (New York: Knopf, 1977), 16.

29. Tulio Halperín Donghi, "Intelectuales, sociedad y vida pública en His-
panoamérica a través de la literatura autobiográfica," in *El espejo de la historia:
Problemas argentinos y perspectivas latinoamericanas* (Buenos Aires: Sudameri-
cana, 1987), 53.

30. Cited by Edmundo O'Gorman in the prologue to his edition of Servando Teresa y Mier's *Ideario político* (Caracas: Biblioteca Ayacucho, 1978), x–xi.

31. Cited in Servando Teresa de Mier's *Ideario político*, x. Other works by
O'Gorman of the greatest interest: "Fray Servando Teresa de Mier," in *Seis estu-*

dios históricos de tema mexicano (Mexico City: Universidad Veracruzana, 1960), 59–148, and "Estudio preliminar," in *Obras completas de Servando Teresa de Mier* (Mexico City: UNAM, 1981).

32. On literary genres in the Mexican Enlightenment, see Jean Franco, "La heterogeneidad peligrosa: Escritura y control social en vísperas de la independencia mexicana," in *Hispamérica*, 34–35, (1983): 3–34.

33. In addition to Leal, O'Gorman and other studies cited, see also: Leda Arguedas, "Fray Servando: la contradicción de la nacionalidad," in *Letterature d' America* 5, no. 21 (Inverno 1984): 29–45; Marie-Cécile Benassy-Berling, "De Sigüenza y Góngora a Fray Servando Teresa de Mier: Vision de l'Indien par le Créole et enjeu politique," in *Les Représentations de l'autre dans l'espace ibérique et ibéro-américain, II: Perspective diachronique*, ed. Agustín Redondo (Paris: Presses de la Sorbonne Nouvelle, 1993), 107–15; Margarita Bera Pierini, "De un fraile heterodoxo en la España de Carlos IV: Las *Memorias* de fray Servando," in *Actas del Congreso de Hispanistas: España en América y América en España*, ed. Luis Martínez Cuitino (Buenos Aires: Instituto de Filología, 1993), 806–15; Guadalupe Fernández Ariza, "Fray Servando en Madrid: Crónica de un romántico destierro," in *Anales de literatura hispanoamericana* 22 (1993): 55–69; José Ignacio García Noriega, "Vida de Fray Servando Teresa de Mier," in *Boletín del Instituto de Estudios Asturianos* 41 (1987): 299–310; Bedford K. Hadley, *The Enigmatic Padre Mier* (Austin: University of Texas Press, 1955); Silva Herzog, "Fray Servando Teresa de Mier," in *Cuadernos Americanos*, 154 (1967): 162–69; René Jara, "El criollismo de Fray Servando Teresa de Mier," in *Cuadernos Americanos* 222 (1979): 141–62; Alfonso Junco, *El increíble Fray Servando. Psicología y epistolario* (Mexico City: Jus, 1959); Luis H. Pena y Magdalena Mais, "El discurso de la identidad y la identidad del discurso. Memorias del padre Mier," in *Secolas Annals* 24 (1993): 50–57.

34. See Lillian Estelle Fisher, *The Background of the Revolution for Mexican Independence* (New York: Russell & Russell, 1934); Doris M. Ladd, *The Mexican Nobility at Independence, 1780–1826* (Austin: ILAS, University of Texas, 1978); David Brading, *The First America Prophecy and Myth in Mexican History* (Cambridge: Cambridge University Press, 1984); David Brading, *Miners and Merchants in Bourbon Mexico, 1763–1810* (Cambridge: Cambridge University Press, 1971); Netti Lee Benson, ed., *Mexico and the Spanish Cortes, 1810–1822: Eight Essays* (Austin and London: Institute of Latin American Studies, University of Texas Press, 1966); Charles Gibson, *The Aztecs Under Spanish Rule: A History of the Indians of the Valley of Mexico, 1519–1810* (Stanford: Stanford University Press, 1964).

35. See also: José Miranda, *Vida colonial y albores de la independencia* (Mexico City: Sep-Setentas, 1972); Francisco Morales, *Clero y política en México* (1764–1834): Algunas ideas sobre la autoridad, la independencia y la reforma eclesiástica (Mexico City: Sep-Setentas, 1977); B. Navarro González, *Cultura mexicana moderna en el siglo XVIII* (Mexico City: UNAM, 1964); Jaime E. Ro-

dríguez O., ed., *The Independence of Mexico and the Creation of the New Nation* (University of California: Latin American Center Publications, Los Angeles; Mexico/Chicano Program, Irvine, 1989); Frank Tannenbaum, *Peace by Revolution: An Interpretation of Mexico* (New York: Columbia University Press, 1933).

36. Raymond Carr, *Spain, 1808–1839* (London: Oxford University Press, 1966, reprinted 1975).

37. Before the end of the seventeenth century, there were seven universities in Hispano-America (at least a hundred years before the establishment of the first one in the United States), all created on the models of Salamanca and Paris. Instruction, despite the religious influence, was on a very high level; the problem was that the Creoles had so few public offices open to them that there was soon a superabundance of lawyers.

38. Nigel Glendinning, *A Literary History of Spain: The Eighteenth Century* (London: Ernest Benn; New York: Barnes & Noble, 1972); W. N. Hargreaves-Mawdesley, *Eighteenth-Century Spain, 1700–1788: A Political, Diplomatic and Institutional History* (London: MacMillan, 1979); Marcelino Menéndez Pelayo, *Historia de los heterodoxos españoles* (Buenos Aires: Espasa Calpe, 1951).

39. José María Blanco y Crespo was a famous Spanish journalist and liberal taken in as a refugee in London, where he wrote under the name of Joseph Blanco White. He was editor of the periodical *El Español* (1810–14), in whose pages he pleaded in favor of efforts to avoid a rupture between Spain and its American colonies by limiting the power of the monarch and giving the New World greater autonomy.

40. In Europe the division of classes among members of the Church was similar. In order to be named a bishop, proof of four aristocratic forebears was required. Later the requirement was even more strict: it was necessary to prove the nobility of sixteen, or even thirty-two, forebears. See Ulrich Im Hoff's *La Europa de la Ilustración*.

41. "As in the mother country, a new interpretation of history contributed to the formation of a new ideology. The study of the pre-Columbian past provided the basis for the notion of a Mexican empire and post-conquest history seemed to confirm the existence of an American constitution. This line of thought culminated in the writings of Father Servando Teresa de Mier. His *Idea de la Constitución dada a las Américas por los reyes de España antes de la invasión del antiguo despotismo* argued that New Spaniards were mestizos who possessed rights derived from two sources: their Indian progenitors, who originally possessed the land, and their Spanish ancestors, who in conquering Mexico obtained privileges from the crown, including the right to convene their own cortes. Mier declared: 'Our kings, far from having considered establishing a colonial system in our Americas, not only made our [kingdoms] equal with Spanish [ones] but also granted us the best [institutions] she possessed.' He believed the early sixteenth century to have been 'the age of the true constitution of America.'" Jaime E. Rodríguez O., ed., *The Independence of Mexico and the Creation of a New Nation*, 32.

42. Ricaurte Soler, *Idea y cuestión nacional latinoamericanas: De la independencia a la emergencia del imperialismo* (Mexico City: Siglo XXI, 1980), 40–41.

43. Cf. David Brading, *Prophecy and Myth in Mexican History* (Cambridge: Cambridge University Press, 1971) and Jacques Lafaye, *Quetzalcóatl and Guadalupe* (University of Chicago Press, 1976). A large part of the references utilized below come from the indispensable collection *Testimonios históricos guadalupanos*, Ernesto Torre Villar and Ramiero Navario de Ande, comps. (Mexico City: Fondo de cultura Economica, 1982) and also from *El heterodoxo guadalupano: Obras completas* [of Mier], vols. 1–3, ed. Edmundo O'Gorman (Mexico City: UNAM, 1981).

44. I owe the part that follows to the generosity of Tomás Eloy Martínez, who allowed me to use the (unpublished) notes of a seminar he prepared on the nation and the Guadalupan tradition (University of London, 1990).

45. Lafaye's *Quetzalcóatl and Guadalupe* is a marvelous study of the formation of a national consciousness in Mexico through these inquiries of a religious nature. It is also worth citing Brading's thesis, according to which the eighteenth and nineteenth centuries in Mexico can scarcely be interpreted as "a mere passive absorption of the currents of Enlightenment thought."

46. This and the following quotation are from Mier's *Ideario político*, 8–11.

47. See also: Ernesto de la Torre Villar and Ramiro Navarro de Anda, comps., *Testimonios históricos guadalupanos* (Mexico City: Fondo de Cultura Económica, 1982); Jacques Lafaye, Mesías, cruzadas, utopías: *El judeo-cristianismo en las sociedades ibéricas*, trans. Juan José Utrilla (Mexico City: Fondo de Cultura, 1984); Bernardo Bergoend, *La nacionalidad mexicana y la Virgen de Guadalupe* (Mexico City: Jus, 1968).

48. See also John V. Lombardi, *The Political Ideology of Fray Servando Teresa de Mier, Propagandist for Independence* (Cuernavaca: Sondeos, n. 25, 1968).

49. See Irving A. Leonard, *Los libros del conquistador*, trans. Mario Monteforte Toledo (Mexico City: fondo de Cultura Económica, 2d ed., 1979).

50. Iris M. Zavala, "Representing the Colonial Subject" in *1492–1992: Re/Discovering Colonial Writing*, 332. She adds: "Within this conception of knowledge based on the natural sciences, the associations and contiguities led to a technology of observing, dissecting and reordering objects (facts) according to mental imaginary constructs, which could then be inserted in the all-encompassing, systematic, ordering of knowledge. Buffon's borrowed language projected an identity of the New World as weak, indifferent, incapable of progress (modernity), because the Americans (Indians) were limited to the satisfaction of immediate needs." (333) Kathleen Ross confirms this sort of interpretation of the facts: "I read the *Memorias* as a natural history of the Old World, a direct descendant of the sixteenth-century histories of Las Casas and Acosta," she writes in "A Natural History of the Old World: the *Memorias* of Fray Servando Teresa de Mier," in *Revista de Estudios Hispánicos* XXIII (octubre 1989): 90.

THE MEMOIRS OF
FRAY *SERVANDO*
TERESA DE MIER

Account of what happened in Europe to Dr. Don Servando Teresa De Mier after he was transferred there as a result of the proceedings against him in Mexico, from July 1795 to October 1805.

I

From the Time That the Resolution of the Council Was Confirmed in Modified Form to My Arrival in Paris

It is certain that I no longer had any intention of bowing to the iniquity of the Council or to the whims of León, whose one thought was also to win time.[1] Promising to do me justice after having forced me to serve out the archbishop's sentence was a mockery.[2] But I had no money to live on. The Council, as a result of the royal decree, issued an order to the representative of my Province to provide for my needs in Salamanca and make arrangements for my journey, giving me the money necessary to meet my expenses. In order to collect this aid, I hatched a plan with a calash driver, who went with me to the representative's; early the following morning I made as if I were leaving, left my cell in the Indies block of San Francisco monastery, received an ounce of gold from the representative and went into hiding. But the calash driver was craftier still; he found the lodging where I was hiding out and demanded that I give him the money, which he told me they were asking him for. How could they have been asking him for what had not been given to him? Out of fear, however, that he would give me away, I gave him twelve duros, which was what I had left after four days. It is more than likely that he kept the money for himself, since he told the representative that I had made him wait for me all day, telling him that

I had a certain errand to run, as I found out because León later confronted me with the calash driver's lie.[3] This is the only plot I ever attempted to carry off in my life, and it turned out as badly as has been seen. My naiveté rules out any sort of dishonest dealings. My friends have always urged me in vain to adopt just a touch of Christian slyness, as they put it. I am incapable of cunning.

I remained in hiding with the help of some Americans,* undecided as to my fate, when I found out that the Council had consulted the ministry as to what should be done with me once I had been caught, and that León, in order to arouse Minister Caballero's wrath against me, had told him that I wanted to kill him. Poor me, a person who, when there are little ants on my path, go hopping about from one foot to the other so as not to crush their little features! To save my own face, which when all was said and done could not be kept hidden for very long, I hired a mule and left for Burgos, to see whether among the friends I had there I could get a little money together and enter France.[4] All I could raise was an ounce of gold, and after two days I decided to go on foot to Agreda, where there was a French priest who was both a smuggler and a friend of mine, so that he could help me out with more money and the means to make my way through France and reach Rome, with the aim of secularizing myself.** As long as I wore the habit I had no doubt that they would be tossing me back and forth as though I were a pelota, since friars in Spain are looked upon with the utmost scorn, as being the scum of society; their honor is of no importance, and they are regarded as proper targets of all the evil done them.[5] All the difficulty in finding the right niche for someone lies in providing him with the means to maintain himself, and inasmuch as the Province has people who can be ordered to offer him such means, oppressors can easily wreak their will.

Just as I was about to mount the mule to set out for Agreda, the Chief Magistrate of Burgos appeared at the inn. On account of the plague that was raging in Andalusia, he was taking many precautions at the time with regard to people passing through the city, and since the wretch of an innkeeper saw that I went out only at night because I was well-known in Burgos, he had reported that I was suspect. I made my

---

* As was common in this period, the term *Americans* was used to refer to citizens or subjects of any country in the Americas. Fray Servando often uses it as a term for his fellow Mexicans.

** Renouncing his monastic vows and changing his status as a priest from regular to secular.

answers brief, believing that there was a warrant out for my arrest; my fear and my replies aroused the magistrate's suspicions; he flung himself on my papers, found the order of the Council sending me to Salamanca, and while he was sending word to the court he had me taken off to the monastery of San Francisco. As I left for the latter, I gave the ounce of gold to the lad who had brought me from Madrid and told him not to go off, because I would be leaving San Francisco during the night and we would be going to Agreda. He reported this to the magistrate, who ordered me confined to a cell in the aforementioned San Francisco. Inasmuch as I was highly respected in Burgos, this caused great scandal.

On the following day a friar offered to get me out by pulling me up to a corridor above through the window. But I did not agree to his doing so because, being as naive and stupid as ever, I had not yet learned everything there was to know about León, and believed that he would be content with having me brought to Salamanca, since I had declared before the magistrate that I was only passing through Burgos so as to collect a bit of money with which to set up my cell there and provide myself with utensils. But that ferocious León, who realized that I had fallen into his clutches once again, went back to his old refrain about making me serve out the archbishop's sentence to the letter, and saw to it that an order was issued to take me to Las Caldas and bury me in a prison cell there for the four years it would take me to serve out the sentence.

That pen pusher from the ministry passed the secret on to don Juan Cornide, my friend, who sent me word of what awaited me through the intermediary of a merchant in Burgos who delivered the letter to me, despite the warden of the convent, who intercepted my correspondence, since friars have no scruples about doing so.[6] A bolt of lightning paralyzed my faculties and my senses for four hours. Everything is going to be lost, I said on coming round; I must risk everything; and I began to ponder ways of escaping. My first thought was to take off with an open umbrella, whose ribs I had opened and made fast, and fly down to the patio formed by a block of three rows of cells, where a door was within sight. But I was very high up; waiting to receive me down below were enormous stones, and my flight risked meeting with the same success as Simon Magus.* I fell back on the monk who had offered to get me out in the beginning but was afraid now, having seen how closely I was guarded, with friars taking turns keeping watch over me day and night.

---

* The Samaritan sorcerer who was converted by the apostle Philip. See Acts 8:9–24. He was often reputed to be the prototype of the Faust legend.

But he suggested to me that I could let myself down with the thin rope that formed the mattress frame of my cot.

Once I had tied the rope from the window, I began to let myself down on the stroke of midnight, the hour at which the friar on guard went off to say matins; and since there were windows on which to support myself, I descended nicely; but then my hands split open from the weight of my body, and before I knew it I came down faster than I wanted to. Just as the thought came to me that I was going to end up on the ground as flat as a tortilla, I found myself astride the end of the rope, which was tied in a loop. I was badly battered by the time my flight ended, and after that I made my way out through a door that opened onto a yard; the door was closed, but with great effort I wriggled through a gap in it. I fled through the yard and ran a good quarter of a league away from Burgos, to the hospital of the royal knights commanders, who hid me that day.

I hung up my habit there out of necessity, and with a hunter's pouch full of provisions and eight duros, I left at eight that night, heading for Madrid, conveyed by Saint Francis's coach, as the saying goes.* It would make a long story were I to tell of the trials I went through, resting by day, walking by night, flinging myself to the side of the road at every noise I heard, fighting off the dogs that occupy the towns in battalions, and trembling from fear of the highwaymen who, led by Chafaldin, were ravaging Old Castile. This was my first attempt at journeying on foot, and my feet and legs swelled up so badly that after walking for two nights it took me nearly a day to go just one league, reaching at last a town three leagues distant from Torquemada, where I burst into tears. Taking pity on me, a muleteer who was going toward Torquemada put me astride a donkey and took me to the house of a good man, his benefactor, who gave me lodging.

The latter, in exchange for my money, provided me with a mule and a boy to guide me to Valladolid. On the way we met several people who were going to Burgos, and they said: "That's the padre who was in San Francisco," which made me quicken our pace, since through them it might become known that I was in the environs of Burgos and the authorities might then catch up with me with a warrant for my arrest. In Valladolid I was taken in by two students, erstwhile pupils of rhetoric of mine in Burgos, and we took the precaution of having me go out into the countryside on the days when the mail arrived in that city, in case

---

*   On shank's mare.

any news concerning me arrived in the morning, until such time as they came to tell me to come eat. I learned there that León had sent to Burgos for all my papers that the magistrate had taken from me, the ones that were most important, which I had been carrying with me; I had left the rest behind in my trunk in Madrid. It had been a constant concern of León's: to take my papers and documents away from me, so as to attack me when I no longer had them in my possession, or find some incriminating evidence against me among them. My letters of holy orders, my certificates of ordination, my defense, and so on, are being kept there; and León did not deposit them in the secretariat, because later on I asked don Zenón to look for them, and they were not there.

After having rested eight or ten days in Valladolid, I went on my way, again passing myself off as an émigré French priest, in a Catalan cart, a most uncomfortable vehicle that addled my brain. On arriving in Madrid, I betook myself to the home of don Juan Cornide, who lived with Filomeno, today the public prosecutor of Havana, his native city. I was told that León, furious that his prey had escaped his clutches, had ordered the arrest of the entire monastery of San Francisco in Burgos; but the chief magistrate had sent word that the monks had shown him my bloody handprints on the wall, which proved that I had escaped without their cooperation. I also found out that León had ordered warrants for my arrest issued throughout Spain. Can such attacks on me be believed? In view of these scandalous events would I not be taken for a murderer, a highwayman or a traitor judged guilty of the crime of lèse-majesté? Later on, León accused me of being the latter, a charge based solely on the fact that I had been brought to trial by two viceroys, even though León had in his possession the letter in which the Count of Revillagigedo gave the lie to the archbishop. Naturally all this was merely evildoing on the part of this wicked pen pusher from the ministry.

The official of the ministry for Mexico, don Zenón, sent me word that he had purposely not issued a warrant for my arrest in Catalonia, in order that I might make my escape to France from there; but in Catalonia I would have no means whatsoever of supporting myself. The lack of money was what put me at greatest risk. My good brother don Froilán, may God rest his soul, kept writing from Monterrey that there were no bills of exchange for Spain to be had there, but that I should get money in Spain and draw a sight draft on it. It is much more difficult to find someone to give money in Spain to be received in America; and in wartime—and Spain had been at war with England almost continually every since I had been in the Peninsula—it is almost impossible.[7] Spain lives off America as Rome lives off papal bulls; and as soon as maritime transport becomes difficult, there is nothing to be found there save hunger and poverty. In order to reach his new diocese, to which he had been given strict orders to proceed on the grounds that he was guilty of being a Jansenist and a friend of Urquijo's, the bishop of Havana, Espiga, had raised the necessary funds to do so by paying 200 percent interest.[8] How, then, was I to find money!

By making my escape by way of Navarre, I could call on the help of the French priest-smuggler who was in Agreda. He was also a friend of don Juan Cornide, who had powerful connections in the region because his brother don Gregorio was a vicar-general in France. He therefore spoke with some muleteers from Agreda to arrange to have them transport me, and he and Filomeno got me out of town via the Fuencarral gate, in a horse-drawn carriage, making a great commotion as they passed through so as to keep the guards from suspecting anything. After proceeding for a quarter of a league, they handed me over in my guise of a French émigré priest to the muleteers, who were already transporting my trunk; and to replace my letters of holy orders et cetera, Cornido gave me those of the late Dr. Maniau, whose executor he was, and they fit me perfectly, since Dr. Maniau had been my age and held the same ecclesiastical rank. The new Maniau mounted a mule, and at nightfall we put up at the muleteers' inn, outside the walls of Alcalá de Henares.

At eight o'clock that night, people arrived in a mad rush, giving me a scare, and it was none other than Cornide and Filomeno, who, having obtained a copy of the warrant from don Zenón, were coming to alter my appearance. And in fact they diabolically transformed me, going so far as to make a black mole on my nose and another on my upper lip with an infernal stone. The mother who bore me would not have recognized me. Nonetheless, in view of the fact that León stated in the warrant that I was good-looking, cheerful and affable, they exhorted me to make myself appear to be taciturn, melancholy and ugly. On spying guards, I therefore contorted my chops, looked cross-eyed and carried out to the letter the last battle cry of the Portuguese army: "Make fierce faces at the enemy!"[9] We did not dare, however, to enter via the Agreda gate, since two warrants had been issued: one by the government and another by the chief magistrate of Burgos; and the muleteer led me through a gap in the wall and home with him.

He was one of the close friends of my priest-smuggler, who came to see me. I entrusted my trunk to him, which he still has in his possession, and he put me in the hands of another confidant of his who was to take me to Pamplona, with a recommendation to a French commercial house, which I too knew of, to get me into France. As I left Aragon for Navarre, I was witness to one of the despotic and ruinous peculiarities of Spain, for a more rigorous search is made for the money that a person is taking from one kingdom to another than the inspection at the frontiers of the country. Even though my only baggage consisted of one small sack of clothing, which the guards emptied out onto the ground, and eight duros that I had declared, they also poked a shoemaker's awl through the cover of my breviary, to see if I had any gold coins hidden there.

I reached Pamplona four days after Urquijo had arrived as a prisoner at its citadel, and from the inn I proceeded to the house of the French merchant. "Don't go back to the inn," he told me, "because they have just arrested two men, believing them to be you and Cuesta, the archdeacon of Avila, a fugitive because of the pastoral doctrine that he preached and his bishop published." This was the crucial period of the persecution carried out against the Jansenists by Godoy (who for this reason was called a *pillar of religion* in a brief issued by Rome).[10] In Europe that is what all men with solid religious training who are friends of the age-old legitimate discipline of the Church are called.

My Frenchman immediately summoned a muleteer who had taken many priests to France across the Pyrenees. He came with his mule, and following along after it, the merchant and I left, handing out a number of pesetas to the guards. I mounted the mule at the far end of the Paseo de la Taconera, and the muleteer advised us to go as far into the Pyrenees as we could, which we did, journeying on till two in the morning, at which time we arrived in Hostia, frozen to the bone. The next day we went through the valley of Bastan, and on the third day we slept in Cincovillas; from there we could see the ocean, Bayonne and all its environs, looking as white as a herd of cows in the countryside. I was not very happy at the inn, because there were guards there and they had the warrant; but the information volunteered by the muleteer, who was very well-known, that I was a French priest, together with the confirmation offered by my physiognomy and my hair, my moles and my Mexican accent (which they said was a foreign one, the one that causes Mexicans to be taken for Portuguese or Castilians in Andalusia and for Andalusians in Castile) got me safely past them.

The following day we went through Ordaz, the last little Spanish village on that side, and I was eager to find out what marked the boundary of France. "That's it there," the muleteer said to me, pointing to a very small, shallow stream. I went across it, dismounted and stretched out face down on the ground. "What are you doing?" he asked me. "I have crossed the Rubicon,"[11] I answered him. "I am not an émigré, but a Mexican, and I am carrying only this passport (the one that had been Maniau's) from Mexico to Spain." "It doesn't matter," he said. "The gendarmes don't understand Castilian, and when they see your grand manner they will take their hats off to you as to a grandee." And that was what happened.

We slept that night in Añoa, the first French village; that is to say, the first Basque or French Biscayan one, for the province of Vizcaya is at once part of Spain and part of France, and immigrants from both sides come to America as Spaniards, just as they do from French and Spanish Catalonia. The next day, in order to enter Bayonne, which is a walled city, the muleteer had me dismount and enter the town by mingling with the people on the public promenade, where for the first time I saw carriages drawn by oxen. This precaution was of no avail, for the guard's suspicion was aroused because of the way I was dressed and because I was wearing boots and was covered from head to foot with dust from the road. He took me to the city hall, where I presented my Mexican passport, and since no one could understand it, they gave me my entry card, or safe-conduct pass. All this was quite necessary at that time because of the disturbances, which still had not died down altogether, in the Republic. It was still a republic, though governed by consuls, with Bonaparte as First Consul.[12] That day was Good Friday of the year 1801.

What to do to make a living, especially since I was possessed of a strong sense of pride, as befitted my highborn station, and incapable not only of begging, but of allowing my poverty to show? I went through some terrible experiences, and would never have survived them had I been a libertine. By sheer chance, I unwittingly entered the Jewish synagogue in the Sancti-Spiritus quarter. The psalms were being sung in Spanish, and the sermon was preached in Spanish. All the Jews in France, and in almost all of Europe, save for Germany, are Spanish by descent and many by birth; because I saw them as they came to Bayonne to be circumcised; all of them speak Spanish, men and women alike; their Bibles, all their prayers are in Spanish, and above all they observe conventions such that, when a German Jew who didn't understand Spanish was married in Bayonne, even though the marriage contract was also written in Hebrew so that he would understand it, it was first read to him in Castilian, and this was the one he signed. And they still follow Spanish customs, and are also the ones who carry on the principal commercial dealings with Spain, which they all have visited. The reason behind this stubborn insistence on preserving all things Spanish is their claim that those who came to Spain because they were sent there by the emperor Hadrian belong to the tribe of Judah.

I entered the synagogue the very next day after I arrived, and that day was none other than the Passover of unleavened bread and lamb. The rabbi preached, proving, as is always done on Passover, that the Messiah had not yet come, because the sins of Israel are holding him back. As I left the synagogue, everyone flocked about me to find out what I had thought of the sermon. They had been surprised to see me, because I was wearing a clerical collar, and because I removed my hat, whereas all of them had kept theirs on inside the synagogue, and the rabbis who were officiating were wearing a prayer shawl over their heads as well. The greatest mark of respect in the Orient is to cover one's head. Only at Kaddish, or the ceremony in commemoration of the dead, which is always recited by an orphan, do worshipers bare their heads in the synagogue. And the way they have of telling whether a person is Jewish is to ask him in Hebrew: "What is your name?" In a moment's time I demolished all the arguments of the rabbi who preached the sermon, and they challenged me to a public debate. I agreed, and since I had at my fingertips Bishop Huet's evangelical proof, I made such an impression at the debate that they offered me in marriage a beautiful, wealthy young maiden named Rachel, whose name in French was Fineta, because all of them use two names, one for among themselves and another for outsiders; and they even went so far as to offer to pay for my journey to Holland to marry there, if I did not care to do so in France.

I naturally refused their offer; but from that day on I enjoyed such credit among them that they called me Japá, that is to say, learned one; I was the first one invited to all their ceremonies; the rabbis came to consult me about their sermons, to have me correct their Castilian, and made me a new habit. When out of curiosity I went to the synagogue like other Spaniards, the rabbis bade me seat myself on their dais or in their pulpit. And once the ceremony had ended at nightfall, I remained behind by myself with the officiating rabbi, watching him as he studied what was to be read the following day. He then brought out the law of Moses, which when the congregation is present is brought out with great ceremony and reverence, as everyone bows before it. It is written on scrolls, without accent marks for the vowels, with only the consonants, and the rabbi would study it, as meanwhile I read it in the Bible with accent marks. And then I would snuff out the candles of the votive lamps, because they are forbidden to do so, nor are they permitted to light a fire to cook or to warm themselves on the Sabbath. They use Christian maidservants to do all this, and I told them that for that reason their religion was incapable of being a universal one.

Since I was still good-looking, I did not lack for young Christian ladies seeking to marry me either, none of whom found it difficult to explain what they had in mind, and when I answered that I was a priest, they would say that that was no obstacle if I were willing to abandon my calling. The horde of priests who contracted a marriage out of terror of the revolution, which forced them to marry, had left them without scruples. In Bayonne and all of the administrative district of the Lower Pyrenees as far north as Dax the women are fair-skinned and pretty, particularly the Basque ones; but I was never more aware of the influence of climate than when I began journeying on foot to Paris, because I saw, quite evidently, all the way from Montmarsan, some eight or ten leagues from Bayonne, to Paris, men and women who were dark-skinned, and the latter were ugly. French women as a general rule are ugly, and physically resemble frogs. Misshapen, short and squat, big-mouthed and slant-eyed. As one goes farther north in France, they get better-looking.

In order to support myself in Bayonne, I had recourse to the priests who had emigrated to Spain whom I had helped move from Burgos to La Coruña. After consideration by the French Government, an order was issued in 1797 directing the poor French priests to leave Spain for the Canary and Balearic islands; those from Burgos were to go by way of La Coruña. I sent a circular petition in their name to the clergy of Burgos, asking them to help raise money for the French priests' journey. It was received so favorably that the clergy went out into the streets with trays to take up a collection, and more than enough money was raised to decently transport sixty priests, who, to show their gratitude to me, came to the monastery of San Pablo, where I was, to mount up for their journey. The poor wretches sent me forty francs in Bayonne, on receiving which I decided, after two months, to enter France. What I needed was a passport; but the Jews pointed out to me that in the one I had from Mexico for Spain the latter word was written out in a shortened form and was followed by a little blank space at the end of the line. I added the words "and France" then, and took to the riverbed to walk to Dax, four leagues away.

From there I set out on foot for Bordeaux, more than thirty leagues away, in the company of two shoemakers who were deserters from the Spanish army. Since the road is nothing but sand all the way, I suffered immeasurably, and in the end I would not have been able to reach Bordeaux, inasmuch as my feet were badly inflamed, had I not taken to yet another riverbed to go the rest of the way. The shoemakers set to work forthwith, and began piling up money as though it were heaps of dirt, whereas I, stuffed full of Theology, was dying of hunger and envy. I realized then how right fathers were to have their sons, however highborn they might be, taught a trade in their early years, especially one that was so easy and so necessary anywhere in the world. This would enable them to earn their daily bread amid all of life's vicissitudes.

I had received a letter from the ambassador of Spain in Paris, don Nicolás Azara, and another from the botanist Francisco Zea, for in the midst of all my trials and miseries I had never lacked for attention from European savants and correspondence with them. In view of these letters, the Spanish consul, who needed to have his accounts approved by the ambassador, ordered the secretary of the consulate to put me up. The secretary was a Spaniard who made every effort to make an atheist of me through the writings of Freret, as though a certain Italian had not reduced his sophisms to dust. I have observed that impious books are read with pleasure, because they look with favor on the passions, and allegations against such works not only go unread, but are viewed with scorn, because the swaggeringly boastful and perfectly self-satisfied tone of those authors who are unbelievers penetrates the minds of their readers. And the truth is that these braggarts are ignoramuses and impostors. They speak with a self-satisfaction they do not possess within themselves, in order to impose their point of view, and if they do possess it, it is owing to their very ignorance. *Qui respicit ad pauca, de facili pronuntiat.**

As soon as the aforementioned secretary discovered that I had money he pretended that by order of the consul I was to pay the sum of twenty duros for my lodging, which he pocketed. The money that I had came to me through the generosity of don José Sarea, the Count of Gijón, a native of Quito, who disembarked in Bordeaux after having invested all his money in Havana sugar, expecting to make a large profit. And in point of fact, at that time there was no sugar in Bordeaux. I talked him into visiting Paris before passing over into Spain, and he took me along as his interpreter. He tossed money about as though he were in America, and I, being of the opinion that he was about to be in very serious straits in Europe, where one and all conspire to fleece a newcomer from America,

---

*   *He who respects little readily pontificates.*

reined him in, even when I was the one on whom he chose to lavish money. This made him angry and he abandoned me almost the moment we arrived in Paris. Later on he deeply regretted having done so, for he was overtaken by all the trials that I had predicted for him. Instead of selling the sugar immediately, the merchant from Bordeaux with whom he had dealt waited until the market was glutted with it, following the peace treaty of Amiens, and then, selling it for nothing, or pretending to have sold it, kept the money as payment for having stored it. The count finally realized that I was a man of integrity, and I have not had a better friend since.

I do not want to neglect to mention that a Frenchman in the service of Spain, who became my friend in Bayonne, sent a letter from Bordeaux to his brother, who had an influential position in Paris, roundly recommending me to him because "despite his being a priest, he is an upright man," as he put it in the letter. The brother showed me this phrase and told me that it was necessary to write that, because all priests were libertines. Later on I noted that this phrase was commonly used when recommending a priest. Unbelievers had inveighed against religion and its ministers as being impostors to such a point that they succeeded in impressing the people, who went out into the woods to which priests fled during the revolution so as to hunt them down, saying that they were going out to kill black beasts.

If the Frenchman had known that I was a monk, he would not have recommended me, because the word *friar* appended to my name made me a good-for-nothing. Among Catholics and unbelievers alike, it is a term of opprobrium, or better put, it sums up all such terms, and when people call someone a friar, they think that they have exhausted their store of insults. It is tantamount to calling him a base, crude, ill-mannered, lazy, begging, abysmally ignorant man, an impostor, a hypocrite, a liar, a superstition-ridden fanatic, capable of any and every despicable deed and incapable of honor and uprightness. It seems incredible, yet it is quite true. Even on Catholic vessels it is necessary to refrain from revealing that one is a friar, because if a storm comes up he is thrown overboard, as has happened a number of times. So in Spain the French killed them without remorse, within and without the monasteries. Hence there are almost none left in Europe. Joseph Napoleon had wiped them out in Spain, and the Cortes* did likewise. In places where there are still a few left, they are looked upon with the greatest

---

* The legislative assembly, which at the time acceded to Joseph Napoleon's demands.

contempt and reviled, and are not allowed entree into any decent house. In Madrid I chanced to go to pay a call on the daughter of a merchant named Terán, because she was a countrywoman of mine, and when I sent word to her that I was outside, I was told to leave her a written message. The worst part is that being a friar is an indelible mark against a person. It does not help in the least if one has been secularized, if one is a bishop or even the Pope.[13] People disdainfully go on calling such a person friar, and in Rome, to show their scorn for the Pope or for some measure that he has taken, men and women say: "Oh è un frate."*

* "After all, he's a friar."

From My Arrival in Paris to My Departure

I am making a separate chapter of my stay in Paris, in order to recount in it many things worthy of note. I said in the preceding
chapter that I arrived in Paris with the Count of Gijón, who immediately abandoned me, and although Inquisitor Yéregui sent me a small
sum of money from Spain, the first aid that reached me was from don
Francisco Zea, an important figure in botany whom I had met in
Madrid. He was one of a group of young scholars of Cundinamarca
(the former name of New Granada) with doctorates who had been sent
to prison by the Royal Tribunal of Santa Fe de Bogotá for having published a short book on the rights of man. The advocate Mariño defended them, demonstrating that all they had done was copy teachings
in current use by classic Spanish authors who had gone much further,
and proceeding to prove each of the young scholars' propositions by citing a hundred of these authors. The judges were at a loss for a reply, but
as is characteristic of the despotism of judges in America, or, better put,
of all the tyrants in the world, they sent them to Spain with their advocate, consigned to the ship's authorities, along with recommendations
that the fewer of them that arrived alive the better. Fortunately, once
they reached Spain the matter fell into the hands of liberals, who all had
a good laugh over Mariño's written argument, since in point of fact the
doctrine of the little book, that is to say the declaration of the rights of

man, already proclaimed by the United States in America, and subsequently by the National Assembly of France, is, in essence, eternal principles very clearly recognized by Spanish authors before the sudden advent of despotism, *which detests the light of day, because it works evil.* The doctors from Cundinamarca were therefore given their freedom, and Zea, having been granted a pension by our government, visited Paris, where he published the famous discoveries by the renowned scholar Mutis regarding the cinchona trees of Santa Fe, and succeeded Cabanilles as director of the Botanical Garden in Madrid.

Shortly after I reached Paris, Simón Rodríguez arrived there, a native of Caracas who, under the name of Samuel Robinson, taught English, French and Spanish in Bayonne when I was there; this latter language was also taught by a discalced Trinitarian friar, named Gutiérrez, an apostate and a libertine, who later was the author of the little Spanish gazette of Bayonne, and was ultimately executed in Seville by order of the Central Junta, because he often went to Spain, by order of Napoleon, to conspire with Ferdinand VII's Lord Privy Seal. Robinson came to live with me in Paris and encouraged me to set up a school with him to teach Spanish, which was very much in vogue.[1]

The reason for this popularity was the fact that Spain had just ceded to Napoleon the island of Santo Domingo (three-quarters of which, the most productive regions, belonged to us), and Louisiana, without specifying the terms of the cession, or realizing that it was ceding a territory as large as the whole of New Spain—all this in exchange for tiny Tuscany, so as to crown the Prince of Parma king of Etruria. Godoy had previously offered Louisiana to Napoleon, simply to win his favor; neither he nor Spain remembered, however, that the king, according to the Laws of the Indies, cannot transfer ownership of even the smallest part of America, and if he cedes it, the cession is null and void.

This cession took place during the brief interval of peace between Napoleon and England, called the peace of Amiens, the city where the peace treaty was signed. The war then went on; and before the English could take over Louisiana and before Spain could cede it to him, Napoleon sold it to the United States for thirteen million pesos or dollars, even though it is claimed that Spain had ceded it to him under the terms of a pact that guaranteed it the right to buy it back. What is certain is that the English in America have taken over territory extending as far as Eastern Florida, the capital of which is Saint Augustine, and have located their Fort Clayborne only sixty leagues away from our settlements in Texas. It will not be long before they take over the eastern provinces in the interior and extend their territory as far as Mexico, as only stands to reason; for through commerce, industry and freedom, the welcome that they extend to all foreigners and the land that they distribute to all families that emigrate from Europe, whom they themselves bring over, they have adopted every possible means of multiplying their numbers, and in forty years they have increased their population to nine million, from the two and a half million it numbered at the time of the insurrection. We, on the other hand, numbered a hundred million at the time of the Conquest, and today there are barely nine million of us, including the kingdom of Guatemala, because we have adopted every possible means of hindering the growth of the population and diminishing it. Among them are the impediment to marriage occasioned by the excessive fees owed priests, the imaginary division of the population into castes, the continual levies of men (on one pretext or another) for the Philippines, Havana, Puerto Rico, for the royal fleet, and for the presidios on the deadly coasts, in addition to the general oppression, the lack of free trade, industry and agriculture, and excommunication from the human species in which we live. Not to mention the butchery of revolution, in which no quarter is given and which has already cost us a million men, and the cruel, perfidious and incessant war waged against the nomad [Indian] nations, with whom the North Americans live in peace and treat as brothers. Spain's own policy will cause it to lose its American territories if it does not change its Machiavellian system.

As for the Spanish language school that Robinson and I decided to set up in Paris, he encouraged me to translate, in order to serve as proof of our ability, the little novel or poem by Monsieur Chateaubriand entitled *Atala*, set in America and enjoying great popularity, which he was about to have printed thanks to the recommendations he had brought with him. I translated it, though I did so almost word for word, so that it could be used as a text for our pupils, and it cost me more than a little effort, since there was no botanical dictionary in Spanish and the poem is full of the proper names of many exotic plants that grow in Canada, and so on, which it was necessary to Hispanicize.[2]

The translation was printed under the name of Robinson, because this is a sacrifice demanded of poor authors by those who pay the costs of having their works printed. Hence the Barcelonan don Juan Pla is the author of Cormón's *Gramática* and *Diccionario*, since Cormón, who did not know Spanish, paid the printing costs. Alvarez, who didn't know Spanish well either, passed himself off as the author of Capmany's *Diccionario*, which he had reprinted in Paris, with an additional second part, in other words the part from Spanish to French, compiled by some Spaniards who lived in Paris. Ródenas wagered in Valencia that he could translate *Atala* into Castilian in three days, and all he did was reprint my translation, omitting the prologue in which Chateaubriand explained the sources he had used for all the characters in the story, though he reprinted even the notes that I had added. And in places where I had provided no notes, he put in some nonsense or other, thinking that he was correcting me. For instance, I made no annotation for the word *sabanas,* since all through the north of America this Indian word for prairie has been adopted. Not knowing that, Ródenas tried to improve on my text and corrected it to read *sábanas.** He was prudent enough, however, to place only the initials of his name on the title page, in case his plagiarism was discovered. This is a very common practice in Europe. In his *Dissentions of Spanish America* [*sic*] the Englishman Walton stole my history of the revolution in Mexico. When Abbot Gándara died, everyone said: Azara's Cicero has passed away, because the life of Cicero was the abbot's work, a translation from the English, which Azara did not know. There have been a thousand other underhanded thefts of this sort. It is common knowledge that the *Apologia Jesuitarum a Fr. Daniele Concina* is the work of a Venetian Jesuit. The ex-Jesuit Zacarías was responsible for the supplement added to Natal Alejandro's work, though he did not sign it, since no one would have believed what he had to say on the subject of grace. And the Jesuits are in the habit of keeping it a secret that they belong to the order, as was the case with Berant Bercastel, who is said in France to have passed off the annals of his Company as a history authorized by the Church. As a history, the work is tolerable up to the twelfth century, at which point he begins to rage against the Order of Saint Dominic; on reaching the sixteenth century he goes on raging, this time against the Capuchins for maintaining that they had improved the nonsecular institution more than the Jesuits, and with regard to the seventeenth and eighteenth centuries, his whole history is nothing but intrigues and impostures. I wanted to insert this here in order to speak out against the wicked tactic of those who do not draw attention to plagiarisms and lies, because there are always people who are easily taken in by them.

As for *Atala,* the first person to come to buy it from us was its author himself, and we had many pupils both within and without our school. At night, I was the one who did the teaching at a set hour, and Robin-

---

* Meaning bedsheets in Spanish.

son gave lessons elsewhere at all hours, since I had to attend to my parish church.

It is quite true that, seeing that in their fits of delirium unbelievers such as Volney went so far as to deny or doubt the existence of Jesus Christ, I wrote a dissertation in proof of it.[3] It came into the hands of the grand vicar of Paris, and I was given charge of the parish of the church of Saint Thomas, *rue filles St. Thomas,* which no longer exists today; it was the church of the Dominican nuns of that name, in the middle of Paris. In the course of my travels, several towns had already offered me their parish churches, because there was a shortage of priests; but I accepted only the one in Paris, where I had settled. And certainly I failed to foresee the amount of work with which I was about to be burdened, with no recompense other than the voluntary offerings of the faithful, which would have been quite sufficient had they been for one priest alone. But I had to pay four clergymen to lend me a hand, the sacristan, the Swiss guard who with his leather shoulder belt and halberd prevents any scandalous behavior or commotion in the church, the two precentors who, wearing copes, lead the choirs of the congregation, and the musician who, with a bass wind instrument in the form of a serpent, gives them the pitch, together with all the other outlays necessary to conduct divine services. Hence I did not have a penny left over, and moreover the office placed a great many restrictions on me, for in France it would be scandalous to see a priest in a theater, on the public promenade, especially on feast days, or even in a café.

Before the revolution there were fifty parish churches in Paris (and forty-four thousand in the entire kingdom), not nearly as immense as regular churches, which are always a great boon. When I was in Paris there were only twelve parish churches, along with a few secular ones, and no fixed parish boundaries, with the result that the faithful attended whatever church they pleased. And since mine was in the middle of Paris, it was heavily attended, owing chiefly to the fact that I was regarded as a foreigner belonging to no party. The Catholic clergy had split into mutually opposed factions, priests who had taken an oath of loyalty to the Constitution and those who had not, Republicans and Royalists, Jansenists and Jesuits or Constitutionals and Recalcitrants, as the former called the latter, or Apostolic Roman Catholics as the latter called themselves.[4]

I was numbered among the latter because I was a parish priest, but I did not think exactly as they did. I admitted to my church those faithful who were Constitutionals, since I did not regard their ministers as having been excommunicated. Nor were excommunications valid *ipso facto* in the Gallican Church, or any other without the approval of their government, nor did the Civil Constitution of the Clergy contain anything heretical (it had been, rather, an effort to return to the early discipline of the Church), nor had it been condemned except by virtue of a judgment brought by the Sorbonne, which in latter days was worth nothing, since persecution by the Molinists and in particular that by the hypocrite Tournelli had driven out the truly learned members who were loyal to it. I knew for a fact, moreover, that the Constitutionals shared a fellowship of ideas with the most learned bishops in Europe, certain of whom had put forth a perfect defense of the Constitutionals—the Dominican scholar and bishop of Noli, Benedicto Solari for one, in his apologia against Cardinal Gerdil—and renowned Catholic universities were supporting them. The Constitutionals held the majority of the parishes; the Theophilanthropists, or Deists, backed by the power of the Government through the intermediary of the Director of the Republic, Reveillère Lepeaux, had taken over a number of them; and the Calvinists, of whom there were some two million in all of France, had purchased the church of the renowned Oratory of Jesus.

In France, besides the regular work of administering the sacraments, the priest must also preach a sermon every Sunday and two if it is an Advent or Lenten Sunday, and likewise on other feast days. The French spend Sunday in church (rightly regarding it as a very holy day, since in their catechism God's third commandment does not read "you shall keep the feast days holy," but Sundays), and consequently, all the priests of each parish and the entire clergy occupy the presbytery wearing surplices, although only the priest wears a stole. The people regard it as an obligation to attend the High or parochial Mass, and likewise vespers. Men, women and children bring their little missals for the divine offices in Latin, with the French translation alongside, and they all sing, as the two precentors pass down the middle of the church, wearing a cope and carrying a scepter to lead the two choirs, and the people bow their heads when the precentors do, and so on. Men and women sit in seats or on chairs that they pay the sum of one sol for, save for a few very poor people who crowd together wherever there is room.

They begin by singing terce, with the priests chanting the antiphony. Then the Mass, which is always celebrated with ministrants, and after it the canonical hour of sext. Once the Gospel has been sung, the priest mounts the pulpit, reads the Gospel in French, which everyone listens to standing up, as when there is singing in Latin, and then he expounds on it for a quarter of an hour or a bit more. This is not called a sermon but a *prone*. The sermons that we read are given in the late afternoon, after vespers, and therefore have no canonically fixed text. The priest then exhorts the congregation to pray for the Pope, for the bishop of the diocese, for the Government, for the one who offers the holy bread, travelers, the sick, mariners, and recites the psalm *Laudate Dominum omnes gentes,* to which the congregation gives the response. He then exhorts them to pray for the dead and recites the psalm *De profundis.* Then he announces the feast or fast days. This is a holdover from the old diptychs of the church. When priests from abroad [*i.e.*, who have come to America] inform us that they preach from memory, this is Spanish boastfulness; they are attributing to themselves what is common throughout Europe. Only the Protestants in England have their sermon before them and furtively read from it. People say that the French preach sitting down. They should say, rather, that they preach leaning back on a sort of half bench, that is to say, half sitting and half standing, save for a passage full of pathos, at which point they stand all the way up, as they do at the exordium; nor do they cover their heads at this time, but rather, after reciting the *Avemaria* they bow three times, once to the front and once to either side. Their biretta is not like ours, but instead resembles a sugar loaf, with a tassel at the tip. This tassel is white for the doctors of the Sorbonne, who always wear it when they preach and when they appear in public to say Mass.

At the offertory of the Mass an upright person, either a man or a woman, who is appointed to do so beforehand, distributes the holy bread. This is a remembrance of oblations of the faithful in the early Church, and consists of a large round loaf of egg bread, which the sacristan, vested in a surplice, places on his head, on a metal plate with a cloth around it, and four lighted candles, holding a lighted candle in his hand as he precedes the person who is making the offering. He mounts to the altar, hands the candle to the priest, and the latter offers him the reverse side of the paten to kiss, this latter being a sort of little plate, the bottom of whose outer side shows Christ at the Last Supper. The person making the offering takes his or her place in the presbytery to one side of the altar, and the bread is taken to the sacristy to be divided into little bits, which will be offered the congregation at Communion.

After this and regularly after the Elevation, the collection for the poor is taken, as ordered by Saint Paul, although when I was in France, it was being taken to defray the expenses of celebrating Mass. On the most solemn days the parish priest or another priest takes it, but at everyday offices the sacristan hands the purse, which is made of silk and gold, to a young lady. She offers her arm and a gentleman takes it, as is the custom in France or England, where women always walk on someone's arm; they are preceded by the Swiss guard, who raps his halberd on the floor in front of each person, she presents the purse, and once she has received the offering, makes a curtsy. The person who chooses to make an offering gives whatever he pleases; but usually everyone gives and as a general rule thousands of pesetas are taken in. At the time of the public restoration of religion in France, when Bonaparte was Consul, the collection was taken by the daughters of the Consuls, and although they made only a brief round of the cathedral, they raised two thousand gold louis. Each louis is worth four duros and a little more than a medio.

The congregation never kneels save at the *incarnatus,* a custom introduced in the Church by Saint Louis, the king of France, although in earlier times it was only at the *homo factus est.* Dominicans too kneel only at the *homo factus est,* their rite being the Gallican one, as practiced at the time the Order was founded in Toulouse, France; and in the church of Saint Jacques in Paris a great book of the Dominican rite was kept, drawn up at the time of Saint Thomas, who was present. People call it the Greek rite, and it is true that the Apostles of France were Greeks, and on the feast day of Saint Denis, the first bishop of Paris, Mass is said in Greek. But it is equally true that the early Gallican rite, like the Mozarabic rite in Spain, introduced by its apostolic members, was the one first followed by the Roman Church, which has frequently made changes in its rite, and has been bent on doing away with the Gallican one since the time of Charlemagne, and in later years the Mozarabic rite of Spain, which today is used only in one chapel in Toledo, by order of Cardinal Cisneros. All these rites are more devout than the present-day Roman one.

French priests, like Dominicans, immediately prostrate themselves at the Elevation, singing the last two stanzas of the hymn of Lauds at Corpus, *O salutaris hostia,* and this spectacle is such a beautiful one that the first time Lord Bolingbroke saw it, he said that if he were king, he would allow no one else to perform this ceremony. They remain thus prostrated until the *Pater noster.* The Italians in Rome do not kneel save at the Elevation. Nor between Christmas and Easter did the early Christians ever once kneel on Sundays. There are always people in France who take Communion at High Mass.

Once Communion is over, the acolytes distribute the holy bread in little baskets, from which one and all take a little piece, cross themselves with it and eat it. These are the pieces of blessed bread* that are used in the Greek Church, as a symbol of charity and fraternity, and a remembrance of the early days when all the faithful took Communion. This is still the custom among those from the Maragatería district in León. And many of the practices of the Church in France are found throughout the kingdom of Aragon, which at one time was under French rule. Everyone gives the responses at Mass and makes offerings at the offertory, and the canons wear purple vestments as do those in France. In this country, after the Mass the congregation sings sext and departs. But people eat their evening meal early on Sundays so as to attend vespers at three or four in the afternoon.

At that time they sing nones, vespers, compline and what they call the *salut,* this latter being the Most Blessed Sacrament in abridged form, like that sung by Dominicans at their Brief Hours, as can plainly be seen during this office. Once it is over, the *salut* is used to give the benediction, which is also given the congregation with the ciborium at the last Mass, which is also before noon, because once the noon bells have rung, it is not permitted to say Mass, although in Madrid there is a one o'clock Mass, with no devotions offered during it. The *salut* is followed by the sermon, such as I have described it, on the days when there is one, after which the congregation leaves the church at eight o'clock in the evening. During Holy Week people attend all the offices and canonical hours and sing at them. On the days when the Mass ends with *Benedicamus Domino,* that is to say when the congregation is not dismissed because it is a day of prayer, the people come back to church at five or six in the evening for the prayer service. The parish priest expounds on the Gospel, and recites a number of prayers. It is usually particularly devout women who attend this service, and for churchgoing they have a sort of black cap with which they cover not only their head but also part of their face.

But the most solemn and tender ceremony in the churches of France is that of the First Communion of the children, whose instruction in religion is not entrusted to just anyone, as it is in our country, but is given, rather, the importance that it deserves. On Septuagisima Sunday, fathers and mothers bring their sons and daughters who have reached the age of reason to the church. Their names are registered, and they come every morning and afternoon to the church to recite the lesson that they are assigned at catechism and hear the explanation of it. To give it, the

---

* Called *eulogias* in the Latin rite and *antidora* in the Greek; in Spanish, *eulogias.*

parish priest wears surplice and stole, as do the priests, deacons or minor clergy who help him if there are a large number of children. They are sent to one or another of the chapels, boys and girls separately, according to their level of understanding, and gradually they make their way up to the chapel of the parish priest, who never entrusts this final instruction to any other cleric. Each day's lesson ends with a very harmonious hymn that they sing. The parish priest decides what the lesson for the day will be, and then they are taught the prayer for vespers in Latin, the hours and the Mass of their diocese, since each diocese in France has its own breviary, missal, ritual and catechism, all of them approved by its bishop, though Bonaparte insisted on setting the text for catechism, in which it was ordered that he be obeyed as the Caesar in the Gospel is obeyed.

When the children have been duly catechized, the parish priests sets the day for First Communion and continues to give them instruction in how to make a proper confession. He himself hears the confession of each of them, and on the eve of their First Communion they receive what are called dry hosts, ones that have not been consecrated, so as to give them practice in receiving consecrated ones. There are any number of people who attend church on the day of First Communion, with the fathers and mothers invariably present. The little girls come all dressed in white, heads covered with their little hats and veils, and they seat themselves in orderly fashion in their little chairs, to one side of the choir, which is in the presbytery, not facing the altar, but rather in the part opposite the choir. The boys, modestly dressed and with their hair worn loose, occupy their little chairs on that side, and both the boys and the girls carry a candle weighing a pound, with a big rosette of ribbon. The parish priest instructs them as to the vows and obligations of the Christian profession of faith, and the children, with great devotion, renew their baptismal vows. Then at the offertory of the Mass they present the blessed bread and their candle, and each of them in turn, in splendid order, goes up to the altar to receive Communion; and since the altar has a great many steps, the long trains of the girls' dresses spread out over them, and they come down very slowly, with their little eyes lowered and their little hands joined at their breast; and it is a most devout sight. At the *Ita missa est,* the parish priest, turning to the congregation, addresses his exhortation to the fathers and mothers, entrusting to their care their children, now instructed in religion, as a precious treasure that the Church bestows on them, and that God will ask them to account for if they do not endeavor to cultivate those tender plants of Jesus Christ in accordance with the doctrine that they have been taught and fail to bring them to the divine offices and instructions of the Church, etc.

In the late afternoon the boys and girls, placed in the same order in the church, with the Most Blessed Sacrament in the middle, on an altar, sing vespers, compline and the *salut,* with their lighted candles in their hands, and so on. All this is one of the most tender and moving ceremonies I have ever seen in my life, and one that rightly captivates all foreigners in whose churches this is looked upon with such nonchalance and indifference.

If the parish priest, at the dawn of reason of the faithful of his parish, looks after them so carefully, the care he takes of them at their death is no less devoted. The parish priest administers the sacraments to those who are ill, delivering to them a brief homily, which is never omitted, before giving them the Viaticum. And from then on he cares for them until such time as he delivers his lamb into the hands of its Creator, who will ask its shepherd as well for an accounting of it. In many dioceses the Holy Oil is delivered today, as it was in the early Church, before the Eucharist, as it should be, since this is the purest of the sacraments, and the Holy Oil, which did not begin to be called Extreme Unction until the fourteenth century, has as its primary object the healing of the body, and to that end ought not to be kept from the believer until his soul is at death's door. This is to tempt God, and has given rise to Calvin's blasphemous sarcasms.

Once the parishioner has died, the parish priest or another priest vested in a surplice watches over him the whole night through, recommending him to God, until such time as, before taking him to the church, they place him in a coffin at the door of his house, with a portable stoup of holy water, and all those who pass by sprinkle him with it and offer a prayer. Neither here nor in Rome is it the custom to wrap the deceased in a shroud, but in a white sheet rather, as in the early Church. Then the deceased is taken to the church, with the closest relatives wearing mourning, all dressed in black with a baize cloak, fastened at the breast with a ribbon. The clergymen receive them and seat them in chairs in the presbytery, while the clergy take their places round the body in the church, dressed in rochets and small black zucchettos with a little cowl. At the offertory all the mourners come to the altar to offer money, and the priests who are standing round about the body also come to the altar, to offer a sum of money that is given them. I did not wish to leave out all this edifying information, because the Church of France, by dint of resisting the constant innovations of Rome, has succeeded in preserving the majority of the devout rites and ancient sacred usages of the early Church.

Among its breviaries, the best is that of Paris; among its missals, that of Sens. In the Paris breviary all the hymns, truly poetic ones, are by the celebrated Santeuil, rather than the ones in the Roman breviary, so dreadful that they are barely tolerable. Only the hymns of Saint Thomas for the office of Corpus, and the hymn for the dead composed by the Dominican Zavarela have been retained, although the *Teste David cum sivilla* has been replaced by *Crucis expandens vexilla,* since it has been proved that the prophecies of the Sibyls are a fiction invented by the early Christians.

As for marriages, there is nothing that is different save for the bouquet, that is to say, the little bunch of natural flowers that the bride and groom wear on their breasts, and it is the bridegroom who gives the bouquet to the bride. The Royalist priests administered the sacrament without making certain that the marriage contract had previously been entered into at the city hall in accordance with the laws of the Republic, because they said that the Pope had not yet recognized it, as though the existence of secular powers depended on his recognizing them. I never imitated them in this regard, and always made it a condition that the contract be signed at the city hall before celebrating the nuptial Mass. The Council of Trent is not recognized in France, and it was the Legislative Assembly of Blois that was responsible for whatever part of its discipline was observed.[5] Once the royal laws became null and void, the contract had to be entered into according to the civil laws, otherwise the marriage was invalid, as it has always been in France without the consent of the heads of family of the two contracting parties. Properly speaking, marriage is not a sacrament: it is a contract, although it is true that there is a sacrament to bless and sanctify it. It is necessary, then, that it be preceded by the matter *circa quam,* which is the contract, over which the State has jurisdiction, as the Church has jurisdiction over the sacrament. This latter is administered in the nuptial Mass, when the priest, turning toward the contracting parties and holding his hands out toward them, prays for them. The prayers are the form; the imposition of hands the matter *ex qua.* This is the most solid and pertinent doctrine to answer the arguments of the Protestants. The proof of it can be seen in due detail in the work *Du Mariage* (two volumes in cuarto) by Agier, the president today of the Supreme Court of Appeal of Paris. Gazaniga, the celebrated Father whose course in theology is widely accepted in Europe, as are his other works, did not dictate his treatise on the sacraments in the schools, but wrote it, rather, after Pius VI had come to Bologna from Vienna and, kissing him on the forehead, had conferred with him for four hours, concerning what is believed to be the same subject that occasioned his journey to Vienna, that is to say the emperor Joseph's laws on marriage, granting to the secular power the right to establish and to dispense with the diriment impediments, in accordance with the doctrine current today, which Launvi restored. Hence it is said in Italy that Gazaniga wrote that treatise *ad mentem Pii sexti,* and for that reason it was omitted in the latest editions of his theology and replaced by Anzualdo's. For the same reason, since Gazaniga, in his treatise on predestination, in order to respond to the argument *voe tibi corozain,* had adopted the doctrine of the Augustinians, amalgamating it with that of Saint Thomas, as Mansolié, the general of the Order of Saint Dominic, had done, Quiñones had a violent dispute with him, sending him an opinion, signed by Roselli and other theologians of the Minerva, that that was not the doctrine of the Order. Gazaniga followed him to the letter when he came to deal with the subject of grace. The Jesuits also challenged more than a hundred of his propositions on this subject. He answered them with a short work: *Breves responsiones ad scrupula contrariae sectae.**

Two noteworthy events took place in Paris during my stay there. The first was a Provisional Council in Paris, which condemned, as contrary to Scripture and the Holy Fathers, the opinion of those who held that the validity of powers and the second National Council of France depended on the Pope's acceptance. The second event was the solemn restoration of the Catholic religion. The proceedings of the National Council have appeared in print, having been recorded by a tachygrapher, that is to say, a man who writes as quickly as a person speaks, an art preserved in England, which in earlier times was used by the Romans and has just been perfected in France, where it has been made more diversified still by the addition of musical notes and in other ways, just as passigraphy, or the art of understanding what is written in any language without understanding that language, has also begun to be practiced; it is an art that has cost scholars many years of cogitation and was finally perfected in Prussia, using very few characters. The characters representing numbers, which we understand in books written throughout the world, furnish some notion of this system. The Japanese thus understand Chinese books without understanding their language, be-

---

* *Brief answers to the doubts of contrary sects.*

cause each Chinese character means only one thing. That is why there are more than eighty thousand of them. The amazing thing about passigraphy is that it has very few characters.

As for the National Council, how edifying it was to me to see those real bishops, extremely poor ones, though rich in virtues and wisdom, who had come from as far as sixty leagues away, some of them on foot! Several of them bore on their persons the marks of their profession of the faith of Jesus Christ, dating back to the days of the Terror and atheism, or of the persecution of those who observed Sundays as the Sabbath. In order to understand this latter, it is necessary to know that one of the innovations of the Republican French was the establishment of a new calendar, with the months divided into tenths or decades. And the Deists, who after Robespierre succeeded the atheists, and under the name of Theophilanthropists, or lovers of God, were now headed (as I have already said) by the director Reveillère Lepeaux, mounted through the use of the power of the Government an extremely violent campaign to abolish Sundays as the Sabbath, forcing people to work on them and take the *decadis* as their day of rest. The Constitutional clergy was opposed, publishing eighty brief works defending Sundays, and they were quite right to do so, because even though it is not recorded that the Apostles established Sundays as the Sabbath day, this became the general rule in the Church very soon after them. The persecution landed a great many priests in prison and banished a number of them to French Guiana in America. But the people, who could read the third commandment of God: "Remember to keep holy the Sabbath," stubbornly insisted on observing it, and even houses of prostitution were closed on Sundays, whereas on the *decadi* they were all open.

The Constitutional clergy were the ones who bore the burden of the Terror and persecutions in France. Had it not been for them it would have ended, and, despite what people maintain to the contrary, almost all the most learned members of the clergy remained in France: in my day their numbers increased to seventeen thousand. Molinism came to the fore, which with the imbroglios and pretexts of Jansenius and of Quesnel, had put an end to all ecclesiastical literature in France, whose learned practitioners, after the Bastille, left the country to die in exile or fled to Savoy or Holland. And the others remained, studying Tournely, Potier and Coller, that is to say, pure Molinism. Molinism also brought scholarship to an end in Spain in the sixteenth century, drowning the nation in a sea of metaphysics, what with the quarrel over the middle way of science. There is no sect more given to the persecution and destruction of solid studies. They use Calvinism as their pretext, and it is evident to me that today all Calvinists and Lutherans, and all Protestants, are Arminians, or simply Molinists.

To return to the Council, it was divided into committees, according to the subjects that were to be dealt with, which were very important ones. Then the reports of the committees were discussed in sessions held in the church of Saint Sulpice, and when the point of final formulation was reached, the solemn plenary session was held in the cathedral or church of Notre Dame, which the Republicans dedicated to the Supreme Being, as though all churches were not dedicated to him, even if they commemorated a Saint. But in the end only one or two general sessions were held, in which the Council declared the primate to be the successor of Saint Peter, and its loyalty to the Holy See, in order to avoid slanderous rumors and libels. The remainder of the proceedings consisted only of discussions, though they were very interesting ones. The celebrated bishop of Blois, Gregoire, was the very soul of this Council, as he had been of the first one, and the pillar of religion in France.[6] In the name of the bishops gathered together in Paris as representatives of the clergy, he reported to the Council on everything that had taken place since the first Council, within and without France, and the article that deals with Spain is mine. He has written many works, among them the *History of Religious Sects in the Eighteenth Century*, which is very curious. Nearly all the entries in *The Annals of Religion*, a very substantial work, are his, as is everything attributed to an anonymous "bishop of France." He told me that it was highly probable that Saint Thomas the Apostle had preached in America, now that he had seen the Latin letter on the subject that I wrote to Langlés, the renowned Orientalist who in my opinion wrote the notes to Carli's American letters, in which the author, though a Deist, says that obviously America was Christianized at a very early date.[7] The notes to Carli, like others to Ulloa, are by señor Wite-Brune. After he had read the brief dissertation on the subject that I placed at the end of my history of the revolution in New Spain, Gregoire urged me to investigate the subject in greater depth when I returned to America, for the glory of religion and the refutation of unbelievers. Baron Humboldt also told me in Paris: "I believed that it was an invention of the friars, and said as much in my statistics; but after I saw your curious essay I see that this is not so."

The cause of the discontinuation of the National Council was the concordat between Napoleon and the Pope, through the intermediary of the legate Cardinal Capra, accepted following the peace of Amiens, for according to the freedoms of the Gallican Church there cannot be a legate in France if that country has not requested one and he may remain only as long as permitted, and must present the credentials of his legateship to the Government, so that an examination may be made as to the extent of it. Bonaparte wanted to make himself Consul in Perpetuity and decided to win the people over by way of the two things that it desired, namely peace and the public restoration of religion.

The bishops of the Council, once they heard that there was a concordat, renounced as one their miters and placed their renunciations in the hands of their metropolitans. The Pope demanded that within three months all bishops who maintained that they were Roman Catholics should renounce their miters; and whether they renounced them or not, he declared all churches vacant posts, and by suppressing many bishoprics and elevating the status of others, he reduced them to fifty, with ten archbishoprics. There had previously been 134 miters. A number of French bishops who were in England refused to renounce their offices, and protested against the Pope's reorganization as being contrary to the freedoms of the Gallican Church, although the bishop of London unjustly suspended them on this account.

Among the new bishops elected by the concordat were a number of Constitutionals, to whom, once the Government had elected them, the legate gratuitously sent an absolution, which none of them had sought from him, from the excommunication they had incurred by not having been elected by Rome and by having followed the Constitution. These are political devices that Rome always uses to keep up appearances as a false decretalistic authority. The bishop of Angoulême took such a firm stand that the legate dared not send him the gratuitous absolution. This bishop and those to whom he had dispatched it, once they read in the proceedings of the legation of Caprara what sort of absolution had been sent them, protested publicly against it, saying that if they had abandoned the Civil Constitution of the Clergy, it had been for the precise reason that it had ceased to be the law of the nation, not because they repented having obeyed it, since it contained nothing contrary to religion. In point of fact, it had simply been an attempt to return to the early discipline of the Church. They also protested against various clauses that had been suppressed in the minutes of the proceedings establishing the legateship, which maintained and safeguarded the freedoms of the Gallican Church. The court of Rome proceeded as it does with papal bulls against which governments protest or accept only with exceptions; it records them in toto and after its own fashion, allows the bull to stand and enforces as much of it as it can; and when it is unable to do so, it temporizes and remains silent. Everything about it is a matter of intrigue and political scheming. I shall cite an example of its characteristic way of proceeding.

When Pius VII arrived in Florence, returning from Paris after bestowing his blessing on Napoleon as emperor, the renowned bishop of Pistoia, Ricci, whose council had been condemned, was quietly informed that the Pope esteemed him and desired to see him.[8] In fact he not only treated him with honor and respect, but offered him his friendship as well, and assured him that he had always regarded him as being orthodox; and that, for that very reason, in order to make people hold their tongues, it would be a good thing for him to present a submission to the Holy See. That is the polite name given to retractions. The bishop replied that he would offer one under certain conditions. He was given a draft copy of a retraction; but once he began writing out his conditions, they kept increasing until they were the size of a notebook. He therefore signed the draft copy of the retraction separately and brought it to the Pope, along with the notebook outlining his conditions. The Pope took all of it in hand, and keeping the signed copy of the retraction, very politely handed the notebook back to him, as though it contained only apologies, saying to him: "No, it is not necessary, it is not necessary: I have always regarded you as orthodox, as most orthodox." The bishop was embarrassed, and the Pope then published Ricci's retraction, pure and simple, in the consistory. The same thing apparently happened to Febronio's. I found all of this out by way of a letter from Ricci himself to Gregoire, who recorded this anecdote in his Universal Biography. Ricci also told him that he had already written down the story of his Episcopate, which was to be found in the hands of his nephew. Religion is all politics, a Jesuit in Rome told me. They are well aware of this, and it is a pity that it involves so much scheming and plotting.

In his concordat with Napoleon the Pope also acceded to the fact that the Republican laymen had taken possession of all Church property, or agreed that the clergy, who had not ceased to burden people's consciences on this point, would not lay claim to such property. And citing the example of Julius II, at the time of the restoration of Catholicism in England during the reign of Queen Mary, he approved all the marriages entered into by bishops, priests, monks and nuns, on condition that they not exercise their ministry. He had already returned the bishop of Autun, Talleyrand, to secular status by means of a brief to this effect, in order that he might marry, as he did. And the legate *a latere* likewise granted his approval of many other marriages of clergymen in the Cisalpine Republic. Celibacy is a matter of sheer discipline, which, despite the Popes, was not accepted by the Greek clergy, who all marry before being ordained, except for the bishops, all of whom are monks. In the Latin Church, at least in Spain, as Masdeu proves against Zacarías, even bishops were married in the first four centuries, and celibacy was not introduced until the decretal to the bishop of Tarragona issued by Siricius. It has not been constantly practiced since then, nor was it approved as the general law until the fifteenth century. The scandals to which celibacy, which was ordained neither by Christ nor by the Apostles, has given rise are evident from history. The reiteration of canons regarding it in the Councils proves that it was not observed, and may it please God that the Popes remove the weight of this yoke, which requires a special gift from God to bear. Wherever I have wandered in this world I have seen nothing but scandals and frailties in this regard among both sexes that have taken holy orders. *Non omnes capiunt verbum istud, sed quibus datum est.**

To conclude: it was formally agreed in the concordat that bishops could wear purple hose, collars and hat ribbons in public, as do the Italian bishops, although these latter wear a green hat ribbon, and only domestic prelates and prothonotaries apostolic purple ones. In France the nonliturgical attire of bishops was a purple tunic with a long train, buttoned down the front from top to bottom, and girdled with a sash of the same color at the waist, tied on the left side, with gold tassels hanging from the ends; a rochet with a collar like a surplice, and a long purple cloak draped over the back; a black three-cornered hat, with a broad gold ribbon, and, naturally, the pectoral cross hanging from a silk ribbon.

Other clergy were allowed to wear noncanonical attire, with all the center part black, like the Italians. Their attire had previously been a black tunic, with a long train, buttoned from top to bottom like that of the bishops, with sleeves like those of a cassock, and a collar that is not like ours. Theirs is formed by the tunic, with a little white band of chambray or silk in the front, with two tips hanging down, each of them two fingers wide, with a black fillet if they are white, or a white one if they are black. A black sash, tied on the side, with ends without tassels falling downward, and a light cloak draped over the back. A three-cornered hat, broader than those of laymen; and bishops and priests, naturally, with hair heavily powdered and arranged in sausage curls in the

---

* *Not all understand this word, save those to whom it is given.*

back, which distinguishes their coiffure from that of laymen. This was an indispensable formality, and no clergyman would dare present himself to his bishop without having observed it. The people are so accustomed to it that when our squadron was in Brest, a monk who was a chaplain went to Paris, and the people did not want to hear his Mass, saying that he was improperly attired, because his hair was not powdered. When I was there everyone dressed as best he could, and insofar as possible was excused from wearing clerical dress in order to avoid being cursed and jeered at. He belongs, worldly people would say, to the *petraille,* a made-up word meaning that he belonged to the priestly riffraff, the way one of our people would use the word *sacerdotalla.*

Leaving ecclesiastical matters now to recount a few things pertaining to the secular realm, the great question of the day at that time, naturally, raised at the suggestion of certain friends who had agreed among themselves beforehand, was whether to give Bonaparte the Consulate for ten years, as recompense for his having brought about the peace of Amiens.[9] But by issuing a sudden drastic order that had destroyed the Directory and the two Councils, of the Five Hundred and of the Elders, whom he replaced by the Consulate, the Legislature and the Senate, he had himself named Consul for Life, already thinking, doubtless, of making himself emperor. I then saw that everything in the world of politics is a fraud. Voting registers were opened so that the people could come to record their vote. Interested parties come to sign the registers; and those who do not come, because they are unwilling to give their consent, yet at the same time do not want to declare themselves enemies, are counted as being in favor, in accordance with the rule *qui tacet, consentire videtur,* that is to say, silence gives consent. And then it is announced that there were this or that many millions in favor. And who could or would dare to publicly give the lie to such news? Poor people! And of a certainty I never saw one flightier, more fickle, more frivolous than the people of France. To win them over and make them tag along, all that need be done is talk to them poetically, and mix in a few witticisms, which they adore, in favor of one party while covering the opposite party with ridicule, which is the weapon they fear the most. The men there are like women, and the women like children. Women are faithful only in matters of religion. Our parishes are in all truth made up of them, and when there were two hundred of them in the church, the men numbered only a dozen, even though the women always ended up attracting all of them, either through their charm, or because they will take over the rearing of the children.

I was also there when the Napoleonic Code was debated and drafted, each law being preceded by two or three magnificent speeches. Each of them was drawn up in draft form by the Council of State, and a speaker from the Council presented it and argued in its favor before the tribunate. The Legislature did not hold a debate; it approved or rejected the law by secret vote, and in the latter case it went back to the Council of State. But in the final analysis there was a trap even in this when the divorce law came up for consideration, since by mutual consent it was agreed that it was intolerable. It could not get past the tribunate. But it passed later on, with a thousand conditions attached, in view of the fact that not everyone in France professed the Catholic religion. But even so it could not pass the Legislature. Then Bonaparte said that if this went on the Code could never be drawn up in final form, that in order to expedite it there would be a commission from each body, which would confer with one from the State, so that an agreement could be reached more easily; and that was how the divorce law passed. Several very curious works against it came out, Monsieur Bonald's in particular. And it should be mentioned that before the draft law was drawn up it was submitted to all the learned societies in France, which sent in their opinions and observations. It is an excellent code.[10]

I shall not speak of other bodies, because the king has changed everything, giving France almost the same Constitution as England, with its two Chambers, the House of Lords and the House of Commons, the latter being the representatives of the people. It appears that he is also going to reestablish the Academies. In the days of the Republic they had been combined into a single national institute divided into various sections: physical sciences, metaphysics, history, et cetera. The most learned scholars in the nation were honored by being elected to it, and others from all over the world were made corresponding members. I was the only American to have the honor of occupying a seat in it as a corresponding member, in the third section, that of History.[11]

As for fashions, most of which were ridiculous, I noted one thing in my day that seemed to me to be most rational, the fact that at that time there was no set fashion in Paris, and each woman dressed differently, as showed her person to best advantage. Since none of them powdered their hair, the coiffeur was a man of taste, who after carefully observing the woman's facial expression, physiognomy, complexion and eyes, proceeded to order exactly the right adornments to bring out her beauty; hair worn long or short, blond or brunette, a turban or flowers, this or that color dress, dangling earrings, choke necklaces and so on. So that at the ball given by the Minister of the Interior for the Prince of Parma, who had just taken possession of the kingdom of Etruria, there were five hundred lady guests, and not one of them looked like any other. So at that time too the women in Paris struck me as being beautiful, whereas in 1814, when I returned, they looked to me like demons with their fashions *à la chinoise,* that is to say with Chinese-style gowns and coiffures. The men were as different from one another as the women, especially their hair styles, and I realized clearly why sometimes the same woman who today seems beautiful to us seems less so tomorrow, or even ugly. Her costume does not suit her physiognomy.

I also noted then how ridiculous apes are. Spaniards perpetually ape the dress and the customs of other Europeans, the French in particular, whose fashions they adopt with no thought for the weather or the occasion, and hence they are more ridiculous. When I arrived in the winter I saw women of the people wearing wooden clogs. That is how we came by the fashion that lasted for so many long years throughout Spain; but there in Paris ladies did not wear them, nor did anyone else, except in the winter, when all the streets are a quagmire, and that is how the city came by the Latin name of *Lutetia**; Spaniards latched on to the fashion and wore it in all seasons. Boots and half-boots came from France; but there they are worn in the wintertime, because of the aforementioned mud; and not even in that season would anyone dare present himself with them at a decent house, nor would he be allowed in, and in England not even in a royal theater. My typical Spaniard wore them for summer too, and turns up everywhere in them. Frock coats, which the Italians call misery-hiders, were invented in the time of sans-culottism and dire poverty; but in France they are a *déshabillé,* informal dress that is worn at home; no one would present himself *en deshabillé* at a social gathering. The Spaniard has made of it a dignified costume for all public occasions.

Something quite noteworthy in Paris, because it is the most popular meeting place, is what is called the *Palais Royal,* built around the former garden of the palace of the Duke of Orléans. It is a square lined with galleries, with apartments above the splendid facade, and trees in the middle, forming a promenade and a little flower garden; it is so large that it takes a quarter of an hour to go all the way round it, and has two walkways through it bordered by fashionable shops. All the notices about various works, novelties and so on are posted on the columns of it,

* From Latin *lutum,* mire.

and in its shops, which are below the galleries, whatever objects are the most refined of their sort, including books, are for sale. There is no one in Paris who is not seen there at one time or another, and the prettiest and most gallant courtesans also stroll about there as though in their houses, and pay a special tax to the Government in order to do so. Without ever leaving the confines of the *Palais Royal* one can come by everything necessary for one's sustenance, luxury and diversion. In it there were eleven kitchens, fourteen cafés, two large theaters and three small ones and even scribes or public clerks with their *bureau* or money-changer's table, and men in wigs who supplied little napkins with which to tidy oneself up, and lavender water, or *alhucema* as we call it, so as to come out with one's behind nicely perfumed.

In the cafés one finds all the Paris daily papers, which are many in number, as well as the official gazette, which is called *Le Moniteur.* And foreign newspapers as well. One can read everything without having to pay, and every café is a refuge against the cold for poor decent folk, because one doesn't feel the cold inside them, on account of the stoves. Since the war with Spain people tend to drink chocolate rather than coffee, except after a meal. And almanacs, some in prose and some in verse, listing women of ill repute by their names, addresses, talents and endowments, are also sold there.

In the Café Borel there was a ventriloquist, a man who spoke through his belly, something that, if it were not an art, one would take for a magic trick. He barely opens his mouth and projects his voice wherever he wishes, far away, up close, in the roof beams, on the wall, as he chooses, and a person would swear with all his senses and all his soul's verities that someone is speaking there in the place where he projects his voice. He varies the tone of it in a thousand ways, and it is enough to drive a person mad. So, a person who took a newcomer to the Café Borel would secretly apprise the ventriloquist of the name and homeland of the latter, and as he was about to drink his coffee, the ventriloquist would enter, ask what his name was and then immediately project his voice into a tall window and call him by his name to come get a letter for him from such and such a place in the country that he was from. The man thus summoned would go upstairs at once, search all about the hallways and find no one. But the minute he returned to his seat, he was again called by name, by a voice telling him: "Come here, I'm here." The newcomer would go back, and the entire café would be amused.

There were other cafés with two rooms, and in one music was played and women sang, while in the other some little play or short comedy was put on, and performances were given in turn in the two rooms, till eleven at night. There was also the spectacle called a phantasmagoria, or the art of the Gentile priests whereby they made the gods and the shades or manes of the dead appear and do things and even go so far as to fling themselves on top of a person. Galvanism or animal electricity had also been recently discovered, whereby the nerves of a dead animal, if touched by two metals at the same time, would make it leap about and jerk its limbs. A dead man's eyes open, and I have seen one move his arms and lie there pulling out his innards, because his body was slit open. I am unable to describe the luxury of the theaters, of which there were thirty. The largest theater, or Theater of the Arts, was very expensive, and was always full; yet even so it was necessary for the Republic to grant it a subsidy of a million pesos each year. It took a thousand young girls to perform the dances alone, and the sum spent on the decor and stage costumes of the opera based on the mysteries of Isis amounted to seven hundred thousand francs, the equivalent of seven hundred thousand columnarias. A Spanish columnaria is what we would call two reals, because the Spanish peseta is worth one Spanish real less than ours. In Spain, there are twenty reals to a peso, which they call a duro, and there are four of these reals to each of its pesetas. So that one Spanish real is worth less than one medio of ours, since it is worth ten and a half cuartos, and a Spanish real de vellón is worth eight and a half cuartos.

It may seem surprising that I leave Paris without saying anything about the city in general, about its population or about France. Such a subject belongs under the head of statistics or geography, and there are books in which to study it. Moreover it varies endlessly, and Napoleon's wars have devastated the population of Europe. Spain once had a population of 10 million; I would be surprised if it has even 8 million today. Madrid was calculated to have 140,000 inhabitants; I doubt whether it has more than 60,000 today. France had a population of more than 30 million at the time of the Republic; I do not believe that it has today even the 24 million it had at the time of Louis XVI, because the annual military conscription led all the young men of France to the slaughter. Paris was calculated to have 700,000 inhabitants in 1801; it was my impression, when I returned there in 1814, that it had less than 400,000, including foreigners. Italy once had a population of 18 million; today I doubt that it has 12 million. Rome numbered 166,000 souls, including 26,000 Jews. I was still there at the time of the first invasion of the French, when 30,000 souls disappeared. Today it has 70,000 to 80,000 at most. Naples, at the time of the Republic, was estimated to have 500,000, and the entire kingdom 5 million. Today it probably has 4 million at most, and the city no more than 200,000 souls. Portugal, including the islands, had 3 million, and Lisbon, its capital, 300,000 in 1807, when I was there. What with the war and the emigration that followed upon that of the king, the kingdom probably has a population of no more than 2 million, and the capital no more than 150,000.

As for the cities, there are none in Europe that can compare to those of our America or of the United States. All of the former appear to have been founded by a people inimical to straight lines. They are all nothing but streets and alleyways that are blind ends, labyrinths with no order and no ostentation. All the houses are made of stone, brick and wood, and the walls are as burning hot as the roofs. The latter are made of tiles, and are not flat, as ours are. In Spain some small measure of regularity and beauty has been introduced in such ports as Cádiz, Puerto de Santa María, Bilbao, Barceloneta that carry on trade with America, by following our example. Churches in Europe are Gothic, except in Rome. In conclusion: in each kingdom little road guides are sold, showing their distances and listing places and things worth seeing along each one. In the large cities a map of them is sold, in the form of a small book, to guide foreigners, along with a list of everything to be found in them. Only in Spain is there no such thing. And such a guide would be useless, because in the small towns and villages only the parish priest and the sacristan know how to read. Everyone journeys like a barbarian through a land of barbarians, trembling at the highwaymen who sally forth to rob travelers, and a carriage is escorted only by troupes of beggars and children, clamoring for alms at the top of their lungs.

What there is not such a great lack of, at least in the capital of Spain, is libraries, for there is the Royal Library and that of San Isidro, where people go to study. In Paris there is the Royal Library, or that of Cardinal Richelieu, whose books number in the millions, and one is given all the books to read that one asks for in the two hours that it is open in the morning. The library of the Institute is very good, and there are others, such as the one at the Collège Mazarin, etc. There are also reading rooms, very neatly arranged and sheltered from the cold, where for a mere nothing one can read not only all the periodicals, but also everything new that has come out. One can also ask for portable books, that is to say, small-sized ones. And if one is not a regular customer, for four sols a day one can go there morning, noon and night, and sit at his own little table, with his own fire and inkwell. And there are also circulating libraries, in which a person can sit down to read and for a paltry sum per month take home as many books as he needs. None of this exists in Spain either. But enough of Paris.

From My Departure from Paris to My Return from Naples to Rome

I never lost sight of Mexico, wanting as I did to return to my homeland. There came through Paris a courier from Spain, who said he
was on his way to Rome to summon señor Vargas Laguna, who was
Minister of Spain there, to serve as Minister of Grace and Justice in our
court, since Caballero had cataracts, although he recovered from them,
to the Spaniards' misfortune; Recacho, the father of the Recacho who is
a judge in Guadalajara, cured them. And inasmuch as Vargas had been
my friend ever since my days in Madrid, I decided to leave for Rome in
order to be secularized and return to Spain in his company. Hence I left
Paris in 1802, accompanied by a Sardinian man of letters, or as his countrymen would say, a former Spaniard, because that is what Sardinians
were; and even today Spanish is the native language throughout their
land, except in Caller (Cagliari), where Catalan is spoken and there is
always a deputy from Catalonia.

I started out on my three-hundred-league journey with an ounce of
gold, twice the sum I had with me when I set out from Madrid for Paris,
and just as I had arrived in the latter via coach, so I entered Rome. My
reader will want to know how that came about, particularly in view of
the fact that I am incapable of chicanery, deception or intrigue. The
story of the adventures to which my poverty and my naiveté gave rise
would be never-ending. But, especially among the compassionate and

devout feminine sex, there was a great deal of charity shown priests, the victims of so much misfortune and persecution during the revolution. They did not accept payment from me in a single inn, and even the coachmen charged me only half as much as the other passengers. In France, apart from stagecoaches, there are many ways of traveling at very little expense. There are a number of lads with little horses, who take people from one place to another for just a few sols (twenty-five sols equal two reals), and particularly on the trip back to their starting point, when they have no passengers. There are also *pataches*, which are little carriages without suspensions, made of wickerwork; they charge very little and are very fast. Since there are villages, or at least little places in the countryside where victuals are sold, almost one after the other all along the roads, and on either side of these there are groves of trees, one can also journey on foot without fatigue. A large part of France has canals and navigable rivers as well, and there are water coaches, that is to say flat boats with bedrooms and kitchens aboard, at most affordable prices, that keep regular schedules, and since they are towed by horses on the bank alongside, they proceed at the pace of these latter and transport passengers for a distance of fifteen or twenty leagues for four reals.

The Seine divides Paris in half, with an island in midstream on which the Cathedral is located, and what is called the Cité, or old Paris, which was very small, when today its circumference, I am told, measures nine French leagues. Water coaches ply the Seine each day in several directions, and I went to Sens on one of these. From there one journeys overland by coach, for one or two days' time, to Chalons, and then one again boards a boat to Lyons and to Avignon, the former residence of the Popes for the seventy years that the Holy See was in France, the period that the Italians call the Babylonian Captivity.

I went by boat as far as Lyons, and from there I crossed Provence in the rear of a coach, scorched by the sun, to Marseilles, and a hundred paces outside of Vienne I saw Pilate's tomb. Since I was, fortunately, in the prime of life still, both men and women were attracted by my physical appearance; the fact that I was from a country as far distant as Mexico gave me a sort of mythological status, which aroused people's curiosity and attracted their attention; my merry nature, my innocence and my openness made people well-disposed toward me, and on hearing me speak, to which end I did my best to find a place to eat at a round table, everyone immediately made friends with me and no one could be persuaded that a man of my upbringing and education was a man without qualities. They introduced me into the homes of the wellborn, and inasmuch as the French in such circles are fond of good company at table, I began to enjoy theirs.

Being a foreigner in France is thus the best possible recommendation, so long as one is not Italian, their perfidy being notorious. I have not been in any large city where some Italian has not murdered or robbed his very benefactors. All Frenchmen, contrary to what happens in England and in other nations, invariably side with the foreigner in any dispute that arises involving their own compatriots, they willingly open their houses to him, they make it their duty to look after him; to insult him is a grave offense, and he is permitted to do a thousand things that they would not tolerate from a Frenchman. Hence every foreigner speaks well of France. To make a long story short: I supported myself with the alms I received for saying Mass, and not by virtue of my credentials, which the pen pusher León kept in his possession, where they remain still, nor by virtue of those of Dr. Maniau, because Cornide, the executor of his estate, on departing for America, wrote me asking me to send them to his family, and I did so; it was, rather, by virtue of my testimonials or letters dimissory* to Paris. In Marseilles I saw women, at least women of the people, with mantillas as in Spain, which is the only place where they are worn. I also saw a colony of Catalans, then later on another in Gibraltar, and wherever there is anything in the sea to fish, they are found there doing just that. Since Marseilles is a city that was founded by Greeks, I set eyes on some of the latter for the first time, for they come there to trade. They do not wear hose, go about in a jacket or cotton blouse, like our Indians, wear their hair short, and cover their heads with a sort of bonnet or cap with a little tassel. The women wear tunics; they have round faces and big eyes. Both the men and the women have the same complexion as our Indians.

A small vessel was leaving from there for Civitavecchia, a port of the Papal State, chartered by two young merchants, and they allowed me to come aboard for a gold louis, that is to say, for slightly less then four and a half pesos. Although the crossing ordinarily takes three days, there was no wind, and with nothing but what the French call a *bonace,* a dead calm, we arrived in twelve, after being boarded by Moors who were pirating along the coasts of the Papal State.

We are now in the country of treachery and chicanery, of poison; the country of murder and robbery. In Italy it is necessary to keep all one's

---

* A letter from a bishop dismissing a clergyman from one diocese and recommending his reception to another.

five senses alert, because people there make their livelihood by what they call *collonarsi*, that is to say, in polite words, by fleecing one another. And there is nothing to equal the delight they show when they have gulled someone. They celebrate it as a feat brought off by sheer cunning. Their language is the one best suited to lying, because it is all politeness and exaggerations. Italy is the homeland of high-flown forms of address and superlatives; it is Your Lordship here and Your Excellency there, such titles being used for anyone halfway respectable. If one orders a pair of shoes made, for instance, they deliver them along with the receipt for payment of them; and it is imperative to take the receipt, because even if they receive payment, they come back another day to shamelessly demand it once again, and without scrupling to commit perjury force a person to pay a second time in a court of law.

The two young merchants, who were on their way to Rome, took me with them in a cabriolet. But when it is a matter of carriages, it is necessary to know that when one asks how much the ride has cost, he is told "such and such a sum, and a *buona mano*." This latter is not a tip that a person is supposed to give voluntarily, but a sum that, if not handed over, he is hauled into court to pay, and if the price for the trip is not agreed on beforehand, it is arbitrarily raised to a figure that nearly equals the price of the carriage, and there is nothing to do but pay it. When agreeing on a fare, then, it is necessary to ask how much it will be including the *buona mano*. And it is also best not to enter an inn, even though one just stops in momentarily to get warm, because one is then made to pay for *la comodità*, the comfort, just as in Spain he is made to pay for the noise and give the servingmaid a tip. In France the only service the latter performs consists of opening the door of the coach when a person is about to leave, and bowing repeatedly.

The carriages in Italy fly, unlike those in Spain, which plod along, and go no farther each day than a man could go on foot, stopping many times as well so as to feed the mules, since as a general rule the coachman's only property is his mules. In any event, when going to Rome or when leaving it, it is imperative to make a thirty-mile run without stopping, or else pay the price, if one stays the night anywhere within those thirty miles, of catching a tertian fever. The entire district is nothing but noxious swamps, though hidden under a cover of greenery. Even in Rome during the summer, monks and those who live in the suburbs have to stay indoors. People do not leave their houses at night till an hour after dark, because of what they call the *aria cativa [sic]*, the bad air; hence in summer the evening stroll begins at midnight. At that season everyone goes about chewing cinchona bark, and people look as if they had just come out of the hospital. The heat is as fierce as in Toledo, for Rome is on the same meridian. So the women wear only a thin little tunic over their blouse, and inside their houses they go about bare naked or nearly so.

The newcomer has difficulty knowing what time it is, since he is told, for instance, that it is fifteen or eighteen o'clock, because they do not reckon clock time the way we do, but rather, like a large part of Germany, they count by periods of twenty-four hours in a row, beginning half an hour after nightfall, and when it is one o'clock they ring a bell. Hence the time of day constantly varies, depending on the hour that night falls. Nor do church clocks ever strike more than six times; and since the one at Saint Peter's strikes twelve like ours do, the Romans say that it never stops striking.

I am now in Rome, without *letters of holy orders*, without acquaintances and without money. The sergeant of Spain, thinking that I had money, put me up for a few days. The sergeant of Spain is the name given to the one who guards the Spanish minister, who has a company of soldiers at his orders, as well as jurisdiction over the district of the Piazza di Spagna, which is very large. The Roman forces of law and order cannot enter it without his permission, and therefore prostitutes, who are not allowed in Rome, and are buried outside consecrated ground if they die in the course of plying their trade, take refuge in the aforementioned piazza. If the constabulary asks the Spanish minister for permission to go eject them, the sergeant gives the prostitutes warning in exchange for the annual contribution that they give him on Epiphany, which is the day when Christmas tips are given in Rome, and then they go off to the Piazza di Venezia, another exempt jurisdiction, until the constables' visit has come to an end. And it is noteworthy that the common people, who in Spain and England are overawed and allow themselves to be shackled by constables, but are enraged and stand up to soldiers, in Rome allow themselves to be arrested by the latter, because they say that they represent the sovereign, whereas they regard it as an unspeakable outrage to be arrested by the constables, whom they stone.

I was on friendly terms from the beginning with very distinguished gentlemen, men of learning in particular; but finding myself incapable of revealing my dire poverty to anyone, more than once I nearly starved to death. My reader will ask why I did not betake myself to a monastery of my Order; [I will answer that it was] because I had no habits, no *credentials;* because in Europe it is necessary to pay for what one eats in the

monasteries; because in view of what I had suffered in them they terrified me, like caves of Cyclopes; and because they were destroyed by the
French, and in those that were not in total ruins the cardinals had taken
refuge, inasmuch as the pontifical table, which had also been destroyed,
was unable to provide the two thousand pesos or Roman escudos
needed to feed them. All of Rome was poverty-stricken.

Cardinal Lorenzana, who was not in dire need because he had
benefices in Toledo, had a habit made for me. But I went without eating
for two or three days; I kept my mind off my hunger either in the library
founded by Cardinal Casanate in the Minerva, the mother house of the
Dominicans, so called because its church was built on top of the old
temple of the goddess Minerva, or in the Biblioteca Angélica founded at
the monastery of Sant' Agostino by an American who was a general of
the Order. These are the largest libraries in Rome. From there I would
go to the Villa Borghese (which we would call the Quinta Borghese), a
good quarter of a league away, wash my clothes and drink water; until,
after having gone without a thing to eat for four days, I fell ill with a
fever, and was taken with a terrible pain in my head to the hospital for
Spaniards, called Monserrate. Spain has two of them in Rome, and used
to have one in Naples, and another in Vienna; but their nationals have
taken over these latter.

They wanted to give me an emetic at the hospital, and I told them to
give me *papa* first (that is what they call soup in Italy) so as to have
something to throw up. In fact, my stomach was so weak that merely
eating the soup made me vomit; but I must have kept some of it down; I
slept and felt fine. While I was there I received news of a bill of exchange for three hundred pesos being sent me by my brother in Monterrey, because as a consequence of the peace of Amiens
communications had been reestablished. At that juncture an Italian, the
son of a former Spanish Jesuit, took me home with him; but I am so
doomed to misfortune that by an odd turn of fate the bill of exchange
failed to come through. I had written to my brother of my hardships,
and that was what led him to send the bill of exchange; but I also wrote
to Dr. Pomposo, of Mexico City, and told him that everything was well
with me, doing so both because he was under no obligation to remedy
my impoverished state, and because I did not want my enemies to re-
joice if they saw a letter from me giving an account of my dire straits.
Dr. Pomposo sent the letter on to my brother, and more readily believing what I had told a stranger than what I myself had told him, he
countermanded the bill of exchange.

When this setback occurred, I got out my brief of secularization, which I had already requested when I was in Spain, addressed to Cardinal Borbón, and another, of entitlement to curacies, benefices and prebends, addressed to the archbishop of Mexico. Nothing of this sort is worth money in Rome, just as relics, even though they be the bodies of saints, are worthless, despite the fact that commercial agents keep asking money for them. With these documents in hand, I decided to leave for Naples, with the aim of getting myself appointed as a member of the escort of the infanta, who was going to Spain to marry Ferdinand VII.[1] The former American Jesuit Noriega provided me with the means to make the journey, and I boarded a little Calabrian boat on the Tiber. The ballast for the vessel was gun carriages, which we left off at a little island called Portolanzó, and we were making for Terracina without ballast when a storm that came up put us in such dire straits that we came within a hair's breadth of drowning. We made our escape and took shelter at the foot of Mount Circeo, where I spent the rest of the night remembering the passages in Homer about Ulysses and the enchantress Circe, who must have given her name to that mountain. In the morning we went to wait out the storm off Poncia Island, which is a rock with a spring and a house well suited for the exile of martyrs, which if memory serves me was the one to which the pope Saint Marcellinus was exiled.

When the weather calmed two days later, we resumed our journey, and disembarked in Naples, whose beauty, as seen from the sea, is surpassed only by that of Constantinople; but the infanta had already left for Spain. I had bought an old habit at the Minerva in Rome; I put it on and a Dominican lector* who happened to come across me in the famous street called Toledo, named after the viceroy Toledo, who hanged the last Inca of Peru, Sayri Tupac, because *it is the proper thing to do,* took me to his provincial** to introduce me. The latter was in fact a Spaniard who from an early age had been reared in Naples, and he recommended me to the monastery of Il Rosario, which is charged with offering hospitality to those who arrive by sea. Italian friars are well mannered and friendly. Having recognized that I was a man of learning, they spread the word, and I was accorded their general esteem. After the reigns of Joseph Bonaparte and Murat the number of friars had greatly diminished.[2] But I had never seen a bigger mob of them, for I couldn't take

---

*   A member of the next to lowest ranking of the minor orders.
**   The director of all the religious houses of a monastic order in a given district, called a province.

twenty steps without meeting one. There were friars belonging to thirty Orders, and within the city the Dominicans alone had religious houses under the jurisdiction of three Provinces, for there were twelve monasteries and fourteen convents, not counting the domestic nuns, because there are nuns who live in their own homes, wear habits like those who are cloistered, and in the churches are given the same preferential places that were always accorded virgins bound by vows of devotion to God. Dominican lay sisters, who are called *mantelatas* in Italy, also wear a long cape and a great veil over their headdress, and look like nuns.

The common folk, who are called *lazzaronis* [*sic*], are very talkative, rude, dirty and so cruel that when, following the first invasion of the French in the days of the Republic, their king reconquered Naples, his commanding general being Cardinal Rufo, who for this reason was called *Cardinalis galeatus,** and the king did not appear at the capitulation whereby the Neapolitan nobles or patricians surrendered the city (on the arrogant pretext that kings are not obliged to attend capitulations by vassals), the *lazzaronis* took the decapitated body of each noble and deposited it in front of his residence, shouting for bread to be thrown out to them to eat with the corpse, which they proceeded to devour.[3] Strips of human flesh, four fingers wide, were sold in the public square for four granos (the equivalent of our cuartos). The only one they didn't eat was a bishop; they had earlier taken it as a grave insult that the king should hang him, when all he did to the secular nobles was cut off their heads.

The accent with which they speak their local jargon is most unpleasant. All the provinces of every kingdom in Europe naturally speak their language with very different accents; but in every city in Italy there is what the French call a *patois,* and the Spaniards a *patán.* Kindly allow me to digress for a moment to explain this. Since the Latin language was the general language in Spain, Italy and France, and these kingdoms were divided into many small sovereignties after the invasion of the barbarians from the North, Latin gradually became corrupted in each of them in a different way, and many terms of the dominant barbarians were adopted. In a number of provinces, because the Court was more refined, letters were more highly cultivated, and better writers were forthcoming, the corrupted Latin forms were normalized and brought into harmony, a greater abundance of terms was introduced, and Latin came into general use among cultivated people over a greater expanse of

* *The helmeted cardinal.*

territory, the inhabitants of which had closer ties to one another, and which today we call a kingdom or a nation. And we call the language of that cultivated province either the language of the nation or of that province. But in each one of them the common people have kept their own form of corrupted Latin, and that is what today we call their *patois* or *patán*.

In France the corrupted form of Latin was first standardized in the kingdom of the Franks, whose capital was Paris, because of its university, and because its king was more powerful than the others. And that is what we call the French language; but their own regional *patois* is spoken by the people of Gascony, of Burgundy, of continental Brittany, where the old Celtic language is still spoken, of Provence and Languedoc, and so on, where Catalan is spoken. In Spain the corrupted Latin forms were systematized thanks to the cultivation and learning of the scholars of King Alfonso the Wise, who ordered that in cases of doubt with regard to the language, the example of Toledo should be consulted. But the language was finally polished and perfected when the Court took up residence in Valladolid and Burgos, thanks to the scholars of the sixteenth century. And that language is called Spanish or Castilian, and from there it spread to the united mountain regions, to Burgos, to Castilla la Nueva and La Mancha, where it is spoken, albeit very badly, especially in Madrid; and in the Andalusian regions, Extremadura and Murcia, although in those parts it is all mixed up with Arabic terms, and *ll* is pronounced like *y*, *s* like *zz*, *hh* is butchered, and the final letter is dropped altogether.[4] Although Aragon spoke the Provençal or Limousin *patois*, brought there with the domination of the French, it adopted Castilian, except for villages along the borders of Valencia and Catalonia. In these latter Limousin is spoken, although in Catalonia it has a very harsh sound and in Valencia it is softened. Since in Valencia everyone prays and hears sermons preached in Castilian, everyone understands it; the contrary is true in Catalonia, where even Latin grammar is studied in Catalan and the Spanish language is thoroughly detested. What with the eight years of occupation during the last war, Catalonians have been Castilianized to a considerable extent because of their contacts with the soldiery. In Asturias they speak a *patán* mixed with Latin terms, and in Galicia what we call Portuguese today, differing from the latter only in pronunciation. This *patán* spread from Galicia to Portugal after the Moorish conquest. Even in the regions where Castilian is spoken, the accent is so different that when I heard the mountain folk speak all I could understand was the final word of whatever it was they said. The truly Gothic people of Madrid talk like this: "Go call the doctu to have them come atone to treat Manolo for his stomachache, and we'll give him twenty *maiz*,"* meaning *maravedís*. There are streets in Madrid that go by names such as "Drag-Ass," "Tumble Doll," "Wide Ninny," "Narrow Ninny," and so on.

In Italy, in Tuscany, under the rule of the Medicis and after the Greeks who had fled Constantinople had been taken in, in the sixteenth century the sciences flourished and the corrupted Latin underwent refinement. Thus what is today called the Italian language is also called the Tuscan language, since it took shape there and only there is it generally spoken by the people, in a pure form, although they pronounce *cc* like Spanish *jj*. It is also spoken—and spoken better—throughout the Papal State, and with such a good accent in Rome that it is proverbial throughout Italy: *Lingua toscana in bocca romana*.** But in nearly every large city in Italy, such as Genoa, Milan, Venice, Bologna, Naples etc, people speak in a different *patán* with a very different monotonous drone; but the Neapolitan one is the ugliest.

Something else happened to me just after I arrived in Naples: on asking a canon in a café whether he knew Spanish (which would not have been surprising, since up until Charles III the laws still were promulgated in Spanish, although attorneys, in that city as in Rome, make their perorations in Latin), he replied by asking what reason there would be for his knowing a language of barbarians. The ill will borne Spaniards throughout Europe is beyond belief. They fought a revolution to regain their honor; but they lost it again the moment they were once more placed under the yoke, as heavy as the former one, if not heavier. It is now said that it was an uprising by barbarians, staged out of rancor and caprice, which has profited them nothing.

I had already seen that French priests who had emigrated to Spain patiently put up with every sort of insult, including being called Spaniards. In Bayonne I saw some youngsters taking a man off to give him a thrashing, calling him a Spaniard; believing that he was one, I freed him. "What part of Spain are you from?" I asked him. And he answered: "I'm French, but they're calling me that to insult me." "It's the same thing"—a Jew who was passing by said to me—"as being called stupid, ignorant, superstitious and slovenly." And, unfortunately, no

---

* The sentence cited by Fray Servando, in Madrileño dialect, reads: *Ve a llamar al médicu que vengan a luna curar a Manolo del estómago, y le daremos veinte maíz.*

** *The Tuscan language in a Roman's mouth.*

matter where I have gone in Europe, there has been some Spaniard who has caused a scandal because of some notorious dirty deed. I heard later on in England and the United States that mothers, meaning to call their children dirty pigs, told them they looked like Spaniards. In all truth, they are indeed filthy pigs; but less so than the Portuguese and even less than the Moors. The Italians are not very clean; the French are, though not as clean as the Dutch, the English and the Anglo-Americans.

The Spanish ex-Jesuits killed themselves writing to defend their countrymen from their general bad reputation as barbarians. But they failed to notice that where they themselves had ceased to be such was in Italy, and the same thing happened to them as happens to our *gachupines*,* who, since they have come to America as children and have never seen Spain through rational eyes, it appears to them to be the best thing in the world; but once they have grown up, when they go back to Spain, they immediately return to America grumbling and grousing. The ex-Jesuits returned to Spain because of the first revolution, when Pius VI was taken to France as a prisoner. They had no sooner arrived in Spain when the Marqués del Mérito, their advocate, published the little opus by the Jesuit Bonola entitled: *Liga de la teología moderna con la filosofía para arruinar la Iglesia y el Trono.*** The Augustinian Fernández replied with *El pájaro en la liga,**** a congratulatory letter to don Cornelio Suárez de Molina, three thousand copies of which were sold in one day. This uproar caused them to be sent back to Italy. Many of them had already taken off *proprio motu* once they saw Spain through rational eyes. The rest flocked together in Alicante and made repeated representations to be rescued for good from the land of the barbarians.

"Good Lord, what barbarians!" Montengón, the author of the *Eusebio,* said to me in Rome. "My pen has fallen from my hand. I am not going to write another word in Castilian. I am writing my history of Rome in Italian." Masdeu recounted with gusto things that had happened to him in Spain, which would not have happened even in Siberia, he said. Hervás told me that what he wrote in Horcajo, the part of the country he was originally from, not far from Madrid, had been set down according to his notes, and once when he needed a Bible in order to quote a

---

* A Spaniard who has settled in Latin America. A pejorative term, in wide use in Mexico in the era of the struggle for independence, particularly by Creoles (Spanish by descent but born in the New World).

** *The Unholy Alliance between Modern Theology and Philosophy to Destroy the Church and the Throne.*

*** *The Bird in the Alliance.*

passage, the only one to be found among the parish priests in the environs was one lacking both the beginning and the end. "A person can't write in Spain; there are no books," he remarked to me.

What else is there to say, save that in the villages only the parish priest and the sacristan know how to read? Sometimes we were unable to find a single soldier in an entire battalion who knew how to read so as to promote him to corporal, and there were captains who didn't know how to read either, and their aides gave them oral reports. In Catalonia during the war, we were asked if the king of Castile that we had was the same one they had. Ours, they told us, is the king of Madrid. In Catalonia this is nothing to be surprised at. In Madrid, when I said that I was from Mexico: "How rich that king of yours must be, seeing as how such a lot of silver comes from there!" In a royal office in Madrid that I happened to go into, when I stated that I was an American they were amazed. "But you aren't black," they said to me. "A countryman of yours came by just now," the friars at the monastery of San Francisco in Madrid said to me, and when I asked how they knew that, they answered that he was black. In the Cortes the deputy from Cádiz, a Philippine priest, asked whether we Americans were white and professed the Catholic religion. In certain hamlets, hearing that I was from America, they asked after señor X or Y; you must know him, they said to me, because in such-and-such a year he went to the Indies. As though the Indies were the size of a small village. When I arrived in Las Caldas, the mountain folk "came to see the Indian," as they put it.[6] "Spain," Archbishop de Malinas says in his *Guerra de España*, "is part of Europe only because of its religion; it is part of Africa, and only through a geographical error is it located in Europe."

To return to the Neapolitans, they call Vesuvius, whose crater is now much lower down, by the name Montezuma. Nowhere have I found more things from America than there. Pine nuts and corn on the cob are sold in the streets, the reason being that in the early days viceroys of America usually became viceroys of Naples later on, and brought with them many things from the territories they had once ruled. But the usual food of Neapolitans is macaroni, day in and day out.

When one enters Naples it is as though one were entering an Indian pueblo, for the people are the same color. The women in particular are swarthy and ugly, and the men much better looking by comparison, something all travelers notice. But in general they are much given to stealing, and are the counterpart in Italy of men from La Mancha in Spain. Their King Ferdinand was a worthy brother of Charles IV; his wife one of the three royal mares of Europe, and Neapolitans weren't sure whether his Godoy was Florentine or English. The king had a separate part of the sea to fish in, and his own stall where he sold the fish and hobnobbed with the *lazzaronis* who bought them. I was there when Isabelita, who came from Spain to marry Franciscone (that was what they called their prince), arrived in Naples. She went with her husband and her in-laws to visit San Gennaro, the patron saint of Naples, in pomp, or *fiochi,* that is to say, the way the Pope goes about in his coach with very long teams of horses, and footmen on either side, with her hat tucked underneath her arm; and the people said of her: "She is beautiful, but she is too stout; she doesn't look like the daughter of a king." How true!

In Naples there is a Greek and Latin priest, who, incidentally, had eleven daughters, for all Greek priests (save the bishops) have been married for some time when they are ordained, and close by the Papal Palace itself in Rome I saw their living quarters and all the balconies full of children and diapers. Since the kingdom of Naples was part of Magna Graecia, it is full of Greeks and Greek churches. I used to attend their offices and the Mass celebrated by their priests, who wear their hair halfway down their back, and a beard just as long, a black tunic and a cloak with purple revers but no collar, and a broad-brimmed hat with a cross made of ribbon in the front part of the crown.

The Greeks allow no images save painted ones. And as soon as they enter the church they go to a large lectern standing in the middle of it, with the Gospel open and a cross on top of it; they kiss both, then cross themselves repeatedly and after that go over to kiss the images of Christ and Mary, of Saint Peter and Saint Paul, which are painted on the partition that closes off the presbytery and has three doors and a small window above the one in the middle. They then seat themselves here and there in the church, on chairs like those in a choir. There are no women seated in the nave, and one sees them only upstairs in the choir or the galleries. The priests always wear a cope when saying Mass, with a sort of little square of cloth with a cross hanging from the sash of it. There is only one altar in the entire church, and only one Mass is celebrated on feast days. The leavened bread that is to be consecrated and the wine are brought from the sacristy by a priest in vestments, and as soon as he shouts that he is bringing the symbols, the congregation bows (because the Greeks never kneel) and venerates the symbols of the Eucharist with such devotion that those who observe the Latin rites are shocked. As soon as the Canon begins, the doors of the presbytery are closed and the only words of the priest that the congregation hears are those of the consecration, which he speaks very loudly, and the choir, still singing, bows deeply, repeating, *Agios otheos,* which is pronounced thus: *Aguios ozeos, Aguios isjiros, Aguios azánatos, Eleyson unas.**

Once the Canon has been recited, the middle door is opened, and the chalice and the bread are presented (the chalice being covered, as it was earlier on in the Latin Church, until the Dominicans introduced the usage of bringing it in uncovered, since they did not use a pall but, rather, large corporals**) for the veneration of the congregation at the little door in the middle of the partition. The congregation keeps coming forward to the aforementioned door until the end of the Mass, and the deacon places in their hand the eulogiae, consecrated bread that he has broken into bits and placed on a tray. Greek Catholics do not say *ámen,* but *amén,* just as Roman Catholics do not say *amén,* but *ámen.*

As for myself, I was well treated at the monastery of Il Rosario, and when I went to see the provincial, who presented me with several gifts of clothing, he called me Your Most Illustrious Lordship. That is proof of how common that title is here. I was the one who accompanied the young novices of Il Rosario on their evening strolls. And at various times they took me to Portici, which is the royal residence; or else to the musical conservatories, of which there are several; or to the large, magnificent charterhouse, which is on the mountain that overlooks Naples; or to the library of Sant'Angelo in Guido, which is open to the public; or to see the great San Carlos theater; or to other more distant places by way of the grotto of Pausilipus, that is to say, a wide path hewn out through a hill with pick and shovel by Cocceyo, that is a quarter of a league long. At its entrance Virgil's epitaph is engraved on a marble plaque:

> *Mantua me genuit; calabri rapuere, tenet nunc*
> *Parthenope: cecini pascua, rura, duces.**** [7]

Above the entrance is Virgil's tomb. On the same hill, not very far away, is the tomb of Sincero San Nazario, famous for his poem *De partu virgineo,**** with the epitaph placed there by Cardinal Bembo:

---

* Fray Servando is referring here to the triple prayer beginning with the words "Agnus dei" in the Latin liturgy.

** The pall is a linen cloth used to cover the chalice, and corporals are Communion cloths on which the sacred elements are consecrated.

*** *On the Virgin Birth.*

Da sacro cineri flores: hae ille Maronis
Sincerus musae proximus ut tumulo.[8]

Once past the grotto I saw Elysium, a deadly place today because of the miasmal air, and Avernus, which today has nothing terrible about it. It was once shaded by a grove of trees.

In the Dominican monastery I venerated the right arm of Saint Thomas, and saw, in his own hand, which is very even and very small, his exposition of Saint Dionysus's *De divinis nominibus.** It is displayed in the sacristy under glass. I visited the chapel where he was in the habit of praying, and I saw the Holy Christ who spoke to him and approved his doctrine. I visited the classroom where he taught; for his doing so the king of Naples paid a substantial sum each year: four pesos, enough to maintain the entire convent. That was how valuable the coin of the realm was before America was discovered. I also visited his cell, so small that there is barely room for an altar and a chair. For this reason another cell was made into a sacristy for him. The cell I saw is not, materially speaking, the very same one that the saint lived in, because the floor of the monastery has been raised; but when they raised the walls, they retained the original dimensions of the cell. The saint's head, the size of which is extraordinary, is in a small chapel that is looked after by a Cistercian nun, and this is all that remains of the celebrated monastery of Tosanova, where he died. His body is in Toulouse, in France, and escaped the wholesale burning of relics carried out by the revolutionaries.

I shall not take my leave of Naples without telling of a notorious lawsuit brought by the Dominican Minacci, a Calabrian and a professor of botany at the University of Palermo, the capital of the island of Sicily. From the earliest times onward, the immense majority of the inhabitants of Europe, both men and women, were slaves. A twelfth-century Pope ordered all Christians to be freed, as Voltaire concedes in his analysis of history. The Romans considered it their pagan right to make prostitutes of their female slaves so as to live off them, as is still the practice today in the Antilles with regard to black female slaves. And in the days of feudalism, in almost the whole of the Roman Empire it was a right of the prince to deflower the brides of all his vassals. Although Christian ethics abolished the practice, it is still the tradition in Germany, and in certain parts of France it was the custom to present the bride to the lord and master, who touched her foot with his, as if to re-

---

* *On the Divine Names.*

mind her of his right. In Calabria, Prince Sguila could claim the right of *cuunatico* (as it was called) with the brides of his vassals, assuming it at his discretion, depending upon the estate or the beauty of the newly wedded wife. Being offended by this continual wrong done his fellow Calabrians, Friar Minacci brought suit against their prince in Naples, a suit that caused a great deal of talk and aroused everyone's curiosity, and he won it.

All this happened in the three months that I remained in Naples wanting all the while to return to Rome to see to my secularization. There was a boat from Mahón in the port, bound for Civitavecchia, held up only because its captain was suffering from a bubo in the groin. I cured him of it, and he gave me free passage in return. As I took my leave of them, there was a great show of feeling on the part of my brothers at Il Rosario, who were very fond of me and sought my advice in all matters. We reached Civitavecchia in three days, borne by a storm that blew itself out, entering port at the same time as two small frigates that Bonaparte was presenting to the Pope as a gift in recompense for the galleys that the French had taken from him previously. I pressed the captain to take me on to Rome, and he did so. I did not suffer grievously there this time, for I was already familiar with the terrain now, and betook myself immediately to the home of my old friend don Domingo Navázquez.

I V

From My Return to Rome to
My Return to Spain in 1803

As soon as I returned to Rome, inasmuch as my return to Spain had come to nothing because the infanta had already left, I began to try to have His Holiness himself issue his rescript, addressed to the archbishop of Toledo, Cardinal Borbón, ordering that I be secularized. It would have been easy to cite the invalidity of my monastic vows as the reason for my petition, and demand that I be restored to the secular state, or as it is called restitution *in pristinum statum,* since I had taken holy orders in bad faith. Having observed ever since I was a novice the moral decline of the Dominican Province of Mexico, although in no subsequent period did I ever again see it keeping up appearances as well as in the triennium of prior fray Juan de Dios Córdoba, I put off taking my final vows for two days, believing in all conscience that my profession was not illicit. But one of the monks whom the master of novices brought in for me to consult was Master León, a padre who was very fond of me, and from orisons till midnight he did his best to persuade me. And certainly the principal reasons that impelled me to make my profession were untruths, although he believed that I put them forward in good faith. Would that I had not taken vows, and I say this as though I were before God's tribunal: with very few exceptions the day that one signs his name to his profession of a morally corrupt religion he signs his condemnation. The vows taken in such a religion are nearly impossible to practice, the temptations many, and in the end bad examples sweep away better ones. I do not wish to pursue the subject so as not to raise a scandal; but throughout that Order religious do not live communally and have their own money, even if it is only that from Masses and sermons, and go about by themselves whenever they like, and fathers who permit their sons to enter it commit a mortal sin, as do the latter if they take monastic vows in it. At the hour of their death they find themselves in a terrible predicament, and many a time I have heard them exclaim then: If only I were a secular priest!

But to return to the subject of my secularization, it did not get me anywhere to prove that my profession was invalid, since I was a priest and therefore obliged to practice continence, though not because it is a vow, as people usually say and write, but because it is a precept of the Church, concerning which one can read a splendid dissertation printed in Coimbra (where the University of Portugal is located) by order of the archbishop of Braga. Hence the only reason I cited was the persecution that I had endured, and had received an ordinary rescript of secularization, in which the obligation *quoad substancialia votorum* still obtained, insofar as they are compatible with the secular status, the vow of obedience owed regular prelates becoming instead that of obedience to the diocesan prelate. The present Pope, who is a Benedictine and was himself secularized, although he returned to his Order later, was aware of what goes on in monasteries, and moreover, seeing the hatred of friars professed all over Europe, he secularized them, on no other grounds than the dissatisfaction that they maintained they felt.

The one difficulty standing in the way of His Holiness's bringing about my secularization had to do with proof that I had fulfilled all the necessary requirements and that I had sufficient means to support myself. As for the first, because distance made it difficult to secure verification from Mexico, my sworn word was accepted as sufficient proof, and my fees as a doctor of theology, which regularly came to two hundred pesos in my day, were accepted as evidence that I had sufficient means of supporting myself; and I proved that this exceeded even the sum specified by the synod, through the testimony of Dr. don José Joaquín del Moral, a domestic prelate of His Holiness and a canon who later left Mexico and today is vice rector of the college of Lille and a lay brother of the Order of Mercy in Havana who was secularized there years ago within days of his being ordained as a priest. On July 6 of the year 1803 I was granted my complete secularization, being forbidden by the terms of the rescript to refuse or to waive the fees due me as a doctor entitled to wear a tasseled cap, since they were what constituted my means of livelihood.

His Holiness had already granted me a rescript of indulgences for myself and my relatives to the second or third degree, with a number of jubilees, altars for souls in Purgatory and the power to bestow four thousand plenary indulgences *in articulo mortis,* half to be applied to medals and rosaries, and half *ad libitum.* To attain this, all one need do is ask for it in a brief petition *pro forma. De rero Coeli,* Rome is as generous as it is niggardly *de pinguedine terrae.** I also obtained a dispensation from recital of the divine office, which has been exceedingly onerous for me because of the fever in my lung, in place of which I was to substitute the brief office of the Virgin, or a half hour of mental prayer. I was also allowed to continue to observe the Dominican rite, through a rescript to that effect from the Congregation of Rites. What caused difficulty, so that my petition ended up on the Pope's desk awaiting his decision (as does everything that presents particular difficulty), was the question of my wearing the Dominican habit when I preached and said Mass. I asked for this indulgence on account of the stupidity of my countrymen, who frown on a priest who is secularized; this greatly shocked the Pope, for in Italy precisely the contrary is the case, and they feel such hostility toward habits that, as I advised Cardinal Cayetano, when regular bishops and cardinals wish to wear one (which is a very rare occurrence) it has to be altered and its appearance disguised. His Holiness finally said that he would permit me to do so, providing that the procurator general of the Order agreed. The latter readily agreed, because I had become well-known in Rome for my writings and my noble lineage, which is held in high esteem there, and a noble in a habit is a rarity. I had already attained the great honor of being named a theologian of the congregations of the Council of Trent and the universal Inquisition, which is not an honor conferred on just anyone. The rescript was sent me, as was permission from the minister of the Papal Palace to read all forbidden books without exception. I had all these rescripts authenticated by the notary for Spaniards, the notary apostolic, the Agency of Spain and a prothonotary apostolic. I also obtained this title of prothonotary apostolic, *extra urbem,* which is accompanied by the privilege of occupying a residence of a Church dignitary in Rome, along with a brief *de non impediendo* issued by Saint Pius V. The prothonotaries apostolic dress in the same attire as His Holiness's domestic prelates, and the latter in that of

---

*   *Concerning heavenly matters ... concerning earthly trivia.*

bishops, and are addressed with the same title of Monsignor and Your Excellency, a title that has spread from Rome and is now used to address the bishops of Spain; those of France are addressed simply as Monsignor and instead of Your Lordship, Your Magnificence; those of Portugal have the title of Excellency, as do the counts and marquises in that country. The Church and the king of Spain restrict the title of Reverend to bishops, that of Very Reverend to archbishops and that of Dear Father to provincials of an Order.

Domestic prelates are distinguished from prothonotaries by the fact that the latter owe obedience to bishops, while the former do not. And prelates are distinguished from bishops by the fact that they wear a green band on their hat, which is a black tricorne, while prelates wear a purple band on theirs. Prelates do not wear a pectoral cross, nor do bishops in Rome wear theirs on the outside, though the fine chain from which it is suspended can be seen. The rank of prelate is immediately below that of cardinal. The latter is the rank of nuncios, and bishops who have been prelates assume it.

The attire of bishops is a purple tunic, bound around the waist with a sash that has gold tassels. The facings of their sleeves are also embroidered in gold, above a short rochet shirred with gum arabic, and on top of it a calf-length purple mantelletta, with openings for the arms. All this is of silk; just as the servants of monsignors are dressed in full-length black silk habits, so the servant of a cardinal who sits at his feet so as to hold his biretta wears a full-length purple habit, though his is made of wool. A bishop's zucchetto is purple, of course, like that of Spanish bishops of the Crown of Aragon (save for the bishop of Vigne, who wears a bright red one, and the bishop of Tortosa, who wears a milk-white one, as does the Pope, perhaps because his bishop had been John XXII, who retained the pontifical habit after he had given up the tiara in Peñiscola. Their collar is purple as well, although the same color collar is also worn by musicians and employees of the patriarchal churches of Rome and Lisbon; and in the kingdom of Valencia by any priest who wishes to do so. And of course every monsignor wears gloves and purple hose. These latter, along with the collar, the hatband and the zucchetto, are a distinction that they wear when they dress noncanonically, in which case their attire is black, although their frock coat has a special cut. When in noncanonical dress, the Pope's chamberlains wear hose and a red hat band, like that of cardinals, except that the hatbands of the latter are edged in gold. This red hatband and the red heels of their shoes are the distinguished signs of cardinals when they are not in liturgical dress, with their lackey following them, whether they are walking or riding in a carriage (which is black, trimmed with gold), with a closed red parasol, which has large tassels of the same color.

Cardinals have three liturgical garments: the one for solemn celebrations, which is a red vestment, cut in the same way as that of our canons, but with a wide, very long train. This is the one they wear in church. Regular cardinals wear one of the same cut, but of the color of their habit, and only their zucchetto and biretta are red. The other vestments they wear when attending assemblies consist of a a little red cape over the rochet, their cardinal's hat and a little red tricorne, edged in gold. This is their most handsome attire. And they wear their third one when they attend literary functions in the churches, or when there are no offices being conducted in them; this one is purely and simply their red cardinal's hat worn above the rochet, and their red biretta. When not attending formal ceremonies they dress in black, as I have already said, with a zucchetto, a red hatband and red heels. They also usually wear a red Spanish cope, with an over-collar embroidered in gold, and wear purple during Lent.

The Pope wears a white cassock, the attire of the clergy in the first centuries, their cardinal's hat and a stole over a rochet, when they are not in full liturgical dress, or as they say in Rome, *in tutto fiochi*, in which case their hat and small cape are the color of bull's blood, both very sumptuous, and embroidered in gold, and their shovel hat is of the same color. Their zucchetto is always milk-white, and I have never seen them in a bonnet with ear flaps, something they wear very seldom.

The clergy all wear noncanonical dress, with a black collar covered with a little white neckpiece. Their principal distinguishing mark is that all their midgarments are black, namely their stockings, breeches and waistcoat. Their jacket may be of any decent color, and in the back they wear a little cloak of black silk over their shoulders that hangs down to midcalf; but it does not spread outward on the sides: it is closely gathered in the middle. This is what people call abbot's attire. It is the papal court dress, and is worn by all clerks and all officials of the Curia, even though they are married, if they choose to do so; priests thus have only one distinguishing mark, which is the tonsure, and usually this is merely a little piece of white cloth stuck on top of their periwig, the latter being very frequently worn. Everyone, from the Pope on down, providing they are not monks, goes about in a powdered wig with a great many curls, and a priest who does not wear one experiences only difficulties or delays when he asks for vestments in which to officiate in church. Black full-length habits, which also have an over-collar, are the distinguishing dress of *servitores,* or servants of monsignors, and it is enough to exclude a person from occupying a place of honor anywhere. In the churches one is given a little tunic to say Mass in, and in Florence a short black skirt. Friars do not wear a fringe around their tonsure except in Spain. In Rome, discalced friars, who are called *secolantes* and have their own convent on the Capitoline, are not regarded as Franciscans; the only ones taken to be such are the conventuals or calced friars, who wear a thin black habit, with a big mozzetta, have incomes and preach in a biretta, as do Dominicans in a zucchetto. The church of these Franciscans is on the Corso; it is called the Holy Apostles and is the church of fops and fashionable ladies.

There are a great many nuns, and they have no difficulty leaving their convents to visit churches on certain feast days, or going back to their homes when they are ill, in the company of another nun to help care for them. Their churches are very small, and very rarely open. Special permission is required to say Mass in them. The convents of San Sixto and Santo Domingo are for Dominican nuns, all of them princesses. Today monasteries have doubtless seen the end of their days, as in all of Italy, now that it is under French rule. In Rome there are also many religious schools for girls, who every afternoon come out for a stroll in a group, as do the youngsters in all the orders, for what they call *moto,* or moving about, something that is essential in such an unhealthy country.

There are those who might wish me to give, before leaving Rome, more specific information about the things to be found there, about its temples and antiquities, both sacred and profane. But there are countless numbers of them, as there are churches, the most magnificent ones in the world, especially Saint Peter's, Saint Mary Major and Saint John Lateran, and there are an infinite number of things to say. I will note down a few of them, and for the rest will refer my readers to books that deal with the subject. Nothing in Rome edified me, because it is all pomp and little substance: *la città è sancta ma il populo corruto,** as the Romans say. There are many good souls, but also countless scoundrels, thieves and murderers, either natives of the country or from every other country, who take refuge in Rome as a sacred asylum. All the churches give asylum, and when the ruffians see that there are a goodly number of coats of arms on the door, they exclaim: *This is a fine church,* because before getting them out of it is necessary to secure as many permits as

---

* *The city is sacred but the people are corrupt.*

there are coats of arms, and meanwhile the malefactors slip away. The Government is extremely lenient, and there is the greatest freedom and impunity.

Bands of filthy beggars and young people of both sexes accost a person everywhere: in the streets, in the cafés, in the eating houses and so on, and they are most persistent. And it is necessary to implore them to leave you alone, *per carità*, because the Romans consider saying *per Dio*, meaning in the name of God, to be a blasphemous oath. Nowhere else have I seen a greater number of maimed youngsters, and they say that their parents mutilate them deliberately, so as to live off the alms they collect. It may also be that their crippled limbs come from the opium of the drugs that are continually given nursing babies so as to put them to sleep and keep them from being a bother. Their parents also castrate them, despite repeated orders forbidding it, so as to get sinecures for them in the pontifical chapels, et cetera. The best way to remedy this evil was to forbid eunuchs to sing in the choir in God's churches. In Rome, people spare no expense when it comes to eating, and Quatrino (a small copper coin) is the eternal god of the Romans, whence the famous couplet:

Est unus triusque Deus, qui regnat in Orbe:
Unus quatrinus regnat in urbe Deus.*

People there make their living from intrigue, from painting and primarily from sculpture and from music, which everyone knows, and from sheepskin (that is to say, the parchment of papal bulls, briefs, and so on). Rome was the richest gold mine in the world at one time, but is nearly exhausted today, because Portugal makes only a small contribution, and Spain some five hundred thousand pesos a year from dispensations and other such flimflam. Despite this, pensions that amounted to twenty to thirty thousand duros were paid to several cardinals and to a princess who was a special friend of ambassadors, and even the lay brother who served Pope Ganganeli had his pension worth six thousand pesos so that he would bring his influence to bear on the matter of the Jesuits. Throughout Italy many other Italians live off Spain; the Duke of Monteleone in Naples, for instance, receives his income from Mexico as an heir of Hernán Cortés, even though when I was in Rome he had been

* *The God who reigns on earth is one and triune*
  The God who reigns in the city is one quatrino.

forced to flee the country because he had espoused the Republican cause, and had saved his neck only through the Pope's intervention. Several cardinals live on their benefices as canons of Spain, and the Pope (like the king) is a canon of Toledo, though by reason of their office canons are dispensed from attending Masses, except on the feast day of Saint Michael, on which alms are distributed, and in order to pay the king and the Pope their due that day, a priest goes all about the church asking people if they have seen them. The courier service from Spain to Rome supports many employees, and the Agency supports countless others. For the same reason, the ministers of Spain in Rome gave up their salaries in exchange for being given the Agency, and ever since they have made every effort to monopolize anything that can be negotiated through the Agency, to which purpose they have secured orders from the Councils so that nothing is valid except what comes by way of the Agency and is channeled through it. When I arrived in Rome, the usufruct of the Agency amounted to as much as twenty thousand pesos. There are bishops, however, who have outwitted the Agency through avarice, and the bishop of Palencia or Sigüenza had everything appertaining to his bishopric dealt with through the Tribunal of the Curia, secretly submitting to it matters rightfully within the competence of the office of the Curia,* a stratagem that Rome willingly countenanced.

The agents of Rome, in general, are rogues like those in every court. And in the court in Rome matters are dealt with as in others, by virtue of patrons, women and money. The monsignors who constitute the Prelacy are the main axis of the entire government of the Church, since they are the ones who head the Secretariats. The cardinals who are ministers attend to matters *ex-audientia SSmi,*** just as royal ministers act *by order of His Majesty,* without the Pope, like the king, ever knowing anything except what his ministers choose to tell him. We kill ourselves pondering the works of a rescript of indulgences, for instance, and yet I have seen a large table full of petitions for indulgences presented at an audience of Their Eminences, and given their blessing without a word being uttered other than "To the Secretariats," where everything is harvested. A learned Dominican, Solari, the bishop of Noli, told me the

---

* The two bodies here referred to (also known as the Penitentiary and the Dataria) had quite different jurisdictions. The Penitentiary handed down decisions regarding such matters as cases of conscience, while the Dataria primarily decided on the fitness of candidates for benefices in the gift of the papal see.

** *By audience with His Holiness.*

story of how, one day when he was strolling about Rome and asked his guide where Simon Magus's famous fall had taken place, the guide replied that he would show him the very spot, and then a few steps farther on he said to him: "This is where he fell." "And what is this enormous edifice?" the bishop asked. "It is the Roman Curia."

The Pope has three palaces: the very old one of Saint John Lateran, named after the Lateran patriarch, as was its church, and long since abandoned; the Vatican, adjoining the church of Saint Peter and full of paintings in tempera by Raphael, in which the Pope resides only during Holy Week; and the palace of Montecaballo, in which he ordinarily resides. This latter is in the center of Rome, a short distance away from Saint Mary Major; his troop of halberdiers, who are Swiss, is on guard there, and the palace uniform is yellow with red insets, or has stripes of the two colors. He also has a corps of life guardians, who accompany him, as they do kings, when he goes about in his carriage, and in church they surround him, wearing their hats with plumes. His carriage is long and black, trimmed with gold, in the front of which two prelates are seated; it is drawn by six mules, in very long traces. There are curtains on either side. When the people are happy because the bread that they call *pagnotta* (which are little round, thin loaves like our *semititas*) is cheap and heavy, they gather as he passes by and shout: *Santissimo Padre, la benedizione.** The Pope draws the curtain aside and gives the people his blessing as they fall to their knees. Since there was such poverty in Rome during my time there, I saw this happen only once, and when I expressed my puzzlement, I was told: *Adesso la pagnotta è grossa; avemmo devozione.***

The Pope wears a cope when he celebrates Mass, as do the priests in the Greek Church, with the facings turned slightly back, but wears a miter rather than a tiara, a most graceful one, as do the bishops of the Greek Church, and the latter also wear a very delicate humeral veil over their cope. Certain priests of the Greek Church still wear the bell chasuble of earlier times, known as a *castilla* or in Spanish a *casula*, which means a little house, because it is open only at the neck, and they roll the sleeves of it back in order to perform their priestly duties at the altar. They also turn around to face the congregation before elevating the Host. Though the Pope does not turn around, he also presents the Host to the right and to the left, and does not turn around because he always

---

*   *Most Holy Father, give us your blessing.*
**   *Right now the loaves are big; we are devout.*

celebrates the Eucharist at the head of the congregation, facing an altar where no one celebrates the Eucharist except him. His little acolytes, in red cassocks and rochets, stand on the steps leading to the altar and the choir of cardinals stands behind the Pope. In all of Italy the choir stands in the presbytery and the altar is at the end of it nearest the congregation.

Once the Canon is over, or rather, once the *Pater noster* has been recited, the Pope returns to his seat, not the one to one side that he occupied during terce, wearing a vestment of a different color, but in the middle of the choir this time, before the altar, and as he sits there the Eucharist is brought to him by the deacon and the subdeacon, who are always cardinals, as are the two priests who accompany them, although the latter are bishops who rank as presbyters. The Pope kneels to receive it, and then seats himself to take Communion, partaking of half the Host, and then with the other half of the Host broken in two administers Communion to the ministers. The latter go back to bring the chalice, and the Pope proceeds as before, except that he sips the sanguis through a gold fistula, and the ministers do likewise. The papal throne is raised, and on its steps a number of bishops are seated on cushions. A sermon is preached in Latin before the Pope, and when he preaches he does so in Latin. Roman congregations always recite the *Pater noster* and the *Avemaria* in Latin, and when the litanies to the Virgin are sung, the congregation does not respond *Ora pro nobis,* but the choir, for instance, says: *Santa Maria ora pro nobis,* and the congregation sings *Sancta Dei genitrix ora pro nobis;* and so on alternately. At every papal Mass, after the Epistle in Latin, a Greek subdeacon sings it in Greek, just as a deacon also sings the Gospel in Greek, after having sung it in Latin. The choral singing is by castrati, who cannot be seen because they are behind a lattice window, accompanied by no musical instruments, because they are never played in a basilica since they were not played there in the early Church, and the seven basilicas of Rome are its oldest Christian temples. A Holy Father of the Church said to idolaters; "We leave you the temples; we have only basilicas," that is to say, universal meeting places. The basilicas inspire great respect in Rome, and one does not offer holy water to ladies, as is the custom elsewhere; each of them takes it for herself. In certain churches in Italy all the women sit on one side and all the men on the other. In Rome they are seated together, and it greatly shocked me to see Roman princesses sitting with their heads bared on a little dais, as they might in a theater, when the Pope is officiating. When kings are present, a special platform is erected for the occasion.

When there is to be a papal benediction, which is given at Saint Peter's on his feast day, at Saint John Lateran on Ascension Day or on the Feast of Pentecost, and at Saint Mary Major on Assumption Day, the Pope comes out of the sacristy seated in a litter, wearing a tiara, his hat being borne in front of it on a pole. Attendants carrying two great feather fans to chase away flies also accompany the Pope. They are preceded by all the bishops in Rome, in chasubles and miters, and all the cardinals also wear miters, even though they may have taken only minor orders, and they go in procession to take their places in the row of balconies located halfway up the facades of these churches. The Pope appears in their midst in his litter, and the people are down below in the atrium. The papal guards dismount, in graceful and orderly fashion, kneeling on one knee as the Pope bows, spreading his hands as if to gather in the people's wishes, raises them heavenward, and as though the blessing descends from on high, gives it to the people. At the same time, when the benediction takes place at Saint Peter's, a salvo is fired by the artillery of the Castel Sant'Angelo, which was once the tomb of the emperor Hadrian, and is therefore called *Moles Adriani*. The marble columns that once adorned it now adorn the interior of the Basilica of Saint Paul, built by Constantine. Once the benediction has been given, pieces of paper with the indulgences granted by the benediction written on them fly through the air. There is no other spectacle to equal it, save for that of Corpus, with a procession that goes all round the square of Saint Peter's; the Pope also makes his way around it in a litter, with his hands joined and bowing as he passes by the foot of the monstrance, and he appears to be on his knees, but he is seated. The illusion is created by a veil all round him that hangs down to his waist.

The square, or Piazza di San Pietro, is magnificent; in the middle of it is an Egyptian obelisk known as Saint Peter's Needle, and a fountain on two of the sides, whose jets grouped in clusters form a reddish cloud, within which, at five o'clock in the afternoon, two rainbows form. There are also two statues, one of Saint Peter and one of Saint Paul; the latter was once the statue of Mars. The piazza is surrounded by four orders of very thick columns. Four other enormously tall ones stand before the facade of the church. The doors are of bronze, and were those of the Roman pantheon. The church forms an immense cross, and between the arms of it, above which the dome towers, or rather, three domes, one atop the other, is the tomb of Saint Peter, surrounded by a bronze balustrade. One descends to it by way of a flight of little stairs of jasper, and Mass is also said in a little subterranean chapel. Above the tomb is the altar with the seven candlesticks on it at which the Pope says Mass, and at its ends are four fluted bronze columns, which reach almost to the cornices, with a baldachin above it, also of bronze, with gold tassels. On the cornices the four evangelists are depicted, not beautifully executed painted likenesses, although that is what they appear to be, but tiny stones, rather, fixed in the wall, which when viewed at a distance form a portrait. When seen from up close they are merely stones placed a certain distance apart. All the paintings in the Vatican are very beautiful, smooth and shiny, because they are mosaics, that is to say, delicate stones of different colors skillfully inlaid in the wall. The tomb of Saint Peter is called the confession of Saint Peter, that is to say, his martyrdom, and beneath the presbytery in all the churches is a tomb called a confession, above which is the altar, for in the early days of the Church they were always erected above the tombs of martyrs, and this is the origin of our altars, which must have a crypt with relics. All the bodies of saints in Rome are beneath altars in an urn.

In the center of the church where we place the side aisles is the throne of Saint Peter, of ormolu, supported by colossal statues of the four doctors of the Church that are so large that in Saint Augustine's miter there is room for an eight-year-old boy. On the perimeter of the church, at a lower level, are the tombs of the Popes, decorated with hieroglyphics and statues, some of them in bronze and others marble, symbolizing their virtues. And up above, set into the wall, are marble statues of the patriarchs of religions, and according to cognoscenti, the one of Saint Dominic is the best. The ceiling is completely covered with gilded stone fleurons, and the walls completely covered with jasper, with the Popes who were saints depicted on them. To the right, before leaving the church, is the baptistery, in the form of a pool of water, with steps leading down to it. In the middle of it is the font, all in porphyry. To the right is the holy door, which is opened by the Pope himself in a jubilee year. Around the dome, along the frieze below it, are the words *Tu est Petrus*, the letters of which, when seen from below, seem to be of an ordinary size, but in fact are six spans high. Toward the arms of the church are the confessionals, and seated in them the confessors, who, if I am not mistaken, are Capuchins in Saint Peter's, as the ones in Saint Mary Major are Dominicans, and in Saint John Lateran Augustinians; and when they grant absolution they rest a long rod on the head of the penitent, a sign of the great powers vested in them. Pius VI had a superlatively sumptuous sacristy with a luxurious interior built to one side of Saint Peter's. Apart from the portion of the bodies of Saint Peter and

Saint Paul in the confession, the most venerable relics in Saint Peter's are the lance that pierced Our Lord's side, and a nail of the Cross. There is a prelate at Saint Peter's who is called the vicar, because he is the Pope's vicar. In certain churches in Spain as well, in Burgos for instance, all the curates are called vicars, because the priest is the bishop. The depository of the Sacrament is in a chapel to the right, and the canon choir is to the left. But they recite the Psalter in it, in a translation from the Greek that dates from before the amended translation of it made by Saint Jerome. The former, corrected for a second time, is called the Gallican Psalter, because Saint Damasus gave it to the churches of France, and it is the one generally used, because Saint Jerome's very beautiful translation of it from the Hebrew original is not used anywhere, even though it is the best one. The cardinals are the titular curates of the fifty parishes of Rome, who are in charge of the regular or secular churches therein, although each of them has its own secular or regular priest. Some of them are presbyterial, and others are diaconal. The gathering of all the cardinals in deliberation with the Pope is what is called a Consistory or a Presbytery, or an Apostolic See, because the one who presides is seated. The Pope is bishop of Rome, archbishop of the seven suburbicarian churches of Rome, of which seven cardinals are bishops, among whom the bishop of Ostia, who consecrates the Pope, has great powers in Rome. He is the patriarch of a large part of Italy and of Sicily, and therefore consecrates all its bishops. And he is primate of the entire Church by divine right. It is extremely important, especially for a theologian, not to confuse these different jurisdictions, for the failure to distinguish between them has given rise to a chaos of abuses within the Church.

The heads of Saint Peter and Saint Paul are in Saint John Lateran on the altar where the Pope says Mass. They were once in silver urns, and to enable them to carry off these urns the French Republicans removed the heads. They were wrapped in cloths dating from around the thirteenth century. Which one is Peter's and which Paul's is not known, but toward the ear of one of them a little flesh and a few hairs remain. This is the oldest church in the West, and the leading one in the world, and above the arch of the presbytery is a painted image of the Savior, which according to Baronius was the first image to have been seen in the West, at the time of Constantine. There are canons there, who are Augustinians, as are those throughout Spain, not all of whom are priests, since they have gradually been secularized. Their vestments, which are purple, are the same as those worn by canons in Mexico up until the end of the last century, when ours adopted the same vestments as the chaplains of the cathedral churches of the Crown of Aragon, who go through the church taking a collection to defray the expenses of Masses. The cuffs that they wear in America are worn nowhere else. A bronze column of the temple of Jupiter on the Capitoline has been preserved in the communion rail of this church.

And to one side is the baptistery, called the Baptistery of Constantine, because it is he who is said to have built it. Everything that is recounted by Saint Sylvester in the Breviary about Constantine's baptism in Rome is a blatant lie. He was baptized three days before his death by a semi-Arian bishop in the East. Since each year there is always a Jew who has become a convert, he is solemnly baptized in this edifice by the cardinal vicar, and then after that he is confirmed, attends Mass at Saint John Lateran and takes Communion. In this church the cardinal vicar officiates, and the bishop vice-regent conducts the rites of ordination. To judge from what I observed, Spaniards, if there be any who present themselves, are given the four minor orders consecutively, as is the custom in Spain, and Latin candidates receive them at intervals. In the first orders, monks precede laymen, as was established by Benedict XIII, since monks are already priests. At the entrance to this church is the statue of Constantine. But the most precious objects in this church, which has three naves, are the statues of the twelve apostles, which are in the main part of the church. The sculpture of their times was doubtless a more highly perfected art than when the statues of the Vatican were executed.

To one side of the church of Saint John Lateran there is also, in a separate edifice, the holy staircase, that is to say, the one Our Lord climbed in order to reach Pilate's residence. One mounts the staircase on one's knees, up stairs of wooden planks laid over the stone ones, and on it one kisses, there where they appear, stains that resemble drops of blood, covered with a little iron grille.

Not far from the facade of the church of Saint John Lateran is that of Santa Croce in Jerusalem, and one can see there the house of Saint Helena, who brought the Cross of Our Lord from Jerusalem, leaving a large piece of it in this house. In this church three long, massive sections of the Cross are preserved, in particular one that is about a yard and a half long. It is black, and a portion of it that was removed in very small bits is in the depository that exists in Rome for relics that will be distributed throughout Christendom. The tiny crosses that are frequently seen in certain reliquaries are made of these bits, which the cardinal vicar places in the reliquaries with tweezers. Also preserved there is the titulus placed on the Cross, *Jesus-Christus rex judeorum,* inscribed in Hebrew, Greek and Latin, and the wood of it is whiter than that of the Cross. The traverse of the cross of the Good Thief is also preserved there, and three thorns of the crown of Our Lord; his entire crown, which is like a skullcap, has been kept in the holy chapel of the Palace of the Tuileries in Paris, ever since Saint Louis brought it back from the Orient. The column to which Our Lord was tied when he was scourged, just a little over a yard high, can be seen in a little chapel of the church of Santa Praxedis. At the foot of the Capitoline is the prison, dug out of the living rock, where Saint Peter and Saint Paul were held.

The basilica of Saint Mary Major, where there is one of the images of the Virgin said to have been painted by Saint Luke, is like a hall with two orders of marble columns. It is called Saint Mary *ad praesepe,* because in a grotto inside the church the holy crib in which the Virgin laid the newborn Infant Jesus is preserved. It is a little bed made of wood, as cribs usually are. The French took the baby Jesus, which was made of silver; but the wife of the Count of Campo-Alange, a grandee of Spain, had a gold one made while I was in Rome. The body of Saint Pius V is also in that church. His cell is in Santa Sabina, an early monastery of the Dominicans, in which the sixty-four cardinals who have belonged to the Order are buried. A very heavy black stone that the Devil is said to have thrown at Saint Dominic is lashed to the top of a column. I saw at the monastery the orange tree that Saint Dominic planted, and after six hundred years, it is fresh and very beautiful, and it has put out an offshoot, which is already quite tall. The Dominicans have nine monasteries in Rome. A statue of Philip II stands at the entrance to Saint Mary Major. That may be because the roof of the church was gilded with the first gold that came from America.

In the Basilica of Saint Paul, outside the walls of the city, where he was beheaded, are, as I have already said, the 160 marble columns from Hadrian's tomb; part of the bodies of both apostles, Saint Peter and Saint Paul, are there, and all round the church, beneath the frieze, are the portraits of the Popes, beginning with Saint Peter, painted at the time of Saint Leo. They go all the way around the church. The second row began with the portrait of Pius VII; he did not want to be placed below Saint Peter, however, preferring to be placed below Saint Linus, his immediate successor. It can be seen there how the Popes have kept adding adornments to their liturgical attire; for many long centuries they wore nothing on their head, and no other vestment but the Roman tunic. Then one begins to see them wearing the tiara of the Greek patriarchs and a single crown, as though they were kings of the Church. A long time afterward they added the crown of the rulership of Rome, and then later the third crown as monarchs of the world. The latter is as authentic as the first two. Nuns look after this church, and one sees the horn containing the consecrated oil hanging at the entrance, the emblem of a patriarchal church, an immense one because Italian bulls have outsize ones.

The catacombs are the burial ground of the early Christians, and because they were persecuted, it was there that they also gathered to celebrate the sacred mysteries. The excavators who have been assigned the mission of disinterring the bodies of the Holy Martyrs, if asked to find a specific body, send word when they discover it; they are known by the palm carved on their tomb, and in particular by the vial containing their blood. Sometimes the tomb has a name engraved on it, something that plays an important part in the ritual of prayer. If the tomb does not bear a name, the body is given the title of cardinal vicar, and this is referred to as baptizing them. The body of a saint entails no expenses; certain nuns in Rome fit their bones together, if possible, and dress the bodies in the [burial] garments we are accustomed to seeing them in.

The secular government of Rome has a monsignor as its head, and the spiritual head is a cardinal vicar of the Pope, whose authority is so great that he sanctions religious orders such as that of the Company of Faith in Jesus, which was a supplementary branch of the Jesuit Order, once the defects of the Constitution of the latter were corrected, according to the founder of the Company, an Austrian colonel named Pacanari. He had the protection of the cardinal vicar Somaglia, because he was courting an archduchess of Austria who was a patroness of that Order, and it was already beginning to flourish, although I was certain that it would come to a bad end once I learned that the Jesuits, out of envy, declared that they were against it and adopted the habit of calling its members Pacanarists. The aforementioned cardinal vicar also institutes special feast days, such as that celebrating the movements of the eyes of many images, when the French Republicans were on their way to Rome. The real ocular movement was the way the Romans gazed with covetous eyes on the guineas of the English, who, using religion as a pretext, tried to incite them to rebel against France. The aforementioned vicar officiates at the great solemnities held at Saint John Lateran, and administers solemn baptism. The bishop who has the title of vice-regent takes his place when other rites are performed. When a child who has not been confirmed is ill, word is sent to the vice-regent, and he goes to where the child lives, be it only a humble shack, and administers the sacrament of confirmation. It is he who officiates at ordinations, even though the candidates for ordination are examined before the cardinal vicar. But the manual of morality used by those who are ordained is the worst one I have seen in my life. Instead of proving what it says by reference to Scripture, to the Holy Fathers of the Church or to Church Councils, which are authentic theological sources, it proves its points by way of declarations of the vicar of Rome, just as Benedict XIV offers definitive proof of his conclusions by reference to the decrees of the Congregations of Rome, as though they were Councils. I fancy the same is true of the theology of the Jesuits on the subject of grace, proofs of which center on the papal bulls against Jansenius, Quesnel, and others that they have secured from the Pope by dint of secret string-pulling. If the Pope is not infallible by virtue of his faith, his bulls are not decisive sources.

Rome is the seat of the permanent Congregation of the Holy Office, which meets one or two days a week in the Minerva in Rome, and its chief inspector is a Dominican; the Congregation of the Index, of which the secretary is also a Dominican, since it was Dominicans who drew up the Index of the Council of Trent, just as the minister of the Papal Palace is always a Dominican, a position first occupied by the superior general of that Order and a post of great authority in Rome, where nothing can be printed without his permission; there is the Congregation of the Council of Trent, that of Rites, that of Indulgences, that of the Religious, that of the Propagation of the Faith; in addition there are extraordinary congregations appointed by the Pope for the examination of extraordinary occurrences. They are attended by certain cardinals who are appointed members of them, and the theologians who compose them are chosen from among the elite of those to be found in Rome. But they are not infallible, and very often they retract their decisions, and certain of them are more highly regarded than others, because of their correct decisions. See on this subject the precious little opus by Tamburini: *Vera idea de la Santa Sede e delle Congregazzioni de Roma*.

It is well-known that the vote cast by the cardinals in the congregations is in fact that of their consultants, a theologian and an expert on canon law, because a number of cardinals, particularly those who are princes, both Roman ones and those from other countries, don't even understand Latin. And the bishops who have held important seats and are regularly given a cardinalate generally know very little more, since they owe that office primarily to their birth or to the connections they have. Cardinal Solís was archbishop of Toledo, and when he returned from a conclave he told the king of his surprise at having noted that in Rome even children speak Italian.

When I was there I saw that almost all the cardinals' consultants were former Jesuits, and I foresaw the reestablishment of their Order, because the present Pope is a simple, dim-witted soul, who does not dare to do anything save what the cardinals want him to. He owes everything to his nephew Pius VI, who made him bishop of Imola and a cardinal, and he returned to the Benedictine Order so as to be unobtrusively promoted to these offices.[2] He owed the Papacy, according to what people in Rome say, to Bonaparte's influence. When the French established the Cisalpine Republic, he made a show of his Republican sympathies, and on Christmas Day he published a pastoral homily, translated into French by Bishop Grégoire, which I read, and in which he exhorts his congregation in Imola to embrace the Republican Government without qualms, inasmuch as it proves to be more in accordance with the spirit of the Gospel, and exhorts the clergy to persuade the people of Imola to do so. Having extended an invitation to Bonaparte and his officers to come to Imola, he tucked underneath his arm the sabers that they had left on a chair, and said to them: "You are my prisoners; what will you do now to free yourselves?" "Take this zucchetto," Bonaparte said, removing the cardinal's zucchetto from his head, "and put it back on inside out," with the white side showing, that is to say, that being the color of the pontifical zucchetto.

The Jesuits are the agents of Rome in the world. With the Roman College or Seminary and the Germano-Hungarian College, they attract to it the most clear-minded young men of Italy and Germany. They have continued to occupy their old houses; they have not stopped teaching yet and have long composed almost all the literature forthcoming from Rome. Nearly all of the most influential houses were on their side. Everything in Rome is Jesuit, and before their election, they made Popes swear that they would reestablish the Company, though later the Popes failed to fulfill their vow. Their existence in Russia was already assured, because at the time of the dissolution of the Company they placed themselves under the protection of the king of Prussia and the emperor of Russia, who were not bound to obey the Pope, the former being a heretic and the latter a schismatic. Now, following their reestablishment, the emperor of Russia has expelled them and the king of Portugal has refused to admit them, because, he said, the reasons cited by Clement XIV in his bull of dissolution still held good, reasons that Pius VII disregards in his bull of reestablishment.

The Jesuits have managed to convince Rome and people in general that they are needed in the fight against the Jansenists, heretics of their own creation, and against unbelievers. And I am of the opinion that their disputes against those who were not Molinists and the cruel persecution that they instigated against them and carried out through the power of the kings of France made religion an object of ridicule, thereby ensuring the eventual triumph of unbelievers. They have likewise managed to persuade kings that if their Order had still been in existence their thrones would not have experienced the vicissitudes that they did, despite the fact that they were expelled from every kingdom precisely because of the conspiracies against the thrones and the lives of kings whose safety they were charged with. Regicide and tyrannicide are a notion that came into existence with them, and Father Mariana's book, *De Rege et Regis institutione*, in which he clearly teaches it, is famous.[3]

This Order will indubitably flourish once again. It engages in teaching, especially that of belles lettres, which is a general and most necessary study, without the other Orders being able to compete with it, because they have abandoned the humanities, which are the very foundation of good writing.

Every Order devoted to teaching forms a staff of scholars who win the respect and esteem of the public. Moreover, its morals are good, since the number of its professed is very small and their profession is made only after they are well along in years, all the others being students, whom the Order unceremoniously puts out in the street without giving them a reason whenever it so pleases; hence the few who remain are an elite. But this purge that is advantageous to the Order is detrimental to the Episcopates, which find themselves burdened with priests without a means of livelihood, whom they cannot reject, because on expelling them from the Order, the Jesuits gave them a certificate attesting to their irreproachable conduct. This was the objection to them put forward by Palafox, who complains that a single provincial of Mexico threw out eighty priests during his four years in that office.[4]

But I am of the opinion that the flowering of the Order will lead it to a bad end yet again. As soon as it accumulates wealth, it will go back to its system where religion is nothing but politics. This is an order deeply involved in deal-making, Melchor Cano said, and also deeply involved, it may be said, in intrigue, arcana and mystery. It has a thousand peculiarities that are foreign to the usual system of the Church and of the monastic orders, such as the rejection of fraternal correction, etc. Since its foundation it has not had fixed constitutions, but was granted permission, rather, to make them up as it went along, as experience dictated. Hence there is no anchor to hold them to the spirit in which it was founded, and time has proved that the constitutions of all orders that have been added to over the years are less holy than the very first ones. Since Saint Ignatius was a soldier, he passed military discipline on to his Company: the obedience promised by Jesuits is blind obedience, and their rule that of the most absolute monarchy. And it is not the Jesuits in long habits who are the most to be feared, but rather those in short mantles, the Congregation of the Annunciation, the two orders with secret vows, that is to say, a vow of obedience to the general of the Company, and another that a person who enters the Company takes in addition to this one if the general deems it advisable. These Jesuits are of every rank, estate and profession. It is the duty of the Company to further its members' interests, to place them in posts and positions suited to the rank of each of them, to procure them wealth and sinecures, to which end the entire Company marshals its forces. They in their turn lend it all their power, and lend it to each other. This is a truly frightening Freemasonry, because by professing blind obedience to the general of the Company, the latter, if he is wicked, can misuse the virtues of his subjects and overturn a whole kingdom, or, even more easily, bring about the downfall of anyone who is not attached to the Company.[5] Their probabilistic moral system serves all these purposes admirably. They do not dare to state today what it is that they are defending, because the universal outcry of the Church and the monstrous opinions to which it has led them keeps them from it; but they continue to extol their authors, call those with sound morals Jansenists, and have contrived to secure the beatification of Monsignor Ligorio, a staunch defender of probabilism,[6] so as indirectly to canonize him, while at the same time they have successfully lent their best efforts to the beatification of Palafox. Finally, they continue to stigmatize the Thomists as Augustinians, as Jansenists, and I am a witness to the fact that they cannot tolerate the former Jesuit Alegre, because in his Theology he advocated vigorous physical activity. Insofar as they can, despite the fact that by the terms of their constitutions they are obliged to follow the doctrine of Saint Thomas, they will revive the disturbances and persecutions of earlier days, they will set all the Thomist Orders against them and in the end they will succumb once again. I know them and have dealt with them; in no way have they changed their former opinions, and are persuaded that whatever the Company has done, in any realm, is the best that can be done. *Sint ut sunt, vel non sint** a general of the Order answered a wise Pontiff who proposed a reform to them so that they might survive.

Of the tribunals of Rome, that of the Rota is highly esteemed for its leniency and its fairness. The presiding judge of the Rota communicates his opinion to the other members and says to them: "Here you have my opinion and my reasons; see if yours can make me change my mind." Can there be anything more equitable? A Jesuit is always the theologian of the Penitentiaria, and an Augustinian the sacristan of the Papal Palace.

As for secular monuments, the Capitoline, the Campo Boario and the villas, or *quintas,* as we would call them, in particular the Matei and the Borghese, are full of them, and full of excellent statues as well. They are everywhere in Rome, although the multitude of nude Venuses in different poses greatly offends the sense of modesty of foreigners; but the Romans laugh at our prudishness because their eyes have long been accustomed to such a spectacle. The bronze equestrian statue of Marcus Aurelius on the Capitoline, where the holm oak of Jupiter stood, is admirable, and the Apollo Belvedere was a wonder among a thousand other curious antiquities in the Museo Pio Clementino in the Vatican. The French carried it off, along with any number of the most beautiful statues, both bronze and marble ones, and the best paintings in Rome and in all of Italy. The pillage and theft were general. Seven hundred choice manuscripts and all the sacred cameos were also carried off from the famous Vatican library (where all the manuscripts are kept under lock and key, and it is very difficult to secure permission to see them). They took even the papal archive in the Castel Sant'Angelo, which contained more than seven hundred scrolls. They have kept everything, even after Louis XVIII was restored to his throne. But when he was restored to the throne, when Bonaparte lost his empire for the second time in 1815, he decided to take what the French troops had stolen away from them, and a large part of it is said to have been brought back to Italy.

Among the edifices of antiquity that inspire respect is the Colosseum of the Romans, where the gladiators fought, outside of which is the sweaty *meta,* where they washed the blood off themselves. That is the place bathed in the blood of countless martyrs thrown to wild beasts. For that reason Benedict XIV consecrated it as a temple to the martyrs, and the chapel of Saint Ignatius Martyr is there. The Colosseum is an

---

* Let them be as they are, or else let them not be at all.

immense structure, in which there was room for 100,000 souls, 80,000 of them seated; at the time Rome had a population of 3,000.000. It is very nearly destroyed on one side, because they say that one of the Popes allowed stones to be removed from it for two hours, and the laborers worked so fast that enough stone was removed to build the magnificent Palazzo Farnese. At the time it was in the middle of Rome, and now it is at one edge of the city, to the east, because after the Longobards (I think it was) destroyed the center section of the city as far as Saint John Lateran, it was never rebuilt. Rome has spread farther west today and is divided in two by the Tiber. The part that is still *trans Tiberim* is a working-class quarter, where people's dress and habits are very different from those of the Rome of the papal court. The people of Trastevere are, in contrast, native Romans.

The other estimable edifice is the Pantheon, or temple of all the gods, today consecrated to all the saints. It is a round building, with no other window save for a very large clerestory overhead, which is always open, and no other columns save for twelve very tall granite ones in the vestibule. The wall and the vault form a single structure, without buttresses. As they were building it, they piled up dirt on either side of it, with intercalated layers of copper coins. When it was believed that that wall had firmly settled with time, the people were given permission to take the coins, the aim being to get rid of the dirt, and in just two hours not a speck of dirt was left. Michelangelo adopted the plan of the Pantheon for the dome of Saint Peter's; it not only has the same height but is three-quarters larger in diameter.

The Antonine column, and especially that of Trajan, are also admirable monuments. They are made of marble and carved with the most beautiful reliefs all round, depicting the victories and battles of these two emperors. But it has been necessary to dig down three yards around the column of Trajan, for the foundation of Rome is built on top of the ancient one, and subterranean temples and precious antiquities are discovered in the city each day. Napoleon had columns made in imitation of these, and erected a bronze one to himself in the Place Louis XIV in Paris, a work that is a superb example of the art. He also had a copy of a triumphal arch built, a marble one this time, in front of the Tuileries, of a certainty a perfect one. In Rome there are three remaining ones: that of Septimius Severus, which is at the foot of the Capitoline; that of Titus, which is very badly damaged, on which there can be seen a relief of the table of shewbreads of the temple of Jerusalem; and that of Constantine, with the Cross that he saw in the heavens. As sculpture was not yet a high art in that era, this arch is built of debris from others that were torn down for that purpose.

As for modern customs, the women in Rome and throughout the Papal State are quite beautiful, and there are many pretty ones, as in Tuscany and in the State of Venice. In the rest of Italy there are very few such women. I have already said that the ones in Naples are ugly and dark-skinned, the ones in Parma snub-nosed and ugly, and the ones in Genoa ugly and potbellied. Roman women have flat bosoms, but good bodies and well-carried heads. Their typical dress is a tunic with a little train, such as the one worn by prelates and cardinals, unlike the one worn by French women, which is very long. They wear their hair short, beneath little silk hats or bonnets. Throughout Italy, though men as a general rule have whiter skin than Spaniards, they have faces that look very much like Spaniards; and it is a well-known fact that when the population of Spain was very nearly decimated by the wars of the Romans, the country was repopulated with colonies from Italy. They have long faces, large nostrils and bulging eyes. The one thing that distinguishes them from Spaniards is the fact that the latter have a fierce, proud air about them, which has made the expression "as proud as a Spaniard" a proverbial one throughout Europe. They carefully choose the emigrants they send to America. Hence in the mountains people asked me: "What do you think of this lad: isn't he good-looking? We're raising him to send him to America to marry a mulatta to whom he takes a liking, and send us money." They believe that there are nothing but people of mixed blood in America, whereas there are more of them in Spain. Bringing up sons consists of teaching them to read and write, by sending them off to a place where there is a school, and the poor lad has to journey three leagues, going and coming, every day. But there is a very widespread custom in Italy, which I confess I don't know how husbands can put up with, that of the *cavaliere servente.* The latter is a man who follows a married woman about as though he were her shadow, accompanies her everywhere both by day and by night, pays what she owes if she loses at the gaming table, and yet the custom gives no offense. It is even stipulated in the marriage contract that the husband will not object if his wife has a *cavaliere servente.* The Italian is jealous only of his lady. The wife goes about with a *cavaliere servente,* and the husband is the *servente* of another man's wife.

There are three or four theaters in Rome, although there are usually no performances given in them except during Carnival, which goes on for three months in Rome. There ordinarily is an opera in one of them and comedies in another, and the performance isn't over until around midnight. The companies that come are first-rate, and they are afraid to come because such perfect Italian is spoken in Rome and because its audiences know so much about singing and music. During the last three days of Carnival, at three o'clock in the afternoon, the bell on the Capitoline announces that it is masquerade time and Rome is suddenly full of people in disguise, with men and women changing clothes and dressing in a thousand different costumes. The Corso, a very long avenue, is hung with damask from one end to the other, and it is there that maskers gather. One sees them passing by on floats, acting out different scenes: here a boat with a crew of sailors; there an orchestra made up of animals, with a donkey acting as the conductor; there a debate on Theology; there another on Philosophy. Everyone goes to the theater, men and women alike, wearing masks, and in the courtyards there is dancing all night long, until Ash Wednesday dawns. I remembered what I had read in a book: an ambassador who had gone from Vienna to Turkey found himself surrounded by Moors telling him that an ambassador of theirs had recounted to them how at a certain time of the year Christian believers and curates alike go mad, whereupon a patch of ashes is dabbed on their forehead. We—the Turks said—know a number of medicaments to make a person lose his reason, but none that we know of to restore it, and we would like to learn about this cure using ashes.

In point of fact, from Ash Wednesday on, the Romans come to their senses again. A number of good preachers who have worked up Lenten sermons in other years ask for a church in which to preach one. Because in Italy and in France the same sermons are repeated, and people extend invitations to one another, saying that this or that preacher delivers a good sermon, and when it appears in print, all the times that it has been preached are noted, as a proof of how good it is and how well accepted. The pulpits are as long as a balcony, and the orator walks back and forth as he preaches. Once the first part is over, he delivers an exhortation on the giving of alms, and men with their faces covered with a veil, except for the eyes, like our penitents of earlier days, go about the church, holding out to the congregation very long reeds, each with a pouch hanging from the end of it, and everyone places in it as many alms for the poor as he chooses. In the last sermon the preacher exhorts the congregation to give alms for him, and this is his payment for his Lenten preaching.

Returning to the subject of Carnival, whose principal festivities take place on the three days before Lent on the Corso, a round of cannon fire is shot off at four-thirty in the afternoon as a send-off for the carriages that parade down the Corso. A second round fired serves as a warning to people on foot, either to leave or to climb up on the benches along the side streets so that the unruly horses won't knock them down; for it so happens that at the beginning of the Corso at the little Piazza del Pópulo four untamed horses have been tied fast or hitched to posts. All four of them are let loose at the same time with the lash of a whip and a thorn in the haunch, and they gallop like mad down the Corso Where the Corso ends, near the Capitoline, they are rounded up again; but the first one to have gone past the halter stretched out on the ground wins, and its master is awarded as a prize one of the three standards embroidered in gold contributed each year by the Jews in return for the privilege of residing in Rome, in the quarter called the Ghetto, where they are shut up at night. There are some twenty-six thousand of them, who wear a bit of red cloth as a distinguishing mark, and the main gate of the Ghetto has painted on the front of it a crucifix with the sign: *Tota die expandi manus meas ad populum non credentem et contradicentem.** I would remove the Christ so as to avoid blasphemies, and I would place there instead Daniel's prophecy concerning the seventy weeks, and Ageus's prophecy concerning the glory of the second temple to which the Messiah was to come. These are resounding proofs, and if they were constantly placed on display, they might eventually have a good effect.

As for the standard won by the owner of the untamed horse, who as a general rule is a prince, it is taken with great fanfare to his house and placed on the balcony as a trophy, whereupon congratulations and invitations follow one upon the other. My reader may wish to know who these Roman princes are. Like our grandees of Spain, they are upright families descended from the Roman patricians of antiquity, or families that have become wealthy because they are relatives of a Pope, or have had cardinals in their family, which in others times made them the equals of kings, and when these latter partook of a meal in the Pope's presence, they ate with the cardinals, the emperor alone being seated at the Pope's table. "Count" and "Marquis" are titles that are come by very cheaply in Italy; they can be bought for very little money, and those who hold them are usually half starved. A handful of pesos buys the cross and the gold key of the Holy Roman Empire; the title of Doctor of La Sapiencia, this institution being the University of Rome, is sent by mail by certain nuns to anyone who sends them fifty duros; and a magnate's house gives its owner the right to use the title of Prothonotary Apos-

---

* I held out my hands each day to the people of unbelievers and naysayers.

tolic extra *urbem*, for very little more or even the same sum. In days gone by, this was a very important title, because all notaries of lesser rank were subservient to him.

At Carnival time the spectacle of the Girandole traditionally takes place at Castel Sant'Angelo. Fireworks are set off there for quite some time, and then, unexpectedly, one sees a great burst of gunpowder rising in the air, forming, for the eight to ten minutes that it lasts, a great show of so many and such brilliant colors that it is spellbinding. This spectacle costs the Government five hundred duros. The illumination of the dome of Saint Peter's is another great spectacle, which takes place on that saint's feast day, or else to entertain a foreign prince who is visiting Rome. The last dome of Saint Peter's, that is to say the outermost one, because there are three of them, has little windows all around it. A great many men hide themselves inside, each with a large, very bright torch in hand, and when a bell rings, each one takes out his torch at the same time and places it in one of the little windows. The illumination is as sudden as it is beautiful; and since the great dome is immense, it is a brilliant spectacle. On Holy Thursday and Good Friday everything takes place inside the Vatican, and people make every effort to go to the Pauline chapel to hear Pergolesi's *Miserere*. In Saint Peter's on Good Friday night there is no ceremony other than the hanging of a very large cross covered all over with lights in front of the Saint's tomb. His tomb is also illuminated on other occasions, but there is wax instead of oil in the votive lamps. Our American Jesuits have introduced the observance of the three hours of devotion on Good Friday in Rome. It was the Jesuits who introduced in America the tolling of bells at three o'clock on that afternoon, something not done anywhere else in the world.

The Pope had done away with the lottery in Rome, because this is nothing but a confidence game on the part of the government to fleece the people without their feeling it. But the people were so fond of this game that they sent their money outside the city in order to play, and the Pope was obliged to reintroduce it. A spectacle is made of it, as Rome is in the habit of making of everything. The people spread out all over the piazza of the Rota, tickets in hand. On the balcony of the Rota a number of monsignors in their episcopal attire, notaries and so on are seated. In the middle of them, nicely dressed and hair neatly combed, a youngster from the Inclusa Foundling Home raises his little hand and shows it to the crowd, draws a slip of paper, which he hands around for the prelates and other dignitaries to see, and then he takes it over to the official crier, dressed in a long red habit, who shouts out very slowly:

Number such and such. This cry is followed by the sudden murmur of those who have won or lost, a sound like the roar of the sea. And the same thing is repeated when each of the three numbers is drawn.

Since the Roman people live in such wretchedness, they dream of the lottery, which has increased to an immeasurable degree the natural superstition of that people. Girls and boys leap out at people everywhere on the streets to tell them a lottery number, because it is believed that God will inspire these innocents, and so people give them a few alms. Others, when they go to bed for the night, place these numbers under the headboard, hoping that God may invest the one they have chosen with special powers in their dreams. Mathematicians make a thousand calculations as to the virtues of certain numbers. A great crowd of people goes at night to climb the hundred steps of the monastery of the Sololant Franciscans on the Capitoline, in earlier times the temple of Jupiter Tonans, so that the Christ Child of that church will help them win the lottery; the madonnas, that is to say the images of the Virgin that are everywhere, are more brightly illuminated, and they provide the only lighting there is at night in Rome, especially the Madonna del Arco, which is the most miraculous of them. People believe in all these images, and a thousand paradoxes that have been written about them make a person blush for shame. The Christs of Burgos have long lingered in my memory. There are two of them: one in the monastery of the Trinità, and another in Sant'Agostino, outside the city. There was a quarrel in the Council as to which was the legitimate one in Burgos. The one in Trinità won the material advantage, the sole right to seek alms within the city; but the one in Sant'Agostino came off with the honors. He is the one whom foreigners visit, and it is to him that by far the larger share of the alms comes. If he were not kept under wraps, or if he were displayed without lights and without money, he would simply be a Christ like the others. Self-interest keeps all these superstitions alive. As in Terence's day, the Romans still kill the hen that crows like a cock, so that someone in the family won't die. In any event, where such devotions are the rule, a person must constantly be on the alert and not allow anyone to approach him at night, or draw closer to anyone else, because he may be killed or robbed. This is the homeland of Cacus, and today his cave is the refectory or the wine cellar of the Dominicans of Santa Sabina.

Before leaving this city of waters, as it is called in The Apocalypse (and, in point of fact there is a fountain in every house, and in every public square, with very showy jets and cascades), I will tell of certain

American and Spanish savants with whom I had dealings. Such information may be of some use for something. I met Masdeu, Montengón and Hervás, former Spanish Jesuits, and the latter did me the honor of ordering Madrid not to print any work of his on American subjects without my prior approval. He and Masdeu had been granted pensions by our Government, and Masdeu had as many as nine pensions. The American Márquez also received a pension in recognition of his great learning in the realm of architecture. He has analyzed in detail two celebrated Mexican monuments: the temple of the Inca and the fortress of Xochicalco. The Americans Juárez and García enjoyed great renown, the former in botany and the latter in medicine. Iturri, an American from Paraguay, was a great friend of mine, who gave Muñoz a thorough dressing-down because within the framework of his history he conjoined some of the ridiculous errors of Paw, Raynal and Robertson.[8] The ex-Jesuit Cavo, from Guadalajara, translated into Latin Gama's notes on the Calendar and the Teoyamiqui, and wrote, in Latin and Castilian, a civil history of Mexico, which I read. He had in his possession an extremely curious collection of letters from Gama concerning our antiquities. I met the Spanish ex-Jesuit Diosdado, to whom Clavijero offered board, and had him read his history, and Diosdado denounced the work to the Council, writing against Clavijero, thereby preventing its publication, although Muñoz, on being consulted by the Council with regard to both works, answered altogether in favor of Clavijero, maintaining that his antagonist was in no way comparable. Masdeu also boldly challenges him, though his braggadocio is as ridiculous as Diosdado's refutation of him. Clavijero translated his work into Italian, and it has been accorded great applause, although as a way of currying favor with the Spaniards, he added at the time certain notes against Las Casas, a weakness he gave in to so that his work would be approved. He also wrote the history of the Californias. In one of his letters to him, Gama pointed out to him how badly he was taken in by Bernal Díaz when the latter maintained that the soldier who joined them in Cozumel was a priest.[9] It is clear, he says, from records of judicial inquiries carried out in Tlaxcala that are kept in the secretariat of the Viceroyalty, that, according to his declaration, he continued to serve as a soldier with his horse and arms and later married an Indian woman from Coatzacoalco. Another American, whose name escapes me and who was already dead at the time, left, albeit in a very incomplete state, a *Diccionario geográfico-histórico* of our America, in manuscript. And in another work that I did not see, he described in detail a number of Mexican manuscripts in the possession of

Cardinal Borja, and another one that was in the Vatican and had been placed in the archives containing Chinese manuscripts or codices.

But the work that caused the most talk in Rome, and everywhere else later on, is that of our American ex-Jesuit Lacunza, who was unfortunately found dead early one morning in a puddle, for he had been overtaken by one of the dizzy spells that he frequently suffered, and there was no one about to help him. The work is about the millennium. It is common knowledge that because of those words of Saint John's in The Apocalypse concerning the first and second resurrection, after a thousand years, there have been many who have believed, since the earliest days of the Church, that Jesus Christ, at the end of the world, would come to reign over the earth with the just for a thousand years, before the last resurrection. Since in the early Church the book of the Pastor of San Papias, a disciple of Saint John, from whom the Pastor says he heard this doctrine, met with such renown that a number of Church fathers believed it, and Lactantius cites it as being the usual and general doctrine of the Church. In another era it had great defenders and challengers as well, although it was discredited because it was confused with the doctrine of Cerinthus and other heretics who took this millennium to be one meant for libertinage and carnal delights. Nonetheless, it was so widely believed in Europe that when the thousandth anniversary of the foundation of the Church was approaching, Europe was so thoroughly persuaded that the end of the world was at hand that countless numbers of them gave their lands to monasteries, and even shut themselves away in them, so that the monastic orders thereby acquired large landholdings and great wealth.

In the Protestant churches millennialism is like a dogma, and they would be greatly disappointed if the events prophesied fail to come to pass. In the year 1813 the London gazettes issued an invitation to people to come to a certain tavern to debate the subject of the millennium, which was approaching. Nor did it lack defenders among Catholics. In the seventeenth century or the beginning of the eighteenth it was supported by the venerable Frías, a famous Dominican from the Philippines, in his rare and most curious collection of prophecies founded on Scripture, and in the latter century it was also defended by the celebrated Jesuit Vieyra, although he paid the price for so doing by being imprisoned by the Inquisition of Lisbon, and from there was sent into exile in Rome. And since it is a maxim among Jesuits to support or favor everything that any one of them puts forward, this opinion has found favor with them ever since, and they have made Lacunza's work immensely popular, with a wide readership, which in my opinion it does not deserve, despite the fact that it is written with the most attractive clarity, order and eloquence.

In his work he is following, he says, the example of the farmers who first clear the field, then sow and then gather the fruits. But when he gathered them—a Jesuit told me—he ruined his work. He dismisses the concept of the empyrean as a Platonist idea, and maintains that our bliss will be on earth, journeying all about it and admiring its beauties. In the days of the millennium, when the Court of Jesus Christ will be in Jerusalem, he would like to see the sacrifices of Christianity conjoined with those of Judaism. For that reason the Jesuits have translated the work into Latin and had the Pope read it, though at the same time reducing it, they told me, to reasonable terms. One of them told me that Lacunza must have originally written against [*sic*] the Jews, because he attacks many of the proofs that we marshal against them and decides in their favor in many instances. Hence they wanted to see his work printed, although he replied that he would not give his consent if Rome did not give its imprimatur. Alvear, the governor of the island of León, had it printed in Castilian in the days of freedom of the press in Spain, and another edition in Buenos Aires, where it has caused a great sensation, and was going to have it printed in London in 1816. When I read it in Rome, it struck me as offering a solution for everything, and I had the impression that the author was not a great theologian, this despite the fact that his work was plagiarized from one by a French Protestant, entitled *The Key, or Fulfillment of all Prophecies*. The renowned Father Ricardo Simón speaks of it and others like it in his selected letters, and says that such works come to grief on their own. The celebrated Bishop Gregoire says in his work on religious sects that because of this work he consulted the famous Tamburini regarding the millennium, and the latter answered that as yet he had reached no definite opinion on the subject. Since the Jesuits have brought it to Mexico, just as they have disseminated it throughout America, and since their lordships the inquisitors have asked me for my opinion, I have spoken at some length about it.

To make a long story short: I decided to leave Rome in mid-July 1803, and just at that time the bill of exchange for three hundred pesos, which my brother Froilán had countermanded a year before, arrived; and the shrewd Italian in whose house I was lodged opened it, pretending to have done so by mistake, and paid himself handsomely for having put me up, leaving me scarcely more than twenty pesos or so for my journey.

I left Rome in a coach, accompanied by a Neapolitan, the brother of the Duke of Dosan who, being as poor as I was, was going to Spain to live, and a Lutheran from Flanders. We promptly left via the Pópolo gate, where there is an Augustinian monastery in which Luther lived, and it is said that the latrines are in his old cell. This monastery was founded to drive away the devils that were said to haunt the site of Nero's tomb, and the Pope goes there once a year to celebrate Mass, because there is an image of the Virgin there, one of the ones attributed to the brush of Saint Luke, the putative painter of the Holy Family, although he was a physician. The Church Fathers of the Seventh General Council, to examine the dogma of the permissibility and veneration of images, did away with copies of images dating from antiquity, not sparing even apocryphal monuments. How could they have kept the images of Saint Luke such a total secret if in the eighth century any plausible rumor about them was circulating? They are by a Florentine painter, named Luke the Saint, who at a very early date took to painting, after much fasting and praying, images of the Virgin, which he gave away for nothing. At best, they may be copies of one, said to have been painted by Saint Luke, which the empress Eudoxia sent to Constantinople in the fifth century, according to Theodore the Lector.

As soon as we travelers had left the Papal State, we realized that we had entered pleasant and gracious Tuscany, for the country people, men and women alike, doffed their hats (the women wear a straw one with a pretty ribbon) and shouted "Buon viaggio" to us. We entered Siena, which is considered to be the town with the most sociable people and the one where the purest Italian is spoken. Thus above the gate to the city one reads: *Cor magis tibi Sena pandit.** A plague at the beginning of the last century had reduced its population from eighty to nineteen thousand souls. For a European city, it is a pretty one, for as I have said, Europe seems to have first been inhabited by a people inimical to straight lines. The cathedral, called the Duomo (because of its dome), is the city's great monument, which the Sienese invite one to go see, and in all truth it is a magnificent church with three very high naves, and in the main part of the church, above the arches, are portrait busts of all the Popes in three rows, shown from the waist up, in their papal bonnets, stoles and red hats, all in marble. The pavement is in mosaic, representing passages from Scripture, and the Sienese are so pleased with their temple that it is not lighted by oil lamps but rather by twelve wax tapers,

---

* Siena opens wide its great heart to you.

day and night. The head alone of Saint Catherine of Siena is there, for her body is in the monastery of La Minerva in Rome. And a person cannot call this saint to mind without remembering those times of madness in which Rome, convinced that its pontiffs were masters of the world, conjoined temporal arms and spiritual ones so as to turn that world upside down. This saint went as an ambassador of the Florentines to Avignon, to plead with the Pope to lift the interdict placed upon that Republic sixty years before, so that when Mass began to be celebrated there again, something that almost no one had seen in his or her lifetime, people laughed as if it were a clown act that was being performed. This saint also was the one who succeeded in getting the Pope to make Rome the Papal See once again, for the French popes had moved it to Avignon seventy years before.

From Siena we went on to Florence; this city is the cradle of modern literature, which it learned of from the Greeks fleeing from the Turks who had taken Constantinople in the fifteenth century. The dukes of Florence were wise enough to take advantage of these circumstances. The famous Academia della Crusca, which produced the purest dictionary of the Italian language, is in Florence. This is the Etruria of antiquity, a center of culture before the arrival of the Romans. After having been a flourishing republic, it fell under the rule of the Medicis, and after that under the dominion of the dukes of Austria. The French captured it and gave it, under the title of a kingdom, to the Prince of Parma, the infante of Spain, which, in exchange for that tiny little province, the duchy of Parma, ceded to Napoleon Piacenza and Guastalla, the island of Santo Domingo, whose three richest and most fertile parts we possessed (and have since taken back), and the immense territory of Louisiana. Then Napoleon robbed the queen of her Etruria, in exchange for a province of Portugal, which she never obtained, and recently the Congress of Vienna returned Tuscany to an archduke of Austria; he gave Parma Piacenza and Guastalla, and the queen of Etruria and her son have been left to live on the alms that Ferdinand VII and the Pope deign to give them. In politics, Machiavelli says, three and three do not make six.

Florence is a large, pretty city, divided in two by the Arno River. Although not all its streets are laid out in a straight line, there are many that are; the buildings, all more or less alike, resemble the simple architecture of Mexico City, which is really Italian. The ancient architecture of the Indians is like that of the French: a patio that the French call a *cour*, trees and then the house. And Mexicans even count in exactly the same way as the French, up to sixty; after that the latter go on by saying sixty-ten, and then four twenties, the way our Indian women always shout when they are selling fruit: four times twenty. The streets of Florence are very clean, and the pavement made of natural slabs of stone fitted together according to their size and natural shape. I did not see any friars, because the French had driven them out; I saw only Dominicans there, and in Genoa, in just one monastery in each city, because its church served the parish, and the French left those. I had the idea that there were nuns; it turned out that since the advent of Archduke Leopold young lay girls had been coming in to replace nuns who died, and wear habits, as do girls in boarding school in France, and in earlier times all the children educated in accordance with the Rule of Saint Benedict. They recite the Divine Office in the choir and are like the canonesses of Germany, who leave their convents to marry if they receive a proposal.

The learned bishop of Pistoia, Ricci, whom I saw in Florence, opened all the orders of his Episcopate to laymen, though he allowed them to take vows only for a year, enough time to enable a man, with constant help from God, to promise without fear to keep the vows, by making an effort to dominate his passions. When the year is up, just as the Carmelites renew their vows through devotion, the others can repeat theirs from year to year, if they feel they have the mettle and the strength to keep them. We who know from experience what the cost of these vows is, and what takes place in cloisters of both sexes, where countless victims forced into them against their will gnaw at their chains, cannot help applauding the bishop's prudence. The Church, in the days when continence was a binding vow only for deacons and those above that rank, and only after the first nuptials, awarded this rank only to those who were thirty or thirty-five years old because, as Saint Paul says, *melius est nubere quam uri. Vidua eligatur non minor sexaginta amorum* [sic]. *Volo autem minores nubere, filios procreare.** Of what use is it to make vows beyond human powers because *non omnes capiunt verbum istud,* Jesus Christ said, *sed quibus datum est,*** and if you do not keep them, it brings you damnation, when without taking them you could save yourself just as surely and more easily?

* ". . . let them marry, for it is better to marry than to burn." (1 Cor 7:9) "Let a widow who is selected be not less than sixty years old." (1 Ti 5: 11) "I desire therefore that the younger widows marry, bear children." (1 Ti 5: 14). (All translations are from the English version of the Catholic Douai Bible.)

** . . . not all understand this word, save those to whom it is given.

Florence is full of cultivated and learned men. I was recommended by Grégoire to the principal scholars of Italy, and in Florence was recommended to Fabroni, renowned for his studies in the field of botany, about which he has written, and custodian of the Museum. The one in Florence is superb, everything about it being luxurious and magnificent. At the entrance I saw an immense geographical globe, like the one in the Bibliothèque Royale in Paris, and I was put in mind of the immense armillary sphere in the Escorial in Spain. When Court is being held there, a Hieronymite friar is appointed to serve as a guide to all the relics and curiosities that are kept there. And when a ground of women asked him to explain what the armillary sphere was, he replied that it was the bobbins of the queen doña Urraca. "How big they are!" they said to him. "Of course," he answered. "They're fit for a queen."

In the Botanical Garden in Florence I saw a maguey cactus in a pot with its label: "Alve messicano"; that is what botanists call it, or else agave, just as they call chocolate (or *cicolatta* [*sic*], as the Italians say) *teobroma*, meaning drink of the gods. It is a proven fact that it is the best food that Nature provides, and that an ounce of chocolate is more nourishing than two of meat. In Europe it is given as a remedy for all ailments and fevers, because it is a mistake to call it hot; we Mexicans confuse its nature with that of the cinnamon that we add to it. Of four ways in which the Indians prepared it, only one, and not the best one, was adopted by the Spaniards, who called it *cacao* and *chocolate* (which means cacao, water and sweet) and took it to Spain with them, and took as well the stone mortar for grinding it, which we call a *metate* and the Indian name of the cup for it a *xicalli,* which they turned into the word *jícara* and the Italians *chichera.* The Jesuits introduced it to the latter and traded in this commodity. Now that it has spread throughout Europe, the way that it is prepared has been improved, and the cacao is ground in a mechanical grinder without roasting it, which earlier on caused it to lose through evaporation most of the fragrance that comes from the oil in the beans. The French have been seized by a mad passion for chocolate, from which they have made a thousand concoctions with Greek names. The Italians have composed a thousand songs about it. Chocolate is one of their delights, one is always invited to have a cup of chocolate as a special treat, and in Florence, in households known for their great refinement and taste, I have been served it in little coconut shell cups, as is still the custom in the interior of our country.

The painting and sculpture gallery is also excellent. Its principal adornment was the Venus dei Medici, which the French had taken off to

Paris; today it is probably back in Florence. The public library is also very good, and in it I saw the collection of vows of the bishops of Tuscany, who in the time of the Archduke Leopold were possessed of great wisdom regarding all the points of ecclesiastical discipline needing reform, on which all the most enlightened churchmen of Italy had to agree. The Council of Pistoia was merely a preliminary attempt at reform, and its 116 Fathers were the crème de la crème of Italy. That was why Rome trembled, created a great furor and made every effort to condemn it, although its condemnatory bull *Auctorem Fidel* is the best possible defense of the Council. The archduke's palace is built in the style of a country manor, which gives it a certain majestic air, and it has a beautiful garden. There are many other avenues with pyramidal tombs. And it is worthy of note that for funerals of people of distinction in Italy not only is the church draped in black inside, but the facade of it as well, and a portrait of the deceased, adorned with black tassels, and the funeral eulogy, in Latin, are hung above the door of the church. This latter is always a tablet inscribed with great care and skill. The bier is placed inside the church, together with perfumes, funeral urns, and so on, as was the custom in antiquity among the Greeks, Etruscans and Romans. There are many book shops, and in the streets and public squares, as in Paris and Rome, many book stalls with very curious little volumes for sale.

I believe that after nineteen days the Neapolitan and I went on our way, leaving our Flemish traveling companion behind, suffering from severe food poisoning brought on by eating mushrooms; I have often seen such mischances, because it is very easy to mistake poisonous mushrooms for ones that are safe to eat. It is necessary to cook them with a silver spoon in the pot, because if the spoon turns green *est morte en olla*.* We arrived in Livorno, because as my reader has seen in this account of my travels, I describe only the large cities in which I stayed for some time. Livorno is a very fine port and quite a large one, a bustling trade center. There are handsome streets laid out in a straight line, and a Greek church there; but the synagogue of the Jews in Livorno, who also have a quarter in Florence, is outstanding, and as there are many Jews there, I saw the lengths they go to so as to eat hot food on the sabbath, a day on which they cannot light a fire. They have an oven or a very large cookstove still good and hot from the evening before, and they set all their food there to be warmed by the heat of the oven. I bought the *Gacetero americano* there; it is a sort of geographico-historical dictionary of all the Americas,

---

* There is death in the pot.

compiled in the United States, with a supplement added in Livorno. There is another one that was brought out in Spain by a Peruvian named Alcedo. The Jesuits sent supplements to it from Rome.

Five or six days later I took ship once again, for Genoa, on a coastal vessel of the sort that are propelled by oars; we passed the famous marble quarries of Carrara, and entered what was once the capital of a flourishing republic, but at the time of my visit was in a state of dire poverty because of repeated sacking by the French and their mad delusions of imposing Republican equality on old and corrupt countries. The Genoese were imbeciles who placed their faith in lofty words and cast envious eyes on the nobility, pulled down its coats of arms, burned its golden book, did away with its luxury and then died of starvation, because that same luxury is what puts food on the tables of the common people by giving work to artisans and craftsmen. The people were filled with remorse, but it was too late. They must now be even more remorseful, because the Congress of Vienna gave that republic to the king of Sardinia, just as it handed over the Republic of Venice to the emperor. The French, who wanted to create republics all over Europe, ended up doing away with even those republics that had existed previously. And how much damage they wrought! During the siege by the troops of France and England that Genoa rashly withstood in the name of its imaginary tree of liberty, its inhabitants died at the rate of five hundred a day, of starvation and disease. Hence the population was as decimated as it was miserable.

As I walked through the streets I remembered Virgil's riddle: *Dic quibus in terris, et eris mihi magnus Apollo, Tres pateat coeli spatium non amplius ulnas*[10]; because the streets are so narrow and the houses so tall that one can scarcely glimpse the sky; as a consequence, the houses down below are very dark. There is nothing worth seeing save for the entrance to the city of the newest street, where the magnificent palaces of the nobles of bygone days are located; the Doria palace is particularly splendid. The hospital for poor orphans is also a magnificent edifice. The entire territory of Genoa is like a broad belt along the seashore, the whole of it rugged and mountainous, and the sea has scarcely any fish in it. They have not been wise enough to preserve their spawn. In England there are periods in which fishing is forbidden, so that the fish of a given species will increase and multiply.

The renowned Dominican Vignoli, to whom I was recommended by Gregoire, had just died, although two other learned Dominicans were still alive, the bishops of Dania and of Noli; as I have already said, the latter denounced the bull *Auctorem Fidel* before the Senate of Genoa, and then defended his denunciation in his apologia against Cardinal Gerdin, whom he triumphantly refuted, and wrote other brief works, such as the one in Latin concerning the indissolubility of marriage, even if one of the marriage partners renounces religion. Another most sagacious Dominican bishop, Becchetti, was still alive; it was he who continued, with equal eloquence, Orsi's history of the Church, wrote on the theory of the earth and refuted Dupuy's work on the origin of cults, which has done such harm to religion, despite the fact that another Dominican scholar, Lambert, also refuted it in Paris. I was also recommended to another learned churchman, Careaga, and met the famous don Vicente Palmieri, a canon of Milan and before that of the Congregation of the Oratory, famous, as I have said, for his dogmatic history of indulgences that was adopted by the Council of Pistoia, a work as solidly argued as it was innovative. Anyone who believes that he knows something about indulgences without having read it is acquainted only with errors. As regards indulgences—the archbishop of Venice said at the Council of Trent—nothing is certain save the fact that the Church has the power to grant them, and that their use is salutary; everything else is debatable, and therefore the Council restricted the definition of them to that alone. In the beginning Palmieri's work was a single quarto volume; he later lengthened it to two so as to reply to the Roman censors. He also wrote the history of the Church in the first three or four centuries, and several lesser works as well. I did not see anything else worthwhile. The gazette published in Genoa is fair to middling, though the one put out in Florence is the best one in Italy. In Rome the only estimable publication of this kind is the *Cracas*, which is a sort of *Mercurio*.

I lived in Genoa with a poor priest who offered people lodging and supported himself, outside of moneys earned saying Mass, by sharpening scissors and razors from daybreak on. A cousin of his was the one who turned the grindstone. He was hoping to become the manager of a country estate, a post that frequently is given to clergymen in Italy. All this reminded me of Spain, where I saw deacons serving their master at table, and acting as pages of their mistress, accompanying her with an umbrella. In point of fact, servants, especially those in monasteries, often end up as priests. And in Seville the Dominican schoolboys of Santo Tomás, which is a boarding school, are followed about by a cleric called a *famulus*, who wears a black cassock with a torch embroidered on it. In Spain maidservants are the ones who become nuns; but when the nuns belong to the nobility, as do those of Huelgas in Burgos, the Royal Discalced Carmelites and the nuns of Santo Domingo, in Madrid, they become so puffed up with pride at the privileges they enjoy that there is not enough room for them in the entire city. When I was in Madrid, a daughter of a tradesman tried to enter the convent of Santo Domingo and they did not admit her, even though she brought a fortune with her. The little Dominican nuns of Saint Catherine took her in and made their convent a really pretty place both inside and out with her money.

Spaniards say that in America nothing is the same as it is in Spain save eggs and Jesuits. And this is all the more true with regard to the nobility. Since those who come to America seldom belong to the nobility, every social status, that determined by purity of blood in particular, that is to say, the fact that a person is not immediately descended from Jews or Moors, has come to be taken to be the same thing as nobility, and yet there is a world of difference between them. In America, therefore, the only nobility is that of the indigenous peoples, that of the descendants of the conquistadors and the first colonists, that of those few whose forebears were nobles in Spain, and that of those who have attained noble rank by virtue of a title, a toga or officer's stripes. But what made me laugh in Spain was to see how Spaniards who come here insist that their wretched families put *don* and *de* in their names, these being a sign of nobility in certain provinces of Spain. It made me laugh just as heartily to see the crafty ways in which people here try to pass themselves off as relatives of the highest nobility of the country. The Countess of Santiago, the most illustrious house in Mexico, died, and my uncle the inquisitor don Juan de Mier told me he had been surprised not to see me among the mourners. I answered that I was not related to her. And he replied that the people did not know that, and are honored at the very sight of him. "I am who I am," he added, "and yet I have been badly snubbed at times and felt deeply hurt." Not long afterward the Count of Santiago died, and at his funeral I saw, in the very midst of the cortege, Father Casaus, a European, who today is archbishop of Guatemala. I was just behind the young count who was the deceased's heir and a friend of mine, and turning to me, he asked me: "What is that Father doing here? You certainly have a right to be present, inasmuch as you and I are nephews of don Cosme de Mier, who as my aunt's husband is the principal mourner." I then realized that what my uncle the inquisitor had counseled me to do was a rule observed by all Europeans so as to give the people the thrill of being in the presence of nobility.

While in Genoa I found myself beset with difficulties, because I had run completely out of money and had no means of support. But a Cata-

V

From My Arrival in Barcelona
to My Arrival in Madrid

Here I am again in the country of despotism, putting myself into the lion's mouth for it to devour its prey. There was no other way for me to get back to my homeland. From here, my reader will be expecting me to provide, as is my habit, a description of the country. There is very little to say about Barcelona, despite its being one of the best cities in Spain; but it is of course made up of a tangle of streets, and the houses have tiled roofs, which on first sight look to be in ruins, and the tiles are all uneven. The Catalans delight in showing the visitor the tomb of the last count of Barcelona, don Berenguer. These counts were sovereign rulers, and Catalonia had its Constitution, its Cortes and its laws, called *usages*. The Customs House is a very fine building, as is the Mercantile Exchange. The post of administrator general of the latter was held by señor Imas, my friend, who refused to allow my trunk to be searched, and extended me a personal invitation. Two other friends of mine, the baron who had taken the Royal Oath and another Catalan whose name I do not recall, did likewise. Several rich merchants decided to follow the example of America and build a district laid out like a grid, and built the Barceloneta at one edge of the city. It is very pretty, though quite small, and the houses have only one upper floor. The most noteworthy buildings in the district are the castle of Monjuitch [*sic*] and the citadel. Monjuitch is a mountain that overlooks the entire city, sufficiently leveled off at the top to provide ample room for a castle. The citadel is a fine one. When taking a city, the garrison of its citadel is sent word that if the city is bombarded its inhabitants will be put to the sword, and in the end it is obliged to surrender. The purpose of citadels, then, is to keep the citizens in check, in places where the Government mistrusts them. And following the war of succession the Bourbons' mistrust of the Catalans could not have been greater. They were not permitted to have arms. The bread knives were chained to the table. It was necessary to have good connections and pay a fee in order to be able to obtain a hunting rifle. And this was a very good measure, because the city dwellers shot at people passing through the city so as to rob them, and if they missed and failed to kill them, they came out of hiding to ask them if they had seen the *conil* (the rabbit). That part of the country was not subject to levies of troops, or conscription, since it was considered to be a country in open rebellion, but people were obliged to pay a tax.

In other respects as well it is not possible to tell the truth about Spain without offending the Spaniards. Since they are not in the habit of traveling and thus are unable to make comparisons, and those who go to America arrive at a tender age, without ever having viewed their native land through rational eyes, Spain is the best place in the world, the garden of the Hesperides, even though most of it is not under cultivation, and three-quarters of the land is barren. A year when there is not a shortage of bread is rare, despite the fact that for the most part Spain lives on maize and bread made of rye or millet flour. Its climate is that of paradise on earth, though in certain parts the cold is intolerable, and for that reason men and women, especially in the vicinity of the Pyrenees, have a goiter that appears on their neck. And in other parts of the country the heat is unbearable. The advent of a new season is clearly marked by sudden deaths, and in the transition between one season and another so high a mortality rate that it seems like a plague. Poxes are always widespread, and the rigors of the seasons create a horde of blind people and another of paralytics, and victims of other cruel ailments. Hence it is necessary to wear three different sets of garments in the course of a year: winter ones, summer ones and between-season ones; to put matting down inside the houses and then take it up again; to move upstairs and down in the same house so as to be able to bear the heat or the cold.

Their cattle are bred from Geyron's royal stock, but the merino sheep were brought from England by the Duke of Alencastre [*sic*]; and even though meat is eaten only in the cities and big towns and only by the wealthy, it is necessary to bring supplies of it in from France, and in wintertime even eggs are imported. The plowing is done with mules and horses, for lack of oxen. And horses are not raised as ours are, in the open fields; there are people whose job it is to spur them on to breed, by exciting them with their hand so that they will procreate. It is necessary to leave the land fallow almost every year, and when it produces a crop it is because of the use of manure; in Madrid the human variety is sold in sacks that are worth their weight in gold; in Catalonia they go about making manure at their very own houses, keeping the inner courtyard flooded almost all the time and throwing out into it all the slops and excrement, which keep the house permanently perfumed.

In the rest of Spain, the first duty of children is to go about with a great basket on their arm and a broom, gathering dung along the roadsides and in the fields, so as to bake bread with it and keep themselves warm, for one can walk for days on end and hardly ever see a tree. And even so there is not enough manure to make the land productive: it is necessary to heap the dirt up in mounds and burn it, mixing in anthills and thorns, then breaking the mounds up with harrows and so on. As a general rule there are no factories or industrial enterprises in Spain, or any workers for them. Almost everyone, men and women alike, wears garments of coarse wool and rough-woven cloth; their footwear is hemp sandals, and their blouses are made of cloth woven from flax.

America the accursed is to blame for all of this, for with the 5,500 million hard pesos that, according to Baron Humboldt's calculations, it has poured into Spain, it has impoverished it. By providing it with a market of 100 million consumers and the entire production of the other three-quarters of the world, and pelts by the millions, it has ruined its factories, which numbered in the hundreds of thousands. A few handfuls of adventurers, who gulled the Indians into fighting each other until all of them had wiped each other out and America fell into the hands of Spain, have destroyed its population, which was once as high as 50 million. As a result, crops have failed and Spaniards have come to know starvation, even though America has given them the maize, the potatoes, as many variety of beans as can possibly be imagined, the chiles, the tomatoes and the chocolate that in general make up its diet and constitute its delight. Why don't the Spaniards leave America?

The wise and impartial Capmany, the author of the history of commerce in Barcelona and of many other works, has published a dissertation in which he demonstrated through arguments and historical documents that the population of Spain has never exceeded 10 million, nor can it exceed that number so long as there is nothing to prove that there has been any change in the mountains that it is full of, the direction in which its rivers flow and the quality of its land, the greater part of it barren; that Spain has never been a great trading nation and has always been indolent and lazy, with no agriculture or industry; that all the things said about its textile mills are canards, with no basis in fact, though by dint of repetition they have managed to impress the nation; that it is now, in our own era, under Charles III or IV, that the nation has reached its apogee in terms of population, agriculture, commerce and industry.

There is a very great difference, however, between the people of each of the kingdoms or provinces of Spain. In each, people have their own distinctive features, so that they are readily recognized by their language (and even among those who speak Castilian, the accent varies a great deal), their temperament, their particular dress, their different customs and different laws, especially their municipal ones. They are alike only in that all of them are more or less proud and arrogant, ignorant and superstitious. In this latter regard I am speaking of the common people, which includes friars and soldiers. As for the others, the same truth holds for them as for the remainder of Europe: deism, not excluding atheism, is predominant.

The abuses and the books of the *philosophes* are to blame for this. By devoting their every effort to combatting the Freemasons, the inquisitors are confusing the issue. If they believe that they can destroy them, they are embarking on a vast undertaking, for in England and in the United States, out of every hundred thousand people, eighty or ninety thousand are Freemasons; in Germany, a little less than that; in France, seventy thousand; in Italy, sixty thousand; in Spain and Portugal, thirty thousand. The Jesuit Barruel has written the history of the Freemasons, wherein he attempts to trace their origin to the heresiarch Manes, in the fourth century, and he attributes to them a general conspiracy against religion and the State. The learned and moderate bishop Gregoire, in his *Religious Sects of the Eighteenth Century,* calls Barruel's history *rêveries,* that is to say, daydreams and deliriums. And the documents that Barruel cites? They are quotations from other Jesuits who are persecuting the Freemasons, as the latter are persecuting the assemblies that are not sponsored by them; for the Freemasons have imitated the entire apparatus of mystery and machination of the Jesuits, and even make the same distinction between novices, students and masters. In books written by Jesuits that cite references, one must be wary, for just as in their books on probabilism they cite "the doctors so-and-so of the university of such-and-such," and these doctors are other Jesuits, and the university one of theirs; in like fashion they cite Count X, Canon Y and Bishop Z, all of whom are ex-Jesuits, who are experts at keeping quiet about their former profession of faith because people would not believe what they say, since it is their doctrine that it is permissible to lie, and to slander as well, in order to defend themselves. As a consequence, in the canonization of Saint Stanislaus of Kotska their testimony was not admitted, at the request of Cardinal Aguirre, but instead they were asked to place the archives in evidence.

I am not a Freemason, but I can guarantee that the first questions asked when seeking admission is: "What is your religion?" And when the person answers which religion he professes, he is asked: "Do you promise to observe your religion?" And when the answer is in the affirmative, the ceremonies and all the rest of it, no longer a secret, continue. Barruel admits that the first three degrees, which are the ones ordinarily received by the English, and by all Freemasons as a general rule, are innocent enough. These degrees have been described in print in England, out of negligence or following the death of the secretary of a lodge. There are two Masonic rites: the ancient one, which is observed by the English, and the modern one, which the French invented. And since the latter cannot keep a secret, I have seen a description of the thirty-one or thirty-three Masonic degrees published in a book in French.

The most likely explanation of the origin of Freemasonry is that it began among the architects that James I, or II, of England, brought from Europe to London, and that owing to the persecution and the exile of the king, their benefactor, they invented certain signs in order to communicate among themselves. The Scotch who had fled their country because they had defended their king added other signs. The entire system became even more widespread following the persecution of the Templars, who were slandered and destroyed because of the avarice of Philip the Fair.

In England the heir to the Crown is none other than the grand master of the Order as well. This was true of the Prince of Wales, and once he became regent, he was succeeded by the Duke of Sussex. The entire royal family are Masons, as are the dukes and the lords. The tavern where they meet is a public building with the appropriate insignia. Those who belong to the Order, be they civilians or members of the military, wear theirs openly in the public processions they organize for the opening of orphanages, et cetera, which they support as charitable institutions, and at funerals, which they attend as a religious community, and perform their ceremonies. In France too their gatherings are public, as they are in the United States. How can all this be reconciled with the fact that their maxims are against the existence of states? Would the despot Napoleon have tolerated them? Acosta, the Portuguese author of the *Correo brasiliense,* has published in London, in three quarto volumes, an apologia in defense of the Freemasons against the persecution they have suffered at the hands of the inquisitors.

All I know is that the Freemasons as a group abhor any sort of association that concerns itself with political matters, on the grounds that this is contrary to their institution. It is a society of universal charity and fraternity, or inviolable friendship. Had I been a Freemason, I would not have endured as many travails and times of near-starvation. No matter what land the hand of fate has brought him to, a Mason finds himself with as many friends and benefactors as there are Masons there. All of them welcome him, help him, take up collections in his behalf, and with the certain knowledge that the rule of secrecy is inviolable, the poor man unburdens his heart. Trying to destroy this institution is a vain endeavor: common interests will sustain it. Men, weary of hating one another and persecuting one another because they are of different nationalities, religions and opinions, or because of the whims of despots and fanatics, have invented this means of fraternizing with one another and protecting one another against the caprices of fortune. I have asked several Freemasons why they took such a terrifying vow of secrecy, which keeps many men from joining them and makes them suspect. And they have replied: If we did not have that oath, we would not have the bond that unites and distinguishes us; no one could open the very bottom of his heart to pour out his woes without fear of betrayal, and finally, everyone would want to be a Freemason then so as to enjoy its benevolence, and by that very fact the institution would be destroyed.

To return to the Catalans after this digression, of all Spaniards they strike me as having the ugliest physiognomy, despite the fact that they are well built, tall and robust. It is said that the name Catalonia comes from *Gollandia,* that is to say, the land of the Goths, and I am of the opinion that it is there that the physiognomy of the Goths has been best preserved. Their noses are all of a piece with their foreheads. The women are mannish as well, and in all of Catalonia I saw not a single one who was truly beautiful, except for a few among the poor people of Barcelona, women fathered by foreigners or by the troops from other parts of the kingdom who are always stationed in that city. Their usual dress is a jacket, breeches, hemp or rope-soled sandals for footwear, and a red woolen cap. These last two items are worn even by decent people and by priests inside their residences. They all appear to be captives; like a part of France they are Catalans, and as such carry on trade with America, and the red cap they wear is the same as the French Phrygian bonnet or liberty cap. By temperament they are rowdy and unruly and rebellious. By nature they are loud and given to making a great to-do over nothing.

But what distinguishes them from Spaniards is that they are not idlers or sluggards. They are farmers, shopkeepers, manufacturers, coachmen, seafarers, and do not give themselves a moment's rest. What can this enormous difference stem from? Just as Europe is the most active of any of the parts of the world and does not leave the others in peace and quiet because it is the least productive, the poorest and most needy, so the industriousness of the Catalans comes from their living in the poorest, most barren and mountainous region in Spain. When a man is poverty-stricken, it is all a matter of scraping by, and the man who doesn't keep on the go doesn't eat. They work the mountainsides in terraces that they call *bancales,* and in each *bancal* they sow a few cabbages that do not grow to much of any size, and the green leaves of them are their usual fare, along with cornmeal diluted with water to make what they call *farinetas,* and bread made of corn, rye or millet flour, millet being a tiny little black seed. They form their loaves of bread either into wheels as big as a shield or in yard-long rolls, and with a knife with two handles, like a double handsaw, they cut a bit off each day to eat, because they make a batch of bread only once a month. At three o'clock in the morning the women are already up to boil the cabbages in salted water, and at three-thirty the men eat and then go off to work till nightfall. From what the sweat of their brow produces they pay two-thirds to the owner of the field and live on the remaining third. They never drink water out of a pitcher or a glass, nor do they ever fail to add enough ordinary table wine to it to give it a reddish tinge; wine must be drunk from a *porrón,* that is to say, a glass jar with a long spout or sharp point that they raise up in the air, pouring the wine out in a steady trickle so as to land just inside their upper lip, and sometimes along their cheek, in order to show off, because this is a matter of pride with them, as is seeing to it that the tip of their red cap falls over one eyebrow. We outsiders are driven to despair because there are no glasses to drink out of, and they consider it really filthy if a person allows his lips to touch the spout of the wine jar. The truth of the matter is that this is one of the sparing ways they have to keep from wasting wine, for even if people have been drinking for a quarter of a hour, in the end they have drunk very little because the trickle that comes out of the wine jar is so scant. But it is such an unfailing habit of theirs not to drink plain water that even nursing babies get running bowels when their mothers drink it.

The one all-absorbing interest there is sols, pounds and deniers, hence the saying that the Catalans have three commandments: *sous, libras and dinés*. It is the one and only subject of conversation, nor does a Catalan take a single step or pull out even one ochavo except with the hope of making a profit; and to collect alms for prisoners, and so on, a raffle has to be held. In this regard there is no difference between rich and poor, gentlemen and ordinary people. When the troops were in Manresa, the Marquis of Albaida, a grandee of Spain, the colonel of Almansa, who was being given accommodations in a house of great distinction, decided, as we were about to go into battle, to have a canvas belt with ounces of gold sewed inside it made for him, so as to wear it next to his body, as is the custom among the military so that they have some money left to get along on should they fall prisoner. When the lady of the house sent his aide to buy the cloth, she told him to buy it in such and such a shop, and the little girl in the house, her daughter, would make the belt. She did a fine job of it, and as the marquis was thinking about the pretty fan that he intended to give the young lady as a present, the lady said to him: "Pay the girl for her work." "How much do I owe her?" the marquis asked, overcome with embarrassment. "Two quincetas"—half a real in our money.

The marquis told me that he felt like throwing his chair at the lady's head. But there is nothing for it; a person doesn't dare take a step around there without a lantern. And the priests, to go say Mass in a church, have to bring their own wine and candles. When people visit their relatives, they are obliged to bring their food for the whole time that they will be staying, even if it is no more than a day. I heard a great to-do in my inn, in Tarragona, and went downstairs to see what was going on. "What do you think this is all about?" the woman who ran the inn, the wife of a shopkeeper, answered. "As usual, it's my shameless father, who has taken it into his head to drop by without bringing anything to eat along with him."

In Olot, a large and prosperous city, I chanced to be standing talking with the owner of my lodgings, and when a beggar asked for alms at the door, he said: "Give alms to my father, and be off with you." "Your father!" "Yes," he answered. "He's a *sobrevenido*."* To understand this re-

---

* Not a usual Spanish word for a person. The meaning is, more or less, "a superfluous survivor," "someone supererogatory."

ply it is necessary to know that, as in all of Spain, only the firstborn inherits an entailed estate or primogeniture; in Catalonia only he inherits from his parents, no matter who they are. The other brothers and sisters are his servants. And everyone doffs his hat at the name of the *hereu;* or if there isn't a male heir, of the female one, the *pubila.* The *hereu* is addressed as master from the day he is born. When he is a toddler, a seat that is attached to the table is made for him so that he may eat sitting down. His sisters, if they are big enough, stand about with their arms crossed ready to serve him, like maids, and that is what they call themselves. "I am only a maidservant," they say, meaning that they are not the *pubila.* When, then, there is a *pubila* and no *hereu,* she must bring a husband into the family; but she does so only in order to produce an *hereu,* just as the story has it that in a certain day and age the Amazons allowed men to join them. When the *hereu* reaches adulthood, he takes over the administration of the estate and throws his father out into the street, because the latter is a *sobrevenido.* When the *hereu* marries, his wife's parents demand that her husband's parents transfer all their property and the administration of it to their son, who then traditionally treats them as though they were *sobrevenidos.* For that reason lawsuits are constantly brought in Catalonia by fathers against sons and sons against fathers. The goddess Matrona is the country's deity, to whom everything is sacrificed. For that reason, no language has more negatives: *il y'a pas, n'y a cap, úy a res.* And what gave me a good laugh over their customary greetings and polite phrases was the fact that to ask after the health of people's children, even though the family is most respectable, one says: "How are the riffraff?"

Large country houses, or *quintas,* as we would say, are called *mases,* and the usual way of building them is to provide them with a large salon with rooms on either side, and then passageways that start from there, with doors on one side and another side like a convent. This is where the riches of the *mas* are. On that side is the storeroom for bread, hams, the pork fat we call lard, and wine put down over many years. Donkeys are the family's usual mounts, and their carriages, called *carros,* which are covered on top, are drawn by mules; they circulate throughout Spain and are so crude and heavy that they ruin all the roads.

There is no nobility there, other than that of barons, a very old and widespread title in Catalonia. I have already said that in America people confuse nobility and purity of blood, the latter being enough to qualify a person for the priesthood, for membership in certain military orders and for applying for an official post anywhere in Spain. What is meant by purity of blood is not being immediately descended from Moors or Jews, from an executioner, a butcher or a meat cutter, from an innkeeper, or from one who practices a mechanical trade or is a shopkeeper, although Charles III ordered these latter stains on a person's bloodlines effaced from his records; even today however, most people consider them degrading. But there is still a great distance between purity of blood and nobility: in between the two are the ranks of *infanzones, hidalgos* and *caballeros.* In the census taken at the end of the last century, there were only 450,000 nobles in all of Spain, 350,000 of whom were in Castilla la Vieja, Asturias, Montañas, Vizcaya and Navarre. And these nobles are not men of wealth; on the contrary, they are wretchedly poor, and in all likelihood barely 200,000 of them have enough to eat. Among these nobles themselves there is a very great distinction, because those who have been raised to the rank of nobles, as are those who have bought Castilian titles without possessing an ancestral home, those with degrees from the University of Salamanca, judges, military officers of a regular army, though not of a militia (in which it should be noted that the rank of subaltern and lieutenant ennoble only the person and not the family), are not comparable to nobles with an ancestral home and a well-known lineage.[2] Nobility of this latter sort is extremely rare, and so precious that the old tower, the haven of snakes and swifts, which is the family's ancestral home, even though it is all by itself in the middle of nowhere, is preserved with the greatest care. And with every step one takes in the mountains, magnificent facades of palaces with a coat of arms come into view, and they are nothing but facades; all there is behind them is a poultry yard, and usually a shabby little dwelling of some sort. Here too there is a distinction, because some of these houses belong to a family of church dignitaries or of grandees, and others do not. Ecclesiastical orders do not confer nobility even on those who hold canonries, and it can be seen from the history of Spain that the chapter of the cathedral of Santiago in Galicia was unable to keep two canons who were commoners from being subject to taxation. An episcopate confers nobility, because it makes those who receive the rank of bishop members of the House of Lords; hence the title of *don* is given to bishops who are friars, these latter usually being commoners, not because they are bishops but because they are members of the House of Lords. In certain localities, members of the nobility enjoy one privilege or another. In Castile "the horse carries the saddle," meaning that the noble husband confers noble rank on his wife, but this is not the case in other kingdoms, and in none of them does the woman ennoble her husband; on the contrary, she loses her rank and has the same social estate as her husband.

The order of Charles III does not confer noble rank; it is a dishonor, rather, to have been awarded it, because it has been given to shopkeepers. I saw señor Muñoz reproach señor Porcel for having accepted it, and the latter replied that he had accepted it only out of necessity, so as to be given a pension. And it is the miters of America that pay for such pensions. The Order of Saint John or of Malta is worth nothing today. Once France abolished its language, because this Order was made up of translators and interpreters, kings seized its encomiendas as well.* Then the Pope named the emperor of Russia its grand master, despite his being a schismatic, and finally, once the English had captured Malta, the seat of the Order, for good, that was the end of it all, and today crosses are awarded by the king of Spain, of Sardinia, of France, of Naples, the emperor of Russia, the Pope and so on, and they are sold publicly for three hundred or five hundred pesos. Outside of the four military Orders of Santiago, Calatrava, Alcántara and Montesa, which each have their council, their priories, their encomiendas, and so on, all the other crosses and orders, both ancient and modern, are nothing but decorations and medals such as the ones that generals gave out by the thousands in Spain during the war. And it was shameful to wear them, as is true of the fleur-de-lis in France today.

In bygone days the great mark of distinction of the nobility was the *don* before their names, and it is still rightfully used only for nobles; but it has become the custom to use it even for the air, as Quevedo once said of the word *donaire*.** In like manner, it is the custom to address all respectable people as Your Lordship when writing to them, and this is always how servants in decent houses address all visitors.

In Spain, on the contrary, colonels, brigadiers and other military officers are not addressed as Your Lordship except by their men, who are obliged to do so because it is one of the Army Regulations, nor are counts and marquises so addressed except by those who need to do so. Barons have no honorific. Judges in the Indies are addressed in that way, because the tribunals there are chanceries; those in Spain are not. Canons do not have that honorific. Grandees necessarily use the informal *tú* when speaking to one another, and they use *vuecencia**** as a term of address only out of scorn for someone they do not consider their equal, since in Spain no one is ever addressed as *excellency*.

---

* An estate of land and the inhabiting Indians, granted to Spanish colonists and conquistadors for purposes of tribute and evangelization.
** Literally, gracefulness, charm, flair.
*** A shortened form of *Vuestra Excelencia* (Your Excellency).

But, the *don* notwithstanding, an honorific that today is used so prodigally, in Spain one can easily recognize a noble, because nobles do not pay taxes nor do they offer lodgings, and have the right to wear a sword. Nor do they billet troops, but when the king goes on campaign, they are all obliged to go to war as distinguished soldiers and ride a horse, a privilege denied commoners. The title *caballero** comes from this. In America, since by the terms of the Laws of the Indies the sons of the conquistadors and first settlers and nobles who possess an ancestral home and a known lineage are *caballeros,* the custom was introduced of not exacting tribute from the Spaniards but from the Indians, who are as good as the Spaniards; a tribute exacted unjustly, inasmuch as it was imposed on them by right of conquest, and this right, at the instance of Casas,** was revoked in the year 1550 in the most solemn assembly of the members of all the royal tribunals and the elite of learned scholars of the nation gathered together in Valladolid by Charles V, and was rendered null and void by an express law that is in the Code of the Indies and can easily be found by consulting the index, for there is no other law under the letter *C.* However, the right not to pay tribute traditionally enjoyed by Spaniards does not make them nobles. There is no other nobility here, then, save for that of those on whom the rank of noble has been conferred by way of the titles mentioned above and by the degree of doctor awarded by the University of Mexico, a specific law in the Code of the Indies; those who are sons of forebears who had already attained the title of noble in Spain, and those who are the sons of the conquistadors and of the first settlers; that of Indian caciques or nobles, which was also a hierarchy with many ranks; and that of their descendants. The rule concerning [inheritance of noble titles by] women, observed in Castile, with which America is included, was retained.

As for ecclesiastical matters, since the French, in another day, held such total dominion over the crown of Aragon, in Catalonia in particular (although in the eleventh century the French suddenly exerted enormous influence on Church affairs throughout Spain), the customs and rites are all French; the entire congregation gives the responses at recited

---

* In earlier days, the term, like the English word *cavalier,* meant literally "one who rides on horseback." The usual translation is *knight.*

** A reference to Bartolomé de Las Casas (1474–1566), a Spanish Dominican missionary and a fervent defender of the rights of Indians in the New World, well-known for his works documenting the abuses the indigenous peoples suffered at the hands of the conquistadors.

Masses; at the offertory women offer the congregation bread and small candles in little baskets, and the priest, after the ritual washing of hands, announces what has been offered or what has been found in the alms box (because in every village there is an alms priest); a wedding ring is not put on the bride's finger at a nuptial Mass, and *mutatis mutandis,* there are similar variations with regard to other things. All the canons in the church wear purple vestments, and number thirty or forty. Large villages where there are no canons have their collegiates or beneficiaries who are present in choir at divine offices. The bishop of Tarragona is the ranking dignitary because it is his see; but the bishop of Urgel holds the sovereign principality of the valley of Andorra, a little valley in the Pyrenees that belongs neither to Spain nor to France. The same thing is true in Navarre, where the bishop is sovereign in the valley of Roncal. But because these sovereignties are so small and so wretchedly poor, no one takes any notice of them, and they are permitted so that they will be heard of far and wide. In like fashion, the king of Spain calls himself the Lord of Molina, which is a miserable hole. For the same reason I saw in the highlands, at the foot of a mountain, a tall crag with a stout band of iron tied around it. And I was told: "This is what the Count of Peñasco,* who is our count, takes his title from." That is the whole of his estate and landed property in Spain.

Note something else: the fact that when we were given lodging in wartime, it made no difference whether people wrote to us or said that we were at the house of the widow so-and-so or at the house of the canon or beneficiary so-and-so. Every priest has a widow as his housekeeper. Consequently, it is widows in Catalonia who are the unlawful spouses of priests. In Spain one finds in every priest's house a good-looking young girl who is spoken of as his niece, and usually she is there to look after her "uncle's" needs and offer the hospitality of his house. Every man of the cloth has his housekeeper, who accompanies him everywhere, even when he travels, and it is the town they visit that pays her fare. Sometimes a priest has two and sometimes three concubines: one is the housekeeper, another the seamstress and another the maidservant, and in general the priest is the best-looking man for leagues around. And with every step you take, the villagers tell you a spicy little story and pass on a bit of scandalous gossip. When the Popes were determined to take priests' lawfully wedded wives away from them, the laws of Spain allowed them to keep concubines, so that, it is said, the

---

* *Peñasco* means crag in Spanish.

wives of the priests' neighbors would be safe. And these concubines are allowed to wear certain distinctive signs on their clothing, which according to the law whores who walk the streets are not permitted to wear, because concubines are respectable women, and by law their children are the heirs of the priests who fathered them. I was in La Montaña in the village of Soñanes, the seat of the very rich Marquis or Count of Contramina, to whom, no matter how many promises he made, the highlanders of the valley of Carriedo refused to grant the honor of being the mayor of the village, because he was descended from Saint Peter. But in order to be granted a title of nobility, he brought suit before the chancery of Valladolid and won his claim that the sons of priests of La Montaña are nobles.

But there is no doubt that Catalan priests and friars do not know Castilian, and their schooling is rudimentary. The University of Cervera is the only one they have, and it is a very fine edifice, built by the Bourbons, because in the war of succession Cervera was always on the side of Philip V; but the university has no reputation in Spain. In Catalonia it is the Dominicans who teach Theology, and the *escolapios** belles lettres, all in Catalan; they detest Castilian and have such a dislike of Castilians that in order to scare children their mothers tell them that "the Castilian" is coming and is going to knock their block off, and the children run away in fear and trembling. In Tarragona I saw that in order to offer benediction to the choir, the deacon raises his hands up only as far as his shoulders, as a priest does when he says *Dominus vobiscum*, and all the canons do likewise, turning to face one another. This was the ceremony observed by Jews and those who followed the Oriental rite to greet one another and wish one another prosperity, and that is where that same ceremony comes from in our *Dominus vobiscum*.

There is a strange town in Catalonia, Tortosa, whose inhabitants never say that they are Catalans, but Tortosans rather, and in fact, since Tortosa is equidistant from the three capitals of the crown of Aragon, namely Barcelona, Valencia and Zaragoza, it is said that people from there are as stubborn as the Aragonese, as fickle as the Valencians, as unruly and rebellious as the Catalans. But this is quite enough about them.

Leaving Barcelona for Madrid presents difficulties these days, because in Spain, as in the rest of Europe, there is no such thing as coaches that travel on every day and at every hour that one would like. It is necessary

---

* Teaching monks. Their name is derived from that of their order, Escuelas Pías, charitable schools.

to wait till chance or a return trip brings a coach and pair that are going your way, or a calash or cart. And after that it is necessary to go about looking for companions to occupy the other seats and help pay the fare, because drivers ask more than a hundred doubloons for a seat in a coach that is going only fifty or sixty leagues. A doubloon is the same as three pesos, and if it is a gold one, four. So it costs more to go sixty leagues within Spain than it does to go three hundred in another country.

Next comes the task of getting a meal, because when a person arrives at the inn and asks what there is to eat, the reply is: "Whatever Your Grace may have brought with him to make a meal of." And at best, the answer is that they have eggs and sardines. It is necessary to take one's own food along from place to place. But, as has already been said, there are no butcher shops except in the big cities and towns. In the others, when someone gets rid of an ox because it has grown too old, and so on, the butcher goes out at night with a trumpet or a drum, walks about the streets playing it, and then shouts at the top of his lungs that So-and-So's ox has been slaughtered, that it was raised in such and such a place, grazed in such and such a pasture and is good meat. The following day people gather to buy it, and there is rejoicing in the town. There is no such thing as pork butchers' shops. Pigs are killed only on All Saints' Day. During the remainder of the year, the neighbor who is more or less well-off raises his piglet and kills it at that time. He then has enough meat for the entire year, because today a little ear of the pig is thrown into the turnip stew, which is people's usual fare; on another day one more little piece is thrown in, and that way it lasts the whole year long.

In the villages where there is a butcher shop and a person needs to fill his stew pot, which he has hung from the back of the coach to bring it to the village, he must hunt up the butcher, because no one else can carve up meat to eat; it is a disgraceful occupation, just as being an innkeeper is. It would occur only to Spaniards to regard as disreputable two occupations so innocent and so absolutely necessary to society. In contrast, there is the registry office of the guards at Customs, who search everything in a most unseemly way as one goes from kingdom to kingdom, making a shambles of every piece of a person's baggage and leaving his clothes strewn about on the ground if he does not grease their palm. If anyone is carrying money and doesn't register it, it is taken away from him. At every step there are tolls that must be paid, that is to say, a certain fee that is exacted for the use of bridges and roads, so as to pay for repairing them. The difference in languages, in laws from one city to another, in money and its value makes travel even more vexing. And to top it all off they ask whatever price they like for a damnable meal, a hard, dirty, filthy bed in a garret, where one is assailed by the smoke from the kitchen, and then they demand payment for the noise a person has made, even if he's been as quiet as a dead man, and then after that comes the pins given to the maidservant as a tip and at the horn post where the horses are tethered. And there is nothing one can do but pay, because if the inn is an isolated one, it is the innkeeper himself who administers justice. So foreigners despair and curse at Spain. And youngsters follow the coach, begging for alms.

I didn't find one for hire, nor did I have the means to pay, but one is not much better off taking one, because they go very slowly, at the same pace as the coachman, who usually walks alongside and after only a few minutes stops to feed his mules, who understand the names they are called by, colonel, captain and so on. The Neapolitan and I struck a bargain with the driver of a Catalan cart. But the jolting in such carts is intolerable, and there is always the risk that it will turn over and the load that it is carrying will kill those traveling in it. This is not an unusual occurrence, and so I went all the way to Madrid on foot, stopping to wait for the cart to catch up at places where I was told we could get something to eat and spend the night.

As soon as we began to see pint-size men, wearing a little short jacket and a hat that in Spain is worn only by Aragonese, we knew that we were in the land of the *coño*. For just as all other Spaniards add a forthright *ajo* at the end of every word, with the exception of the Valencians, who say *pacho*, which is an indecent name for the business of procreation, so the Aragonese use *co*—*] with every word. And this is the way the boy called out to his sister when I arrived at a house with a billet for lodging: "Co—, go on, tell our co—of a mother that the co—of a soldier is here." In certain other countries *ajo* and *col* ** go together. Is it not scandalous that the Spanish people cannot say three words without interjecting such a lewd word, something that is not done in any other country?

In general the Aragonese speak a very ugly Castilian with a heavy beat; they look like rats, though these rats have a great deal of courage; and they are so obstinate that just as a man hammering a nail with his forehead is a symbol for a Basque, so a man hammering it with the end

---

*   Euphemistic form of *coño*, cunt.

**   A double entendre, since *ajo* and *col* are vulgar terms for, respectively, the male and female pudenda, and in decent language *ajo* means garlic and *col* cabbage.

of it pointed toward his forehead is a symbol for an Aragonese. Some of the women are rather pretty, but in miniature, the way dolls are, because they have very tiny faces and their hair is very black. The region is arid, the mountainsides barren because the soil is calcareous. On the outskirts of the villages there is a pocket in the earth, where rainwater collects; it is covered with a green crust, and this is what constitutes the water supply of the village. There is good wine in Aragon, although it is a bit weak, and the wine of Caviñena is famous. But they are such oafs that when Charles IV was in Catalonia around the year 1802, the mayor of Caviñena sent a group of men with torches out two or three leagues beyond the town so as to light the king's way should he come by night. But as soon as the king had lunched in another village, he went on toward Caviñena. The *"tíos,"** which is what commoners who are workers or men who are not *caballeros* are called, shouted, "Light your torch, he's coming," as soon as they spied him; and at two in the afternoon, when the summer sun is hottest, the monarch was racing along in his coach, and the men who were escorting him on either side kept shouting to each other, "Run, run, you *co*——; you're falling behind," and the king arrived in Caviñena in a blaze of light and sweltering. And then the *tíos* asked the king how the kids were. I did not set foot in Zaragoza, though I saw the maze of its streets, and saw nothing else that was noteworthy save for the church of Nuestra Señora del Pilar, and inside it her little round chapel, many years old, and held up by columns, except for the back. To one side is the image of the Virgin of Pilar, in the middle the altar where Mass is said, with an image of Our Lady, in marble, up above, who is pointing out to Saint James (a statue of whom is on the other side) the place where the Virgin of Pilar is. Nowadays no one, except for the common people of Aragon, places any credence in this tradition.[3] It was not only denied by Benedict XIV and Natal Alejandro, and rejected as false by Ferreras, along with countless others who deny that Saint James ever preached in Spain; learned professors of History have told me that it was an absolutely untenable belief. "I have in my possession," I was told by Dr. Traggia, an Aragonese and the Church chronicler of Aragon, "the oldest extant document and it dates from the fourteenth century." When on the Church calendar the day came to recite the prayers to the Virgin of Pilar or the Virgin of Loreto, Dr. Yéregui, the inquisitor of the Supreme Tribunal and the tutor of the infantes of Spain, recited instead those of the eighth day of

---

* Literally, *uncles*. Familiarly, *guys, chaps,*, etc.

September,* because he said that the stories of their lives were intolerable fables. At the time when the city was besieged by the French, people said that three palm trees had been seen above her temple; but when Zaragoza was captured, after more than sixty thousand souls had died from the siege and from an epidemic, the image lost a great deal of its reputation. Today the city is a heap of ruins, because of the resistance, as stubborn as it was foolish, that its inhabitants put up, thanks to thirty thousand men of the Army of the Center, who had taken their stand with them.

We passed through Daroca, where I went to see the famous Communion cloths tinged with the blood that had flowed from several consecrated Hosts, and we entered Castile by night. For that reason my Neapolitan did not have a chance to see the typical dress of Castilians, who wear a pointed woolen cap on their head, a small tight-fitting black waistcoat with buttons, black knee breeches and long stockings of the sort that were worn before Philip II, the first person in Spain to wear hose, presented to him as a gift by a very rich lady from Toledo. They are also in the habit of carrying a pilgrim's staff or rod. This is precisely the costume worn by the Three Wise Men in all the theaters of Europe. The Neapolitan lay down in the feeble light of a little lamp, and had dropped off to sleep when I sent word to him by way of the "uncle" who was the innkeeper to come have dinner. The Neapolitan, who on awakening found himself alone with that figure, leaped out of bed and began running about shouting: "A Wise Man, a Wise Man!"

In Castile there is bread and wine and nothing else; the stew is made of turnips; and the lack of trade because of its distance from ports keeps it poverty-stricken, and its villages are wretchedly poor and filthy. The architecture of the houses made me laugh; the wall with the door is a high one, and the one in front so low that the roof touches the ground; and nearly all of them are made of earth and have one story lower than the street. The door is secured by one or two boards tied together with a rope. The piglet, the hen, the cat and the dog live inside the house with them. In the wintertime, people wear a dark-colored cape of very coarse wool. The women either cover their head with a mantilla of coarse cloth or else they wear a cap like the men, and a shawl in place of a mantilla. This latter is the usual attire of the women of La Montaña, which they wear even to church, although the women from Vizcaya and from the Pas valley wear a kerchief tied around their head. Speaking of these

---

* September 8 is celebrated as the feast day of the Nativity of Our Lady.

women from the Pas valley, who are highlanders of La Montaña, almost from the moment they begin to walk they are given panniers, that is to say, a basket to sling over their back, which they always wear as an adornment, whether full or empty, and always when they are sent out to earn their dowry. From France they hurry about, heavily laden, all over Spain, and often make their way across the mountains to hide their contraband. In their own way these women are the equivalent of the Galicians who are to be found everywhere, working as harvesters, porters or water carriers, because their part of Spain is so miserably poor, or like the highlanders from La Montaña, who go about selling *agua de aloja** or dried fruit, and the Asturians, who are lackeys. The women from Vizcaya are often seen outside their own province as well, because they run on foot in front of coaches, like the boys who are muleteers' helpers, as far away as Madrid. In their home territory they are the porters, the sailors and the mule drivers. I have seen them departing from Bayonne in France on foot, leading their mule, with a passenger seated on either side of the animal, in a sort of little side saddle. The women of La Montaña who are not from the Pas valley do not leave home, for they are working the land. They are the ones who do the plowing and the sowing; nearly all the men take off for America.

I did not see Castilians doing the plowing, although the poor wretches dress in the same way as all other Spaniards, in ordinary thick flannel garments that make them look very roly-poly, with shirts and white shawls thicker than our Indians' blankets. This cloth is called homespun. Fine linen cloth made in Brittany was almost unknown even in Madrid; and in order to wear a shirt of fine cloth in Spain, it is necessary to be someone with a great deal of money. Their feet and legs are bare, of course, or else they wear wooden clogs. The petticoats of Valencian women usually do not go below the knee. At the slightest movement a person can see everything they have from there on up, as is true also of Valencian men in their *enagüilles* or *zaragüelles*,** if when they sit down they do not carefully tuck them to one side. One thing I noted in the towns of La Montaña is that the women look like identical Capuchin nuns, all dressed in one-piece outer garments of the same color and made of the same cloth. A nail in the wall that catches up this gar-

---

* A soft drink made of water, honey and spices.

** *Enagüillas* are kilts, and *zaragüelles* wide-legged breeches with pleats or loose folds. Once the traditional costume of Valencia, they are still sometimes worn by men who work in the fields.

ment from behind serves them as a *desnudador*,* and once they have removed this garment they turn out to have been as naked underneath it as the day they were born.

We are gradually approaching Madrid, but whereas in other countries one can tell that one is close to the capital because of the villas, the country residences or little villages that are more refined, Madrid is surrounded on every side by miserable villages in ruins, with all the dwellings made of earth, and full of wretchedly poor people; there is not a tree to be seen anywhere about; the arid terrain assails the eye until one reaches the very gates of the city. The first time I entered Madrid I came by way of the Fuencarral gate, and just as in other cities one spies marble columns, I saw two very tall ones and asked what they were. Dung for making bread. I stuck my head out of the coach, and on every corner I saw pairs of billboards with huge letters that read: "Don Gregorio Sencsens and don Somebody-or-Other make trusses for both sexes." I fancied that Madrid was a town full of people with hernias, but it is merely a town peopled by a degenerate race, for native-born Madrileños look like dwarfs, and every once in a while I had a fine time romping with some little girl or other whom I took to be eight or nine yeas old, and it turned out that she was over sixteen. It is commonly said that natives of Madrid are big-headed, runts, gabblers, broad in the beam, founders of rosary processions and second-generation jailbirds. And then there is the mark on their neck of the Hospital of Antón Martín, the mark left by the Gallic disease,** since in Madrid the first signs of it appear on people's necks.

On almost the same day that I arrived I saw a procession on the calle de Atocha, and when I asked what it was, I was told that people were going to pay their respects to the p——*** Virgin. And it so happens that since the image of her is a very pretty one, a procuress was displaying it between the bars of a window so as to attract customers. The language of the people of Madrid reveals them for what they are, the crudest in Spain. One of the streets is called Arranca-culos, Grab—Ass Street, another Tentetieso—Tumble Doll Street, one Majaderitos Anchos—Broad Stupid Idiot Street, another Majaderitos Angostos—Narrow

---

* Probably a word made up by fray Servando, meaning a device that serves to strip off their outer garment.

** The term, in common use until modern times, comes from the title of a Latin poem by Fracastoro, entitled "Syphilis sive Morbus Gallicus" (1530), after the hero Syphilus.

*** Fray Servando's euphemism here stands for *puta*, whore.

Stupid Idiot Street. A man selling milk goes down the street shouting "Who will buy this milk or this shit from me?" Women cry out: "A dozen eggs: who wants my very own eggs?"* Everything is sold by the *maíz,* meaning *maravedís.* The Castilian they speak sounds like this: "Manolo, que lijiste al médicu?" "Lije que te viniera a curar del estogamo aluna, y le daríamos cien maís."** I have heard a beggar asking for alms say: "Sir, toss me an alms penny for love of the little God; it's the day of the procession of the Good Shepherd"; the day of the "big God" is Corpus Christi. They call any corner the "main corner," and the door of a house a "portal."

Well-bred people from every part of the monarchy live in the center of Madrid; but they can't go out to the barrios, because decent people are insulted there. In the barrios people live the way they do in villages. The men shave themselves and the women do their sewing out on the street. The most heavily populated and insolent barrio is Avapiés. And when there is a row*** between *manolos**** in the barrios, one from Avapiés is the caller. They earned this privilege in a stone fight in which the combatants were mounted on donkeys. Even kings are afraid to go into the barrios, and one day when the queen was out riding in her coach along the Manzanares River, where the women from the barrios do their washing, they called her a p—, because the price of bread was high. The queen took to her heels, and some thirty women were arrested, but were immediately released, because the whole incident was already only too public.

What are *manolos?* The same thing as *curros* in Andalusia. Manolo is short for Manuelito, and Curro for Francisco. They are people who were born in the region, people who have no education, insolent, blowhards and in a word, Spaniards *au naturel,* who with their knife or with stones do a person in, if necessary, after hurling a thousand insults. They are the dandies, the braggarts and show-offs who are pimps for women like themselves, just as shameless as they are; among such women are all the fruit vendors and old clothes peddlers. They do not wear tunics, but pet-

---

* A play on the Spanish word *huevera,* meaning ovary.
** In standard Castilian, the passage would be pronounced: "*Manolo, qué le dijiste al médico?*" "*Le dije que le viniera a curar del estómago a la una, y le daríamos cien maravedís.*" The meaning is: "Manolo, what did you tell the doctor?" "I told him that he should come treat you for your stomachache at one o'clock, and we'd give him a hundred *maravedís.*"
*** Making a pun, Fray Servando uses here the slang word *fandango,* also a popular dance.
**** A typical Madrileño from a popular quarter of the city. See the following paragraph for fray Servando's explanation of the origin of the word.

ticoats, a little short jacket and long hair with ribbons in it. The men wear a tight-fitting waistcoat, trousers, a three-cornered hat, long hair caught up in a big knot and a cape with sleeves slung over their shoulder, decorated all over with gaudy ribbons, tawdry dangles and fripperies, and a cigar in their mouth. These are the real people of Madrid, and they are born police magistrates who hand down decisions by way of stone fights and riots. Sometimes the women have wanted to dress better or change their traditional costume, abandoning the look of black beetles or scarabs, the difference between them and Castilian ladies being that the latter wear a white mantilla of muslin or some other cloth, and Andalusian women black silk ones; but the *manolos* won't allow them to change. In this regard they are on their worst behavior on Holy Thursday and Good Friday, which are the real Carnival days in Madrid. Since coaches are not used on those days, and great ladies have to walk, they order dresses for church made for them that are sometimes truly scandalous, and at times they have tried to dress in purple. Although they had life-guardsmen accompanying them, when I was there the *manolos* stoned them, and in order to calm the populace down, General Urrutia ordered the guards to be locked up in their barracks. The women withdrew to their houses, and the councilors of the Crown were barely able to save them by surrounding them with their constables, the only ones whom *manolos* respect, because the sight of troops teaches them a lesson and the constables attack them. So each year the king's ministers are obliged to put up handbills on Shrove Tuesday ordering the women to dress discreetly. And it is fortunate that the *manolos* have assumed the role of policemen, for there would be no limit to the licentiousness and the women would appear in public naked.

In no part of Europe are women as determined as are Spanish ones to show off their breasts, and I have come upon women on the public promenade with their breasts all the way out, and wearing gold rings on their nipples, and likewise on the toes of their naked feet, just as their whole arm is bared from the shoulder down. And since they cannot go bare-legged, they wear flesh-colored stockings. *Manolos* are not permitted to stroll about the Botanical Garden and the Paseo del Retiro, where no one is allowed in without a cape or a mantilla because it is a royal estate, and no one can enter in a carriage save the intendant of the royal residence; this is where the most striking spectacles are to be seen: women dressed as goddesses and priestesses, or with such a light dress that every last detail of their body shows through.

After vespers the Puerta del Sol (that is what people call a little public square in front of the post office, and it is the most public spot in Madrid) and all the adjoining streets are taken over by countless numbers of young prostitutes, very smartly turned out with their fine outer pettiskirts and white mantillas, who spend the evening simply walking back and forth at a very brisk pace, as though they had business other than the sort that they are really looking for, and they bustle about like that till ten o'clock at night. Once a bargain has been struck they hurry off to the hallways and stairs of nearby houses, and when I entered mine at night there wasn't room to set my foot down, because of the diphthongs on the landings. There is a great deal of procuring, but this is for the more decent men. All this makes for many surprises, because the hallways of Madrid are public pissoirs and privies, and one must make one's way inside a building by a narrow little path down the middle, holding up the bottom of one's garments so as not to get dirtied.

There is as much disorder everywhere. Even in Church precincts this is so, because of the multitude of exempt jurisdictions. The jurisdiction of the patriarch of the Indies is exempt, because it is military, as is that of the Crusade, of the Inquisition, of the military Orders, and of the monastic Orders as well. If they care to do so, friars can attend theaters openly, and on the bill of publicly posted admission prices that is printed at the beginning of each year, one of the items listed is "such and such a price for religious," this price being one real more than a vellón, a Spanish real not amounting to even half a real in our money. The reason behind this was the fact that one night at the Opera there was a very large audience and it filled the entire amphitheater, that is to say, the seats that go all the way around the courtyard below the first ring of boxes. In the silence of an intermission, it being already nearly midnight, a clown of a friar, intoned in the middle of the courtyard *Domine labia mea aperies,* * as at the beginning of matins. There was such laughter and it caused such a scandal that the friars donned their hoods and decamped. Cardinal Molina, the archbishop of Toledo, then added that real to the price everyone else paid, in order to discourage religious from attending: that is how miserably poor they are.

The life-guardsmen are the stallions of Madrid. Four companies of one hundred noble youths each, called the Spanish, American, Flemish and Italian companies, are called life-guardsmen. They stand guard at

* Lord, open my lips.

the Palace with their carbine, and in groups of five always precede the carriages of the members of the royal families, galloping ahead in front of them with their swords held on high. In Godoy's day, at the suggestion of Beristáin, the American company was organized, and wore bandoliers with purple checks, since that was the queen's color; the Spanish company wears bandoliers with red checks, the Italian with green, and the Flemish with yellow. Today there are almost no American life-guardsmen left; but there were many of them in the beginning, and they were the ones who introduced a note of luxury, for before they arrived, life-guardsmen wore simple cotton stockings and narrow bandoliers. As a general rule, they are libertines who corrupt young girls.

But the ones who are the biggest corrupters and deflowerers of young girls who come to Madrid seeking work as domestics are the grandees of Spain. And who are they? The lowest men in the nation because of their ignorance and their vices. They are the tycoons, called in bygone days the *ricós-homes,* of the nation. Because of the disturbances that their arrogance caused in the kingdom each time a king was elected, the kingdom of Spain was made hereditary, less by means of the passage of laws as through the common accord of the people, so as to avoid such disorders. The grandees took their stand against the people, in favor of the despotism of Charles V and his successors, at the time of the wars of the *comuneros* to uphold the Constitution of Spain. Because of the fear that the kings had of them, they obtained any number of possessions, in particular what were called "Henry favors," and took over nearly the whole of Spain. Once seated on the throne of despotism, the kings summoned the grandees to Court with the aim of making them go bankrupt trying to equal their magnificence, and they succeeded in doing so; but they also managed to ruin the towns of which they are the feudal lords, because they overburdened them with taxes and sucked them dry in order to keep themselves in luxury at court, so that money has not flowed back into the towns, where the grandees do not reside; hence the people of feudal towns in Spain are the poorest of all. The kings gave the fifty grandees posts at the Palace, where they succeed one another in turn as chief stewards, so as to train them thereby to be obedient and learn their place as servants, and demeaned them thereby. But at the same time, since they have money, they have given themselves over to vice. They do not have honorary titles or positions at Court, nor does anyone else outside of the royal family.

They fall into three classes; but the difference is simply that those of the first class don their hats before greeting the king, those of the second class greet him and then doff their hat, and those of the third don it after greeting him. This ceremony takes place only on the day when the king receives the grandees. To be received, a grandee must have an income of thirty thousand pesos. But there are grandees who are very poor. The richest and most respectable of them were the Dukes of Medinaceli, who had an income of thirteen million; the Duke of Alba, who had eleven million, and the holder of the infante's appanage, with four or five million. By this I mean sums in millions of reales; fifty thousand pesos is a million reales; although all the grandees are debt-ridden, because their incomes do not suffice to pay for their luxuries, and they keep securing royal orders so that they will not be compelled to pay their creditors. They are the patrons of countless churches in their domains; they give out canonries, benefices and a thousand salaried posts, in addition to the influence they have at Court that enables them to obtain them. Thus almost all those employed in the royal offices are servants and lackeys of the grandees or relatives of the latter's concubines. One of them offered me a handsome benefice that he had in his domain so that I would provide him with a means of pulling the wool over the eyes of a young lady by having me perform an invalid marriage, for the purpose of satisfying his lust, a proposal that horrified me. In their own way, the wives of grandees are usually as corrupt as their spouses, and in my time *reginae ad exemplum*;* the entire Court and the Sitio were a brothel.

The *camaristas*, the queen's maids-in-waiting, are the Palace nuns; they live very well, however, on the top floor, though no one can see them or talk to them except in most ceremonious fashion, as they do toward their duennas, who are grandees or ladies-in-waiting to the queen, once they have reached the age of discretion. These noble young ladies destined to serve the queen and princesses on days when ceremonies are held leave the Palace by marrying men who are seeking official positions, because they have as their dowry the best posts in the nation. A German woman around the age of fifty, a servant of the queen, was given as a dowry the right to appoint the director of the Mexican lottery. Several candidates competed for the position; but the elderly lady took a liking to Obregón, a Mexican twenty-six years old, because women who are well along in years are always fond of young men who cannot love them, because nobody can love death, which is what an old woman represents. And all of a sudden, there was Obregón, director general. That was the only way in which a Creole could get a top post. There are

---

*   . . . following the queen's example.

ladies-in-waiting to the queen who are all grandees of Spain, and Godoy's sister had great influence; but the queen's closest confidante when it came to her scandalous love affairs was Verdes.

The Palace servants have uniforms trimmed with gold braid, yet they are poor as church mice because they still receive the same salaries as in the days when they were paid by a thrifty king. Today valets (whose uniform is of silk, with no trimming, and their insignia an iron key on the pocket of their jacket, hanging outside by the eye from a silver chain) are usually *caballeros*. But by their letter patent one can see what they once were: "inasmuch," it says, "as you are a man handy with a needle and thread, and know neither how to read nor how to write, I make you my valet." Chamberlains have a gold key embroidered on their pocket, on the left side of their jacket. A kitchen chef is called a gentleman of the mouth, and each one of the infantes had all these sorts of servants, so that along with the salaries of the counselors, who are considered to be members of the Palace staff, the daily expenses amounted to a million reales, or fifty thousand of our pesos. Ferdinand has limited all the infantes to one tableful of servants. Most of the employees supported themselves on the perquisites of their office, because in order to give the king just a couple of eggs an entire basket was examined, and so on with everything else, and what was left over went to the kitchen chefs. When the king emptied his bowels, a valet held in front of him three yards of household linen for him to dry his hands, and this linen cloth, which was discarded, became a perquisite of the chamberlain of the lavatory, and so on. The king's cup is paid the same honors as a grandee of Spain. It is carried from place to place with four halberdiers in attendance, and everyone doffs his hat.

Charles IV, like Charles III, spent his days hunting on the royal country estates, within whose bounds no one save the king can hunt, and any number of beaters (all of whom are from a village in Castile called Espinosa de los Monteros) accompany him so as to flush the game and herd it past him. And in the time of Charles IV a syringe was also brought along so as to give an injection to a beater named Montril, who pretended to die of embarrassment when the king ordered him to be given the injection, and he managed to support his whole family very well with his melodramatic playacting. A great many spaniels are also brought along for the hunt. And the king would go out hunting rain or shine. Sometimes he was obliged to proceed on foot because his carriage got stuck in the snow. When the hunt was going to take place a long way off, everyone left the royal estate at three in the morning, in cold that numbed the dogs. But the ones who had the worst time of it were the life-guardsmen, who even though it rained buckets or was freezing cold, always had to go about without a coat, and always at a run, because that is how the horses draw the king's carriage. The royal Sitios, or country estates, are: Aranjuez, seven leagues from Madrid; La Granja, or San Idelfonso, fourteen leagues distant, which is the best Sitio because of its gardens. The crystal factory was located there, and its abbot is mitered. There is also a collection of ludicrous figures there, ancient gods of the Spaniards; the Prado, abandoned after the death of Charles III; the Retiro in the Prado in Madrid, abandoned since Philip II, inside which is the China warehouse; and the Escorial or San Lorenzo, which was built by Philip II to fulfill a vow made to that holy martyr, in thanks for his victory at the battle of San Quintín. It is a vast monastery, with very beautiful paintings by the best painters of Italy and Spain at the time. The so-called pearl is the best one. Hieronymite monks live in half of the Escorial, and the king in half. The Spaniards consider it a marvel, but to me it seemed no more than a heap of stones. What there admittedly is in the Escorial is a great store of luxuries, amassed there by Philip II in the days when he ruled over half of Europe. Money, which came in large part from America, was worth four times as much as it is today, and the price of things had not gone up: so that the pay of the master builder was a real and a half a day, which amounts to half a real and a cuartilla in American money. All the nuns in Italy worked at making religious adornments, and the number of chasubles alone that they made added up to two thousand five hundred. There are many relics, a Host in particular, that is said to be incorruptible, kept inside a Moorish gold watch case in the shape of a little tower.

The library of Arab manuscripts, seized from a Moorish king, was also located there. This library burned down, though a large part of it was saved. A Hieronymite monk is the librarian, and merely by saying that he is a Hieronymite he betrays the fact that he is a lout, for it is an Order of singers and gluttons, and that is why Hieronymites are called Jesus Christ's fattened pigs. I had the same opinion of the librarian as an ambassador of France, who, on being asked by the king what he thought of his library, replied: "Excellent; but Your Majesty ought to make your librarian Minister of the Exchequer, or comptroller general, because he never touches anything deposited with him."

The royal tombs are also there, alongside the sacristy. They are in a little vault all lined with veined marble, which one reaches by going down stairs made of the same stone, and in several marble urns, each with its inscription, are the bones of kings, queens and infantes who left issue. I have said the bones, for once they die the kings are taken to the rotting vault. There they are put under an open water tap that trickles down drop by drop, rotting the flesh until the bones are as white as paper. When I was there, I was told that Charles III was still in the rotting vault. I visited that vault, making the appropriate reflections on the fragility of things human.

While I was there, one of the Palace staff, a man well along in years, married a young girl, and I saw the charivari that is the custom in Spain in such a case: a crowd of pranksters gather and ring cowbells all night long and make a tremendous racket around the house of the elderly groom so as to keep him from sleeping. From a balcony, the queen was presiding over the teasing by the whole Palace staff, life-guardsmen and Walloon guards. Because in addition to the life-guardsmen, there are other corps of Spanish Walloon guards, who do not wear bandoliers; but officers wear velvet cartridge belts. The sergeants are officers, the cadets receive the rank of captains, the captains that of colonels, and the colonel is a grandee of Spain, a lieutenant–or captain–general. The royal corps of guardsmen have many privileges, but they are also in the front line on the battlefield. When they are on duty, the life-guardsmen wear red hose, as do the halberdiers, and also the pages. These latter are youngsters of the nobility who are educated in a special school. When the king goes out for a ride in his carriage, they follow after him in one or two carriages, crowded together like souls in Purgatory. They serve at table, and bow in the Spanish fashion of long ago, bending their torsos and parting their legs without moving their feet apart. The grandees and lords also have their well-bred little pages, as do the viceroy and the archbishop here in our country. Footmen in livery are called pages; and in Mexico it is disgusting that rectors of the university (since Francisco Cisneros, nicknamed Pancho Molote) outfit footmen with swords and place them behind their carriage; it is crass ignorance and an outrage. The sword is the distinction of nobles and knights, and even though they are nobles, the very fact that they serve as footmen would degrade their wearers. On ceremonial days the queen's ladies-in-waiting and other gentlewomen also wear hooped petticoats with big bulging pouches at the hips to put their arms in. I have never seen an uglier and more ridiculous thing, yet I have seen the same attire in England.

The king's ministers are the ones who head the four secretariats of State: the first secretariat of State, that of Pardon and Justice, of the Exchequer, and of War, which is usually combined with that of the Navy, but not always; and all of them have their share of pen-pushing bureaucrats, who go from there to the Councils when they fall from power, except for those of the first secretariat of State, who end up at the secretariats of the four embassies that used to be under the jurisdiction of the Bourbons: Portugal, France, Naples and America. The others are ministers in the Cortes, and when the authorities wish to honor them, they are appointed envoys extraordinary.

In order to understand what the Councils are it must be remembered that long ago the king was the only judge, journeyed throughout the kingdom rendering justice and was accompanied by the Court Council, made up of bishops, abbots, grandees, members of the military, legal experts and statesmen, treasury officials, etcetera. In the thirteenth century the Constitution of Spain was changed in this regard, through the municipal charters that the kings granted to cities and towns, as a reward for the services they had rendered in the wars against the Moors. Inasmuch as the towns already had mayors, the Court Council then had no other function than to hear appeals and was divided into branches according to its members' professions. For civil cases the Council of Castile was established; it is the supreme Council of the kingdom, with its magistrates' court for criminal cases. Although the Council of State, which meets only once for political affairs, is considered to be on a higher level, and is composed of ministers, grandees, generals, and the like, and all of them have the honorific title of Excellency, whereas the members of the Council of Castile bear only the title of Your Lordship and the chamberlains Your Most Illustrious Lordship. The Council of the Exchequer is made up of people who understand the handling of public funds. The members of the Council of the four military Orders are knights of those Orders. There are other Councils as well: the Council of the Inquisition; the Crusade Council; the Supreme Council of the Indies, instituted at the instance of Bartolomé de Las Casas in 1525, that does not have a magistrate's court but has its chamber and a governor. The Council of Castile has a president only when its head is not a grandee of Spain. If he is a grandee, he is called the governor. Councils before the reign of Charles V have the honorific Highness, which was the one reserved for kings up until that time. This is the honorific for the Council of Castile and that for the third court of the Council of the Indies; the courts of the Council of Government have the title of Majesty, as do the other councils. In earlier times all the independent kingdoms of Castile, such as Italy, Flanders, Portugal and Aragon, had a council, up until they were made part of the kingdom of Castile.

Of these councils the only remaining one is that of the Indies, proof of the fact that the Indies are an independent kingdom of Spain. The members of the councils of each kingdom were native-born, and according to Solórzano the Council of the Indies should be composed only of Americans. But through a legal fiction officials of the secretariats of the Indies, and the deans or other judges who have been naturalized because they have been in the Indies for ten years, are promoted to it. Since, unfortunately, a legal fiction does not change people's inclinations, they do not love America. On the contrary, having conceived here the same hatred that their countrymen have for us, they are our greatest enemies. The regular salary of all Council members is fifteen hundred pesos, and thus it is no wonder that they sell everything they have to support their family.

The Chamber of Castile is like the Council of the Kingdom of Navarre, the only one that has a lieutenant viceroy as America does, because although it is incorporated, that is to say, dependent on the king of Spain as king of Castile, as is our America, its Constitution (which now has the force of law) provides that a session of the Parliament be held each year, which the king is to attend as its presiding officer, swearing to uphold the Constitution. Every three years the king grants the viceroy special power to open and adjourn it. Ferdinand VII agreed that it should continue to hold sessions as in the time of Charles IV. But since the Parliament had declared one of Ferdinand's orders to be contrary to the Constitution, as it has always had the freedom to do, at the time when I took off for America the king had ordered all the deputies imprisoned, because the words *Cortes* and *Constitution* terrify him, when today nearly all the kings of Europe have instituted parliaments and a constitution; so that in countries with a population of ninety million, which is more than half of Europe, kings today are constitutional monarchs. Godoy had already dealt the law codes of Vizcaya, governed as a republic of which the king serves as a sort of president, an equally strong blow.

I don't know of there being any other viceroy in Spain save for the one of Navarre, although Portugal had one in another era, and Aragon. They are called either governor, as in Valencia, or general, as in Catalonia and in Valladolid. For in addition to the Council of Castile, Valladolid, the Court of Castilla la Vieja, and Granada, the Court of the Moorish kings, enjoy the privilege of having chanceries, that is to say, a pretorial Tribunal, which uses a royal seal, the keeper of which is called the chancellor and decides cases in its name. Like the old Councils, as a body it is addressed as Highness, and appeal is made to it from all the

Tribunals of the district, and its decisions are without appeal. The only recourse is to petition the king or his Court Councils, because the king too is a council. All the other tribunals of Spain are simply tribunals or assemblies of gentlemen of the robe, to which appeal is made from the municipal councils, as appeal is made to these latter from the magistrates' courts, and criminal causes are tried there on appeal. The tribunals have the honorific Your Lordship only when addressed as a body; the individual judges have none.

In our America all tribunals are chanceries, and in the capital of the viceroyalty there is a magistrates' tribunal. It is composed of three courts. In the other chanceries the judges of the second court act as magistrates. Hence our judges are addressed as Your Lordship and can be promoted only to the Council. And this shows how nonsensical it is to use the word *colonies* for kingdoms that enjoy all the prerogatives of the most distinguished kingdoms of Spain. In accordance with the Laws of the Indies we also have assemblies or congresses of cities and towns, in which their right to vote is registered. Mexico City has the first, Tlaxcala the second, and no authority can keep us from appointing deputies for the general Cortes of the nation.

With regard to these legislative bodies, what I have already said must be kept in mind: the fact that in earlier times the king was the only judge of the nation with his Court Council. In each city there was a count (from the Latin *comes*) to fulfill the same function, because he belonged to the company and entourage of the sovereign. The chief authority in a province was called a duke (from *dux*, captain). These names, which in the beginning were *ex officio* titles, became hereditary, because those to whom they were given were able to remain in command and attain enough independence to force the king of Asturias and León to recognize their power, even though they had the duty of coming to the general Cortes of the nation. That is the origin of the grandees of Spain; for that reason, although dukes in England, Portugal and France are princes of the blood and a marquis is above a count, in Spain this is all a matter of indifference: the title of grandee depends on one's relationship with power, not on one's name, although there is no duke who is not a grandee. Certain of these governors who had become independent succeeded in crowning themselves king, as did the governor of Navarre, of Castile, of Aragon, of Galicia, of Portugal, and under the name of count, those of Catalonia, of Valencia and of Majorca. Since then they have ceased to attend the general Cortes, and each of them had the Cortes appertaining to their kingdom; there were also Cortes appertaining to the various independent counts who each had their own, such as the one in Aragon, which was attended by the counts of Catalonia and Valencia. Each kingdom had its own Constitution, as well as a Cortes whose composition varied from kingdom to kingdom. The Cortes of Castile had three branches: the grandees, the bishops and the deputies of the cities and towns. The three together constituted the real sovereignty of the nation. And legislative power resided in the three of them as well as in the king: royal decrees or orders between sessions of the Cortes were considered only as temporary fiscal provisions. After despotism destroyed the Cortes, and the king with his Council of Castile arrogated to himself the right to make laws, the kings nonetheless refer to the old Constitution of Spain when they say: *let this be regarded as a law passed in the Cortes,* as if by so saying the authority of the Nation had been replaced. As for sources of income, the king had only those of his own royal house, and certain fines or pecuniary penalties that were his by right. Only the nation as represented in the Cortes could levy taxes on itself, as is done in England today by its House of Commons. In Spain too this could only be done by the branch of the deputies of the cities and towns. This law was an article of the official Code of Laws* of Castile. Minister Caballero has committed the wicked deed of suppressing it in the *Novísima Recopilación* in order to make the nation forget it.**

When the king needed funds for a war or some other necessary expenditure of the nation, he asked the Cortes for subsidies, and the Cortes might or might not grant them for a certain period of time. And they trod very carefully when doing so, so that the same thing would not happen as with the *alcabala,**** which the Cortes granted the king for the siege of Algeciras, and it was continued to be levied in perpetuity, and he even introduced such a tax in America, where (Solórzano says) there was no reason for it.[4] A holdover of the old right of cities and towns to levy a tax still exists in the case of the deputies of Castile, called *millones,* who attend the Council of Castile. The king was granted the right to collect a tax on everything that was brought into the cities of Castile or sold in them for a period of six years. But every six years he requests that it be renewed, the municipal council of the cities meets, and the intendant has a standing order: if any councilman speaks against the renewal, he is to ad-

---

*   In Spanish, the *Recopilación,* which was established in 1567.
** This new version of the *Recopilación* was compiled in 1805.
*** An excise tax.

journ the session and send word to the authorities to have that poor wretch sent to prison, and secretly garrote him, an order that in Godoy's time was still carried out, by night, in the royal prison. This is the same as asking for alms the way a highwayman used to ask for them on the roads in Spain, by placing his pistol belt or his hat in the middle of the road, as meanwhile he stood around a bend, rifle in hand.

How were the constitutions of Spain and its Cortes destroyed? The despotic Cardinal Cisneros began to pay officers to take Ceuta in Africa and use cannons. Charles V came to power, and as he needed funds for the war with Germany, he began to disregard the Cortes that would not grant them to him or delayed them, and filled it with Flemish supporters of his. Philip II came to the throne, with the money from America in his pocket, which made him the most powerful king in Europe. He paid troops who had previously been conscripted, paid and commanded by Municipal Councils for a certain period; and because the Municipal Councils were once called regiments, that is how that word came to be used for corps of soldiers. With these armed and paid slaves the kings now did as they pleased; and since they were in the process of inheriting all the other kingdoms in Spain through marriage, the same thing as happened in Castile happened all over the country. The nation took up arms, and the groups of insurgents were called communes; but the accursed grandees came to the aid of Philip II. The chief justice of Aragon died on the gallows, as did the constable of Castile and the bishop of Zamora, and the vanquished nation was cast into chains forever. It now tried to cast off its chains, but Ferdinand, with the aid of the grandees and of the troops who in Valencia placed O'Donnell and Elío under their orders, occupied the Cortes, and filled nine prisons in Madrid with its deputies and the flower of the nation, and after that the monasteries of Spain and the prisons of Africa, although a great many of them managed to escape.

There is only a simulacrum of a parliament for swearing in princes and kings, a precious remainder of the old rights of the nation, since the crown of Spain is constitutionally awarded by election. This is how it was in the beginning, and has been several times since, because, less by force of law than by popular consensus, it gradually became hereditary, although not in any one manner. For centuries heirs to the throne were not determined by primogeniture, and only under the Bourbons was the exclusion of female heirs introduced. Thus it does not suffice in Spain to be the firstborn son to be the heir to the crown: he must be sworn in as a prince of Asturias. Even so, it does not necessarily follow that the heir will ascend to the throne, for the infanta doña Juana was sworn in twice before the Cortes; the grandees and the kings of France and Portugal upheld her rights. Since she was his legitimate daughter, her father Henry named her sovereign in his will. But the people took it into their heads that her father was impotent and that she was the daughter of don Beltrán de la Cueva. The people, therefore, through their deputies in the Cortes, kept her from ascending the throne, and the infanta doña Isabel was crowned queen. That is the reason why, when a king or a prince is to be sworn in, the ceremony of convoking the Cortes takes place and the deputies assemble to pay their respects, wherefore titles and crosses are handed out to them. The king transmits his royal letter patent to the Councils, advising them that he has been sworn in before the Cortes, and the councils, after administering the oath to him before each of them in a body, send orders for him to be sworn in in their districts. The councilors then raise pennons in the cities and towns and swear him in. Until that time he is not constitutionally the king.

Speaking of what the city of Madrid is like, the reader can well imagine how higgledy-piggledy, narrow, labyrinthian and tortuous the streets are, without a single bench, such that they are without an equal anywhere in Spain, except for the calle Ancha, in Cádiz. They are paved with chips of flint, little blue stones, sharp-pointed and standing up endwise, that ruin one's feet. The houses, of wood and stones, uneven and unmatched, are all ugly and seemingly ruins because of their roof tiles and garrets. Above the ceiling, so that the sun won't make the room below an oven, there is a sort of loft or attic, above which is the tile roof, and it has a window opening onto the street so as to ventilate it. This is called the garret, and some unfortunate usually lives there, as other poor wretches often live in the cellars that the houses have. There are no buildings worth seeing. The king's abandoned palace in the Retiro, where there is a Hieronymite monastery, is not at all impressive. The palace where the king resides today was to have had three stories; but only one has been built because of the mad expenditures of Godoy and the queen, whose secret annual purse amounted to fifty-six million reals to pay for their love dalliances and to build a palace for her family in Parma. The councils are jammed into a large old run-down mansion. The royal printing press and the post office are sensible buildings, built almost in my day, although the architect forgot that the latter had to have a stairway, and a wooden one has had to be tacked on to one side. The houses of worship are also inconsequential: the best one is San Isidro el Real, which formerly belonged to the Jesuits and today is a collegiate church. Churches there are not lofty, magnificent houses of worship as in Mexico, but little chapels. None of them has a tower, and the much-praised Giralda of Seville is not as high as the tower of Santo Domingo in Mexico City. Monasteries are blocks of monks' cells, and the convents, except for one or two, are low-lying buildings with an oratory that hug the street; and for two years I happened to walk down a certain street without realizing that there was a convent there. The houses do not have, as they do here, one family living on each landing, but on each one, as one goes up the stairs, one family lives behind each of the doors on either side of the staircase along the hallway. Nor are the blocks of flats each a street that is closed off, as is the case here, but a series of little rooms crowded together, with everyone smelling everyone else's breath. Chamber pots used to be emptied into the street, with the shout "Water coming down," as is still done in Portugal. Charles III insisted that this filth in the street be removed; the Madrileños were against it, for the corps of royal physicians said that since the air was very thin it was advisable to impregnate it with the vapor from the filth. Hence Charles III said that Madrileños were like children, who cried when their bottoms were wiped. Finally in each house a privy with one hole was built that is called a *Y*. It is in the kitchen, and it serves to empty the chamber pots into because nobody can sit down on it; it is always wet from the kitchen slops that are also thrown down it. All the pipes of the *Y*s empty into a tank. This is cleaned out by Galicians, every month or so, at night, so that no one gets any sleep, and for a week the stench is so bad that many people fall ill.

In Madrid there is a greater multitude of thinking beings than in any other city in Spain, because they come there from all over the country to apply for jobs; but all of them live alone, each hidden away in his dark little room. The Dominicans of Santo Tomás teach their scholastic jargon there; the monks of Escuelas Pías, belles lettres and certain other subjects at the Royal College of San Isidro, whose expenses are paid by the king; but there are no literary functions, even in the monasteries. Usually these do not even have a library, and if they have a few books, they are full of dust, and one chokes on it if one enters the room, as happened to me in the great monastery of San Francisco, in Madrid. I attended Divine Offices at the cloister vault of San Ginés, where missionary-style sermons are preached, and when the padre intones *apprehendite disciplinam* as a sign to them to take up their whips to flagellate themselves as penance, each monk grabs his, and then the padre shouts: "Capes underneath your knees!" because otherwise, as some of them flagellate themselves, others rob them while they are entirely absorbed in this rite of contrition. I was in the habit of reciting my prayers at the Prado, and then going back to San Francisco, where I lived, a distance of about half a league, and had to go on reciting my prayers the whole way and even inside San Francisco, because each church rings its bells for the canonical hours only if it so pleases. Each church exposes the Holy Eucharist when it wishes to, and this is done by a friar wearing a stole, on an altar with two little candles. In order to win a lawsuit brought by the Benavente family against another family of grandees, the Holy Eucharist was exposed in two churches, and people went to see which of the two Eucharists won out. There does not seem to be a bishop, and the bishop of Toledo fulfills that function. Madrid has a vicar and a bishop *in partibus infidelium*,* who is present in choir at every office with the canons of San Isidro, over whom he presides.

The royal chapel of the Palace is the mother church, and is a chapel attended by a number of priests in choir, and these latter are called royal chaplains. There were two monstrances there, small ones but richly adorned with precious stones. The patriarch of the Indies, to whom they are subject, is the Palace curate and always has the rank of cardinal. To understand why this is so, the reader should know that when it was decided that to make the Americas independent in the spiritual realm (since the archbishop of Seville was previously the metropolitan of the Indies, and therefore that Church was called a patriarchal one), a patriarch was elected. But Rome objects to the title of patriarch because of the prerogatives that accompany it, and he was granted only the honors appertaining to a cardinalate. He is the vicar-general of all the armies of the monarchy, and the miters of America pay a certain amount for his maintenance. I have seen the king attend a ceremonial Mass in his chapel. He sits with a table and a lectern before him, and behind him, all around, are the grandees and other dignitaries. The patriarchal cardinal brings the book for him to recite the Gloria and the Credo in Latin; before he reaches the king, a priest wearing his robes and his bonnet comes out from behind a curtain, which is why he is called the chaplain of the curtain, and performs the ritual of placing the register alongside the book, and the patriarch places it before the king. In Mexico City the royal preachers would barely pass for students practicing their rhetorical skills on Saturdays. They are idiots. I attended the sermon of one of them, a Basilian monk who was highly thought of, and it nearly made

* A bishop who ministers to regions inhabited by infidels.

me split my sides laughing to hear fray Gerundio de Campazas. People said to me: "You are laughing because he preaches to your liking, isn't that so? He has a silver tongue." On Sundays the king goes to the church of the Virgin of Atocha, where he hears the Dominican friars sing the litany; and the friars sometimes tell lies about this image, stories of the sort generally told in Madrid about the Virgin of Almudena, whose festival Mass is attended by the Council of Castile, and I have heard a sermon preached before it, to the effect that, having at one time been placed in a niche in the wall of Jerusalem, she came to Madrid to escape from the Moors, and that candles lighted to her did not go out in I don't know how many years. I cannot fathom why the most absurd frauds must be tolerated in such matters, nor why people get all upset when someone criticizes these abuses that are unworthy of religion and do it harm.

While I am on the subject, the only clergy in Madrid worthy of esteem are the fathers who are priests of the monastery of El Salvador, and the canons of San Isidro. Floridablanca established these houses with the idea in mind that they would serve as a model for all the cathedrals in Spain, because canons are nothing but an abuse, particularly when they are very wealthy, as in Toledo, whose archdeacon has an income of eighty thousand ducats.[5] A ducat is worth about four and a half of our reals.

In Spain in former times, alongside his church the bishop had his canonical school where he lived, that is to say, a residence or college where children offered to the Church by their parents were educated according to the canons of the Church, from whose numbers the necessary ministers were chosen. The vicar of the bishop in the latter's parish church, which is called a cathedral because that is where he has his *cátedra* or seat, was called the *arcipreste;* the priest in charge of the deacons, or first deacon, was called the *arcediano;* and the first priest or the one in charge of the priests, that is the subdeacons (who in Spain belonged to a minor order), acolytes, et cetera, was called the *primiclero* or *primiciero.* But in the eleventh century, during which the French occupied all the cathedrals of Spain, they introduced the institution of San Crodegando, a bishop of Vienne who brought Augustinian monks to his church, to help him administer his parish and educate young ecclesiastics. Since the bishops served as generals in the armies and the clergy barely knew how to read, from the tenth century on these monks began to usurp the rights of the Presbytery or Senate of the Church. The office of sacristan or *sacrarium* was made a priestly office, and abandoning their appointed duties as schoolmasters, as precentors, as sacristans, as lectors, and so on, they retained only the names of these offices, which they transformed into ranks, the legal term for which was therefore *ventosas.** Since it is a French institution, the names are French: Dean is *Doyen,* and in France, that is what the head of each faculty is called: there is a *Doyen* of Letters, and there is even a *Doyen* of cobblers. A *maître d'école* is a schoolmaster. *Chantre* means cantor and so on. And once they were entitled to tithes because they sang, as though the faithful were rightfully stripped of the tenth part of the fruits of the sweat of their brow and their labor to provide cantors with carriages, the latter have been able to hold their own against the bishops, and have gradually become secularized, although they still retain such terms as cloister, conventual Mass, *cabildo* or chapter; and in Mexico they kept their habits and chapels until the end of the last century. The priests or pastors whom the people have the obligation to maintain have had to overburden them by selling the sacraments to them; and the fees charged for them are nothing but simony authorized by the government, which has set aside for its own use four-ninths of these fees, as well as the income of the first year brought in by canonries, estates left by bishops, vacant offices, etc.

The canons of San Isidro have their yearly salary, but all of them are equal, all of them attend Divine Offices in choir, all of them preach, all of them hear Confession, and the diocesan bishop, who performs the same duties as they do, presides over them. This is tolerable, and the idea was to organize all cathedrals in this way. All canons enter San Isidro by competitive examination, and all are clever, although as a consequence they are accused of being Jansenists. I was very well received by them, and in San Isidro I said eleven o'clock Mass for six reals.

The *Gaceta de Madrid* is the most wretched one in Europe, and merely apes those in France and Italy. As a general rule there are two compositors, who send it in manuscript form to the Secretariat of State, which edits it and sends it back with permission to print it in Madrid. The *Mercurio* is sometimes worth something, and sometimes nothing at all. The idea of this gazette originated with an American who needed enough money to be able to eat, because when Americans have just arrived in the city they are fleeced in no time at all; hence people in Madrid say that Americans start out by living in the calle de los Preciados, then go on to that of Desengaño and end up in that of Hospicio,**

---

*   Cupping glasses or suction pads.
**   Roughly translated, respectively: The Street of the Highly Valued, of Disenchantment and of Hospice.

there being streets with these names in Madrid, where I know for a fact that there is a hospice for orphan girls, just as outside of Madrid there is a shelter for girls called San Fernando. There is also a museum of natural history, with an especially large collection of fish and birds of America. On display there are two mummies of the first inhabitants of the Canary Islands. There is the skeleton of a mammoth, an animal found in America that is bigger than an elephant, other bones of which are sometimes found; but the species has died out. Precious vessels of the Incas are on display there, and a metal plate that rings like a bell when it is struck because of the metal amalgams of which it is composed. It also comes from America. There are whole rooms full of precious vessels. To house the museum Floridablanca began to construct a magnificent building in the Prado, adjoining the Botanical Garden, whose director, [Francisco] Zea, was American. The museum collection was begun by an American who died in Paris and bequeathed it to the king. Next to the royal palace is the Armory, with a collection of armaments used in former times, among them the sword that Francis I of France surrendered when he was taken prisoner by Charles V. Bonaparte asked to have it, and took it to France.

Almost all the works published in Madrid are translations, especially ones from the French; extraordinarily bad translations paid by the piece, done by hungry job seekers, to whom the booksellers pay a mere pittance. They need to be translated, one author says, because they speak Spanish in French, and are corrupting the nation's language. That is not the worst of it, but, rather, the fact that nearly all the works are cut, especially when they are not very favorable to Spaniards, and the text is changed without informing the reader, as is the case with the Batteux wherever the subject is Spanish letters. The translator of Hugo Blair, whom Capmany calls a chatterbox, speaks three or four times as much as his author, and does not tell the reader so.

But I must tell a story about don Pedro de Estala here that has to do with us. Don Pedro was a former *escolapio* who did translations to keep food on his table. He therefore began to translate a book by a French author entitled *World Traveler*. He thought up the idea of selling it for a peseta so that people of few means could afford to buy it, and made a bundle. But once the author's strength was exhausted and his account had come to an end, Estala, not wanting the same thing to happen to the pesetas he was making, decided to travel all through America. To do so, he kept asking countless questions of any *gachupín* in whose company he was pretending to travel, and also garnered information from a number of dictionaries, works that by nature are incomplete and inaccurate. The moment he embarked on the subject of Havana, he began to make dreadful mistakes, and a native of Havana turned up at the newspaper and beat him up badly enough to force him to retract every word he had written about the city. For Mexico Estala had recourse to don Luis Tres Palacios, a highlander from La Montaña full of his own importance who had come here to have a look around; he had made a number of observations concerning ordinary people typical of a highlander who is seeing the world for the first time, and who after having been here for twenty-six years took Estala on the sort of sight-seeing trip that Anacharsis had taken in Greece in the middle of the fourth century. Dr. Maniau, a Mexican, also provided him with a few notes on the world of letters, and lent him the memoirs of the Count of Revillagigedo;* but he did not want to be Estala's traveling companion as the latter proposed, so that people in Mexico would not take him to be the source of all the nonsense and all the lies that Estala had put in the book.

I wrote to Tres Palacios complaining of the blasphemies that the traveler had written against the venerable bishop Las Casas, and of his complete ignorance concerning the geography of America. Tres Palacios sent the letter to Estala, telling him that that was what all of us Mexicans were like, and to go after us with a heavy hand. Estala then copied all the absurdities and stupidities of Paw and his fawning followers Raynal, Robertson and Laharpe that put America and Mexico in a very bad light, as though they hadn't already been pulverized by Valverde, Carli, Clavijero, Molina, Iturri, Madisson and their like.[6]

Garviso, a European, bought a number of books for Father Berstad, a Dominican of the monastery of San Fernando, and the latter wrote an open letter against the traveler and presented it to the Council to be printed. It was sent to the vicar of Madrid, who sent it to Estala himself to censor; naturally, he was against publication of the book because it made him look ridiculous and put an end to the pesetas he was making. That is how it goes with everything in Spain. I began to write a newspaper piece against the traveler, entitled *Cartas de Tulitas Cacaloxochitl Cihuapiltzin Mexica*, in other words, letters from a Mexican señorita, to the world traveler. But I did not publish them in the newspaper, because I was already beginning to be persecuted because it was thought that I was the real author of Father Berstad's open letter. Estala and his

* The viceroy of Mexico from 1789 to 1794.

*lazarillo** were out for vengeance, and I had need of the latter, who was a relative of mine. But the *Traveler* was translated into Portuguese, and then has served as a guide to the English geography by Guthrie, who has copied all of Estala's claptrap about Mexico. Thus are insults and errors perpetuated.

The most estimable institutions in Madrid are the Academy of History and the Spanish Academy. The number of members is limited to forty, and usually there are several learned scholars among them, especially in the Academy of History, which has its librarian who is also the antiquary. Each member receives a duro for every meeting he attends, and their total honorarium amounts to about two hundred pesos. There are corresponding members who are clever and bright, and honorary members, that is to say, idiots. When the *Gramática española* was compiled, I was told by Muñoz, all the great men who were members of the Spanish Academy were already dead. Their dictionary is very incomplete and the derivations from Latin very badly done. The Terreros *Diccionario* is better.

The climate of Madrid is extreme, and they say there that it is nothing but eight months of *invierno* and four of *infierno*.** The cold is greater than in any other country of Europe, except Petersburg, because close by is the Guadarrama range, which is almost always snow-capped. The air is so thin that one seldom walks down a street without getting an agonizing pain in the side. And one feels the cold more because there are no fireplaces, as there are in England and in France, and no stoves, as in the north and in Paris, only a miserable brazier in the middle of the room, which burns all day. So the person paid to poke it up is told that he is costing the household too much money, because he is destroying the bed of hot coals, and I am talking about the brazier in fairly well-off households, and even they are hard put to it to afford coal. Poor people either rage against the cold or buy the ashes of sulphurous dung, and I don't know how they can tolerate the stench. Even the brazier, though it is never thoroughly extinguished, causes terrible headaches, and sometimes it suffocates and kills people. In the lower town there was nothing but dire misery, and I was amazed how people could live on pig's tripe from the slaughterhouse, which is made into blood sausages.

The heat is most unbearable and even the water is hot, hence in well-off households ice is always put in it. All the tall doors of the houses

---

* The word comes from the hero in the Spanish picaresque novel *Lazarillo de Tormes*, a rascally guide to a blind man.

** *Winter* and *infierno*, respectively.

have above them large mats or blinds, and the houses are purposely kept so dark that when one enters one can see nothing. The rooms are washed down with water for the same reason, and everyone lives on the lower floors all summer. The young ladies stay inside, almost stark naked, wearing only a sort of shift, like a loose-fitting petticoat that covers them from the neck down, from which their bare arms stick out, and that is how they are turned out when they receive callers. I don't know if they wear a chemise underneath, because I didn't see any of them wearing one despite the fact that their costumes have such low necklines that when I was seated next to them I could see their two naked breasts. At six in the evening one is still not able to go out into the street, because the paving stones are still burning hot.

Hence the evening promenade begins between eight and nine o'-clock, in the Prado, which is a broad tree-lined avenue, and there are two fountains there: one at the beginning of the avenue, called the fountain of Cybele, and another at the end with a statue of Neptune in his chariot; on one side there is also a statue of Apollo. There is nothing especially noteworthy about them. This promenade is next to the Retiro, where there are gardens, a pond, a wood with a number of animals, the warehouse of goods from China, the Observatory building, a parish church, and the playing field for pall-mall, that is to say, a contest where the ball is driven with a mallet, and on either side of it there are planks so that the ball doesn't go out of bounds, and the menagerie. This is a small round building, where a lion, a tiger, and up above some large birds are kept. Outside of the Retiro are the bullring, which is round and made of boards. Bullfights are held there several times a year, because Madrileños are very fond of this barbarous diversion. The people of Madrid ask for nothing but bread and bulls.

The other promenade in Madrid is on the other side of the Manzanares River, and consists of only a few trees. The river is like all the others in Spain, except for the Ebro, the Tagus and the Guadalquivir, rivers that in America we would call brooks or little streams; they carry water from the winter rains, and in summer one can get across them in one jump, and on the other side of the river, opposite the palace, is the king's country estate.

The Madrid fair is in the plaza in front of the monastery of La Pasión, and even if the entire Court attends it, the articles for sale are limited to chamber pots, potties, pots and pans. At the same time bed-bugs come flying out of old pieces of furniture into all the streets of Madrid. Used-clothes vendors also set up shop. The *manolos* go about the streets in procession, reciting the rosary, with a holy image painted on a banner; the venerated statues themselves are not taken outside the churches. Corpus in Madrid is not at all impressive, although the Councils attend the ceremonies; on the night of Corpus I saw a rosary being recited in procession by what appeared to me to be *caballeros,* all of them wearing periwigs and dressed in black, which is the Court costume, but it turned out to be a rosary by rag pickers. These are men who go about with a sack and a hook collecting all the rags in the streets and the rubbish dumps, which they poke about in with their sticks. The dogs so despise them that when people hear a whole chorus of dogs barking they naturally think that the rag picker is passing by. I still am surprised at their putting out *peleles* at New Year's or for Carnival; these are big dolls stuffed with straw, very well dressed, that are set out on the balconies, from which they are thrown down into the street on the last day, and that is why there is a saying: *The* pelele *is the man that always dies every year.*

I forget to mention that neither in Madrid not in any other city in Castile is the Birth of Our Lord celebrated with the doors of the churches open. The common people were in the habit of coming to church dead drunk and vomiting there, and their great delight was to throw fruit, the pits or stones of them and cabbage stems on the altar. Several times they hit the priest reciting the Mass straight in the head. In the shadows men and women hope to earn indulgences by thrashing each other, and they form rings and go to it with their staffs. Hence the French, who in 1808 were unaware of this, on finding themselves in the dark all of a sudden in church in Barcelona, and thinking that the people were going to kill them because of Ferdinand VII, began shouting, in despair of their lives: *Long live Ferdinand VII!* and were discovered clinging to the walls screeching *viva.*

With this and the other things I recounted in chapter I, I have given, it seems to me, enough of an idea of the Court as I knew it during the reign of Charles IV and the end of the last century, when it was at its most splendid. The French tore down many houses in order to halfway straighten certain streets, and everything is now in even worse straits, doubtless, since in 1816 the people could scarcely even put food on the king's table, for he demanded that they contribute a thousand pesos to this end each night, and they sweat like mules to do so.

I often used to say when I was at Court that everything was tripe, alluding to a joke about what happened to a country bumpkin in Mexico City. Among all the events he heard about that took place there, nothing made as great an impression on him as the meeting of the Royal Tribunal. On arriving in the city, the thing he was most eager to do was attend this session. A scribe gave some thought, in fact, to making it possible, and for fifty pesos offered to place him behind the partition, where at least he could hear what was being said. The viceroy was late in arriving at the meeting, because, he said, the tripe he had eaten had made him ill. A judge spoke up and explained how tripe had to be prepared so as not to make a person sick. My wife is better at preparing it than anyone else in the world, another chimed in; but inasmuch as the viceroy was ill, there was no meeting of the Tribunal and it all ended up as so much tripe. Just think of my bumpkin who had spent fifty pesos and all he got in return was tripe. After that, however much people would insist that something was very impressive, he would answer: "That's tripe." And I say the same about Madrid and our Court. Moral and political things are the opposite of physical ones. Distance makes the former appear smaller and the latter larger; but when seen from close up it's all tripe.

Addendum

Seeing as how I have this piece of paper left over, I shall tell a little story that happened in Madrid at the time of my first stay there. A young woman whom Capuchin nuns sent away from their convent before she took vows acquired a reputation as a saint through her mother, her Franciscan confessor and Canon Calvo, the head of the Molinist party who was later put to death in Valencia. As an invalid, she was confined to her bed, swathed in veils, and that was where her profession as a Capuchin nun took place, thanks to a brief in her favor secured from the Supreme Pontiff. The queen herself very nearly came to commend herself to the nun's prayers; but all the nobility did in fact frequently come to visit that oracle, and a mere suggestion from her sufficed to cause the Countess of Benavente to establish a hospital for the disabled, of which she had promised to be president. The mother assured everyone that the only nourishment her daughter took was five orange seeds a day. And the nun often said that to bring an end to the revolution in France and Europe's ills, it was God's will that the Jesuits be reinstated, and that the feast of the Most Tender Heart of Jesus be made a solemn holy day. She was very well informed of the desires of the Molinist party that favored her. The auxiliary bishop of Madrid went to say Mass at her bedside, and she received Communion in bed. She was the saint of Madrid, whose only relatives were her mother and a little niece.

The niece went back to her homeland, and told her priest at Confession how the saint of Madrid, as soon as her visitors left at night and the door of her house was closed, arose from her bed and gorged (as did her mother) on the ample food supplies stored in her larder, thanks to the alms offered her.

The priest informed the Inquisition, and there our holy one was, in the clutches of another one. The Holy Office was nonetheless afraid of pitting its reputation against hers by falsely accusing her of imposture, and her testimony was taken in the presence of persons who knew her, as they remained hidden from her sight by a veil. She was thereupon heard to declare that, at the time when she took her vows in bed, a privilege that by virtue of the brief had been granted her because of her illness, she was well. I have learned nothing as to her whereabouts at present, but I understand that she has probably been shut up in the convent of Capuchin nuns.

I have no desire, a former Jesuit told me in Rome, to go to the Piazza Colonna, a place where ex-Jesuits meet, because all they talk about is the visions of nuns and pious women. And, indeed, whenever any of them spoke to me they always told me of the revelations that such persons had had. And I was amazed at how credulous people who in other respects were so enlightened were when it came to such a slippery subject, which has caused endless scandals and fiascos in the Church.

V I

About What Happened to Me in Madrid Until I Escaped from Spain to Portugal to Save My Life

As soon as I arrived in Madrid I sought out in the calle de la Salud my Aunt Barbara, the first person who had offered me lodging when I arrived at court, and someone who had always been fond of me. But she had died. The celebrated Dr. Traggia had met his end too, by having overworked himself preparing to deliver Campomanes's funeral oration, entrusted to him by the Academy of History.[1] My noted benefactor Yéregui had gone to France for the ostensible purpose of taking the waters at Baguières, but in reality in order to publish, as he subsequently did, his national catechism, which is very good, and send to Bishop Gregoire, the author of the celebrated letter against the Inquisition addressed to the Inquisitor General, the refutation of the reply to it by Villanueva that he had composed. Villanueva later retracted his reply in the Cortes of Cádiz.

In view of all this, and because I had no money whatsoever, I had no idea what to do next, whereupon I happened to run into a lay hospitaler, a counselor-at-law from the province of Quito, his homeland, an old acquaintance of mine, who had been at court ever since he joined Beristáin's entourage. To secure me lodgings, he put in a word for me at a private home and also at a lodging house with mattresses for rent, to see if they would give me one. I stayed in the lodging house for only five days. Then my friend don Manuel González de Campo, an official in the Postal Service, took me in. And after that I rented a dark little room in a hostelry run by an Italian, eating my meals with Canon Navas, one of the cleverest men of the cathedral chapter of San Isidro. My only visits were to the home of the botanist don Francisco Zea, an American from Santa Fe, the present editor of the *Gaceta,* with whom I lunched several times; to the home of the Count of Gijón, also from Quito, who lived in the calle Mayor with a life-guardsman, a cousin of Mayo's, in the queen's entourage, who was Godoy's successor; and to a shop in the calle del Carmen, owned by don Magín Gomá, a Catalan, who was an old friend of mine.

While I was there, my indefatigable persecutor and longtime cat's paw of Archbishop Haro, Jacinto Sánchez Tirado, recognized me by my voice as he was passing by. He came into the shop on the pretext of asking after someone, to make certain that I was his man and take a good look at me so as to send a description of me to his accomplice, the vilely venal and vicious pen pusher don Francisco Antonio León, who was the chief clerk and right-hand man of Minister Caballero, and his closest confidant, because the one was as cruel as the other. I was dressed in black, with a rather dark greatcoat and a round hat. But since it was nighttime and my eyes kept staring into his, Tirado didn't get a very good look at me.

What was this man's object in persecuting you, I will be asked, if the archbishop was now dead? Spaniards, tenacious by nature, do not waver in their hatred once they have conceived an utter dislike of someone, nor do they stop persecuting a person, even after they have sent him to his grave. I have already said that in the years following my arrival in Spain, Archbishop Haro, frightened off by the deaths of my provincial and the two canons who were censors, wrote to Tirado to leave off persecuting me. But Tirado said that he was doing it *ex officio,* in order to do something worthwhile in exchange for the ten thousand reals a year that he was paid. Once that evil archbishop was dead, Tirado kept up his persecution of me so as get himself hired as a go-between, making the Americans believe that he had a great interest in Our Lady of Guadalupe and writing to them of his harassment of me as though it were to his credit. In 1803 I saw in Rome a letter of his to Dr. Moral, in which he told him that he was doing his best to catch my sermon, so as to have sermons preached against it. And he had not only my sermon, but the soul of León, the petty official at the ministry, in his pocket. The scoundrels know that, just as America was subjugated by using religion as a pretext, so the Virgin of Guadalupe is the halter with which Mexicans are led to drink at the asses' fountain. And just as Haro cleverly waved before the people of Mexico the cape of Juan Diego,* which he ridiculed, so as to hide beneath it the persecution of a countryman of theirs, precisely because he was a brilliant man, and just as in order to get their hands on Iturrigaray (who did not hate Americans) they maintained that he had tried to burn down the Sanctuary of Guadalupe with candles impregnated with gunpowder, so all of them there in Spain do whatever they can so that Mexicans will allow themselves to be ridden and robbed like horses. That is why that clever scoundrel Branciforte had his daughter christened Guadalupe here in Mexico, but as soon as he went back to Spain he changed her name.

That rogue Sánchez Tirado also had his bit of a money-pouch relation to the Virgin of Guadalupe. I have already recounted how, in the last century, our blessed peasant don Teobaldo founded, in the Augustinian monastery in Madrid, called San Felipe el Real, a congregation to aid indigent Americans that bore the name Nuestra Señora de Guadalupe. Twenty brothers could change the articles of its constitution, and twenty Spaniards who had entered the congregation ostensibly out of devotion changed the aim of the brotherhood. In no part of Spain or Europe is there any such thing, be it real or ideal, as devotion to our Virgin of Guadalupe—or to anything else from America save hard Mexican pesos. So almost as soon as it was born, the congregation died. When I was there, there had been no brother of the congregation for many years. But Haro's agents bequeathed to one another the administration of this unofficial prebend, without having to render accounts to anyone, and it passed from Ribera to Tirado. The latter laid out a little money for music on the Virgin's festival day, and a sermon and a Mass in honor of her image, a half-length painting of her that is on an altar in a chapel, reserving the remainder of the money for his own most devout pocket. When the Cortes moved to Madrid, the Americans apparently took the administration of it away from him. That was no doubt the end of devotion to her. But the entire malicious campaign against me was waged at the direct instigation of Haro, who persuaded this scoundrel and León that I had denied the tradition of Guadalupe, his aim being to get them to persecute me on that pretext, as they have done here in or-

---

* Juan Diego was the Indian peasant to whom the Virgin of Guadalupe appeared, leaving the imprint of her image on his cape.

der to make my compatriots hate me because of my supposed calumny, when in point of fact my object had been to cover them with glory and exalt the Virgin.

The four years at the end of which the king had ordered the council to render me justice, as the public prosecutor and the Academy of History had requested, had gone by. And if I sought justice myself now, there was nothing they could do. The only recourse left them was to throw me out of Madrid, and to that end Tirado wrote to León, who had no jurisdiction whatsoever over me since the official in charge of the Mexican desk was don Zenón Alonso, my friend, to whom I had paid a visit when I arrived. What way will the infernal pen-pusher think of now to get me thrown out of the court? The usual shuffling about of secret reports from Haro, naturally, to make him appear to have been an infallible oracle, and his word irrefutable. But what the venal officials of the ministry needed was to find some pretext justifying the order that they drafted in the king's name, and that the minister had signed without looking at it, in order to have an official document to back them up if things did not go as they planned.

Evildoers know one another very well and (like demons, Saint Thomas says) have no love for each other, but they put their heads together nonetheless in order to do evil. So, then, in order to carry out the diabolical order that he had invented, León chose Marquina, a royal magistrate, the corregidor of Madrid, to execute it. That was what a troublemaker, liar, and brute he was. When I went to Madrid he was an absentminded trial lawyer, who used to sit smoking cigars in the Puerta del Sol, which is called that because many people go there to take the sun. He must have done some dirty work for Godoy, who made him a royal magistrate. He fawned on him so basely that he went morning and afternoon to tell him of everything that was happening in Madrid, and one day when Godoy was at the Sitio, he sent him one or two couriers to do the same. The more men grovel before superiors who feel the need of that, the more high-handed they are to the ones who are beneath them. This barbarian was therefore entrusted with the execution of any order that required despotism and acts of violence, and carried out his assignment to perfection. He was the *timebunt gentes** of Madrid, whose populace, when Godoy fell, gave him his just deserts by rending him to pieces. If all despots met with such success, we would see fewer of them in this world.

---

* Terror.

León sent to this savage a royal order against me that could be dispatched to no one save the Devil, for it said that it was of great concern to the life and tranquillity of Their Majesties that fray Servando Mier be arrested immediately, using the inexact description of him forwarded by Tirado to identify him. Such an order would have sent the most placid man into action. Imagine, then, the commotion that Marquina must have caused. He filled the entire town with spies and officers of the peace, and in the calle Mayor and in the Plazuela de San Juan de Dios he posted numerous groups of constables, whom everyone noticed as they stood elbow to elbow in the middle of the street looking as though they were standing guard over a bull or a band of thieves. I myself asked them what all that meant, for how could I have imagined that their quarry was myself, when my conscience was perfectly clear. One morning as I stepped out into the calle Mayor, on leaving the house of the Count of Gijón after two hours with Mayo's cousin, I had asked that very same question of some hundred constables who were posted out front, and after we had gone a few steps a constable caught up with us and said to me: "By order of señor Marquina, come with me." At the name Marquina, as terrible as that of Nero, my companion took to his heels, and the whole mob of constables followed after me. The order that had been given was that if they saw anyone who seemed to them to fit the description given them, they were to ask him if he were so-and-so, and no matter what his answer, he was to be taken to his house. They had not asked me anything; but the minute we entered his house he asked me: "Who are you?" "Servando de Mier." "I've been looking for you." Whereupon they tied me down like a rocket, and when I told them that they should remember that I was a priest, they put a cape over me, and Marquina ordered them not to allow me to speak, so as not to cause any trouble.

Surrounded by that multitude of pharisees, I was taken at a trot to the public jail. Once we were inside, they untied me, and when they were about to search me at the door of one of the cells, noticing that I had a little piece of paper in French that I had wrested away from a life-guardsman, I tore it in half. The prison warden flung himself upon me to take the paper away from me, and I had a good laugh later when I saw it carefully filed away in my dossier. It was a little letter that when read straight through was very good; it was entitled *Letter of a vicar general to a young female convert,* but if read only halfway down the page, with the paper folded lengthwise, it was a most indecent letter from a prick to a cunt. The stupid warden had thought that it was a matter of State or a conspiracy.

As I said, I laughed, because I remembered a story about the prior of the Hieronymites of Valladolid. French priests were lodged in monasteries by royal patronage when they emigrated because of the revolution in France. The prior took a dislike to one of the three who were lodged in his monastery, because he spoke well of his nation. And he ordered the postman to pretend to be picking up that priest's letters to take them to the post office but to bring them to him instead. He opened one that the priest had written to Madrid, and seeing that it contained a sketch, the prior took it into his head that it was a drawing of the bridge of Valladolid, which the priest was sending to the French to make it easier for them to capture it. With this idea in mind, the prior went off to inform the Chancery of Valladolid in public session of the existence of the letter. He claimed he knew French, but the entire letter turned out to be nothing but an order for a truss, because the priest had a rupture, and after setting down the specifications that the truss must meet, he had made a drawing of it. This was what the prior of San Jerónimo had taken to be the bridge. There was a tremendous amount of joking and ribbing in Valladolid, and even the youngsters gave out with catcalls taunting the Hieronymites about the truss.

Then the warden asked me my age, and I answered that I was forty years old. "You've been very well preserved," he said to me. When I left Mexico I was twenty-three, although I looked twenty-five at most. At forty I looked thirty-two; but I left that terrible prison an old man with gray hair. Spanish prisons are not meant to keep men looking their age; they are meant, rather, to kill them.

The following day the magistrate summoned me for a hearing and ordered me to make a statement. I did not know, nor could I imagine, the contents of the royal order, and I answered that I had nothing to say. He wanted me to at least tell where my trunk was, for they had taken the key to it from me; but I answered that it was a key I had found by chance. As I had spent a very bad night stretched out on the floor, I begged that I be brought my mattress. "Yes," the judge said to me, very affably, "just tell me where you're keeping it." "I don't have one," I answered, "but in such and such a place they rented me one, and they can bring it to me from there." They went to inquire, and since the poor lay hospitaler from Quito had put in a word for me so that they would rent it to me, they went to arrest him, and kept him in the stocks for forty days, even though he had taken holy orders as a tertiary. How could I have imagined such a thing? One cannot do good unto a man who is persecuted without risking sharing his misfortune. The lay brother was more conversant with the court than I, and even though he did not know that I had left that lodging five days after he had secured it for me, on learning of my imprisonment as soon as it occurred, he had gotten rid of his trunk containing his papers. The constables followed him, and made such a thorough search for him that they finally met up with a woman who was a *comadre** of the poor lay brother. They doubtless put together information provided them by the friars, who are always one another's enemies, and though his relations with me were judged to have been innocent, León ordered him banished to Quito.

What with this outrageous harassment of the lay brother, all my friends who had been charitable toward me were trembling in their boots, but not only had the brother forborne to mentioned their names, but I too did not mention any of them, no matter how closely the judge questioned me. I already presumed that it was all part and parcel of León's wickedness, and that I ought not to involve anyone in my misfortune, nor do I believe that the oath I took in court obliged me to be pitiless toward my friends. The oath concerning truth-telling does not bind one to do evil. Even so, when it came time for making statements, I evaded the judge's "Do you swear?" et cetera. I answered him with pat formulas of the sort that my reader can imagine; let's get to the subject at hand, for one. He presumed that this meant I was taking the oath, but I had had no such intention. The one friend of mine about whom he plagued me was don Francisco Zea, though I have no idea how he learned that don Francisco knew me. He summoned him at ten-thirty at night, and kept him by himself in a garret, with only a feeble light, until midnight so as to intimidate him and make him tell how he came to know me, although don Francisco admitted only that he had met me in Paris, at the home of the Spanish ambassador. The judge's greatest concern was to seize my trunk. I had nothing in it save for books and my briefs, which numbered seven, and an engraved print that had been presented to me at the Council of Pistoia. This was enough for León to do me harm, and I knew that he would ask for all my papers, as he did in Burgos, so as to keep them, leaving me without documents, whereupon he could attack me and leave me helpless, without a means to earn enough to eat on by saying Mass, or find something in them that would enable him to incriminate me. Can anyone believe that in the charges that he brought against me later was the fact that he did not find my doctor's diploma among my papers seized in Burgos, so that my doctor-

---

* A fellow godparent.

ate would appear to be an imposture? I had presented it to the Council. He also accused me of being the author of that ridiculous little bit of paper that I had wrested from the life-guardsman because it appeared to be in my handwriting. What proof could all this be that putting me in prison was a matter of importance for the life and tranquillity of Their Majesties?

When I answered on the first day that I was summoned that I had nothing to declare, Marquina ordered me taken to a worse cell, and they took me to one so narrow that when I was sitting down I could touch the walls with my two hands outstretched. The prisoners in the cells, which all have a little grille in the upper part through which they communicate with each other by shouting, spoke to me in gypsy cant. The gypsies, as thieves by profession, always occupy respectable quarters such as these, and in the salutations that are exchanged from one dungeon to another in the morning and at bedtime, the formula they recite is: "I tell you, handsome gypsy . . . ," whereupon there follows a long recital and a very close little embrace, and so on. And when they hear the judge approaching, they say like the Freemasons: It's raining. I asked them why I had been brought to that cell that was so cramped, and they answered that it was "so as to give me eau-de-vie." As a matter of fact (since I heard them being worked over later), it was the torture chamber. I answered that they couldn't do that to me. "Are you a nobleman?" they asked me. "That is immaterial. I am a priest." "Señor Marquina will face the consequences for having kept me here," one of the prisoners said then. "I'm a servant of His Excellency." The latter was a bishop *in partibus infidelium*,* a Capuchin, who had served as an auxiliary bishop in Havana and then was exiled to a monastery of his Order in Catalonia. But he strolled about as he pleased in Madrid, for he was the one who had joined in marriage, or in an invalid marriage ceremony, Godoy and the well-known Pepa Tudó, whose father was aware that Godoy already had a lawfully wedded wife, and it was common knowledge that he had had three children by Pepa. Who knows which was the real marriage: the one to Tudó or the one to the infanta.

On the following day they took me out of the cell again to make my declaration, and since I answered that I had nothing to declare, the judge asked whether there wasn't another cell that was worse. I was then taken to the "bedbug trap," where they had tortured a woman. I suffered while there was still some light in the cell, despite which the walls were

---

* In regions inhabited by infidels.

covered with bedbugs, and there were clusters of them in the corners. But I was overtaken by a dreadful sense of horror as I paced about in the dark, for when I bumped into the walls, I began to crush them with my hand. I then said I would confess. They were no doubt waiting for me to make a confession that would justify the severity of the royal order, and the following day I found myself in the presence of the judge, the vicar of Madrid and the scribe.

As I reached the point where I declared that my father was the governor and commanding general of the New Kingdom of León, the judge turned and looked at me in surprise, because I was being accused as a monk and it was extraordinary that I should be a man of distinction.[2] Then he proceeded to ask me very long questions, and I replied that I would give him an account of my entire life; and as I did so, he had the scribe make a note that I was the one who was dictating it. My story seemed like a novel to him, and surely one I had made up, because nothing about it fit the accusation in the royal order. So I went back to my bedbug trap and fell asleep on the brick floor, with no other covering than the clothes I had on, and with my handkerchief as a pillow. The judge goes the rounds to inspect the prison at seven at night and again at twelve. I lay stretched out in the middle of the cell so as to get away from the bedbugs; but the odor of my body attracted them, and they came down the walls and bit me all over. The judge, on his round at midnight, usually squashed underfoot the procession that filed down to attack me. Around four in the afternoon I was given, as were the other prisoners, an inedible chunk of cow's palate, as hard as a rock, and a piece of black, ill-smelling bread, which at times was missing, for the famine in Madrid was so severe that a third of the population left the city; the rest ate bread made of corn and bran, and when a bread wagon entered Madrid, the starving people flung themselves upon it pell-mell, despite the troops escorting it, and made off with the bread without paying for it. The cell was isolated so that inside it one could never hear a human voice.

I spent more than forty days like that in it, until León submitted the charges. Two men carried me downstairs one afternoon to hear them, for I was now so weak that I could not stand up. With my scraggly beard, since those who are held incommunicado in the jail are not shaved, I must have looked like a dead man, because after having fallen into a faint as soon as I arrived in the courtroom, I heard the judge say to the vicar of Madrid: "This one must be transferred to the royal jail, otherwise he's going to die on us here and then people in Madrid will have something to talk about." The judge himself sent out for wine and biscuits for me and revived me: he laughed as he read me León's ridiculous charges, then went off and left me alone with the scribe to answer them.

León discarded the rest of his hand at this point, keeping only one miserable jack. He began with the Guadalupe sermon, as though this were not a subject over and done with since my case had already been heard. He then followed this with the archbishop's secret reports, in the shadow of which, as though they were true, proven charges, he had been playing a game of ball with me for ten years. I have recounted and refuted all of them, and the fact is that my retraction was not a sincere one. It is evident that it was gotten out of me by violence and trickery. And I had no reason to retract my statements, since, as the Academy of History declared, I neither spoke against the tradition nor was there anything in my sermon that was of theological importance or merited censure. [He charged] that I was inclined to attempt prison breaks: in what jails had I been confined in my life for him to know this? [Another charge was] that I had been tried by two viceroys: Revillagigedo and Branciforte. I learned of this report in Burgos, and wrote to the Count of Gigedo asking for a letter on the subject that could be presented in court. And he sent it to me, saying in it that I had done nothing untoward during his rule as viceroy; on the contrary, he had always heard nothing but good about my talent and my writings, and León had this letter in his possession. Besides, all it takes to be put on trial is the calumny of a rogue. The way one gets out of a bad spot is the best testimony. If I had come off badly, why hadn't the viceroys punished me? If I had come off well, what was it that the archbishop was accusing me of? These were the things he reported, along with the charge that I was proud and arrogant, which León said nothing about now, so as to have something to latch on to later on.

The pen pusher added on his own that I had escaped from Las Caldas; that the provincial of Castile had written that I spoke ill of persons of lofty character (Godoy and his beloved), and that he had written that it was necessary to keep me in prison, since I did not have a religious spirit because I failed to come kiss his whip to bid him farewell; that when I left Madrid I played the dirty trick on the calash driver of making him wait all day. At this point the judge laughed. I had been so far from doing any harm to the calash driver that, simply because he had arranged with me to pretend to be taking me somewhere, he did me out of twelve pesos. Why had I not presented myself to His Highness Prince León when I arrived? [There were other charges]: That I had maligned Minister Caballero, whom León, in order to get him up in arms against me, had warned that I wanted to kill him. That the little piece of paper that I tore up appeared to be in my handwriting; and that I was dressed in layman's clothing when I was a monk in holy orders, and that among my papers seized in Burgos my doctoral diploma had not been found. And for all these reasons it was important for the life and tranquillity of Their Majesties that I be kept incommunicado in a cell of the public jail.

As I have just said, I have already recounted and refuted all these stupid accusations, and I refuted them yet again, citing in answer to the charge that I was a monk in holy orders my briefs of total secularization that I had. The following day the judge again summoned me, and in the presence of the vicar of Madrid my replies were read aloud. The judge told the vicar: "Sire, the charges are nothing but a collection of passages whose meaning has been twisted. It is obvious what this is: persecution on the part of the official from the ministry." And since I had said that no attention should be paid to the reports of a bad bishop, reprimanded by the king and by the Apostolic See, who never preached sermons, who rarely visited his diocese, and never all of it, and who lavished on his family all the income of the archbishopric and spent large sums to secure secular honors, the vicar, who was straitlaced, told me that I should not speak ill of the prelate. But the judge said that my defense was just, so as to weaken his testimony. Turning to me, he said: "Say that you have something very grave to reveal to the minister in person. You must go there and tell him of the wicked thing that his scribe has done." "It is useless, or might well make matters worse, because León is his oracle," I answered; and he said to me: "Well then, if you know that, there is nothing to do but be patient." "But, Your Excellency, I ask your permission to go to the infirmary." "That is not possible," he replied. "Because of the benevolent association established a short time ago, even grandees of Spain come here, and León is afraid that word of all this will get out. They will cure you upstairs in your cell; I shall see to it that you are given the best room, and His Excellency the viceroy will come to your aid."

I was wrong not to have taken his advice and done as he proposed, because even though I believe that León would have caused trouble and passed on false information about me to the minister, I could have had a word with the relatives I had at the king's country residence, and gained time, and so on. There is no doubt that I was given a better cell, without as many bedbugs; but in order to give me the one with the most light, although there was still not enough to be able to read, they gave me one whose window was exposed to a strong north wind, and the cold was unbearable. The vicar of Madrid had clothes made for me, which I laid aside for when I got out, and had them give me a mattress and a blanket. Inquisitor Yéregui had returned from France, had some tobacco brought me, paid to have a modest little supper sent up to me, and collected my trunk from the inn where I was keeping it, although it would appear that all the curious books I had brought from Italy, which were not inside the trunk, were lost.

I spent that entire rigorous winter, without a fire or a cloak, in that icebox of a cell. My clothing had rotted away on my body, and I became ridden with lice and filled the bed with them, such big fat ones that the blanket walked about by itself; the worst of it was that because of the cold and because I had no outer garments that were warm, I had to stay in bed most of the time. I asked for an earthenware bowl full of water and threw whole handfuls of lice into it; and I truly came to believe that my whole body was being eaten away by lice on account of some ailment, the way other people get eaten away by worms. Although I always kept my handkerchief tied around my head, my left eardrum ruptured from the cold, and I was in such pain that I lay in the bed shrieking for hours on end. I saw criminals, thieves, men condemned to death and miscreants sentenced to a public lashing go down to the infirmary; and I could see myself dying in that cell, even though I had been found innocent.

Finally, at the end of January 1804, that scoundrel León handed down the royal order to have me taken to the house of Los Toribios in Seville. Five or six days before I left, the inquisitor got the judge to have me taken down to the infirmary in secret so as to be able to give me the briefs from Rome, which in fact he did hand over to me. In order to go downstairs I took all my clothes off and put on the ones that the vicar of Madrid had had made for me. That was the end of the lice; but the whole bed, along with the clothes that I had taken off, had to be burned. I was given a shave in the infirmary, and instead of a bear I began to look like a human being. I was still very ill, however; nonetheless, very early one morning I was obliged to climb into a calash with a constable, escorted by three light-infantrymen. I was dying from the pain in my stomach and my ear, and we spent the night in the vicinity of the royal Sitio in Aranjuez, where the Court was at the time. That night I suffered such severe pains that I asked for a confessor and a physician. "Sire," the constable said to me very sarcastically, "put yourself in God's hands and ask of him that he relieve your pain and give you patience, for even though you are dying, you will do so without confession and without a physician." "For the love of heaven! Why must I be dealt with so cruelly?" "The reason is clear," he replied. "León knows that everything that he is doing to you is utterly wicked; you have relatives in the Sitio and in the royal Palace itself. If they find out, it will go hard with León; but tomorrow, if you are still alive, once we are a couple of leagues away from the Sitio, I give you my word that we will stop until you are well." He kept his word, and I drank mother's milk to relieve the pain in my ear, although it grew worse again on the road, becoming so severe that, not being able to wait patiently for the malva visco with which I was treating myself to cool, I put my entire head in the boiling water, and the part of it that I plunged into the water has been bald ever since. By the time we reached Andújar I had finally recovered; and as we journey on to Seville, driving through snow, which kept us on the road for sixteen days, I am going to tell about the place that people in Seville call Los Toribios.

This was the most barbarous of the Saracen institutions in Spain. A man named Toribio, an elderly bookseller in Seville, though he was an Asturian, a tertiary of the orders of Saint Dominic and of Saint Francis, seeing the horde of nameless youngsters who prowled around the marketplace in Seville stealing, decided to take them in, educate them and give them a trade. To do so he sold his books, leased a house that would suit his purpose, and with biscuits and meringues gradually attracted the youngsters to it, so as to teach them doctrine. When he had attracted a considerable number of them, he seized them by brute force and shut them up in his house; and by giving the biggest boys little presents and cosseting them, he got them to serve as guardians and escorts of the littler ones, whom he subjected to very frequent thrashings. He fed them and took them to the archbishop's palace every day to recite their catechism lesson in chorus, and to the palace of the auxiliary bishop.

Although it was all done by violent means, the auxiliary bishop and the archbishop dissimulated because of the good that followed, for those boys were merely seeds in the hotbed that produced the highwaymen with which Andalusia was infested. Toribio went out at night with his older boys to catch nameless youngsters, not only in Seville but in its immediate environs. Mothers brought complaints in vain; there was no one to hear them. Toribio had organized his young prisoners into a senate. He presented before it any new prisoner who had fallen from virtue and accused him of a multitude of misdeeds. The sentences the boys handed down rivaled each other in cruelty. Toribio would lighten them, promising that the young proselyte would mend his ways, and reduced them to twenty-four lashes, which became by tradition the newcomer's admission fee. Now and again some braggart hired by a widowed mother would come swaggering by and arrogantly demand the release of the woman's son; but Toribio would let loose his mob of youngsters on him and they would throw him to the ground, take him prisoner, and not let him go until he had performed certain spiritual exercises. The undertaking gradually prospered, taking in more and more alms, and the boys little by little learned to read and write, and were taught a trade as weavers, craftsmen, cobblers, and so on. But it also became increasingly cruel, and acquired such a reputation for brutality that all unruly and badly behaved boys and eventually even men began to be sent from all over to this Barbary.

A certain Mier, Toribio's successor, enhanced the reputation of the institution. He had at his orders a number of disabled veterans, called broadasses there, and even today as soon as a woman complains about her husband, a sister about her brother, and so on, to the superintendent of Los Toribios, the highest-ranking judge and the police magistrate of Seville, provided the women are willing to pay the peseta per day it costs to maintain the prisoner, he sends his broadasses and they bring him in, tied down like a rocket. His head is immediately shaved; in the old days they gave him the twenty-four, and after that he is put in irons, and begins starving and praying. In the past all sorts of abuses followed. A greeting was answered with a punch in the face that left the greeter badly bloodied. A reasoned argument was answered with a kick in the teeth. Then double shackles, the rack, a gag, chains, iron bars, beatings, the lash. And there is no one to complain to, because writing or receiving letters, or communicating in any other way, is not allowed there. It was a rung up on the ladder to be taken out of the madhouse and made a Toribian brother. The former asylum inmates, who are called *arraeces,* Moorish chieftains, as a joke, told me that they were terrified at the excessive mistreatment they received at the hands of the Toribians. This earned the madmen quite a few knifings from various people who ran into them on the street after they had left Los Toribios. And if one of them died in the encounter, the Toribian brothers fulfilled their obligation by sending on his burial certificate, the way muleteers hand over the traces of the pack animal that dies on them from being overloaded. Isn't the archbishop of Malinas right when he says that in Europe Spain is considered a geographical error?

Just as today, following the return to the throne of Ferdinand, the flower of the nation has ended up in monasteries and prisons in Africa, in the era of Godoy, Los Toribios was one of the depositories used by the barbarous Minister Caballero for putting away all those who had committed no crimes serious enough to earn them a prison sentence, but whom the authorities wished to torment by sending them to houses of correction. At the time when I was being sent to Los Toribios, the celebrated Minister Jovellanos, the honor of the nation, was lying in a charterhouse to learn Christian doctrine; the famous Dr. Salas Salmantino was in a monastery in Guadalajara; and the renowned Padre Gil, a Minorite, who later on was a member of the regional government of Seville was in Los Toribios, which he left shortly before I arrived. *La vida secreta de María Luisa* was attributed to him. León was sending me there so that they would dispatch me from this life; for owing to my delicate constitution, my age and the extreme weakness that I came with from the prison in Madrid, it was clear that I would not be able to withstand such mistreatment.

To my good fortune everything at Los Toribios was now altogether different. By royal decree the Toribian house of correction was now a residence hall; the priest in charge, the former head and superintendent of Los Toribios, had sold off whole cartloads of irons; and in order to separate the youngsters or the respectable persons from the Toribians and the commoners engaged in spiritual exercises at the cost of a peseta a day, since they had all been herded indiscriminately together, he set up a house or a section apart, with a garden and so on, to which the Toribians had no access whatsoever, this residence being headed by a priest with the title of chaplain, for the guidance of distinguished retreatants doing spiritual exercises.

This would have been a fine arrangement in the former royal residence hall. But when I arrived, it had been moved to a large old mansion in the barrio of La Macarena. It had its own patio, where the priest in charge lived. It had several large rooms teeming with bedbugs, and a yard for the Toribians, along with others for the school, the cobbler's shop, the wool spinners and weavers. On an upper floor was the chapel, the living quarters of the chaplain, and an inside corridor with several little windows with no panes, and three gloomy cells, a refectory and several latrines on one side. This was the residence for the distinguished retreatants, who paid ten reals or half a peso a day; they had their own doorkeeper and a servant, a big hulk of a Toribian who was a fatuous imbecile. There were no lashings any more, not even for the Toribians. The distinguished retreatants were greeted by clapping them in a pair of irons or a shackle, to be worn for a few hours or a few days, depending on the recommendation that they came with, a couple of hours spent shut up in one of the three little cells, and that was all. All this was at the pleasure of the priest in charge, however, who could (if he so chose) re-institute all the cruel practices of the past, because everything there was still as arbitrary as in the beginning.

On the morning I arrived at Los Toribios, I immediately presented to the priest in charge my briefs and what in Rome is called the *discessum,* in other words the letters dimissory of the Supreme Pontiff, which certified that my conduct was irreproachable; the man was openmouthed with astonishment. The royal order of the blackguard León said that I was being sent there because of my overweening pride, and because I had been discovered dressed in layman's attire, though I was a religious. And he then instructed the priest in charge of the need to keep me in close confinement under the most severe conditions, going so far as to advise him that there were not sufficient safeguards in that house to deal with such vicious criminals as myself. That great rogue León was out to take my life or cause me to leap to my death, or else make certain that I would be unable to bring all of his evil deeds to light.

The accusation that I was arrogantly proud had been brought by the archbishop, but he himself had gainsaid it by including in his edict and his final verdict assurances that I had made a voluntary retraction, had humbly asked to be forgiven and had offered every satisfaction. Even if I was overweeningly proud, so are all of us sinners, for the Holy Spirit says that "the beginning of all sin is pride." But the passions are not grave sins, so long as they break no commandment of the Lord's, nor is it within the competence of any judge on earth to punish the affections of the spirit. In such a case it would be possible to answer with Jesus Christ: *Qui sine peccato est, primus in eam lapidem mittat.** It is evident that these were nothing but pretexts, and pretexts that seemed very grave to the ignorant, such as the lay brother of Los Toribios who, when later on I answered in those words, was as scandalized by what I said as if it had been a blasphemy.

As for my having been discovered wearing layman's attire, though I was a religious, why was it that León did not dare go so far as to call me an apostate? Would this evildoer have failed to accuse me of so obnoxious an offense? I had already declared before the royal magistrate that I was secularized. The answer, if León did not believe it, was to ask for the briefs that I cited. But he took great care not to do so, because then he

---

* "Let him who is without sin among you be the first to cast a stone at her." (Jn 8:7)

would have had no way of sending me off to an arbitrary destination, for it was necessary to provide for my maintenance, and funds in the keeping of the secretariat of the Treasury were not available to him. It suited his purposes, then, to presume that I was a religious (though he did not dare go so far as to call me an apostate) and therefore order the procurator of Mexico to pay for my transportation and my board at Los Toribios.

This wicked deed caused me to be persecuted later on by the aforementioned prosecuting attorney, who wrote that from then on I was to be held to the strict vow of poverty of a friar, and be obliged to wear a woolen tunic next to my bare skin, even though no Dominican wore one in Mexico, since its Province has a dispensation from Rome not to do so. This was a *gachupín* who brought with him to Spain the envious hatred that his countrymen here have of me. Since I had been sent to him as an apostate friar, the priest who was warden of Los Toribios could not be persuaded that the briefs were genuine, even though they had been authenticated by three notaries, and had nineteen official seals in all, and he was thunderstruck when he saw me send the king my written defense against León's accusation; to all of which León, who was acting in bad faith, merely turned a deaf ear.

Nonetheless, since the *discessum* was magnificent, and was a printed one, the Toribian did not dare shackle me, or subject me to the usual brief imprisonment. There follows a description of the companions that I was destined by fate to have. There were eight of them; six assigned to three little cells along the passageway or corridor, and two outside. The two outside were a lad named Clemente, who had four heels, the son of a doorman from Medinaceli at the house of Pilate in Seville. This is the name that the Medinaceli palace in Seville goes by, because the Duke had the nerve to use Pilate's residence in Jerusalem as the model for it; even today there is not a single detail that is missing save for the little pillar that was on the balcony where Pilate presented Jesus Christ in the *Ecce Homo*.* The other Toribian, who had been there for two years, was a young man named Gaspar Montoya, an honorary captain because he was a royal page. He was allowed to leave the building and go out onto the street, and enjoyed the complete trust of the priest in charge, because he had made the latter believe that he was going to marry one of his sisters, all of whom led the dim-witted priest around by the nose.

Those inside the cells were: a stupid young counselor-at-law, who was deeply aggrieved because God had not made him a woman, on ac-

---

* Behold the man. (Jn 19:5).

count of the honors and attentions that women enjoy; an American slave trader, who had been sent to Los Toribios by one of his brothers, no doubt because he had robbed him, for he was such a good man that when he received from his brother a letter without a cross on it, my comrade sent him a terrible reprimand; a life-guardsman, as ugly as he was thick-headed; a young Hieronymite friar from the Escorial, half mad, and another Hieronymite, as fat as a pig, of whom it can be said that he had sprung at birth from the head of the Devil, as poets said that Minerva had sprung from Jupiter's. It fell to my lot to share my cell with this demon who was to do me immeasurable harm. I have never seen a more evil, more violent or more tireless troublemaker and schemer.

He was at one time in holy orders at the monastery of Salamanca, from which he was expelled; he went to a town in Extremadura, where he had been born, and incited the townspeople to rebel against their overlord. He then went to a monastery, of which a brother of his was the prior, and prodded his brother and all the monks into causing such scandal and so much commotion that the entire monastery was sent into exile by the king. He himself was banished to a monastery outside of Burgos, from which he wrote screeds against the friars to all the sovereigns of Europe and all the grandees of Spain. He finally caused so much mischief that the friars locked him up. He made his escape, and appeared before the intendant of Burgos to accuse them of smuggling. Doubtless the friars kept small deposits for certain poor wretches. Since everything in Spain is contraband, and taxes, duties and pensions keep the people in direst poverty, the instinct of self-preservation and concern for their well-being spurs them on to take up smuggling, with everyone with good sense lending a helping hand or closing their eyes to it, and there is no end of it in sight, despite the light troops engaged in waging a war to the death against smugglers.

Since the intendant paid no attention to the friar, he went off to the cathedral and, clinging to a bar of the choir grille, preached against the friars at the top of his lungs. The canons gently led him away and turned him in to the authorities. Such episodes are not unusual among Spanish friars, since they are commoners. Within the Franciscan order the Observantists are the sworn enemies of the Alcantarines or Diegans, whom they call *descalzillos*.* In a procession on Corpus these latter filled their sleeves with stones, and since all the Franciscans were intermingled, to tell a Diegan to move on, an Observantist made his meaning clear by

---

* Insignificant little discalced Franciscans.

throwing stones at his head. This started such a violent stone fight that the archbishop of Burgos halted with the Monstrance and said: "Good Lord, they're killing one another!" As the abbots of the Order of Saint Benedict were celebrating a pontifical High Mass, the prelates of the other Orders were annoyed on Saint Benedict's feast day in Oviedo, because the offices lasted so long. "We'll see each other again on Our Father's day," the guardian of the Franciscan monastery said; and that day the prelates were astonished to see it celebrated pontifically, with double the escort that the Benedictine abbot had had, that is to say, twelve friars in copes. The bishop and the abbot joined forces to have the friar exiled. Just as the monks of the Hieronymite monastery, outside the walls, succeeded in getting the king to order their accuser sent to Los Toribios.

Through the intermediary of the little tattletale doorkeeper Clemente, the friar also accused me of having penned a description of Los Toribios in verse. Outside of hunger, our principal martyrdom there was the boredom of having nothing to do, no work, not even a book to read for diversion. The intendant of the Navy, don Juan Antonio Enríquez, had recommended me to his brother, the royal treasurer in Seville, who used to come visit me, and recommended me to a priest, the former warden of Los Toribios, who lived in retirement there with the title of administrator. The latter gave me an inkwell and paper, and to amuse myself I began to write verses with the following title: "Cries from the Purgatory suffered by the distinguished retreatants of the house of correction of Los Toribios in Seville. A brother wrote them in the Lenten season of 1804 in order to arouse the compassion of pious souls." It was a joke, naturally; and to make it more humorous, I mixed features of the old system, which no longer existed, in with those of the new one. It was nothing but a way to make time pass and have a good laugh among ourselves. It had thirty-six *décimas.** I shall set down some of them here as a sample.

-I-

Our renowned Toribio
A devout man and bookseller in Seville,
Seeing so many moths
Flying about in his market,
Sold everything in his old bookstore
That he had bought;

---

* Stanzas of ten octosyllabic lines.

And with pious,
Albeit miserly, intent, stockpiled
All the nameless boys he found
Or those who seemed so to him.

-2-

He shook the dust off
The codex he grabbed,
Or because that was his pleasure,
Filed it away in his house.
He fed the boys and lodged them,
Taught them doctrine, and even how to read:
And was allowed to do as he liked.
And by dint of such effort founded
The holy house where I
Have come to suffer.

-3-

He was an Asturian, and founded
This house of prison chains
In the first year plus a double dozen
Of the century just ended.
It became famous for its cruelty;
And from all over the nation
People were sent there for correction.
Today it is a royal residence hall,
And though still a touch brutal
There is a great difference.

-4-

The little candidate
Who is nabbed and sent here
Gets off cheaply
With twenty-four lashes.
But quite other treatment is given
Those well-off people
Who wear colored stockings
That come from Vizcaya.
Religious in holy orders
Are granted certain exceptions.

-5-

In accordance with the initiation
Dealt out freely,
At the slightest infraction
The jailers survive in their profession.
But my song does not deal with
The natural sons
Of Toribio, nor other such
Who, by paying one peseta,
Are incorporated in the recipe
As co-naturals.

-6-

I weep for the retreatants
Set apart by the fees they pay
And because they are divided
From the poor self-flagellators.
The latter, free to wander in the courtyards,
Are not as closely confined;
We up here who are shut away
In a black passageway,
Are completely excluded
From human co-relations.

-7-

The father of the living
Though we can see he exists
Never casts his eye on the sad prison
Of such miserable wretches.
Only cold drafts
Can come and go as they please
And with murderous breath
Spread corruption
From a garden on a ship*
Never cleaned in its life.

---

*   On ships, the heads are called the garden. [Author's note]

-8-

Save when the sun in Lion
Roars as it spews fire
Which settles in immediately
To devour the prison,
There's no hope for redemption.
It's a real inferno outside,
Because from the cauldron
After being thoroughly roasted
Like the condemned in hell
We go to an ice chest.

-9-

The dreadful passageway
Is barely eight feet wide,
And forty paces long
And is used for recreation.
Like cannonballs
The soldier is there, the priest
Who is a woman-chaser, without good sense,
A shopkeeper, a friar, a toper:
Could the devil make a gazpacho like that
If needed in a hurry?

-10-

With no other exercise
No books, nothing to see, no recreation,
The tedium of nothing to do
Is our eternal ordeal.
Each one talks of his vice
That idleness feeds and even suckles.
And in such sainted company
And good conversation,
Instead of with mended ways, one leaves
More corrupted than when he entered.

-11-

Each madman with his own obsession
Soldiers and clergy pray

And the blasphemous band
Forms a mixed lot.
The one from Cyprus burns incense
To Venus, a Cypriot custom;
Bacchus grumbles without his wineskin;
Mars swears and despairs;
The galley burns with vows
That are not those of pious souls.

-12-
Finally, when the sun has gone down
With a handful of iron keys jingling
As though they were cowbells
They then round up the herd
In three cow pens to one side
With no furniture save ourselves,
Handcuffed together two by two,
Or more, if we are many or few;
And in these cages full of madmen
They shut us up, and off they go!

-13-
Farewell, we say; patience!
O wretched retreatant!
Every bug that bites
Mercilessly trains your spirit.
I've never seen such a plague of bedbugs
Or of Pharaonic mosquitoes,
The Inquisition did not have
Such an enormous fleabag;
Nor do dogs attack with more determination
A rag-and-bone man.

-14-
For everyone to roll out his mattress
They provide a plateful of burning oil
For a short time
A sepulchral wick.
The poet who as such
Cannot afford a bed

Climbs up on a tall, hard, narrow
Refectory bench,
Whence he will go to purgatory
If he has no right to be there.

-15-
At six in the morning
The door bolts clang again
And we hear Mass with our eyes
At the bars of a window.
Then most unwillingly
We mumble to ourselves a part
Of the rosary, and leave
Another part for the night
With one decade
Not yet said when we leave.

-16-
This most devout daily office
Is said in the refectory,
That we make into an oratory
For it has a Calvary there.*
And it is not a daring opinion
That because of our praying so badly
Christ is in a nasty mood,
Quite annoyed, and because she's weary
The Virgin is seated
Not standing, as in Scripture.

-17-
Only to some trifle
Is any attention paid,
If, for instance, one attends
Orisons bareheaded.
No matter if this leaves one with a head cold
In such a blast of icy air.
Or that one's noggin turns into a skull;

---

* An apprentice retreatant painted this Calvary, in which Christ is there, very much against his will, and the Virgin, seated at the foot of the Cross. [Author's note]

With the sending of a burial announcement
The duty of the house is fulfilled,
As with the passing on of the trappings
Of a pack mule that dies.

-18-
To round off the prayers
Chocolate and bread carefully measured out,
The bread doesn't come in the cup, though.
And the chocolate is peanut-shell cocoa
And floods of hot water:
It doesn't break one's fast,
Though it breaks one's bones;
And though most have been shriven
They still must endure such torture.

-19-
As for our meals, we get better treatment
Doubtless, and more variation;
Benediction, grace, a lesson
And squash on a plate:
In another, for trimmings,
Grace and benediction,
With no risk of indigestion,
To put us to sleep, soups;
And at lunch and dinner
Glasses of water *ad libitum.*

-20-
By Bacchus, out of here
You muses with your Castalia
For poets in Italy
Go like Horace to Falerno;
They swim a great deal in the Avernus,
Like frogs in a marsh
Be they Manichaean or Mohammedan;
But, 'sblood, 'tis a heinous crime
To smuggle in wine
For a Christian.

-21-

O, Hispanic-Moorish house
Of merciless spiritual exercises,
A site for them out of necessity,
The art of an early death.
Why do you usurp, you tyrant,
The name of house of correction?
You amend people's diet
But hunger's the wrong remedy
Where there is no one
Suffering from indigestion.

-22-

If with such a pitiless diet
A person's health declines,
He will die without medicaments
For there is no infirmary.
Sangría* is the one thing not lacking
If we send out to buy some
Because our rascal of a doorkeeper
Knows how to administer it,
The one we call old Cacus**
A most appropriate name.

-23-

The buyer for the house
Is not a thief, but a blind man
Can there be anything, I ask you,
More absurd than that?
He is sold cat for rabbit,
Both wholesale and retail,
By merchants in the market
As he blindly fingers their wares;
The worst part is when we wretches shut up here
Have to pay the bills.

---

* A play on words: *sangría* is both the well-known bloodred wine punch and a medical bloodletting.
** In Roman mythology, a thieving giant, son of Vulcan.

-24-

But it's imperative to keep quiet
About all one's objections; write nothing
Because even if you're amid scribes
You're not allowed an inkwell.
They have the right
Or dispensation of conscience
To open without your permission
Whatever comes to you sealed
Sending you things that way is a sin
That brings inevitable punishment.

-25-

There are infernal storehouses
Of shackles, of chains,
Of gags and other torture devices,
With iron bars from royal vessels.
The broadasses and other such lazy louts
Ministers of despotism,
Who like those of the infernal abyss
Do not enjoy full satisfaction
Save when, in wreaking their bodily harm,
They smash a person's head in.

-26-

All this and all the staff
Are at the orders of a warden,
Who is chief constable of lead
And galley sergeant of Tetuán.*
Woe unto those who have
Such a priest-warden in charge:
He's a Cato, and in all truth
The strength of his lungs
Is a perfect match for
The thickness of his head.

---

* Another name for Los Toribios.

-27-
His sister winds him around her little finger
And his entourage leads both by the nose.
And whoever is the tattletale
Gains the greatest favor.
And for both of them
The top brass around here is a captain,
Who after a two-year stay here
As a retreatant or a galley slave
Without breeches or a cape
Has ended up a sacristan.

-28-
Captain Bajá has
His constables and informers,
And his choice of scoundrels
Recruited here:
There's a rascally doorkeeper*
Who comes from Medinacelli
And suits him to a T
(With two feet and four heels
Like a cock with spurs)
When it comes to singing, the knave.

-29-
He has another one, our manservant
In truth an innocent
Because he's mad; but guilty
Of sheer maliciousness.
Keeping everything shut up tight
Is his obsession; and I hold him to be
A liar because he is a talebearer.
He loves no one, hates no one,
And money does not concern him,
He was born to be a jailer.

---

* After 1811, I saw him in a lieutenant's uniform in Cádiz, because any rotter was an officer in those days. [Author's note]

There followed stories of souls in Purgatory, though without naming names, and it concluded with the lament uttered in Spain on behalf of the souls in Purgatory.

It is obvious that the whole thing is only a joke, and among rational people it would have been laughed at and hailed as a clever bit of tomfoolery; but I was in Tetuán. It was all still in rough draft form when the friar told the little doorman, who ran to tell Honorary Captain Montoya about it; and that night, while we were in the chapel, the latter came with the supervisor to search me and they found the *décimas*. Montoya was very annoyed at the part about his lacking a cape and breeches, because even though it was true that he had been obliged to borrow both so as to go out onto the street, he was very vain and extremely arrogant. And since he had the stupid priest in charge under his thumb, he set him against me. The priest came upstairs the next day, and with his mouth full of bread dunked in soup and half an Andalusian tongue, he said to me: "Zeñor, you make everything your businezz, even the Mozt Holy Virgin: whether she is ztanding or zitting; she'll be in whatever pozition she pleases. And why is it any conzern of yours if my head is big? With this big body of mine, would you want me to have a head like a pinwheel?" When I saw that that idiot didn't understand that what I was calling him in *décima* 26 was stupid, I slyly replied: "Sir, the whole matter can be remedied simply by changing the last four feet of the *décima*. "Where are you from?" "From Alpechín, and I used to be an acolyte here in this parish church of Santa María, where I'm a cantor now." "Because it's all composed already. Here it is:"

> This fine specimen is from Alpechín,
> An acolyte by profession;
> A mere man, so Plato says
> With two feet and his head held high.

Everybody knows that Plato defined a man as: *An animal without feathers, with two feet, with its head erect,* and that Socrates, plucking all the feathers from a live rooster, tossed it into the Academy, saying: *"Here comes Plato's man."* But my priest in charge, who had never been ragged like that in his life, said to me: "So before you wanted me to have a head like a pinwheel and now you say I have one like Plato's? I'll keep it the way God gave it to me. Wait, I'm going to put you in irons." They put me in a pair of them for the first time in my life, even though I warned him that by the terms of the *Si quis in clericum* he was risking being excommunicated. "This is a royal residence hall, and therefore I have the king's permission to do whatever I please." And except for the imaginary king of the Mandarins in America, the king never puts priests in irons. I was then sent off to a tower two stories high, and they added to the irons a shackle attached to an iron bar that weighed some thirty or forty kilos.

He visited me at evening orisons, thinking that he would find me in very low spirits, and was amazed to find me cheerful. I was taking all of this with the mockery it merited in the eyes of a philosopher who finds himself among Hottentots, or like Anacharsis when the tyrant Mecrotion ordered him to be ground up in a mortar: "Crush the garments of Anacharsis," he said to him, "but you won't touch him." I have always had on my lips, amid all the abuses I have endured, this beautiful saying of Saint Cyprian's: *Non facit martyrem paena [sic], sed causa.** Irons and imprisonments dishonor no one, for Jesus Christ, the Saints, the greatest men, endured them, and it has always been the heritage of virtue and merit. The cause that makes for martyrdom is what brings dishonor, and I had none, though I was ever mindful of the irons that Montezuma had worn.

Then they removed the irons and two days later the shackle with the bar, because my leg swelled up, and suddenly I found that I had turned into a prince, for in the top part of the tower I had four balconies that overlooked the rooftops of the entire neighborhood and had lovely views of the nearest gardens. The one in the bottom part had an opening with a grille that gave on an unwalled garden, with thin bars that had such wide gaps between them that I could have spread them apart and escaped, just as I could have from above. Why didn't I make my escape? you will ask me. I myself am amazed, and I don't know what to answer except that I am the greatest simpleton in the world. The archbishop had reported that I was inclined to attempt to escape if I was incarcerated, and León always made a point of this so as to keep me in chains. And in fact I am so inclined to suffer the most unjust imprisonments so patiently that it has been necessary to drive me to utter desperation before I even think of saving my life, in obedience to the counsel of Jesus Christ: *cum persequentur vos, fugite.*** The friar was very pleased that I was being mistreated, because he was extremely envious, cruel and vengeful and could not bear it that they had left him with a shackle for a week when he first entered whereas they had done nothing to me. He

---

*   *It is not the punishment but the cause that makes for martyrdom.*
**   *When they persecute you . . . flee . . .* (Mt 10:23)

did not see the difference of subjects or of causes. Moreover he had come to be on the friendliest of terms with Montoya, who had declared himself my enemy; so that with my imprisonment the same thing happened to those two blackguards as to Herod and Pilate with the imprisonment of Jesus Christ: *et facti sunt amici ex illa hora.** One Sunday as I was leaving my tower to go hear Mass in the oratory, the friar asked me how I was getting along; I answered him that things were going fairly well, but that he should ask someone to bring me my hat that I'd left behind in our room. I said this for no other reason than to have all my clothes with me, because that was the only thing I had left behind in the tower. The friar told Montoya, and both of them intimated to the priest in charge that I was trying to make a getaway, as though I had such great need of my hat, since I was so well recommended in Seville, that not having it was enough to keep me from trying to escape. Carpenters came immediately to nail the doors of the four balconies shut.

I could just as easily, or even more easily, have left through the barred window after garroting him, and I had already begun to consider doing so, though I hesitated. I have never been able to persuade myself that men do evil for evil's sake, nor do they fail to keep in mind the account they must render God for having harmed their neighbor. After so many proofs that León was out for my life, or in any event to keep me far from court so that justice would not be done me, I believed that he would be content to keep me in Los Toribios for a time. This is already being too naive; but there is nothing for it; that is how I am; a child has more guile.

Opposite my window there was a guard who was keeping watch on several prisoners who were in a house adjoining Los Toribios. But it was turned into a hospice for poor women, and when the guard left one afternoon, though I didn't think he had departed for good, a soldier came over to greet me and offer me his services if I wanted something. The thought occurred to me to have him get me a file just in case trouble came my way, and I gave him a peso. The scoundrel warned them at Los Toribios that I was thinking of making my escape, and pocketed the money. I was immediately sent back to the block of cells where the distinguished retreatants were confined. But I fell sick at once; and as I told the doctor that I would offer him proof of my gratitude, he gave his assurance that it was necessary that I be taken to a hospital if I were to recover completely. Everything was all arranged, when the accursed friar

---

* *And [they] became friends that very day.* (Lk 23:12)

and Montoya persuaded the priest in charge that I had bribed the doctor. Hence this way of getting out came to nothing.

The ones who had bribed him were the ones who had eight duros to buy the freedom of the life-guardsman on whose behalf (because the guardsman was from his part of the country) the friar had had a word with Montoya, and Montoya with the priest in charge, because the guard had a silk sash that the captain coveted. The guard got out, in fact, on the pretext that he was ill; but that was after he had fulfilled an iniquitous condition that the friar had imposed. I am so decidedly against talebearing, troublemaking and gossipmongering that I have never recriminated anyone for slandering me, or taken the trouble to go put matters straight with the person whom it was claimed that I had spoken ill of. I have contented myself with the witness of my conscience, and disregarded all idle talk. I was wrong, doubtless, because by my so doing the slander spread unchecked, discredited me and made me many enemies. Only once did I try to recriminate anyone, and that was the friar of Los Toribios, for the evil he had done me. And that viper told the life-guardsman that he would not get out through his intercession if he did not wreak revenge on me on his behalf. Since I had not offended the guard in any way, I was caught unawares when he grabbed me by my neckerchief and twisted it till I turned black in the face. The little porter Clemente, who saw this, ran off, shouting that I was being killed, to summon the friar who was close by, and he answered that he was praying, because the whole thing was obviously all being done at his orders. When I had but one last spark of life left in me, I bit my torturer's hand; he let go of me, and they carried me off to my bed. The friar managed to turn the tables so that, instead of its being the guard and the friar who were punished, I was the one they put in irons and locked up.

It was summer, in Seville, that is to say that the sun's rays there are molten, and my cell was always scorching hot. At lunchtime or dinnertime, in order that the mad Toribian servant who brought me my meals would not keep it open for any length of time, Montoya, of whom the madman was deathly afraid, because the latter beat him, meanwhile stationed himself at the little window at the end of the passageway.

The servant would set the plate with my lunch or my dinner down in front of me, and immediately leap out of the cell, shouting, "Fire! It's an inferno in here!" That was how much steam that crucible gave off. So as to be able to breathe, I sprinkled water on the bricks, and stretched out naked on top of them. I finally made up my mind to save my life.

One night, at eleven o'clock, soaking the wall of my cell with water, I began to chip away at it with a nail round the small window with the bars and barbed wire. On the stroke of one, I managed to yank it out. But I then was confronted by a big iron grille. Nonetheless, it seemed to me that by tying a rope to it, I could easily get out; and taking the wool out of the mattress, I threw the bedclothes and the entire bed down onto a flat roof so as to get a little money for it later, keeping only the pillow-cases to make the rope with. Imagine my fear when I found that because the bars, and the crossbars as well, were very close together, the grille barely gave at all. The thought of the abuse that I would no doubt suffer when dawn came gave me inspiration and determination; I therefore tied the pillowcase strips to the other grille, and seeing that my head would go through, I pushed with all my might; my chest was squeezed against my backbone, I gave a terrible, involuntary cry of pain, so loud that I have no idea why the broadasses who were sleeping within sight of me failed to hear me, and found myself on the other side. It was two o'clock in the morning on Saint John's Day, 1804, and it was already getting light. I collected my clothes, and a gardener who was already at work in the garden set up a pole for me so that I could slide down it to the ground.

I put atop my head my bundle of clothes, which was not a small one, though I had taken no other clothes with me except for my shirt, my breeches and my shoes, and began running along the outside wall till I came to the door of San Fernando. I sat down nearby to wait for it to open, and I now think they never do open it. It was already seven o'-clock, and seeing some mules come by, I followed them and left by the Chiclana gate, in the gypsy quarter, which is separated from Seville by a pontoon bridge over the Guadalquivir. Seeing the coat of arms of Saint Dominic on the door of a monastery called San Jacinto, I stopped and waited for it to be opened. Once inside, I asked which padre was the best-tempered, and when they told me it was the sacristan, I summoned him and told him my troubles. "Clear out of here," he told me, "and head for the towns where boats put in for the night." He let me out by way of a monastery door and sent me on my way. I was sweating with my load, but I ran without stopping and after one or two leagues lay down in the shade of the first house I came across. The women invited me in, and I waited there till nightfall, whereupon I went down to the bank of the Guadalquivir to wait for boats to come in. Many sailed past, heading for the open sea sixteen leagues away, but all of them told me they were making for San Lúcar. Noting that there were fewer and fewer of them, and not one was going to Cádiz, because the boats that ply the river are only small feluccas, I asked for passage on one of them. "Is that bundle you have your clothes?" "Yes, sir." "Let's have a look at those blunderbusses of yours, those shotguns." That is what the boat-man said, because many times thieves, pretending they want passage, rob the boatmen when they dock.

I went aboard, and we sailed for six hours, because the boats go downstream from Seville with the outgoing tide every six hours, and likewise go upstream from the sea with the incoming tide, laying over, therefore, every six hours. I sold my bedclothes to some passengers and made a little money. When we reached San Lúcar I bought a hat and went on with the passengers headed for the Puerto de Santa María in two old coaches, one of which broke down, and we reached the port on foot. I immediately embarked for Cádiz; when the boat docked in its bay, I took lodgings on the Plaza San Juan de Dios, not knowing what to do with myself, because there is nothing more embarrassing for a man than to have a sense of shame and no money.

As I was walking along the Alameda, around nine that night, I saw a Dominican friar, sitting by himself, and because of my abiding affection for the habit I went over to speak to him and inquire about the outcome of the lawsuit brought by the provincial of Castile over the matter of the old vicar-general of the Order, and in the course of the conversation I said that I was a Mexican who had just come from Seville. He suspected who I was. He was the procurator of the Dominicans of Mexico, and to get me to tell him more, he told me that he was a friar from Ronda. This was true, for he was one of the two brothers who came to Mexico with a boatload of missionaries, because he had fathered a daughter in Ronda, thereby causing a great scandal. The money of the Province of Mexico would provide her with a dowry. Just as they let out all the prisoners in jails throughout Spain to populate the colony that Columbus founded on the island of Santo Domingo, first called Española, so today they are still emptying the prisons of its monasteries so as to bring over missionaries and rotating friars, that is to say, clergy to take turns enjoying a prelate's honors and benefices, leaving the Creoles nothing but the burden of supporting them. This law is based on nothing but intrigues and false reports submitted by the Spanish friars here so as to recruit for their cause. I believe that the friar who succeeded me in the post that I held in the Order of Saint Dominic in Mexico was one who was able to come take my place because he was let out of the jail of Santo Tomás in Madrid, where he had been serving five years for having committed apostasy and become a soldier.

The suspicions of the friar-procurator that I was the former Dominican who had been sent to Los Toribios were confirmed when I proved to be very knowledgeable about the affairs of the Order. Had he not been a malicious *gachupín*, he would have been forthcoming with me, I would have shown him my briefs, explained the whole affair to him and spared his Province the expense of my maintenance. But what does a *gachupín* care about the Province of which he is the stepson? The business at hand is to persecute the Creole, and he proposed to do so. To that end he told me that he took great pleasure in keeping company with well-educated men; that on another day we would lunch together, if I would tell him where I was putting up. I told him, and he wanted me to point it out to him so he wouldn't mistake it. With my blessed simplemindedness I went with him so as to show him which one it was, and on the way he tried to have me arrested, for he asked me to wait for him for a moment just outside a certain door, while he exchanged a word with a friend of his in passing. I then discovered that it was the house of the chief constable, but that he wasn't home. I finally showed the friar my inn, and from there he went to the house of the governor to ask that I be put in prison, as an apostate and a fugitive from Los Toribios, where I had been confined by order of the king.

At midnight the chief constable came to arrest me, and took me to the public jail, because the clergy in Cádiz do not have a separate one. The friar also wrote to Los Toribios to tell them of my whereabouts, saying that the arm of justice has a very long reach, and I would not escape, for he had already had me put in prison. Just look at what a zealous constable the king had found. He was the one who ought to have been put in prison. I sent a letter of protest to His Excellency the bishop, writing as a secular elder, under the name of Ramiro de Vendes, an exact anagram of my name and surname, the name I used at the inn, and also the one that I gave to the chief constable.[3] The vicar-general came to see me, with a scribe. I explained my case and handed my briefs over to him. Had it been only a matter of the friar's denunciation, I would have been a free man; but since that wretch had mentioned the royal order to have me put in Los Toribios, he was not able to let me go; all he could do was notify the court, that is to say, put me back in León's clutches. Meanwhile I was sent to the infirmary.

The Cádiz jail is an edifice well suited to the function it fulfills. It has a pretty covered patio with a vault of iron bars, with its glass-enclosed chapel in the middle, visible to all the prisoners. The infirmary is very spacious. I had a very large salon all to myself, with three windows overlooking the sea, which kept the room cool. The food was very good, and in addition to the patients in the infirmary, I was visited by the doctor, who became a close friend, a canon and an English hospitaler who was most charitable toward the prisoners.

I wrote to His Excellency the inquisitor Yéregui; but he had died, and my grief put me in bed. Nonetheless, my friend don Manuel González recommended me to the vicar-general, who came to visit me and provided me with clothing. I had recourse to the house of Vicario, through whose intermediary I received money from Mexico, and was given twenty-five duros that Dr. Pomposo had sent me. If I had asked for help before, I would not have found myself in such an embarrassing position because of my lack of money, but instead I do things backwards. I wrote a long memorandum to the court while I was there; but in the end I didn't send it, because it was useless: that accursed León knew very well that I was innocent and formally secularized.

While that villain, as my reader already suspects, is sending me back to Los Toribios, I shall tell a bit about the prisoners. Among those in the infirmary there was one with the finest and most respectable presence in this world, who had made himself out to be a minister of the Holy Office seeking to arrest a sly priest. He arrived in a carriage, with his prison wardens, alerted the forces of law and order to come to his aid if need be, and went into the house. It was a commercial establishment that made fat profits; and since he asked for a quiet and secluded room, they put him in the back room, begging him to think of the honor of the family and not take the priest away. He told them that they knew the ways of the world, and things could be arranged if they kept their eyes closed. They tried to do so; but the inquisitors were not satisfied, and since they were alone and there were sacks of pesos there, they stuffed their pockets full. "Thieves and inquisitors," the family said the minute they discovered the money was missing. "It's not possible." They sent word to Seville, and the inquisitors of my story were caught midway on the road, their carriage having been recognized because of the luxurious saddlebags loaded on the front of it.

It was not the first time he had foxed someone. Because of his fine presence other foxes made use of him. An attorney had forged a letter patent of nobility for someone who wanted to be made a member of a knightly Order, but since the forger was not satisfied with what he was given, he sent the inquisitor of my story to pass himself off as a commissioner who had come from the court to look into certain flaws that had been found in his letter patent. The man who coveted a knight's cross thought that he was lost and threw himself at the commissioner's feet. "I am an honest and charitable man," the commissioner told him, "but you know what makes the world go round and how matters get settled." The would-be knight emptied his strongbox, the attorney who had forged the document sucked at two teats and the interested party got his cross. How many things like that I have seen in this world! An executioner in Málaga received a knight's cross in America. A relative of mine said to me quite rightly: "Nobles of ancient lineage like ourselves have no need of knight's crosses. When you see one, recite a *Pater noster* and an *Ave-maria*, for it is a sign of decline." My inquisitor had the signatures of all the ministers and pointed out to me that after becoming a minister, Caballero had changed the *v* of his name to a *b*. And he showed me how a letter of the alphabet is forged, by placing a light underneath a pane of glass between two chairs, and a thin paper over the letter that the forger wants to change. It is not that hard if one has mastered the principles of draftsmanship.

Among the prisoners in the infirmary there was also an Italian picklock, a very skillful one, who carefully fingered the lock on one of the doors of the salon where I was, and when he managed to get into the kitchen for a moment, fashioned a lock pick out of two nails that opened the door as easily as though it were the right key to it. But on the night the prisoners planned to escape, at the end of August, the chief constable came to get me and take me to Los Toribios, and by so doing saved me from having a great scare, for if the prisoners did not manage to escape, or the sentinels stopped them, I would have had cause for regret for having allowed them to make their escape by way of my room.

I boarded the boat in the bay of Cádiz in the company of a corporal and two soldiers, because to do me honor and ease his mind León always provided me with such an escort. A sailor took such a liking to me that he offered me his house if I ever found myself in a tight spot, and told me where it was in the Chiclana quarter of Seville. The soldiers also became friends of mine; they provided me with a good file, which they hid by sewing it inside the back of my waistcoat; they also sewed sixteen duros inside a canvas belt for me to wear next to my skin, and I hid away a good knife and a pair of scissors, as well as my briefs, inside the facings of my frock coat; and here I am, back again, two months later, in Los Toribios, owing to the evil designs of the *gachupín* friar-procurator of Mexico.

I was put in a cell and clapped into a pair of irons, not to mention being shackled to the iron bar. This, however, was after four hours, during which I would have had time (had I been craftier) to lift up a brick in the floor of the second room, because there were two of them, and hide all my belongings there. After supper, in order to catch me unawares and half naked, the madmen came, along with Montoya's satellites and the Hieronymite, and searched all my belongings. But the only thing they found was the file, because I had taken off my waistcoat after supper.

The wretched friar was not satisfied, and thought I still had at least the briefs in my possession. Perhaps on the friar's advice, a son of the Order from Bilbao, a recent proselyte, whom we called *Rompiendas,* because the Basques, speaking of what we would call *calzones rotos or rompidos,** say *calzones rompiendas,* became a fast friend of mine. He came to tell me that they were going to search even my privates, and therefore I should give him everything I had with me for him to keep for me. All this was on the advice of the friar, since no one was thinking of making such a search. Though I already had a way of keeping everything quite safe, either by hiding it underneath the bricks or placing it in the hands of the porter, who was a very honest and discreet man, I fell into the trap and handed over briefs, money, knife and scissors. The friar demanded in return that he be given a lunch and a big spread for supper paid for with my money, as I, hearing him laughing and downing his feast, remained in my cell, raging with hunger.

Following the friar's advice, the aforementioned Basque made his escape, with my money, by stealing out at nine o'clock at night behind the chaplain, who went home at that hour. The friar thereby killed two birds with one stone: depriving me of all help and ousting the chaplain, since the latter had allowed the Basque to make his escape, so as to take his place, as he succeeded in doing later on. When he took off however, Rompiendas left my briefs and papers with the friar. I dashed out of my cell when I learned that and went to see what the fugitive had left behind in the friar's room. And finding myself without briefs, I burst into tears. My tears did not move in the least that reprobate with a fringe of hair around his tonsure; he kept the briefs hidden, and since Montoya was going to Madrid, he gave them to him to take with him. Such a wicked, cruel deed! Leaving me with no proof of my secularization and with no defense against León! Leaving me without letters dimissory and with no proof of all my privileges! How to secure other briefs, and ones as well authenticated? They had cost me many steps, efforts and labors to acquire. Where to get money to secure others? It would occur only to

---

* Torn breeches.

demons to wreak such evil against an unfortunate victim in desperate need, one who had never done them the slightest harm. Hence the friar pretended, to my face, to be my friend, inasmuch as he did not have the slightest pretext for being my enemy. I later got some of my rescripts from Lisbon, through the intercession of the secretary of the Spanish embassy. As for the rest, Montoya answered that he had burned them. What wickedness!

After a few months they allowed me to leave my cell, to my misfortune as it turned out. A Spanish lad who had fallen into heresy and libertinage was brought to Los Toribios from London. And the exhortation delivered to him by the priest in charge, as we were having supper, was limited to reproaching him for having lived among those heretical dogs who denied the Conception in grace of the Most Blessed Virgin Mary. Such a reproach to a lad who had abandoned religion was quite enough to make a theologian like myself laugh, for the Conception in grace is merely an opinion. The friar asked me why I was laughing; I told him the reason, adding that Dominicans maintained the opposite, in accordance with the doctrine of Saint Thomas, and had a brief from Pope Gregory XIII granting them permission to defend it in their general Councils.

The friar told the priest in charge, who called me a heretic and an enemy of the Virgin. I told him, to no avail, that the point in question did not concern a venal or mortal sin that had been committed but had to do, rather, with a sin that had been inherited; it was not a matter of a sin on the part of an individual, but, rather, of the nature of Adam *in quo omnes peccaverunt,** as the Apostle said; that that was the doctrine of Saint Thomas and that of all the Church Fathers, as he could verify in the opuscule of Cardinal Cayetano to Leo X; and the same doctrine was held by all the theologians of antiquity, as was demonstrated at the Council of Basel in another opuscule, by Cardinal Torquemada; that the Greek Church, in its Council General against the Protestants, protested that it had always believed that same doctrine; that the Council of Trent renewed the order of excommunication issued by Sixtus IV against anyone who maintained that affirming or denying the Conception in grace is heresy, error, impiety, temerity, scandal or mortal sin; that while allowing the prayer, the Supreme Pontiff protests that this should not be taken to mean that so much as a grain of weight has thereby been added to the opinion of the pious as opposed to its contrary. The altogether uncultivated priest neither believed me nor understood me. I lacked all

---

*   *. . . in whom all have sinned.*

credit in his eyes in matters concerning religion, and the friar later abused his authority in order to heap as much calumny upon my head as he pleased, for this demon feared that I would compete with him for the chaplaincy that he was already trying to take away from the chaplain. He was from Extremadura, like the majority of those who bathed the Republic in blood.

I ought to have remembered that Seville is the most fanatical place in Spain, and that the spectacle of burning people at the stake had been so common for forty years that the ring where they were burned, as solidly built as the bullring so that the public could witness the ceremony, is still standing. And that that was where the *bendito** was invented. They must have criticized it in the Dominican monastery, and a theologian with a garrote or a lay brother of the Order ordered the lad who sang it to be silent and he refused. The lay brother used his garrote to give him a syllogism in the Barbara mode** so long it shut him up forever. The amends to the Virgin for this death, the scandal, the ruckus were enormous. And the king ordered that every preacher say the *bendito* in the pulpit before the sermon or be hauled down from it by some village constable. This is the reason why it is still recited today. The Dominicans submitted a denunciation of the *bendito* to the Holy See, maintaining that it was superstitious, because it conjoined an article of faith, which the Eucharist is, and mere opinion concerning the Conception. And the Supreme Pontiff Julius III, if I remember correctly, issued a brief ordering an *amen* inserted between the Eucharist and the Conception. This *amen* is preserved in the *bendito* that is sung, because in canticles old junk is better preserved. "May the Divine Sacrament be praised and extolled, amen, and the immaculate conception," etcetera. This *amen* placed there made a lasting impression on me as a youngster, because to me it cut the canticle short. Today it is not said in the recited *bendito*, either out of ignorance, or because the *bendito* has been changed, and one says: " . . . and Most Holy Mary, Our Lady, conceived in grace," etcetera.

As punishment I was made to go sleep at Los Toribios every night, in a cell two paces wide, without a breath of air. And I got hardly any sleep, because I have always had difficulty sleeping, and the rosary recited by the Toribians and the shouting of their madman "Moorish chieftain" kept me awake. Between two of them they go on singing the rosary all

---

* A prayer that begins in Spanish with the words *bendito y alabado*: blessed and praised.

** *Barbara* is the first word in the mnemonic lines that represent the valid modes of the Scholastic syllogism. Here it is also a pun on the word for *barbarous, barbarian,* etc.

night long, while the others sleep. But apart from the first two mysteries, I noticed that they never finished any of them. The hapless creatures, roused at five in the morning for the office in the oratory, which lasts for an hour, and another at night, which also lasts an hour, dying of hunger and exhausted after working all day, fall fast asleep on their beds. The priest in charge awakens them, shouting, the poor youngsters go back to sing a few *Avemarias,* and fall fast asleep on their beds again. This goes on all night long, and I didn't sleep a wink.

A son of a clothier from Madrid, so wicked, such a liar and scandalmonger that he had caused his parents to divorce, was sent to Los Toribios, yet was free to wander all through the place, and came back to the house of the distinguished retreatants only to sleep. I did him a thousand services, and through him managed to write a letter to the vicar-general of Cádiz, asking him for a little money to help me get by, to be sent to me through the chaplain. He sent me an ounce of gold through him; but the friar, playing the saint by pacing up and down the corridor so that the priest in charge would see him praying all day long, though he was a most dishonest man, had ousted the chaplain and taken over his living quarters, along with his post and the salary that went with it. The chaplain kept six duros for himself and sent me ten. Since I am charitable and generous by nature, I threw copper coins through a little window to the famished Toribians. The friar realized that I had money and informed on me, and they came to search the little cell where I slept. They found nothing, and the friar suggested that they should pry up some bricks in the room where I spent the day. They found eight duros and kept them for themselves.

The evil that man did me is immeasurable. I suddenly found myself locked up, with two pairs of shackles, without my having the least idea why. I asked the priest in charge to tell me, but it was not possible for him to be wiser than God, who even though he knew how trivial the excuses that Adam, Eve and Cain were about to give him were, did not punish them without first hearing them out. But I never found myself without the friar at my side, who in this instance never left me, both so that the priest in charge would not tell me of the slanderous stories he spread about me, and so that I would not tell the priest about his villainy. That man was even malicious enough to see to it that a kitten, my only diversion because it could do everything but talk, was taken away from me. I was born to love, and my sensitivity is such that I must love something in order to live. Hence whenever I have been imprisoned, I have always cared for some creature, if only a little spider, a few ants, any living being; or if there was no such thing, any sort of little plant. I missed my kitten a great deal. In short, that blackguard offended my sensibilities so deeply, and made me suffer so much physical abuse because of the sheer stupidity of the priest who was the warden, that I was found on the floor, knocked out flat. When they bled me in the foot they were astonished to see that my blood was as black as coal; my soul was that badly burned. The doctor ordered that I be given the last sacraments as quickly as possible, and this was done. But the confessor was bewildered to see me in Los Toribios merely because of a sermon I had preached, when, he told me, only totally recalcitrant young men doomed to perdition were sent there. In fact, no greater misfortune could befall a decent man than to find himself in that pigsty of scoundrels, recruited from all over Spain, who took advantage of my natural naiveté to satisfy their inclination to do evil, and gain, by mortifying me, the indulgence of the priest in charge, who had been left with a bad impression of me because of the calumny heaped upon me by the friar and Montoya.

I was aware that my illness came from being overheated and dehydrated, and I sent out for some prickly pears, on which I gorged myself, and since my body is as docile as my soul, on the day after I had been given the sacraments, the doctor found me out of danger and asked me in amazement what I had done. On discovering that I owed my recovery to the prickly pears, he ordered some brought to me every day. I was so ghastly pale and weak when I got out of bed that there was no knave who would not have dared insult me, especially a doorman of the General Treasury, the son of the king's boot maker, as vulgar and ugly as he was evil. I finally found a way, through the clothier's son, who was let out shortly thereafter, to write to my friend don Manuel del Campo, to have him plead in God's name with don Zenón, a member of the General Council for Mexico, to get me out of that pigsty. To justify the order, don Zenón sent word to the priest in charge of Los Toribios to submit a secret report. That barbarian, without ever hearing me out with regard to what the rogues were saying about me, or commending himself to God, reported that even though he had not given me a hearing, he knew, through persons whom he thought he should believe, that I often spoke ill of religion and of the Blessed Virgin Mary. These trustworthy persons were the villainous friar and the depraved clothier's son, who (as I later learned from the friar himself), once he had become aware (in all likelihood thanks to a hint from the latter) of the priest-supervisor's weak point, his prejudice against me, after humbly kissing his hand whenever he saw him, begged him, with tears in his eyes, to spare him from having to listen to my continual blasphemies and irreverent remarks directed against Jesus Christ and the Blessed Virgin Mary, which had horrified him. And that was the reason why he was free to wander about wherever he chose, coming back to the cell block of the distinguished retreatants only to sleep. I for my part had gone so far as to act as his servant there, without ever once opening my mouth about religious matters. What greater villainy or more outrageous behavior could there be than to take the word of a pair of scoundrels against that of a priest of my high degree, who, pen in hand, had defended the faith against unbelievers and heretics? How right the wise man in Ecclesiastes was when he declared: "I have seen under the sun another evil . . . a fool put in lofty position. . . ."*

The indignation of the distinguished retreatants at Los Toribios at such a terrible report to the king made me aware of its existence. And I could see then that there was no other way out for me save the one that the Gospel recommends: *fugite.* The distinguished retreatants themselves urged me to do so, because they were persuaded that in order to keep me safely shut up they too had been put under lock and key, and that if I were gone they would be given permission to wander all about the place. I managed to yank a little window out, and they found me a rope made of esparto grass with which to let myself down. I managed to throw my clothes down below; but I did not dare let myself down, because it was too far to the ground. God was watching over me, because I would have been dashed to pieces: the rope was rotten.

Since the patio into which I had let the rope down was a poorhouse, they took my clothes to the priest in charge of Los Toribios and locked me up, but only for a little while, because Montoya had already left. The priest was very annoyed, because Montoya had let the priest's sister down by not marrying her as he had promised. The clothier's son had also left, since his slanderous stories about me had earned him an excellent report from the imbecile of a priest in charge, who was now in a rage because he had found out that the clothier's son had taken letters out for me. The friar was able to go out whenever and wherever he pleased, and was having a fine time, and even having a love affair, because a shopkeeper who had a pretty wife had been sent to Los Toribios and had gotten the friar involved with her so that he would have re-

---

* Eccl 10:7.

course to that Asmodeus* as an intermediary and thereafter be under obligation to him. So there was no one left in Los Toribios who was determined to persecute me.

A priest finally arrived who had been sent to Los Toribios because he was a Jansenist and he was still confined there. He doubtless came well recommended. He was dominating, and dominated the whole crew of Toribians, especially the porter of the Treasury, who was from Murcia, as he was. The latter had a file, with which he filed off the shackles of the son of a shopkeeper who had just arrived, and the shopkeeper's son and the priest opened up a good-sized hole through the latrines at eleven at night, using the bolt from my cell, which was long and pointed, and the three of us took off, with me lugging along my bed-clothes to sell them and have a little money. It had now been thirteen months since my return to Los Toribios. The gardener who took care of the garden next door, hearing footsteps on the flat rooftop, came out to see what it was, and put a ladder up so that we could get down. We spent the night in the Alameda of Seville, which is like two streets lined with trees, and when it got light we went to the Chiclana quarter. My priest, who liked dealing with gypsies, got us lodgings in a house of theirs, and began selling all my bedclothes for an ochavo, so as to go on a spree. Since I knew the aforementioned family, I left and went to find the house of my friend the sailor who had brought me from Cádiz, and though he wasn't there, I stayed at his house till nightfall.

I no longer had a hat, because the supervisor of Los Toribios had kept it along with all my other clothing; but in a rubbish dump I saw a hat without a crown, placed my handkerchief on top of it, as if I had just been bathing, and went by night to Seville to see the royal treasurer, Enríquez, to whom I had been recommended. He gave me an ounce of gold and asked me if I wanted more. I, who am very timid about asking for things, answered that that was sufficient, and that night I boarded a riverboat for Cádiz. I ought to have gone overland to Ayamonte, which is close by and is divided from Portugal only by a small stream. But I have not learned the topography of Spain except by way of canings and thrashings.

I went off to Cádiz to a shabby inn, where I had as much to fear as I had had before, because the patrol searching for sailors came round two or three times each night and it was necessary to tell each of the men

---

* In Jewish mythology, the evil spirit of anger and lust; later the king of the demons.

who I was. So I moved to the Posada del Sol, and after three days, when I arrived at a barber shop on the Plaza San Juan de Dios to get a shave, the barber asked me if I had been in Rome, because someone had come by to ask if he knew where a padre who had been in Rome was staying. I asked him to describe the man who had questioned him, and it was the chief constable. I therefore surmised that I was the padre he was looking for, on account of a request to detain me sent from Los Toribios through the friar's influence.

This greatly upset me; but that same day, most unexpectedly, I ran into my friend Filomeno from Havana on the street, which at that moment was a godsend to me. He was not able to take me to his inn because, since it was a public place, I would be running the same risk; but he took me to the home of another Havanese who made his living as a moneylender, where I stayed for two days, while Filomeno got me passage on a boat bound for Ayamonte. A German shopkeeper, who had been a friend of mine since the days when I had come from Mexico to Cádiz, lent me twenty pesos. I was so upset and so frightened that I didn't go looking for the boat that Filomeno had found for me, but instead went aboard the first one I came across as night was falling.

That night we put in at Rota, because the boat was hugging the coast out of fear of the English, who were within sight with twenty-nine ships of the line and forty-four armed frigates. The following day we went on, and the English fleet and the combined fleet of Spain and France joined battle almost within sight of us, with thirty-two warships and five frigates.[4] This was the famous battle of Trafalgar, in which countless officers and crewmen died, because in our squadron alone there were thirty thousand men, and Admiral Gravina, who was in command of it, lost his life. The English admiral, Nelson, also died, having been fatally wounded by a rifle bullet; but the English won because of the tactical skills of the latter, who deployed his armada at an angle, and with his ship at the apex, broke our straight line, and left half of our squadron out of action. The English did not capture many of our ships, because a terrible storm finally came up, and except for four or five of them, the few ships of our fleet that hadn't gone down, though they were badly battered, came in to Cádiz. But by winning this battle the English finished off the remainder of the maritime forces of Europe. There was no need of such a battle; but Bonaparte already was planning to occupy Spain, and he wanted to get his ships and ours out of Spain and make them head for his ports; and so he gave the order for battle to make them put to sea, which was what the English wanted.

Because we were fleeing from that same storm, we put in at the foot of the Tower of Umbría, because along the entire coast there are watchtowers a certain distance apart, and in each of them there is a man called the tower keeper who is a fisherman. My heart beat faster when I spied from there the monastery of La Rábida and the little port of Palos. The head of the monastery was fray Juan Marchena, Queen Isabella's confessor, who caused her to decide to sponsor the discovery of the New World on behalf of Castile. To this end he borrowed eight thousand pesos from the treasurer of the Crown of Aragon; and Columbus, taking one-eighth of this sum as his share, left the port of Palos to set out on the unknown open sea with two wretched caravels and a brigantine. What miserably small forces by comparison to the ones that our money has given Spain, and the ones that we saw fighting the English!

I feared that the boat and its passengers might be searched when we reached Ayamonte, although boats that ply the coast have never been searched, and I persuaded a passenger aboard, the son of a seaman who lived in Ayamonte, to proceed overland with me, because the boat would not be sailing till the next day. We went on our way on foot, following the coast and growing very tired as we made our way through the vast stretches of sand, till we arrived at a tower where the fisherman, who had taken minor orders, spoke to us in Latin. We rented donkeys there, which we rode to Ayamonte that same day. I slept at the seaman's house, and in the morning, as many people were crossing over the border to Villanova de Portugal because there was a fair there, I went across the little stream that divides Portugal from Spain in a small boat.

And here I am in a foreign kingdom—not knowing my way around, without clothes, without money, without diplomas, without briefs, without a single acquaintance and without resources. This is where hunger and hardship and new labors begin. But freedom, more precious than gold, makes them more tolerable. It is necessary, however, not to think of oneself as being free from the royal talons because one is in a foreign country. At the slightest demand from an ambassador or a consul the authorities seize a person and hand him over, even though there may be more or fewer difficulties, depending on the country. Only in the United States and in England, where by merely setting foot in them one is under the protection of the people, and not even the king of England can throw a person out or arrest him, much less ambassadors. In the reign of Charles IV, the Spanish ambassador was sent to prison in England because he owed a small debt. In both countries there is no power that can prevail over the civil authority; and not even a general who is head of an entire army is possessed of power superior to the little crown with which a constable in England lightly taps a person, or the tap of the hand of a mayor in the United States.

General Washington was once marching with his troops, and because some of his men had not paid a small sum they owed at an inn, a mayor of a little village came to the general and tapped him on the shoulder. "Aren't you afraid of this army that I can order to tie you up and shoot you?" the general said to him. "That may very well be," the mayor answered, "but meanwhile you are my prisoner." The general paid what his men owed, and pointed out the power of the rule of law to his army. In that country and in England, the military, in all matters except for war, are subject to the civil authority. There can be no liberty where there are persons not subject to it.

To return to the subject of the asylum given by those countries, when Bonaparte surrendered to an English warship, so as not to fall into the hands of the kings of the Holy Alliance, the Cabinet of England, by common accord with them, decided to banish Napoleon to Saint Helena, an island in the Southern Sea, and keep him confined there like a lion in a cage, and did not allow him to disembark.[5] The opposition party, which wanted to spare him, sent an order to the mayor of a town to arrest him, on the pretext that he owed a debt. All the king's power and the entire Royal Navy would not have been able to keep Napoleon from landing as a prisoner under arrest. And once he had set foot on land there was no human power that could have gotten Napoleon out of England. The whole of England would have taken up arms. This is what it means to be a free people under the rule of law alone.

Let us halt here without entering Portugal, because as is my habit I must set down what I noted from the time of my departure from Madrid until I left Spain.

From the Apologetic Manifesto

What Followed Thereupon in Europe Until My Return to Mexico

When Napoleon's crime against our monarchs galvanized the wrath of the nation, I myself, breathing the same indignation, went to the aid of Catalonia with the Spanish troops who had been taken prisoner by the French in Portugal, as a chaplain, a military priest attached to the battalion of light infantry of volunteers from Valencia.[1] But I rendered such distinguished service that as a result, when I returned to the army, after having been a prisoner and having rendered great services even in that state, in 1809 General Joaquín Blake recommended me to the Central Junta for a canonry or a dignity of the cathedral of Mexico City; this did not come about, however, since the Junta was dissolved.

Having earned more merits, for there was almost no battle or combat that my battalion entered in which I did not obtain honorable mention, not only for my charity but for my valor, I went to Cádiz in 1811 with the proper letters dimissory from the vicar-general of Catalonia, señor Fivaller; and the Regency, in view not only of my military services but also of the justice owed me following my winning of a lawsuit regarding the Guadalupe sermon, ordered the Council of the Indies to give me preference for a canonry or dignity of the cathedral of Mexico City, as General Blake had already requested. There was no vacancy except for a half prebend, which was offered me and which I did not accept.

Since among the documents I lost when I fell prisoner was my rescript of secularization and others as well, although my colonel had already endeavored to make up for my loss with a certificate, attesting to the fact that I had presented this rescript at the office of the vicar-general of Cádiz, along with others against the Dominican procurator of the province of Mexico, who in 1804 had brought suit against me in the belief that I was still a religious, I secured from the office of the vicar-general a document certifying that I had presented the aforementioned rescripts. I presented this notarized document to the Inquisition, as well as the certificate from my colonel, don José Torres, concerning my services, etc. to His Excellency the viceroy, and neither the latter nor the former has returned anything to me despite the request I had submitted for the return to me of all my documents.

While I was last in Cádiz, my battalion fell prisoner at Figueras. Cádiz was about to be bombarded, and, in a word, Spain was lost. I therefore proceeded with the proper passport to London in order to arrange for the publication of a number of my works, in particular the *Historia de la revolución de Nueva España*—which is a collection of documents in defense of Mexico City against Cancelada's calumnies regarding the events of 1808.

When Ferdinand VII returned to his Court I too set out for it, and was the first American to obtain in Paris the highest literary honor in Europe, namely being made a member of the National Institute of France. But I met most distinguished Spaniards who were fleeing pellmell from persecution by the absolutism that had taken power. And I thereupon hurriedly returned to London, before the roads were closed once Napoleon disembarked from the ship bringing him back from the island of Elba. It is the custom of the Anglican Court to award a pension or to give financial aid to subjects who have displayed outstanding talent, and I was given a respectable sum of money to go to New Orleans, where contact was said to have been established with the Interior Provinces of the east of New Spain, where I was born. I wanted to establish communication with my family and receive funds that had been continually promised me but very rarely transmitted owing to the difficult conditions that obtained.

I had already arranged for my passage when I received a message from don Javier Mina, whom I knew only by reputation, offering me free passage on the ship of a friend of his that was about to set sail from

Liverpool.[2] Mina himself arrived there. This young man of twenty-six had sent his former officers from London to raise troops in Navarre, which he was readying himself to go take command of in an attempt to reestablish the Constitution, and had already recruited a thousand men, at the same time that Porlier was attempting to do likewise throughout Galicia. Since the attempt in Navarre had come to nothing, and since Mina's officers could not find ships on the coast to transport their men, they were on their way through France to join him when complaints from our king regarding the third conspiracy, which was also attributed to maneuvering by Spaniards residing on the other side of the Pyrenees, reached the French king. The officers were dashing through the country so fast that they aroused suspicion and were detained in Bordeaux. Hence Mina took ship for the United States accompanied by almost no one save myself.

His object, according to him and according to what he said in his manifesto, was to establish, if he could, the constitutional rule in Mexico proposed by the liberals or give it the freedom that, once established in as important a territory under Spanish rule as Mexico, would rapidly spread to every corner of its domain. Europe, he said, must be liberated in America. This was where war against despotism must be waged, as at its very roots, since it was with money from America that Philip II had paid his troops and enslaved the nation. Mina did not think that Spain would lose anything if the Americas became independent. England, he said, thought that it had lost its right arm when its colonies won their independence, yet its wealth and commerce has simply increased five-fold. America would be free one day, for in the annals of history there is no colony that has not emancipated itself, just as do all sons when they reach manhood. If we Spaniards ourselves give generously to Americans what in the end they are bound to secure by way of a violent rupture that will forever separate kindred spirits, in return for this generosity they will forgive us for the wrongs done them in the past, and even closer, more useful and more profitable ties of blood and friendship will be established, and liberals will find asylum. These ideas were very well set forth in a long letter sent [by Mina] from Soto la Marina to Arredondo, the commander general of the Interior Provinces of the east.

From Baltimore, in the north of America, where Mina disembarked, I went on to New Orleans, and not finding there the means of communication with my homeland I hoped to find, I took ship for the island of Galveston, which was said to have good communication with the Interior Provinces, and in fact a number of families from Texas had come down there by way of the Trinidad River. A small town had been formed there, governed by the Frenchman Aury through powers granted him by the Mexican Congress, and given financial aid by the admiralty which, at 12 percent of the prizes captured, brought in fourteen thousand hard Mexican pesos in three months.

On arriving there I met up once again with Mina, who had left the United States of the North in October of 1816 for Mexico, with two thousand rifles that he was bringing from London, two hundred fifty officers and thirty artillerymen and a number of artillery pieces. In other words, he was bringing officers and arms, the only thing that might be needed by the Mexican Congress, which he believed existed in Tehuacán. Having received news of its dissolution because of an insurrection led by Mier y Terán, he went on to make inquiries on the island of Santo Domingo, where some of his men died and others deserted.[3] He replaced them with islanders and Frenchmen, and in order to confer with the minister of the Congress who he had been assured was in Galveston, went back there in search of him. He arrived with about five hundred men, the majority of them officers from the best families in the United States who had been attracted by the high repute of his name, which still served to rally round his cause a number of followers from New Orleans.

There arrived in Galveston shortly after me the Caracan don Mariano Montilla, the same person who had been exiled to the United States by the Republican government of Venezuela because of his intrigues against General Miranda and then, having gone to Cartagena and begun his scheming once again, brought on the war between Cartagena and Bolívar that destroyed both. I have never seen a more imposing, charming, talented man. But he is a disaster for any party that he is allowed to join. Mina, who was gullible and naive, made him his chief of staff, and left him in command while he went to New Orleans. I never learned the real cause of this journey, although I later heard that Montilla had been behind it, in order that certain Spaniards of his party whom he had left there could try to induce Mina to take his expedition to Caracas, and in any case win people away from Mina in the meantime by getting Aury's people to come over to his side.

As soon as he succeeded in doing so, he instigated an uprising that resulted in Galveston's being burned to the ground, so that no one would come back and settle there again and all the pirates would head for Caracas, for which, in reality, once all the Galveston settlers had boarded ship, we began to leave. But to all appearances, we were leaving

Galveston because the entrance to it was so shallow that four ships had been lost, and we were heading for the island of Matagorda which, when sounded, proved to have an entrance eighteen feet deep, and two little islands that could be fortified to defend the port that lay in eight and nine feet of water.

We were just leaving when Mina returned from New Orleans with an old transport ship and found himself without an expedition. Since the recruiting of forces had been done in his name, however, he was able to take command again and with only a little over two hundred fifty men went on, escorted by Aury. In New Orleans he had found a young man from Soto la Marina, an insurgent from the time of Hidalgo; he brought him back with him as a guide for the disembarkation there, and I still think Mina led him on with his story. The young man was not yet aware that his home territory had been moved sixteen leagues away from the port, and the latter wasn't even a port anymore, since sands and flooding of the lagoons had cut it off.

When I suddenly found myself ashore there, on April 21, 1817, exactly a year after leaving London, I was amazed. Landing in New Spain with a handful of men made little sense, but to do so in the poor, unpopulated Interior Provinces, two hundred leagues away from the theater of war, was absurd. I was not the only one who thought so, for Mina too was aware of the state of affairs because correspondence being taken by a courier from Tampico to Spain had been intercepted and we had read it as we left Galveston. When I remonstrated with him, he answered that he was counting on his countrymen, as though the Spaniards here were the same as the ones in Spain. "I began there with twelve men," he said, "and I will not leave here even if I find myself all alone with my rifle on my shoulder." I would have boarded ship again, as did fifty Americans from the North who had been as surprised as I was and had taken off overland with Colonel Pery to Louisiana, had Mina, that rashly daring young man, not given orders, like Cortés, to sink one transport, leaving another with no one aboard. This old transport was the one that sailors in the royal fleets made off with, with only a cat on board, and the redoubt they claim they destroyed was the hull of the one that had been sunk, which the current had driven ashore. They were given a bonus of one escudo for their exploit when what they deserved was punishment, for if they had disembarked they would have taken everything that Mina had brought with him, which was still lying abandoned on the beach with only a few seamen to guard it, who took to their heels as soon as they spied the frigate and two corvettes from the war fleet. They also let the sailors make off with an American corvette with a cargo of clothing and ammunition worth fifty-six thousand pesos.

The new Soto la Marina, to which Mina immediately marched, is nothing but a few huts, or as the people there call them, *jacales*. Mina was there until the beginning of June, organizing his cavalry and replacing the Anglo-Americans who had left for Louisiana with some fifty cowboys from the region. Then he decided to go into what people there call "the outlands," leaving for the defense of a little fort that he had built on the riverside some thirty raw recruits, enlisted men, who still didn't even know how to shoot a rifle; although later, after they were joined by other men from the region and some of the seamen (the rest of whom were isolated at the mouth of the river), the garrison came to number more than five hundred riflemen.

Mina had had me sign a number of his officers' letters patent, which he had brought with him already printed and which were provisional until the independent Government of Mexico approved them; I protested that I was not his secretary; he answered that his signature was not a known one, and if I too signed them, people could at least tell that the other signature was his. Since mine in no way validated his, which in and of itself was of no value either, I gave in; nor was I entirely free to refuse to do so. But I did not accept any letter patent for myself even though his officers were addressing me either as vicar-general, or vicar of the division, or headquarters chaplain, as they pleased. I was in command of nothing and so far from playing an active role that they were annoyed because I put up this sign on the door of my quarters: "Thank you for coming, but callers are not received here."

For that same reason I refused to accompany Mina and stayed behind, despite the fact that Arredondo and his troops were only eight leagues away and the fort could not defend itself, as I told Mina. It had no provisions, or coal, or water; it was unfinished and almost entirely exposed on the side facing the river, which was only ten yards across. The high ground on the opposite bank dominated it and had behind it a hollow that was an invitation to install with impunity an artillery battery, which would rake the fort. Mina answered that he believed it could readily be defended for the two months that he would be gone. The commander of the fort, a young Italian named Salardete, was a treacherous man, like almost all Italians; what he did the minute he spied Arredondo was to come round with another countryman of his and advise him how he should go about attacking the fort with the aforementioned artillery battery.

The post commander, an honorable and courageous man, told me that he would not surrender the fort entrusted to him by his general without a fight, so as to capitulate with honor. He did in fact put up a fight for four days, beginning on June 11, and would have held out longer even after three artillerymen had died, had almost all the others, who were French, not passed over to the enemy between the second and third parleys. After advising the townspeople to retreat from danger (and there were only a few wretched families left, who moved inside the fort out of fear of the violence and thievery of Arredondo's troops), I placed myself in a hole that I dug outside the fort, awaiting the first opportunity to present myself for amnesty. Arredondo had already published the amnesty in the name of the king, promising on his word of honor, "which had never been broken," to pardon all those who presented themselves to him or to one of his officers. It was combined, as was customary, with insults and malicious slander, such as the statement that I had been tried by the Holy Office, which I had never had anything to do with. At the same time, the viceroy of Mexico had an announcement placed in the government gazette to the effect that I was an apostate, when it was widely known that I had been secularized for fifteen years. It would seem that the only way the satraps of America know how to fight is with insults and slander, like women and cowards. A long silence of our artillery, on June 14, owing to the fact that the small cannons had overturned and the gun carriages of all the cannons had broken down, though six of them were soon repaired, gave rise to the first parley with a party sent out by Arredondo, who lacked ammunition. Then, on the pretext of going to the aid of a wounded Frenchman at the forge almost next to the site of the parley, I presented myself, amnesty in hand, to Captain Martínez, Arredondo's aide-de-camp. But since on withdrawing, after having spared the lives of those in the fort, he had granted an hour for deliberations, with his permission I went to get dressed and, with a few of my belongings that I needed most tied in a scarf, I went on to the second parley, having already secured Sardá's permission. At the third, at which I was granted as many favorable conditions as were in the commandant general's power to authorize, two majors proceeded to his camp to stipulate the terms of the capitulation.

Since Arredondo presumed that it exceeded his authority to receive them as prisoners of war, as they demanded, they surrendered, according due trust to his word of honor, which in addition to the pledge that their lives would be spared, had ensured that they would be treated decently, as befitted their ranks and titles, and Arredondo had further promised to recommend them to the viceroy. The officers' baggage would not be held. Officers and foreign troops would be sent back to their homelands as free men. All the native-born who had embraced their party would go free and be pardoned.

These promises were kept as our pashas usually keep their word of honor, "never broken." The first thing Arredondo's guard did was rifle the pieces of baggage and one of them was mine, worth some thousand pesos, not counting three boxes of books that I recovered later; this was utterly improper since I had voluntarily presented myself to be amnestied. The thieves belonged to Arredondo's guard because they were the ones who returned a chalice that was in my trunk. Nothing was easier than to recover everything by searching their knapsacks because they were all well-known articles that had come from abroad. But the troops are allowed to take booty to keep them happy, and their chiefs, who have enriched themselves outrageously through pillage, devastation, cruel extortions and even executions by firing squad of peace-loving priests to obtain money, set the example for them.

The pasha of Monterrey immediately ordered me kept incommunicado because in that vacant see he had obtained one of all the many ridiculous decrees of excommunication against me that have been so generously forthcoming since the beginning of the insurrection. Every excommunication motivated by political concerns is an abuse; and every excommunication against many people as a group is null and void according to the rule of canon law repeatedly inculcated by Saint Thomas: *Multitudo non potest excommunicari**; but the one that that mere overseer applied was typical of a vicar-general among Indian savages; for by virtue of it he maintained that I was a domestic prelate of the Pope and a prothonotary apostolic, and it was stated that I had officiated at confirmations and granted indulgences; and he notified me of the excommunication provided for by canon law against a bishop who performs pontifical rites in any diocese other than his own. And without further ado he decreed a full excommunication *ipso facto incurrenda* against any person who communicated with me in any way whatsoever. He did not fail to cite the much-crowed-about excommunication of the Fourth Council of Toledo against those who made an attempt on the life of kings of Gothic blood. A person must be very stupid to confuse a domestic prelate of His Holiness or a prothonotary apostolic with a bishop. It is true that there is no outward distinction, neither as regards

---

* *A multitude cannot be excommunicated.*

the way in which they are addressed nor their attire; but the former wear neither a green hat ribbon nor a pectoral cross, the distinctive signs of archbishops. And I not only did not wear anything of the kind, but in fact wore nothing but noncanonical vestments, and only for a short time on certain Sunday mornings, but not all of them. My dress was the same as that I wore in Spain and before the Cortes of Cádiz. Through the testimony of the religious who was vicar of the settlement, I proved to the chaplains who came to tell me about the nonsensical rumors spread by the canons of Monterrey that I had not performed any ecclesiastical functions except for celebrating a recited Mass on Sundays in accordance with the Dominican rite that I observe, and granting, to eleven persons, a plenary indulgence for those on the point of death, advising the chaplains that I had special permission from the Supreme Pontiff to do so. So then, without regard for the fact that every excommunication is *ipso facto* an abuse and in substance amounts to no more than a threat, if I was not excommunicated, how could those who communicated with me be excommunicated, when excommunication applies only to those communicating with a person who has been summoned for trial or has had his name publicly posted as being officially excommunicated?

As for the excommunication authorized by the Fourth Council of Toledo, inasmuch as such abusive use had been made of it in order to fanaticize entire peoples and steep insurrection in blood, I shall point out to the canons of my homeland that, even in view of the fact that our sovereigns have the blood of Goths in their veins, a fact that very serious historians of the nation deny in dissertations on the subject, they should be aware that these were assemblies that the Goths called councils, because that was what they also ordinarily were, and in the councils of Toledo that are cited, the legitimate king Suintila was deposed, he and all his family were excommunicated, he was stripped of all of his possessions, and those who might make an attempt on the life of the new king Sisenando whom the council had elected, and whose party they feared, were also excommunicated. Masdeu says that the bishops who met together, with Saint Isidore of Seville presiding, would have left a better opinion of themselves had they not lent their consent to a decree marked by nothing but violence and injustice. The only thing that that canon, like several others of the Toledan councils, serves for is to demonstrate that the Cortes always believed that they possessed the power to depose the king, as the Cortes of Cádiz threatened to depose Ferdinand and the Cortes of Madrid ordered that it not be recognized.

This is not a very good excommunication to bring up in this particular case, senōr Vicar-General among the Indian savages.

Despite my having proved that the excommunication in no way applied to me personally, Arredondo kept me incommunicado, but it is a well-known fact that the very persons who seek such an excommunication from fawning ecclesiastics place no credence in it. They are farces that they take to be an opportune way of discrediting their neighbors and fascinating the plebs. But in two days' time Arredondo could not think of any way of getting round his word of honor concerning the amnesty that he had granted in the presence of the officers of his troops, almost all of whom were my kin, as were the leaders of the town. On the third day, he sent his chaplains to take away from me, as though I had no right to wear them, several articles of purple apparel that were among the few possessions I had brought out of the fort in a scarf in order to present myself to him in the only clothes I had left, the ones on my back; and they also took even my set of eating utensils away from me. They found in my possession a copy of the aforementioned *Historia de la revolución de Nueva España,* and even though it does not bear my usual name, and as I have said, supports the king, the title alone of history of the revolution was enough to mislead people and cloak the shamelessness of Arredondo's having broken his word of honor.

According to Cerquera, his judge advocate, he wrote the viceroy that he had not granted me amnesty because I presented myself only out of necessity, and because after the amnesty I intended to win over the simple-hearted townspeople in Soto la Marina. But Arredondo knew of no such necessity, nor did the commander of the fort himself, who was still attempting to defend it. And if such a necessity were a valid reason for not granting amnesties, no one would still be alive, for it would be the rare combatant who would expose himself to the notorious bad faith of our pashas if he were certain of victory. As for my winning over the people in Soto la Marina, how could I have even attempted to do so when I was being held incommunicado because I had been excommunicated from the moment that Arredondo entered the fort? Whom would I have won over if in Soto, up until the time I left for Mexico City, the only inhabitants were the very same people who were with us in the fort? And to what end, to what intent or with what powers would I have tried to win over a few poor wretches? To lie convincingly it is necessary to invent plausible lies. It is evident that these are nothing but ridiculous subterfuges to justify Arredondo's not fulfilling genuine promises made to people whose influence our pashas fancy they have reason to fear.

Hence Arredondo did not dare go there where his lies were obvious so as to continue bringing false charges against me, and taking as his pretext the fact that a copy of the *Historia de la revolución de Nueva España*, whose contents supporting the king those people had no knowledge of, had been found in my possession, three days later he had me placed in a pair of irons, without regard for my character, rank, position and birth. He was the one who was excommunicated! And he sent me off, on a saddled mule at an unearthly hour of the night, to Mexico City, with an escort of twenty-five cavalrymen headed by a certain don Antonio Ceballos, a European, who informed me later that he was a devotee of mysticism. I immediately realized that I had to contend with all the cruelty of a fanatic, because there is no man more fierce than one who hides his inherent evil nature beneath the mask of religion. He pitilessly slits the throat of his victims so as to offer them to God.

Forced to journey two hundred leagues and being fifty-five years old, I was no doubt doomed to succumb to such ill treatment; and in fact a violent fever overtook me in Huexotla, yet he would not have dreamed of removing my shackles merely for that reason. On the contrary, he subjected me to the further punishment of refusing to trim off the beard that was torturing me: and it was cut and thrust between the two of us all the way.

Because I had tired of this, and of the words *traitors* and *rebels* that this stupid boor repeatedly used as insulting epithets for Americans, I was tempted a thousand times to answer him with this argument: from Valencia, in May of 1814, Ferdinand VII issued a solemn decree declaring all the powers that had undertaken to govern Spain in his absence— the Cortes, a handful of rebels—illegitimate; and the Constitution a crime of lèse-majesté. And the Cortes of Madrid, by virtue of the article of the Constitution that decrees that no king shall be recognized as such without having sworn a formal oath, issued another decree ordering that Ferdinand not be recognized as king. Which of the two decrees is valid? If it is Ferdinand's, all of you who recognized those governments and parliaments and swore to obey the Constitution are rebels and guilty of the crime of lèse-majesté: and you insurgents who did not recognize them and did not swear to obey the Constitution although you recognized Ferdinand as king are loyal subjects. If it is the decree of the Cortes that is valid, insurgents who no longer recognize him as king are doing what all of you should have done had you not been traitors and rebels against the nation represented in the Cortes whose sovereignty you swore to recognize, and you have taken the name of God in vain, having sworn before him on the Constitution not to recognize Ferdinand as king if he did not swear likewise. In any case, therefore, it is you, and not the insurgents, who are traitors and rebels.

But the military, like the Mohammedans in defense of their law, unsheathe their scimitars as their only argument, and the *arraez* Ceballos threatened to have me shot at any moment, or as he put it, to have my heart split open with two bullets according to the instructions given him. I still believe one of his instructions was that I should not appear to have been done in deliberately but rather to have died accidentally; for people in Huexotla tried their best to convince him, to no avail, that the road he was taking me by, one just opened across the Andes, which people in those parts call the Sierra Madre, was not a road but, rather, a series of mighty, swift-flowing rivers, cliffs and precipices that the horses and cavalrymen were scarcely capable of negotiating, especially at that time of year, during the rainy season. And I was even less capable, what with my shackles and the fact that I could not grab hold of anything with more than one hand because the other was in bad shape, than any of the others.

We were sometimes at such a high altitude that we went on amid the clouds; and having already fallen off my mule several times, I begged the *arraez* who had me in his custody to put me, if he was still all that afraid of an elderly sick man under such heavy escort, in some other sort of bonds that would not keep me from riding the mule, so as to escape death. I would not have escaped it had the porters and soldiers not taken pity on me, for, cursing the "Jewish *gachupín*," they helped me over the hardest spots when I had to cover open ground.

In Zacualtipán I was inhumanly put on a horse that had violently bucked when it was saddled up, and on repeating its nasty trick sent me flying through the air, leaving my right arm shattered, so that even today I can scarcely use it. Will I be believed when I say that as I lay there on the ground, stunned almost senseless by the blow and the pains in my arm, since one half the bone was on top of the other half, that barbarian began to hurl insults at me? They laid me in a sort of stretcher then, because I kept falling into a faint; and that day he bared the depths of his evil heart because he was in unbelievably joyous spirits, thereby scandalizing the cavalrymen escorting me. The following day he made me follow him at a trot on that same fractious horse so as not to miss Mass at Atotonilco el Grande, as though charity did not come before the fulfillment of a precept of the Church.

He was to make his way back from there because a captain with twelve hussars from Tulancingo had arrived from Mexico City to relieve him. But he asked permission to go present some purple rags and tatters to the viceroy, among them a much-mended Polish campaign cap made out of some very old facings from a dress coat of mine, which that brute, no matter how hard I tried to explain to him, had taken to be a bishop's biretta, as though they wore purple ones. He was particularly bent on presenting three letters that Sergeant Treviño had perfidiously handed over to him after having urged me to write them in Huexotla, giving me gratis the necessary materials for writing them. They were addressed to three persons in Mexico City, relatives and old friends of mine who were known royalists, to ask them to intercede on my behalf, if I should get there alive, so that I would be granted the amnesty.

To Ceballos this was a crime, the discovery of which should earn him a promotion. These tigers, not being Christians, do not know that according to the teachings of Jesus Christ one ought to abhor sins yet still love the sinner. They accuse the latter of seeking compassion and their neighbor of offering it to them. In Pachuca, where five days after my arm was broken they tried, though to no avail, to mend it, the American officer, the new head of the party escorting me, on seeing me lying face up on the bed, in irons and helpless, let it fall that he felt compassion for me. And Villadea, the commandant there, reproached him for his remark, ordering that despite my condition and my being within view of a sentry, I was to be kept locked up by order of his commanding officer, Concha.

So I was kept there for two weeks, because the government of Mexico was colluding with the inquisitors to have me admitted to their jails. Meanwhile, I will recount the memorable words uttered by Umana, the viceroy's secretary, to the officer of hussars, on sending him to escort me on the remainder of the journey from Atotonilco. "What Arredondo should have done with that padre is shoot him. It is true that there was a capitulation, and so on, but even so all this shilly-shallying has gotten us nowhere; we would have approved of it [the execution] here, rather than having him send us this nuisance." The official remembered them literally because they shocked him.

Once the viceroy had reached an agreement with the Inquisition to free himself of the nuisance of my person, in the words of his secretary Leyano, I was taken out of Pachuca and sent on my way via Perote, on the road to Veracruz, with the aim of fooling Mexicans as to my route and the place where I was to be immured, as they say, in the caverns of the Cyclopes with blue cuffs. I spent a night locked up in the castle of

Perote, shivering on some planks, and in the morning we headed back toward Mexico City by a back road. We were already close to the city when I was made to go back to Texcoco by order of Concha, who received me at a hacienda and placed me in such an awful dungeon that the soldiers, on seeing it, embraced me, saying affectionately: "Farewell, Little Padre, in case we never see each other again." I had to swallow hard on seeing myself in such straits, in the power of a man who, starting from a tavern, had managed to get himself handed the baton of colonel by imprisoning Morelos, and is famous for the frequent execution of priests by firing squad and the horrible tortures he has used to extort confessions of supposed crimes from a number of poor devils, leaving them mutilated.

But I was soon transferred with obsequious courtesy to better quarters because Concha had seen the light, thanks to my documents, with regard to the apostasy that the Government had accused me of in its gazettes. This is all the good it does the Government to slander its victims, and something almost as bad as that had happened to me in Perote; though I don't know who puts the military up to punishing monastic apostasies.

It must have been eight o'clock at night on August 13, 1817, when we again took to the road leading to Mexico City in Concha's carriage, which we changed at the little post in San Lázaro. From these secret moves by night it was easy to deduce that the dark shadows of the Inquisition awaited me; I entered them on the morning of the fourteenth at two o'clock. They removed my shackles then and politely requested that I hand over everything that I had brought with me. In the name of the viceroy, Concha also demanded my gold watch. I suspected that it was to see the seal in relief on it, something important to Englishmen, who use it as a signet. But it did not have any markings on the chalcedony; it had gone through a storm at sea, however. The custom of taking booty has left our military entirely without scruples.

When I found myself in cell number seventeen, a spacious and neatly painted one, though it does not have much light despite their installing glass windowpanes as soon as I suggested it, I was given food, wine and sweetmeats the moment I asked for them, though the other prisoners were not given any, and the inquisitors themselves urged me to ask for anything I had a craving for, just as nothing is denied those who are about to be hanged; I had a foreboding that my stay in the prison of the Inquisition was destined to live up to the name of *Perpetua* that it had given to the street it was located on. Since I had committed no crime whatsoever, the inquisitors treated me not only with courtesy but with affection and friendliness. For diversion I read, though there were few books among people who studied nothing but complicated lies, and I tended a little garden set aside especially for me. In it, I managed to set up a secret mail drop underneath a mint bush, inside a hollow nut shell, so as to be able to correspond with other prisoners, whom I supplied with ink made from walnuts.

Though in the end there were nine of us, to judge from the number of chamber pots that were taken out each day to be cleaned in the patio as Dr. Verduzco watched from his little window in cell number eighteen, I did not manage to find out for certain which of the nine were there because they were insurgents, except for Father Luna, a Franciscan who had been there for two years when I arrived, Canon Cardeña, who had been there seventeen months, and the aforementioned doctor, who had been put in prison six months after I was, and with whom I kept up a continual correspondence without the warders suspecting. A universal silence was the rule even with regard to the most trivial things, despite all my preaching that the secrecy of the confessional, which makes a priest as isolated as though he were no longer in this world, does not apply to such matters; nonetheless, through many a cunning stratagem, Dr. Verduzco and I managed to penetrate the wall of secrecy that surrounded many things. For the details, I refer the reader to a note. I will merely say in general that just as a fellow countryman of mine who lost his case when he brought it before a chapter meeting after having been dealt with kindly by each of the canons individually, said afterward that canons were good but canonries bad, in like manner I can say that the inquisitors were good and the office was what was bad, even though it was called the Holy Office.

At each one of the visits that an inquisitor pays to its prisons on the last day of the month, I vehemently insisted that I be told the reason for my imprisonment and that my defense be heard. The judges had already used their workload and the snail's pace typical of the Tribunal as excuses, shrugged their shoulders and protested that the matter was not in their hands. The one thing they had not done was to tell me straight out that my case was closed by order of the Inquisitor General of New Spain.

When a year had gone by, in order to see whether, despite my crippled arm, I might perhaps contrive to write, I asked for an inkwell and paper, even though the other prisoners were not allowed them, and as a test I sent them this sonnet, taking as my epigraph the words of Jesus

Christ at the Last Supper: *Exemplum dedi vobis, ut quemadmodum ego feci, ita et vos faciatis:**

> Adam sinned; he ate forbidden fruit:
> he killed Cain, his brother; God knew
> what ridiculous, vain, and groundless
> excuses each would give him
> and yet before he heard them out did nothing.
> My judge knows not what I will tell him
> and though as yet I've not been charged
> I've done a year's hard time here in this prison.
> What to do? Neither eloquence nor reasons of State
> can save us on Judgment Day:
> what has not been fairly settled following God's example
> will then be condemned as dereliction,
> either let our Holy God be here imitated
> or cease to call yourselves the Holy Office.

I then sent them a memorandum, and during one of the three general visits that the three inquisitors made on the three Pascuas of the year,** I handed them a brief: each of the two documents was four or five pages long. In the brief I emphasized the same point as in the sonnet, reproaching them for their wickedness in cooperating in vilifying their neighbor in the realm of what was most sacred, for they were lending the government a hypocritical religious veil to allow it to accuse me of committing a crime against faith, when the only crime I was accused of was a political one. An accusation on religious grounds is so serious, because of the abominable and indelible stigma it leaves, that even among the pagans an Athenian against whom such a charge was brought could not escape the death penalty, which he incurred even if the charge was not proved. To maintain that they were acting under orders did not excuse them, I told them, because in that case the executioners of martyrs and the crucifiers of Christ would be exonerated. We are duty bound to face death rather than violate one of God's precepts.

At the beginning of May of the current year we prisoners noted an unusual agitation in our usually slothful Tribunal. Could the liberal party in

---

*   *For I have given you an example, that as I have done to you, so you also should do.* (Jn 13:15)
**   Three major Church festivals of the year, commemorating Christmas, Easter and Pentecost.

Spain have triumphed, and once again toppled this bulwark of despotism?[4] One after the other, the prisoners were hurriedly summoned for a hearing, and saw in the courtrooms the signs of a breakdown: books and gilded statues packed in boxes, documents that had been torn up, and the extraordinary gentleness, mingled with sadness, of the satellites. Without waiting to receive the new instructions that the prisoners were issuing him for their defense, their attorney, of the two advocates of the Tribunal the one who had previously been chosen to defend them, took upon himself the task of concluding his arguments in one night, and the cases were all brought to an end with only a bill of indictment from the public prosecutor, no further answer to the charges being permitted. All this so as to send the prisoners off immediately to serve their respective sentences, and then publish in the official gazettes the trumped-up story that no prisoner had been found in the Inquisition prisons.

The worst was that even though they knew that the Inquisition no longer existed in Spain, and that consequently its proceedings in America were null and void, since all inquisitorial powers were vested solely in the Inquisitor General, who received the Pope's bull, and the others were only royal counselors, they continued to sentence prisoners with their usual outrageous abuse of power, basing the proceedings on nothing more than a bill of indictment brought by the public prosecutor, when the defense had not yet rested its case. Dr. Verdusco's advocate was not permitted to finish his arguments for the defendant, and with only a bill of indictment that he petitioned in vain to answer, Dr. Verdusco was forced to accept an absolution from heresy, which he resisted, and sentenced to ten years in Ceuta, the loss of his curacy, disqualification for any sort of benefice, fasting for seventeen Lenten seasons, a retreat of forty days in San Fernando and who knows what else, as though he were Luther; merely for having accepted the Constitution of the Mexican Congress.

In May the lords with the blue cuffs summoned me for a hearing after keeping me in utter oblivion for three years. And the proceedings began with my acknowledgment of documents in my handwriting, including a number of pages with no beginning or end labeled at the bottom "document submitted by His Excellency the viceroy," who had obviously seen to it that the holy armory was supplied with wads and cartridges; but as everyone knows, the Little Stag has never smelled gunpowder in this war because none of the shots fired at me with that ammunition ever hit me.[6] My opponent, the inquisitor Tirado, kept stubbornly insisting that

I acknowledge that I was the author of a letter written in my name and apparently in my handwriting, to two Creoles in Veracruz designated by the initials of their names, against whom he must have borne some holy* will. I denied having written it, although I confessed to others found in my boxes of books, and not in notebooks for rough drafts, because on finding myself obliged to write them, I pretended to send them off and hid them there.

It is true that I took advantage of my being in the Tribunal's clutches to get three boxes of books that I had brought with me out of Arredondo's, for inasmuch as I knew nothing of Mina's planned expedition, my baggage was not campaign equipment. One box contained almost nothing but works of mine, and the other two contained books that were very useful and highly prized even in Europe, along with scores of opuscules, scholarly essays, memoirs, manuscripts and documents that I had used to write my *Historia de la revolución de Nueva España*. I foresaw very clearly the enormous quantity of mephitic gas that could be extracted from this material by the cunning and malicious tribunal, bent on making me out to be a criminal so as to please His Supreme Excellency the Inquisitor General of Anáhuac. But I preferred to fight the battalion of his official examiners or heretifiers, rather than abandon my books as prey to the satrap of my homeland.

In any event, the letters could in no way harm me; for it stands to reason that when one joins a cause he must willy-nilly do his share, and all this was included in the amnesty. Moreover, since the existence of those letters was not known when I was taken to the Inquisition, they could not have been the cause of my being put in prison. Nonetheless, even though the inquisitors knew beforehand that it was useless to present them as evidence, they were still determined to get a detailed acknowledgment from me of every last scrap of paper they had found! Their aim in so doing was to pass these documents on to the government, as they in fact did, since the heavy seal of secrecy of those panders of despotism was not compatible with government policy.

The term *panders* is not a noble one; but neither was that dark depository of gossip, denunciations and spying, where there were probably few citizens who did not have some sort of record opened against them. Since the questions asked were cunningly framed in anonymous and general terms, deponents who feared that they would be punished for

---

* A common euphemism for its opposite: *ill* will, with a bit of wordplay on "Holy Office" as well.

not having made complete statements concerning everything they knew or had heard regarding religion or the government, they kept endlessly and successively accusing one another as they were summoned as witnesses at one another's hearings. In time this inevitably resulted in a store of malicious gossip so immense that even the Devil could not have imagined such a thing.

Once the acknowledgment of the papers in my possession had been taken care of, Inquisitor Tirado, who had no accusation brought by the public prosecutor nor any other formula, announced the charges against me, a procedure that along with my replies proved to take no more than two hours. Ever since I had made the general confession concerning my entire life that is demanded of all prisoners two or three months after their incarceration, they were already well-disposed toward me and fully satisfied, because in Inquisition proceedings no conclusion other than the will of the inquisitors was predetermined. Hence the charges that were made against me now were frivolous and brought only for form's sake. The first charge amounted to nothing more than some cavil or other concerning my rescript of secularization, so pointless that it does not deserve mention and that dissipated like the wind; although now, in view of the persistent efforts of the Cortes to destroy the friars, I cannot help laughing at the determination on the part of "Arredondo, the Inquisition and the viceroy to make me out to be a friar still, so many years after my having been secularized." They longed to find me guilty so as to excuse their unjust persecution of me. The second charge was limited to their asking me why I had brought so many forbidden books with me; and the third to objecting that by taking advantage of the titles of domestic prelate of His Holiness and prothonotary apostolic, I allowed myself to be addressed in Soto in terms befitting a bishop, since even the military leaders called me Your Most Illustrious Excellency; I granted indulgences; and, following the Dominican rite that I observe, I gave the episcopal benediction, *Benedictio Dei Omnipotentis*, at the end of Mass, etc.

If I had dismissed the congregation with *pax vobis*, I answered, a charge could be brought against me, but what other benediction could I have and ought I to have pronounced if I was celebrating Mass in accordance with the rite of the Dominicans, which is that of the Church of France in the twelfth century, the place and the time of the foundation of the Dominican Order? The formula surely matters little, and to give benediction is the proper duty of priests. "It befits you," the bishop tells them at their ordination, "to preside, to bless, to baptize," and so on.

As for my being addressed as Your Most Illustrious Excellency, that is the proper title for me, both as a prelate and as a prothonotary; and as in my case, it is a right granted by Rome to bishops, having later been extended by kings to their lay ministers in the councils of Castile and of the Indies, because it was they who appointed bishops. The form of address proper for those in the Church is the one our sovereigns use for them: "Reverend in Christ" if they are bishops, and "Most Reverend Sir" if they are archbishops. In times when they merited it all bishops were addressed as "most blessed" or "most holy," terms which have been reserved for the Pope, as is this title, which in earlier times was common to all archbishops. Our sovereigns use the honorific "devout" for provincials of monastic orders, and it is the proper one for them. The members of cathedral chapters are addressed as "venerable," because this is the proper term for elders, as that of all the faithful is "brothers" or "friars," from the Latin word *fratres,* which is still used for them today at the beginning of the Epistles.

As for the granting of indulgences, I repeated what I had told Arredondo's chaplains, that I had received from His Holiness the power to grant several thousand to persons on the point of death. And surely, if granting indulgences merely signifies shortening the time for doing penance as determined by the early canons, following the example of Saint Paul, who granted this dispensation to the Corinthian who had committed incest, priests grant such dispensations in the confessional every day, since they have the power to *bind* or to *unbind.* The penance that they impose and that we call sacramental, is simply that first part of canonical penitence, regarding which the Nicene Council forbade the granting of indulgence. When Saint Cyprian complained to Rome that the presbyters of Carthage were shortening the time of penitence for trivial reasons because of the altogether too numerous recommendations of martyrs and confessors, he did not say that such indulgences were null and void, but that by their being so generously granted they thereby lessened the salutary rigor of canonical discipline. It had pleased God to have had the dogmatic history of indulgences further studied by Canon Palmieri. No one has brought more solid scholarship to the task of getting to the bottom of this subject both full of abuses and made even more obscure by the Scholastics through their countless mistaken interpretations and errors.

I concluded by stating to the inquisitor that the categorical proof of the fact that I did not pass myself off as a bishop in Soto, although perhaps Mina's men called me by that title since it seemed to them to be appropriate, was the fact that I did not wear a green hat ribbon but a purple one, nor a pectoral cross, which are the designations of office of bishops. (A green hat ribbon is also worn by certain inquisitors, the inquisitor of Majorca, for instance; and a pectoral cross, a staff and a miter are also worn by Cistercian Benedictine abbots and others, priors of canonical and military orders, cardinals, even if they are ordained in minor orders, and canons of several cathedrals in Spain itself).

Hence the submission of certain purple articles by Arredondo, Ceballos's stubborn determination to turn them over to the viceroy and their transmission to the Inquisition by the latter. The Inquisition transferred them in turn to the archbishopric, wherefrom, grumbling all the while, the viceroy himself returned them to me after all the great to-do over them. On hearing of all that fuss, anyone might think that purple attire was not as appropriate for all the clergy as black. If bishops and many canons, all those of the crown of Aragon for instance, have taken to wearing it because it is a more attractive and less gloomy color, it is one of many usurpations of the rights of the Presbytery. In the early days of the Church, naturally, no distinction was made between clerical and secular attire. To have observed such a distinction would have been tantamount to a presbyter's deliberately offering his life as a martyr in those times of persecution. White attire was later adopted as a symbol of innocence. And it had remained since then the color of the amices, albs, surplices, rochets and chasubles worn on the days commemorating virgins and confessors, and the color of the habit of certain religions. Thus it was the color worn by all of them before the seventh century, by which time the use of inner tunicles of white wool had begun to be introduced, and therefore the color of the outer tunic was gradually changed to black because it was better suited for the physical work the monks did. They thus conferred esteem upon this color, and to share in it, clerics little by little began to imitate them, and for that reason they were called monastics and later on lay brothers. But the Councils of Toledo allow the entire clergy to wear so-called modest colors such as black, blue, old rose, dark purple. And in the Pontifical State all members of the clergy in general, content with wearing a habit that is black, wear accouterments of some modest color.

As for the accusation concerning the forbidden books, my reply to the judge-inquisitor is contained in a letter that on October 6 I wrote from this castle to don Félix Alatorre, the most reverend archbishop's vicar-general. His Excellency the viceroy had officially communicated with him concerning my books, which the Inquisition passed on to him and I reclaimed the night I left Mexico.

When I was done replying, the inquisitor Tirado, rising to his feet, said to me with great satisfaction, "I have finished with you. And you see how well we have treated you. That was the only thing within our power." And I was no less satisfied to see that the charges against me had been limited to such mere trifles. No further words were exchanged. No sentence was pronounced, I was not given absolution or the slightest reprimand. As I came downstairs from the Tribunal I received my last visit in its cells, the general visit of Pentecost. I was complimented on my cheerfulness and the inquisitor Pereda said: "It is common knowledge that you were not guilty of anything. Such abiding happiness over a period of three years' inquisition is unprecedented." "Innocence and philosophy," I replied, "are a life-restoring balm. Ever-present in my memory and on my lips is this maxim of Saint Cyprian's: 'It is not the punishment but its cause that makes for martyrdom (*non facit martyrem poena sed causa*). The cause, and not the chains, bring dishonor.' The Carranzas, the Luis de Leóns, the Marianas and so many other great men dragged about the chains of the Inquisition in Spain that I can look upon mine as a mark I needed to appear to be a martyr. For this reason in foreign nations pensions are awarded those who have suffered in the power of the Inquisition, and since this implies outstanding merit, you have provided me with an income if I leave Spanish territory. In Spain itself, the only Catholic country where it exists in the same form that it has always had, the Inquisition no longer discredits: it is what is discredited."

And didn't it deserve to be? Because of such ridiculous charges? Because of those accusations on such trivial grounds, which I had answered satisfactorily from the day I entered, yet had been held incommunicado in a solitary cell for three years, at risk, as a person who had seemingly committed a crime against faith, of losing my reputation forever and eternally dishonoring my kin? How can inquisitors justify themselves before God's Tribunal, in which reasons of State, which His Holiness Pius V called reasons of the Devil, count for nothing? And why in human tribunals must their complicity with tyranny still remain unpunished? It is certain that if the east wind that began to blow on the island of Lyon had not extinguished the green candle throughout the monarchy,[7] the Inquisition would to all appearances have been my grave, despite my innocence and even despite the lack of competence of the inquisitors to judge me, because as a domestic prelate of His Holiness I enjoy all the privileges of bishops. They were not unaware of this; I told them so, although I did not insist too strongly in order to prevent their using it as a pretext to exile me so that I could be tried in Europe, for I had come back to my homeland to die.

On May 30 at nine at night the Commander of the City and three adjutants transferred me to the royal jail and left me in the solitary confinement cell, called the *olvido*, three paces wide by seven paces long, and so dark that I could not read my breviary to recite the divine office. I fell into Scylla after having left Charybdis. The door of my cell was located in the chapel, and I immediately noticed that it was the same cell from which they led those who were about to be hanged. I asked if I had been sent to the chapel because it was the eve of my execution, and despite the reply in the negative, I was not at all certain. As a result of this apprehension and the foul-smelling air I had to breathe in such a small space, perfumed as well by the chamber pot, I was taken ill with a fever on the same day that people swore to prattle about, if not to practice, the Constitution.

On the general visit of prisons that according to the Constitution must take place on the following day, the Royal Tribunal, curious to meet a man who has become famous by reason of the persecutions he has endured, demanded that I be shown to them, despite the viceroy's orders that I be kept incognito. I briefly set forth to them, from the sickbed where I was lying, how much it pained me to find myself subjected—three years after having been granted an amnesty—to such outrageous treatment. Its chief justice, as renowned for his servility as I am for my liberalism, told me to notify my Tribunal, the Captaincy General, of this, whereupon visitors from it would come immediately to see me. And the inspector did in fact come, in the name of the viceroy, but he left me as outraged as he had found me, nor did the visit as a whole have a better effect in the rest of the national jail.

At the next ordinary visit that the Royal Tribunal makes on Saturday each week, accompanied this time by its public prosecutors, its learned judges and a great procession of curious petty magistrates, I was already on my feet, receiving the visitors in the chapel. I began by expressing my satisfaction at speaking with a Constitutional Tribunal, since I was obliged to have recourse to the most essential part of the Constitution in order to support my protest against the oppression that I had endured for three years. I told them of my surprise when I disembarked, the amnesty that fell through, my stolen baggage, my death journey across the Andes and my being stowed away for three years in the Inquisition prison. I left as I had entered, unscathed, because I was simply a political prisoner who had been buried alive.

I therefore demand first of all, I told them, due obedience of the royal decree of March 9 last ordering that all those who were in Inquisition prisons because of their political opinions be freed immediately. I demand due obedience of the decree to the same effect, on the same date, circulated to all the captains general, ordering that all those who were taken prisoner anywhere be given their freedom immediately to enable them to return to their homes.

The viceroy did not publish this second decree until August 2, even though it had been sent to him by name as early as March 9, but both decrees had already appeared in the June 15 issue of *El Noticioso* of Mexico City, the day that I had demanded that they be duly obeyed. The viceroy persists in arbitrarily deciding whether or not to publish the royal letters patent granted the viceroys in accordance with the Laws of the Indies. I should point out, first, that those were powers appertaining to this office of royal deputy, which the viceroys in fact have not only been stripped of by the Constitution, but had already been deprived of a long time before, as I shall prove later. Second, that these powers apply only in the event that the royal letters patent may cause scandal and irreparable harm. In this case precisely the contrary is true, in that the real irreparable scandal lies in the fact that publication of decrees favorable to Americans is delayed or suppressed. Such oppression is the reason for their insurrection.

According to the Constitution (article 293), as I proceeded to tell the visitors from the Tribunal, the jailer must be given notification of due cause as each prisoner is handed over to him, without which, even though it was within his right to receive me because I had entered prison on the eve of the swearing of the oath of loyalty to the Constitution, once it had been sworn to, he had no right to hold me.

To date the cause of my imprisonment has not been explained to me, although (article 300) such an explanation should have been forthcoming within twenty-four hours at most following my imprisonment. I was not asked to make the deposition required of me by article 290, which should have been taken down within those twenty-four hours. Therefore, the trial proceedings have not been made a matter of public record in the manner and form prescribed by law in accordance with article 302.

"The king cannot deprive any citizen of his freedom, or subject him to any penalty whatsoever. The secretary of the office who signs such an order and the judge who executes it will be responsible to the nation and punished as accused criminals found guilty of an attack on individual freedom. Only in the event that the welfare and security of the State require the arrest of an individual does the king have the power to issue orders to that effect, but only on condition that within twenty-four hours he will have had that person placed under the jurisdiction of the Tribunal or of a legally competent judge." This is a literal citation of the eleventh of the king's powers, article 172, chapter 1, title IV.

And can the king's viceroy do what the king is not empowered to do? By the decree of the Cortes of June 23, 1814, as head of government he is granted only the right to hold a person caught *in delicto flagrante** for twenty-four hours before handing him over to the competent judge, one-half the length of time granted the king. My judge or tribunal is the ecclesiastical one, since clergymen have the right to remain under its jurisdiction (article 249). It is evident, then, that by keeping me prisoner, incommunicado, in a cell after sixteen days and by failing to meet any of the provisions of the Constitution, the viceroy has violated it and gone beyond all the powers granted him. I shall now sum up my case, I said, and improvised this sonnet:

> I was granted amnesty and surrendered
> in Soto, and was robbed of my baggage
> and by transporting me in irons they maimed
> one of my arms. I was then handed over to the Inquisition.
> With no other cause save an order
> of the government, I was imprisoned for three years
> and finally was transferred to this jail
> where I was held incommunicado still.
> Has the Inquisition ended? No, only its location,
> the name varying with the edifice:
> what today is called the Captaincy General
> was once known as the Holy Office.
> Under the Constitution everything is as it has always been:
> the name is now changed; the despotism continues.

I concluded by lodging an appeal with the Constitutional Tribunal as an appellate court empowered to review cases overseas (article 268), doing so in the only terms possible for me, and taking my hearers as my

---

* The Spanish text has "*caught in fraganti.*"

witness, since I was being held completely incommunicado. To make my appeal official, I asked for an inkwell and paper and asked that a defense attorney and an advocate be appointed for me or that I be allowed to appoint them. The visitors answered that what I had set forth would be taken into consideration; they then left, confessing that everything I had said was the gospel truth, and officially notified the viceroy.

During this interval, taking my ease for a while after supping, in the chapel, an avocado seed fell into it with some interesting news inside, signed, "Hollow shell underneath the mint bush." I understood immediately that it was the doctor, one of my secret correspondents in the Inquisition prison, who after a seventeen-day spiritual retreat in San Fernando, had come to share my fate, though not my solitary confinement, and supplied me with a means of writing using avocados the way I had used nuts in the Inquisition prison. I did not take advantage of the opportunity, however, to secure legal aid or to give the public an account of how unjustly I was being dealt with, so as not to compromise the jailer, a good and charitable man. Hence the document that came out in my favor, entitled *Alerta a los mexicanos,* was falsely attributed to me. I owed this favor, as I have been told, to Attorney Gallegos, to whom I extend cordial thanks.

On the second visit from the Tribunal, when I repeated my petition, they informed me of the official notice that they had sent to the viceroy, who, thirteen days after receiving it, sent a scribe to notify me that I would be judged by a joint military and ecclesiastical authority. In what section of the new legislation, I retorted, does this hermaphrodite Tribunal exist? According to the Constitution, the king cannot exercise judicial power or assign himself a case (article 243), nor can he suspend the execution of the laws (article 246), or have anyone tried by commissions but only by the competent Tribunals as previously provided by law (article 247). A military Tribunal is competent to try only members of the military (article 250), just as the ecclesiastical Tribunal can try only ecclesiastics (article 249). There is no mixed Tribunal provided for in the Constitutional Code.

Article 30 of the Law of Tribunals of October 9, 1812, stipulates that viceroys, captains general and military governors "are strictly limited to the exercise of military authority and nothing further." And by the terms of article 31 the advisors that the viceroys had were done away with, since viceroys are to consult with legal advisors only "for the exercise of the military authority that is within their competence." I am unable to understand by what right or reason His Excellency the viceroy is seeking to exercise such authority over me.

Even in the decrees issued during the six preceding years in which absolute authority, emerging as suddenly as a bull driven from its pen at the bullring, knocking down all the barriers erected by the Cortes, no justification will be found for this with respect to insurrection. Having been consulted by the viceroy of New Granada, Montalvo, as to the proper procedure and the proper authorities for trying crimes having to do with the present insurrection in America, the king, after reviewing their court-martial, issued, in 1817, a decree, dated July 28 and circulated in the issue of August 9 of the *Gaceta de Madrid* by the Ministry of War, in which he divided those to whom it applied into eight categories: in all truth, I do not fit in any of them. But no one would endeavor to include me in the first four or in the eighth, which have to do only with members of the military, and they are the only categories in which the king orders that those included in them be tried by court-martial. He wishes the rest to be tried by civil Tribunals. And in which category are those granted amnesty included? In none; he orders, rather, that those who have been granted them enjoy their amnesties. Will His Excellency the viceroy perhaps try to exercise his military authority over me precisely because of the amnesty granted me? He did not grant it to me in his capacity as Captain General but rather in that of viceroy, or in constitutional language, Head of Government.

The scribe answered me that there was an order of 1810 by the Regency that certain cases were to be tried by joint military and ecclesiastical authority; I forbear to mention, I said to him, that that Regency whose decrees you now wish to take advantage of, which, moreover, it would have been a crime of lèse-majesté to cite seven months ago, has not only been declared illegitimate by Ferdinand but even the Cortes of Cádiz conceded that it had been illegitimate; but who is there who does not see that that order was a temporary one conforming to the old rule of law that was still in force; and by that I mean to say that not only that order but the entire body of law prior to the Constitution, which is the fundamental and sacred code, is now null and void by the very fact that it is contrary to one or another of its articles, and no more need be said?

I protest, then, against that joint authority, which is unrecognized and condemned in the Constitution; in accordance with the latter I ask to be tried by my own rightful Tribunal, the one that has authority over me, and my own alone; and in any event to be heard, with paper, ink and an attorney and advocate to defend me. The scribe fretted, stuttered and wrote down my request in very brief, equivalent terms.

I did not insist on being tried by my own rightful court in the hope that my case would be settled more promptly there than in the military one. The black Tribunal, like the blue one, is an acolyte of Government.[8] Even in England people call their bishops pillars of despotism; and they will not cease to be that until the right to elect them is restored to the people, a right that is theirs by virtue of the early, pure and legitimate discipline of the Church. Who if not the bishops in our America have ignited, with excommunications as unjust as they are null and void, the firebrand of fanaticism in order to multiply the horrors of civil war, prostituting themselves by violating even the secrecy of the confessional so as to betray people to the authorities and leave dead bodies unburied? Who but a Bishop Queipo would have dared to declare the insurrection "clearly and evidently heretical"? Saying such a thing is the true and evident heresy, as I shall prove to you in the notes. In a word, since the archbishop is a European and I am a Creole, I had more reason to expect persecution than to expect protection, and so it has been, but at least, I thought, certain forms would be observed and the whole Constitution not be trampled underfoot by a vizier whose brazenness is rooted in the same purblind and slow-witted servility as that of the Janissaries of the Sublime Port.

During the subsequent visits of the Tribunal, when each time I had to explain the reasons for my petition yet again because the justices were new, I thanked them for having taught a deaf-mute to speak even though all he did was babble on about how nonsensical it was to have my case assigned to a hermaphrodite Tribunal; I pointed out to them that since such a Tribunal was infertile, like all monsters, it had still borne no fruit after a month and a half. And, finally, I begged them to allow me to explain myself in detail to show them the justice of my cause and thereby enable them to hand down a decision at last.

They did not allow me to do so because this was not my visitors' responsibility. Is a visit, then, by a Tribunal with public prosecutors and learned judges a courtesy call, a doctor's visit to look after my health or a police visit to check on the quality of the food and the cleanliness of my cell? "You have your Tribunal. It is the ecclesiastical one. Take your appeal to it." "By what means, if I am being held incommunicado? That is the abuse that I am complaining of and that the Tribunal can and must put an end to." "That is to criticize us wrongly. As far as your case is concerned, this is not our responsibility inasmuch as the viceroy has assigned it to the Captaincy General." "That merely shows me that your not protecting my rights is motivated by the same outrageous miscarriage of justice that is the burden of my complaint before the Tribunal that the Constitution offers to citizens oppressed by the arbitrariness of power. The Tribunal is doing itself scant favor. There is no military Tribunal except for members of the military. I have my Tribunal and after that the Royal Tribunal to appeal to against the violation of my right to by tried by my own court and against the viceroy's encroachment upon that right: Is it in his power to deprive a citizen of his legal right or of his lawful Tribunal so as to hold him fast in the iron meshes of military despotism? *Sic volo, sic jubeo, sit pro ratione voluntas?* *

The visitors in judges' robes were necessarily brought up short when confronted with the evident truth of such arguments. And depending on which of them thought of some subterfuge, now the chief justice, now the public prosecutors spoke up, and in order to be heard over the loud murmur and enable the whole crowd of them to hear me, I raised my voice like a trumpet. Accustomed as they were to the age-old shadows of the judiciary and to the language of servility, they took offense at my outspoken arguments and remonstrated with the jailer for having let so many people visit me, although all of them belonged to their profession, because, they said, the general public might get wind of the case. As though the Constitution did not decree that beginning with the prisoner's first deposition after being taken into custody or within twenty-four hours thereafter, the entire proceedings are to take place in public, so that respect for public opinion will make it incumbent upon the sultans to do so. If a leopard can change its spots, the judges of old in their starched white collars will cease to be the cadis of the Ottoman Empire.

Hence the visitors were almost unaccompanied the last time they came, and as I fell back into my old habits, when the chief justice left he asked one of the amanuenses of the recently appointed judge-advocate, Cerquera, why he had not come to take down my deposition. He answered that because he was familiarizing himself with the records of proceedings that the Inquisition had transmitted to him, consisting of an enormous number of sealed documents and manuscripts, as though these were any concern of the military authorities or as though in order to take down my deposition as decreed by the Constitution there were any need of being familiar with the proceedings of the Inquisition. The members of the military Tribunal had to begin with the first deposition because the proceedings of the Inquisition were of a very different sort, just as when I was first imprisoned by the Inquisition a confession con-

---

* *If I so wish, if I so order, you may oppose my will by the force of your reason?*

cerning my entire life was demanded of me, made under oath and under threat of excommunication. And be it noted in passing that the Inquisition publicly revealed that in accordance with the decree of the Cortes it was transmitting its archives to the archbishop, and my example proves that cases were subsequently turned over to the government. *O pleni malitia et dolo filii diaboli!**

The chief magistrate sent orders to Cerquera that he should come to take my deposition at once and without fail, because my appeals were repeated and well-founded, and the Royal Tribunal could not get out of handing down a decision. Those cowardly accomplices of despotism should have done so a month and a half before.

Do not seek to be a judge, the Holy Spirit says, if you do not have the courage to dash iniquity to pieces: *Noli querere fieri judex in si valeas virtute irrumpere iniquitatem.* I told them so clearly, and these were my last words: "If you had been willing to use your authority, I would be free by now."

The viceroy understood perfectly the import of what was passed on to him during the last visit, and before the next one could take place, a half hour after midnight on July 19 the post commander went with the captain of police to get me out of solitary. Once we were in the police station, to which I had been taken, the commandant read me, very confidentially, a legal opinion handed down by Cerquera, the judge-advocate, and Alatorre, the public prosecutor of the episcopates, and therefore a provisional sentence of the viceroy.

Those apocrypha, collected in servile obedience to a despotic whim, said: "that the amnesty of November of last year (in all likelihood the one granted on the occasion of the king's third marriage) cannot be used in my defense because the rebels and traitors of America are excluded." They would have to prove that I was one of them, or I would prove to them that they did not know what they were talking about in their shameful legal opinion, rather than telling them that they were the real traitors and rebels. "Nor could the amnesty that Arredondo granted me be used in my defense since at the time it had not yet been made public and since I presented myself only out of necessity." Then Arredondo committed a felony in Soto la Marina by granting us, in the king's name, on his word of honor, an amnesty that was not yet valid. I have already said that viceroys are stupid to think that they have the power to thwart royal decrees, replacing them as suits their fancy. I have also proved that no necessity whatsoever compelled me when I presented myself, at the

---

* O the sons of the devil are full of malice and guile!

first parley, to Arredondo's aide-de-camp, and absolutely none when I presented myself to Arredondo himself at the third one, nor did that make the amnesty invalid. Cerquera and Alatorre conclude: "that nonetheless, in view of the fact that I presented myself when the commander of the fort was still blustering and threatening to blow it up, it [the amnesty] could be applied to me by sending me to enjoy it in Spain, where I had previously been confined." They ended with a lie, as is evident from what has already been set forth in this Manifesto, and none of the rest of it is true.

In the document from which the Commander of the City read me the legal opinion of Cerquera and Alatorre, along with the provisional sentence of the viceroy, only a small space was left blank at the end. And so, though I was not able to answer at as great length as I would have liked, I said a great deal in the following brief passage: "That everything that had been read to me was full of lies and mistakes: that it was all illegal, unconstitutional and null and void, since the Tribunal did not have proper jurisdiction and had granted me no hearing whatsoever, despite the fact that I had never ceased asking for one. That I demanded the return of my books, manuscripts, documents, clerical collars and zucchettos, along with other things that I handed over to the Inquisition on the night I entered prison: my clothing, my doctoral ring and my gold watch that Captain Ceballos and Colonel Concha had taken away from me so as to present it to His Excellency the viceroy. The Constitution prohibits the imposition of the penalty of confiscation of belongings (article 304).

It must have been one o'clock in the morning when the Commander of the City and the captain of police took me away in a carriage to the little post at San Lázaro, from which it was necessary to dispatch two orderlies on foot and on horseback to summon a lieutenant with thirteen provincial dragoons from Mexico City who were to escort me, since despite the fact that the viceroy had alerted the lieutenant as early as eight o'clock the night before, he had not told him what post he was to come out to in order to receive me. That was how secretly they went about things. When matters are taken care of so silently and so secretly, it is rightly presupposed that the people will disapprove, just as injustice and fear on the part of the one who gives the orders to proceed in this way are likewise presupposed.

The viceroy told the lieutenant, in so many words, that he was going to be escorting a wild beast. And that wildness was proved by the fact that after keeping me buried alive for three years in a cell of the Inquisition prison, I had asked him, in no uncertain terms, to tell me the reason and to listen to me. Alexander also called Calixthenes a wild beast because with philosophical ingenuousness he refused to adore him as a son of Jupiter Amnon, whereupon, once his hands and feet had been cut off, he was shut up in a cage. Nothing should have come as a surprise from a viceroy made as vain and arrogant by the license offered him by the Mexicans as was Alexander from that offered him by the Persians. But since there are others who are also oddly mistaken about my character, I beg them to question all those who have dealt with me on fairly intimate terms; they will doubtless learn that the principal source of the life full of misfortunes that I have had is my childlike innocence and naiveté. My friends have exhorted me in vain to have, as they put it, a little Christian cunning. It is not within my power to be malicious. And those who mistake for malice the extreme penetrating perceptiveness of all my features do not remember that this is quite compatible with the candor that has almost always been noted in all men of great wit and discernment. *Laissez ce pauvre betela* [*sic*], La Fontaine's famous Swiss told the missionaries who were tormenting his master about matters that were his own affair, *Laissez ce pauvre betela, le bon Dieu n'aura pas le courage de le damner.* I defy anyone who comes to know me to be my enemy. He would see that the very acrimony of my speech comes from the ingenuousness that causes me never to be able to disguise the truth and to be surprised even today to find that I have given offense because of it.

In my writings as well, a certain anger that is feigned makes it impossible for me to write without vehemence. My indignation is a fire, but my heart is above all a region of thunderclaps. I am incapable of hating even my enemies. Because where my friends are concerned none, naturally, has suffered or passed away without my offering the homage of my tears. So as not to crush little ants underfoot it is my habit to hop lightly from one foot to the other when I am on the road, and when I am imprisoned—for by my reckoning, of a total of twenty-four years of persecution eight have been spent in prison at one time or another—I have carefully seen to it that they have food, considering the company of little living creatures in the solitude of a prison cell to be a precious thing. In a word, God is my witness that never in all my life have I tried to do evil to anyone or deliberately done any person harm.

This is the wild beast that the viceroy handed over to the dragoons to be taken to his grave, just as in order to break me I had previously been

---

* Leave that poor beast alone, the Good Lord will not have the courage to damn him.

made to travel across the Andes in chains. For sending someone to Veracruz in the torrid heat of the dog days is in all likelihood to send him, rather, to his death. Others who had arrived at the same time died. On August 4 I was put aboard a ship in Veracruz bound for San Juan de Ulúa, exactly twenty-five years after having been put in prison here because of Archbishop Haro's persecution of me, and held as rigorously incommunicado, with equal injustice and equal usurpation of authority over me.

I was placed in block number 7, to which, because it was so hot it resembled a steam bath, I gave the name *Temascaltepec*, and the name stuck. There were other priests there who had been imprisoned as insurgents and like me were being sent to Spain, and one of them, an Augustinian, died of fright on the day they were preparing to put him aboard ship. Then, as a favor, I was transferred to the one I am in now, where I have replaced a captain of artillery who had just arrived from Perote, who was taken from this life in a few days by an attack of the black vomit. Of all the ones I have known here, none lived to the age of twenty. God's mercy has kept me safe thus far, and I thank him with all my heart because it has never occurred to the authorities to give me an artificial apoplexy such as the one they gave my kinsman don Cosme de Mier y Trespalacios, the regent of the Royal Tribunal of Mexico City, because he opposed the royal will regarding charitable works, or in other words, his destruction of the National Bank of New Spain, for all its dealings revolve around the forty-four million hard pesos that the possessions of the Church represent.

Finally, on June 11 the Cortes granted an amnesty to all Americans taken prisoner from 1814 until March of this year because they had participated in the insurrection. The Spanish Americans who surrendered at the fort of Soto la Marina, which I left in order to be granted amnesty, and who were sent to Ceuta, are free now in Havana. The corvette *Diamante* brought them there. Will His Excellency the viceroy, who obeys nothing save his own caprices, announce this amnesty publicly? Or will I be obliged to go to Havana, along the route of fatal ports of call that we Mexicans who are coming down from the high plateau to the Andes are forced to follow till they reach Spain?

While this is being decided, kindly allow my tender and tormented heart that has been obliged to see my compatriots dumped in heaps in those murderous places to ask: why is it that one and two lots or gangs of men leave Mexico City each month, sent off to Veracruz and to this castle, to Acapulco and other penal colonies on the deadly coasts, to Havana, which is no less so, and to the Philippines, not to mention those taken away by the ships of the fleet? Is it to defend Veracruz? In the meeting of engineers and so on that Iturrigaray convened here, it was agreed that it could not be defended. And its importance is nil because its bay is an open roadstead and there are better ports, such as Antón Lizardo and Villarrica, within sight of it. This castle that is all falling to pieces and to ruin, serves no purpose, in the final analysis, save as a place for ships to tie up, and a place to waste money and men. Can the vast coasts of New Spain be guarded? Or are they not well enough defended by their very unhealthiness? Does Havana need settlers when it already has a population of more than half a million? Do the Philippines need settlers when their population already numbers three million, of whom a million and a half are subjects of Spain? Mexicans are hated there as oppressors, since once they are levied here by force they are already trained soldiers by the time they arrive there. Why are these young, robust men, most of them artisans, not sent to populate the completely deserted frontiers of the interior provinces threatened with invasion by the United States, which Spain, by ceding Louisiana to it, has placed in immediate proximity to us? To the east United States territory touches Texas, and to the west its settlements along the Missouri surround New Mexico. If Mexican young men were sent there, they would be soldiers and tillers of the soil, who could be provided with women to marry from among the countless orphan girls whom the insurrection has left in dire straits and who must take up prostitution in order to eat. Why give preference to expatriation and death rather than to such a useful course?

I shall say it straight out. If the murder of prisoners during the insurrection is a direct means of destroying the population in order to be able to subject it to an iron scepter, as Cortés's mass butchery succeeded in doing, that other murder of which I am speaking is one of the many indirect means adopted since the Conquest to decrease the population or keep it from growing. "The great multitudes that there were in this America," Torquemada said, "are dying off because of the enormous burdens and different sorts of mistreatment and heavy labors with which they have been oppressed."

To the same end, the classification of men by color was then put into effect, giving different names to the monsters resulting from the copulation of different species of brutes—as though all men did not belong to a single species. I know very well that this is not sanctioned by the Laws of the Indies, quite to the contrary, but the Congress of Cádiz has sanctioned it in the Constitution by excluding, contrary to what is provided in the Laws of the Indies, those born in any part of Africa (which allegedly produces only monsters) not only from the number of those who are citizens but also from those counted in the national census and even from the number of rational beings, for the sole purpose of reducing the representation of America, in the utterly stupid belief that the majority of its inhabitants is made up of mulattos. There are more of them in Spain. This constitutional sanction has just made marriage, to which public opinion was already an impediment, even more difficult; if indeed, with time, it will not serve to bring on an attempt by mulattos, already angered by whites, to wipe the latter out, as in Santo Domingo.

The excessive fees paid priests increases the difficulty of marriage among the poor. A real and a half is enough for a nuptial Mass in Spain; here many pesos are required because in order to live the priests must sell the sacraments at prices fixed by the schedule of fees and tariffs owed the king. The tithes, or the tenth part of the fruit of the sweat of their brows, that tillers of the soil give to maintain their pastor, are divided among the king, pensioners awarded a cross by Charles III, the palace curate or nominal patriarch of the Indies, the successors of the poor fishermen of Galilee, so that they may live in princely luxury and regularly enrich their families in the Peninsula, and cantors who are hauled around in carriages.

Notes for the Memoirs

CHAPTER I: FROM THE TIME THAT THE RESOLUTION OF THE
COUNCIL WAS CONFIRMED IN MODIFIED FORM TO
MY ARRIVAL IN PARIS

1. The reference is to the useless appeals Mier made to the Council of the Indies, the body responsible for overseeing from Spain the execution of decisions regarding the colonies. Mier tried to get his case reviewed because—according to him—he had been condemned without allowing him to speak in his own behalf and as a consequence of an illegal trial. He managed to secure support for his cause from Minister Jovellanos and Dr. Muñoz, a chronicler of the Indies, but in practice it was agents of the Indies who had the real power. They were the intermediaries between the Council, the ministers and the king; according to Mier's testimony, all of them were corrupt. The only one he excepts from this charge is Ramón Soto Posadas, the public prosecutor of Northern America, whom he considered to be an honest man. However, Mier's case did not fall under the public prosecutor's jurisdiction, but rather under that of one of the allies of Archbishop Núñez de Haro y Peralta in Spain. The person in question was Francisco Antonio León, a minor official whom Mier mentions continually, "an ignorant, bumbling man, corrupt and venal, whom [Haro] trusted not to allow me access either to the court or to the Council." (Mier, *Memorias*, vol. I, 225).

Núñez de Haro made his mark on the history of the Mexican colony in its last years: he was archbishop of New Spain for nearly thirty years (1771–1800) and took over as viceroy of Mexico in 1787; he was the person mainly responsible for the persecution of Mier as a heretic.

The system of administration in Madrid denounced by fray Servando functioned as follows: the king depended on his ministers, and they in turn on their first- and second-rank officials, who in turn allowed secretaries to run the ministries. These secretaries were called *covachuelos*, because they worked in the *covachas* (cellars) of the palace. Each of them was responsible for the administration of a province or kingdom of Spain or of the Indies. To Mier's misfortune, León was the secretary in charge of New Spain; influenced by the virulence of Haro's reports concerning the Mexican priest, León never left off persecuting fray Servando, with an intensity that would appear to stem from a personal hatred.

2. Mier's case was sent from the Council of the Indies to the Royal Academy of History to be reviewed. After Mier had endured the trial and travail of six years' imprisonment, endless red tape and appeals to various authorities, the Academy rendered its verdict: his sermon on the Virgin of Guadalupe did not deny the tradition concerning her nor did it contain censurable elements, and Haro was deemed to have acted unjustly. But the Archbishop's representatives mobilized, bringing the subject to a dead halt for over a year. The *covachuelo* León succeeded in getting Mier transferred to the Dominican monastery in Salamanca by interpreting the Academy's decision according to his own lights: he gave assurances that "no harm is being done him" by sending Mier to a monastery, since he was in holy orders (hiding the fact that Mier had been given the right to choose the place of his detention), and keeping him there for four more years (the time required to serve out the ten years' imprisonment ordered by Haro).

3. With regard to the identity of León, see the previous notes.

4. The escape to Burgos took place in 1800, the same year as Archbishop Haro's death.

5. On the situation of priestly castes in the New World and in Spain, see the introduction. Mier is alluding here to the difference in education between the friars of the Peninsula and those of Mexico, finding the latter better educated. For example, when the commander of the Order of Calatrava, Francisco Corbera, made a recommendation that Minister Jovellanos intervene in Fray Servando's behalf, he warned the minister that "[Servando] was not a Dominican, because in Castile what is meant by that appellation is a man whose education is as rudimentary as his manner is coarse. . . . There is a phrase used by men of learning in Castile to express the fact that a certain individual is very crude and [his language] macaronic: he is said to be very Dominican. And certain Dominicans who had emigrated from France told me that having left it at the end of the eighteenth century, they were amazed to find themselves in the middle of the fourteenth century in Spain." (M 235) With the intention of defending his own social status, Fray Servando takes no notice of the fact that the low clergy was equally ignorant in both regions.

6. Juan Cornide was a priest from Veracruz who was based for a time in Madrid. Along with Mier, he suffered from slander at the hands of the wife of Saturnino de la Fuente, the agent of the Indies, a swindler, and deeply in debt. The wife denounced Mier and Cornide to the Minister of Grace and Justice, accusing them of being engaged in hatching a plot to kill the king; both priests were arrested and sent to the Royal Prison. The mayor began an investigation, the woman confessed her calumny and was taken off to the prison for mad-women in Madrid. Cornide and Mier were freed after a week, with a royal certificate attesting to their innocence.

7. Manuel de Godoy, Queen María Luisa's favorite, was again at the head of the Spanish government. After Louis XVI was guillotined (1793), Spain declared war on France. The following year, the French invaded Bilbao, San Sebastián and Figueras. Godoy feared the spread of the ideas of the French Revolution, but he was even more afraid of England. He signed the Treaty of San Ildefonso in 1796, becoming the ally of France and declaring war on Great Britain. Among its basic revenues, Spain had the monies obtained from the American colonies, but the war made communications difficult and eventually opened the New World market to the English. The Franco-Spanish armada was defeated by England in the battle of Trafalgar (1805), which Servando Teresa de Mier witnessed.

8. The Jansenists—members of an unorthodox Catholic movement—were opposed to Jesuit ethics, advocating a more Augustinian evangelical compromise, but this was no longer a matter of importance, since the Jesuits had fallen into disgrace and been expelled from America. During the French Revolution the Jansenists were opposed to the ecclesiastical hierarchy based on the caste system, dissociating in the eyes of the revolutionaries the image of an alliance between the monarchy and the Catholic Church. At the end of the eighteenth century and the beginning of the nineteenth, a "Jansenist" priest was regarded as an extremist, as a threat to the reestablished social order.

Mariano de Urquijo was prime minister of Spain during the brief period when Godoy was barred from holding the post (1798–1801). A man of great learning, he backed Humboldt, securing for him the permits necessary for beginning his voyage to America with Bonpland. Manuel de Godoy Alvarez de Faria Ríos Sánchez Zardosa, also known as Prince of Peace and of Basano, Duke of Alcudia and Suca (1767–1851), was the favorite of Queen María Luisa of Spain and twice Prime Minister (1792–98 and 1801–8).

9. There was great tension between Spain and Portugal. In 1801 Godoy succeeded in invading Portugal, in the War of Oranges; Charles V allowed French troops to cross Spanish territory to invade Portugal, an ally of England. In 1814, Portugal was among the countries that forced Napoleon Bonaparte to sign his first abdication.

10. In 1795, Godoy had received the title of Prince of Peace for having negotiated the Peace of Basel between France and Spain. But during this period his

power had grown weaker: the aristocrats did not like him, nor was he popular among the people, especially because of the inflation that his policy had brought on. The persecution of the Jansenists formed part of his strategy for holding power. Famous for his intrigues, he contributed indirectly to the Napoleonic intervention: Ferdinand, Prince of Asturias, was plotting against his father, Charles V, to remain on the throne and incidentally to throw Godoy out of power. Taking advantage of the confusion and the unrest, Napoleon expelled the three of them and placed his brother on the throne of Spain.

11. The movement of Julius Caesar's forces across the Rubicon River (Italy, 49 B.C.) began a three-year war that ended with his being named Caesar of the Roman world. "Crossing the Rubicon" became a popular phrase describing a step that definitely commits a person to a given course of action.

12. In the wake of 18 and 19 Brumaire, in 1799, a conspiracy led by Bonaparte and Abbot Sieyès put an end to the Directorate and named a new government, the head of which was Bonaparte himself as First Consul. This marked the official end of the French Revolution. An enlightened dictatorship came to power, giving the appearance of being a constitutional government, but with no guarantees either of the "rights of man" or of the famous principles of "liberty, equality and fraternity." Servando Teresa de Mier is here referring to the events of 1801, but in a way that reveals that he is writing from a perspective that dates from long after the events themselves. This text was in fact written in 1818; on questioning the nature of the French Republic at that moment, he is doing so retrospectively, with the knowledge that Napoleon would be named Consul for Life in 1802 and Emperor in 1804.

13. The Catholic Church had suffered a severe setback during the French Revolution, whose leaders demanded that it submit to the civil authorities except in matters of doctrine. Just three years before Mier's stay in Paris, Pope Pius VI (1775–99) suffered the humiliation of being driven out of Rome by the French army and taken as a prisoner to France, where he died. By 1801 the new pope, Pius VII, had bettered the position of the Church with Napoleon, but he did not succeed in recovering its secularized land holdings or in completely reestablishing either its image or its influence.

CHAPTER II: FROM MY ARRIVAL IN PARIS TO MY DEPARTURE

1. Known as "the preceptor of Simón Bolívar" and the instigator of the famous Oath of Monte Sacro that was to mean so much to the fight for independence in Latin America, Simón Rodríguez (1771–1854) was the Socratic teacher who wanted to *teach how to live* and make citizens through education. An early conspirator against Spanish colonialism, a Venezuelan expatriate for twenty-seven years, going by various other names, most importantly that of Samuel Robinson, he was one of the freest and most original writers of the

first half of the nineteenth century in Latin America. Simón Rodríguez was one of the fathers of emancipist thought in America; nonetheless, like Mier, he is not so much read as remembered for his most eccentric behavior and outlandish adventures in many corners of the globe.

2. The 1801 translation appeared under the title *Atala o los amores de dos salvajes en el desierto; escrita en francés por Francisco-Augusto Chateaubriand*. The translation and a brief introduction were signed S. Robinson, one of Simón Rodríguez's pseudonyms. Historians differ as to the identity of the real author, since Mier maintains in the *Memoirs* that it is his work entirely; nonetheless, it seems quite unlikely that Rodríguez would hire him as a "ghost writer," since the two of them were equally penniless. Rodríguez's biographers usually prefer to regard it as a case of coauthorship, taking no credit away from Mier despite his not having signed his name to the translation.

3. Count Constantin-François de Volney, a historian, a philosopher and a Girondin, was the epitome of eighteenth-century rationalist thought in France.

4. This period was as difficult for the Catholic Church as that of the Great Schism and the Babylonian Captivity of the Pope. Not only did the prestige of the Supreme Pontiff suffer, but the religious orders were placed in question by Enlightenment thinkers and at the same time they were manipulated by the kings of Europe, who wanted to use them in order to get rid of the Pope and enhance their own power. During the papacy of Pius VI, the Church was completely divided (see chapter 1, note 13) between republicans and monarchists, between rationalists and traditionalists. The entire ecclesiastical hierarchy was being called into question, and Mier himself questions the power of bishops (see the introduction).

5. The Council of Trent (1545–63) was very important for the Catholic Church because it issued edicts for self-reformation and clarified dogmatic definitions called into question by Protestants; this strengthened the Church in Europe, but fray Servando observes that it did not do so in France.

6. The invocation of the name of the celebrated Bishop Gregoire in favor of his cause clearly reveals Mier's position with regard to the conflicts between Church and State. Gregoire was the great defender of the Constitutional or nationalized Church during the French Revolution: in 1789 he was an active participant in the Revolutionary Assembly attempting to bring about the union of the clergy and the Third Estate and the abolition of slavery; in 1790 he was named the Constitutional bishop of Loire-et-Cher (the diocese of Blois); two years later he proposed the abolition of the monarchy. He was opposed to the coup of 18 Brumaire, the proclamation of the Empire and the reconciliation with Rome proposed by Napoleon. Like Mier and despite the loss of prestige suffered by the priesthood, he continued to wear clerical attire and openly professed his religion.

7. On Carli, Humboldt and the early presence of Christianity in America, see the introduction.

8. Mier is here referring to the Synod of Pistoia (1786), presided over by Matteo Ricci, the bishop of Pistoia-Prato, under the tutelage of the Grand Duke Peter Leopold, which was very important in the history of Jansenism (see chapter 1, note 8).

9. The Treaty of Amiens (1802) was a peace accord signed by France, England, Spain and the Netherlands, which brought peace to Europe for fourteen months during the Napoleonic wars, but strengthened Bonaparte's absolutism as First Consul. Two years later he proclaimed himself Emperor, a fact known to Mier at the time that he writes this.

10. The Napoleonic Code was the first civil code in history to be founded on a rational idea of the law, based on common sense; adopted in France in 1804, it had a decisive influence throughout the entire nineteenth century, both in Europe and in Latin America. Father Mier's support for the Code is revealing, since it not only permits divorce but in fact also replaces the previous legal system, based on principles of the Catholic Church.

11. Mier was made a member of the Institut National de France in 1814.

CHAPTER III: FROM MY DEPARTURE FROM PARIS TO MY RETURN FROM NAPLES TO ROME

1. In 1802, the infanta Isabel of Austria was about to marry Ferdinand VII, Prince of Asturias and heir to the throne of Spain. Ferdinand ruled as king between 1808 and 1833, although his reign was interrupted by the Napoleonic wars, when he was sent into exile in Bayonne. The rebels—both in Spain and in America—who were against the French occupation, staged an uprising to secure the return of Ferdinand, now called "Ferdinand the Desired," in whom the Cortes of Cádiz believed they had an ally who would support a liberal constitution on his return to the throne. But history took a different turn, and Ferdinand was not to accept such a constitution until many years later, under pressure and foreseeing that his reign was approaching its end. The marriage alluded to by Mier did not bear fruit; the king fulfilled the obligation of fathering an heir only with his fourth wife, María Cristina I of the Kingdom of the Two Sicilies, who gave birth to Isabel II in 1830.

2. The reference is to the brief reign in Spain of Napoleon's brother, Joseph Bonaparte (1808–13) and to Joachim Murat, one of Napoleon's marshals, who was made king of Naples (1808–15).

3. Father Mier is really referring to the Catholic cardinal Fabrizio Ruffo, the leader—along with the legendary Fra Diavolo—of a popular-royalist counterrevolution, against the Bonapartist forces in Naples and in support of King Ferdinand IV (1798).

4. Correct grammar and pronunciation were one of the obsessions of the learned men of the nascent American republics, as a way of obtaining both au-

tonomy and national homogeneity. Mier returns to the subject more than once; in, for example, his *Carta de despedida a los mexicanos,* written in the castle of San Juan de Ulúa in 1821, he attacks the "ugly" Spanish pronunciation of the letter *j,* advocating the restoration of the "soft x" in the name of Mexico. Both he and Simón Rodríguez, and later Andrés Bello and Domingo F. Sarmiento, attempted to simplify the alphabet, reducing the number of letters to the same number of sounds as in the spoken language. The proposal did not succeed.

5. Catholic priests wrote grammars, dictionaries and catechisms in the New World during the seventeenth and eighteenth centuries. Lorenzo Hervás y Panduro writes about this period in *Idea dell'universo* (1778–87).

6. Las Caldas (diocese of Santander) was the monastery in Spain to which Servando Teresa de Mier was banished by Archbishop Nuñez de Haro. For his sermon on the Virgin of Guadalupe he was sentenced to ten years' imprisonment there, accused of heresy by the Inquisition. The Holy Office, let it be said in passing, formally came into being as an institution in Mexico in 1569; Mier was to live to see its definite eradication in 1820.

7. The epitaph is in dactylic hexameter in Latin:
Mantua gave birth to me; the Calabrians snatched me away; now [Mount] Parthenope holds me [i.e., I am buried there]. I sang of pastures, leaders.

I owe this and other translations from Latin to the generosity of John Bodel, Department of Classics, Rutgers University.

8. *Give flowers to the sacred ash: that true [ash] of the [muse of] Virgil is next to this tomb.* (Trans., John Bodel).

Maronis is cited in place of Virgil's whole name: Publius Vergilius Maro.

CHAPTER IV: FROM MY RETURN TO ROME TO
MY RETURN TO SPAIN IN 1803

1. The Jesuits' fall from grace began with the theological adventure in China of Matteo Ricci, who—in a way that calls to mind the Franciscans in New Mexico and the myth of the Virgin of Guadalupe—persistently maintained that he had found evidence of Catholicism in Confucianism. Popes Clement XI and Benedict XIV condemned these theories, and in conjunction with the condemnation, resentment against the political power of the Society of Jesus grew more intense. The crown of Portugal expelled the Jesuits in 1759, France declared the Society of Jesus illegal in 1764, and in 1767 Spain and the Kingdom of the Two Sicilies took repressive measures against it. In 1773 Pope Clement XIV issued a decree abolishing the society for the good of the Church in Rome— the majority of the priests expelled from the colonies had ended up in Italy and Portugal—thus accounting for Mier's surprise on noting the power of the Jesuits in Italy. The society continued its clandestine activities until 1814, when Pius VII restored the order's legal status.

2. Pius VII, whose baptismal name was Barnaba Gregorio Chiaramonti, was pope from 1800 to 1823. Mier here treats him with contempt, but in point of fact the Church—devastated by the French Revolution—was restored during his papacy. The Mexican friar could not forgive him for having restored the Society of Jesus, for having concluded the Concordat with Napoleon and for his attacks on those who were attempting to liberalize the Church. Despite his great efforts to modernize the papacy, the Papal State was reestablished, and his death was followed by a "government by priests."

3. Father Juan de Mariana, a Spanish Jesuit, maintained in his *De rege et regis institutione (The King and the Education of the King*, 1598), that overthrowing a tyrant was justifiable under certain circumstances; he was accused of inciting tyrannicide when Henry IV of France was assassinated in 1610. His *Tractatus VII* (1609), one of a series of political and moral treatises that included the defense of the heretic Arias Montano, was banned by the Inquisition. Mier attacks the Jesuits by invoking the example of Mariana, but in point of fact Mariana was a great critic of the Society of Jesus, as is evident in his *Discurso de los grandes defectos que hay en la forma del gobierno de los jesuitas (Discourse on the Great Defects that Exist in the Rule Governing the Jesuits*, 1625). On the Jansenists and Molinists, see chapter 1, note 8, and chapter 2, note 4.

4. Juan de Palafox y Mendoza, bishop of Puebla and viceroy of New Spain, a Jesuit regarded as a model of the secular priest and the initiator of the Herrerist style of architecture in the sixteenth century, the author of works such as *Virtudes del indio (Virtues of the Indian), Vida interior (Inner life), Direcciones para los señores obispos y cartas pastorales (Instructions for the Reverend Bishops and Pastoral Letters)* and *Relación breve de la venida de los de la Compañía de Jesús a la Nueva España (A Brief Account of the Coming of Members of the Company of Jesus to New Spain)*. The mention of Palafox is interesting, since in his diocese of Puebla—adjoining Cholula, the holy city of Quetzalcóatl—he had ordered the destruction of the last remaining statues of Mexican divinities in public places. It must be remembered that among Father Mier's polemical theological theses was that of Saint Thomas–Quetzalcóatl as an apostle to Mexicans, developed at greatest length in his *Apología del doctor Mier.*

The Jesuits were expelled from Mexico in the second half of the eighteenth century, at the very height of their power; they had been responsible in large part for the triumph of the national cause of the Virgin of Guadalupe, as well as for restricting the power of the viceroy over the missions and preventing the beatification of Palafox, proposed by the missionary bishops, a prelate for whom Mier must have felt a certain sympathy.

5. Accusing the Jesuits of being Freemasons was an unreasonable charge on fray Servando's part, since the Freemasons were not even a Christian institution, their belief in the existence of a Supreme Being notwithstanding. In general, in the world of the Enlightenment and in Latin America, the Masons were freethinkers and anticlerical. Many leaders of Latin American indepen-

dence, such as Francisco de Miranda, Simón Bolívar and José de San Martín, were associated with freemasonry. Mier himself was accused of being a Mason—an accusation he always denied, as can be seen in the chapter of his *Memoirs* entitled "From My Arrival in Barcelona to My Arrival in Madrid," despite the fact that he expressed his gratitude for the "infinite" aid that the lodges contributed toward "overthrowing Iturbide and establishing the republic." ("Carta a Cantú," August 31, 1826, in the Ayacucho edition) Moreover, there are documents extant that establish the affiliation of Servando Teresa de Mier with a lodge: "In the middle of September, 1811, he was initiated into a society that met in the San Carlos district, in Cádiz, founded by the Argentine military leader Carlos Alvear and made up principally of Americans troubled by the situation of Spain and the misfortunes that would befall its American dominions if it surrendered to Napoleon. The society went by the name of Los Caballeros Racionales [The Knights of Reason]. . . . The obligations of its members were to defend the fatherland, to aid other members and to keep its existence secret." (Virginia Guedea, "Las sociedades secretas durante el movimiento de la independencia," in Jaime E. Rodríguez O., ed., *The Independence of Mexico* . . . , 52–3).

6. Probabilism was first formulated by the Dominican Bartolomé de Medina in the sixteenth century and later developed in detail by the Jesuits. The central premise was that when a person does not know if a certain conduct is licit or illicit, he can have recourse to a "probable opinion" based on logical argument or on the views of authorities. The Jansenists, who believed that it was imperative to adopt the strictest point of view in case of doubt, attacked Jesuit confessors for having set forth a relaxed system of morality.

7. Francis Xavier Alegre was the first serious historian of the Jesuits and was expelled with the others from Mexico to Italy. He was the author of works such as *Alexandrias, Homeri Ilias, latino carmine expressa (The Iliad of Homer, Expressed in Latin Verse)* and *Institutionum Theologicarum.* His *Historia de la Provincia de la Compañia de Jesús de Nueva España* contributed to the Guadalupan tradition; in Mexico there was an aura of supernatural *signs* that should be read; Alegre was stricken with the plague of 1725 and of 1736; as a consequence of the latter epidemic, the Virgin of Guadalupe was declared the patron saint of New Spain. Fray Servando maintained that Alegre fell out of favor with the Jesuits because he defended "vigorous physical activity" *("promoción física")*: I am inclined to interpret this statement in the light of the fact that Alegre was in favor of sports and against activities such as chess, since "it is foolish to devote a great deal of attention and effort to a fictitious thing of no importance which produces mental fatigue." (*"Stultum enim est in re umbratili, et nullius momenti maximam attentionem et studium cum capitis defatigatione collocare,"* Institutionum, III, 479). Arnold Kerson says: "As a man possessed of good logic and practical sense, he recommends games requiring less mental concentration and more physical activity." ("Francisco Javier Alegre, humanista mexicano del siglo XVIII," in *Cuadernos americanos* 160 (1968): 174; and Mauricio Bechot, "La ley natural

como fundamento de la ley positiva en Francisco Xavier Alegre" *Hispanic Enlightenment Aesthetics and Literary Theory* 14, nos. 1–2 (Spring-Fall 1991): 124–29). It is my impression that, given the context, Mier is poking fun at the Jesuits themselves, who have no idea whom to attack next.

8. Mier writes Paw instead of Pauw: this is not the only name whose spelling he changed. On the discourse of Pauw, Raynal, Robertson and Clavijero, see the introduction. It also contains a discussion of the influence on Mier's works of fray Bartolomé de Las Casas and his *Brevísima relación de la destrucción de las Indias*, a work that began the "black legend" of the Spanish Conquest and Spanish colonialism.

9. The Spanish soldier Bernal Díaz del Castillo was one of the first to offer a version of the Conquest from a nonofficial point of view in his *Historia verdadera de la conquista de la Nueva España* (1632).

10. These are a pair of verses from Virgil's *Eclogues* (3.104–5): the better texts have *tris* for *tres* and *caeli* for *coeli*. According to John Bodel's interpretation the translation is: "Tell me in what lands, and you will be a great Apollo to me, the expanse of the sky is not more than three ells wide [Ell is a unit of measurement, from palm to elbow; while the original word ulna equals about five feet.]

There are several possible solutions. One is that Virgil is referring to the tomb of Caelius, a bankrupt who in selling his property reserved only enough ground for a tomb. The other is that it may refer to the well at Syene (Aswan) used by Eratosthenes, who is not, however, mentioned, in calculating the earth's circumference. According to Asconius Pedianus (9 B.C.–A.D. 76), Virgil is said to have told him that by writing this passage he had set a trap for interpreters *(hoc loco se grammaticis crucem fixisse)*. Now the majority of interpreters relate this with the sphere of Archimedes or with that of Posidinous (a friend of Cicero's); the measurement of the construct establishes a contrast between the dimensions of the sphere and the immensity of the sky. (This interpretation is derived from Wendell Clausen, *A Commentary on Virgil Ecologues* [Oxford: Clarendon Press, 1994, 116–77]). Given fray Servando's context, I believe that his use of it is more in accord with the first interpretation, since the space described is so limited.

CHAPTER V: FROM MY ARRIVAL IN BARCELONA TO MY ARRIVAL IN MADRID

1. On Freemasonry, see chapter 4, note 5.

2. Servando Teresa de Mier is here making a clear distinction between purity in the Peninsula and that in America, obviously favoring the latter as being more authentic, turning topsy-turvy the polemic regarding the inferiorization of those born in America (see the introduction). By attesting to the authenticity of his "well-known lineage," he was defending the privileges of the Creole no-

bility, which had so little access to jobs and honors. Hence, in his *Historia de la revolución de Nueva España*, the reasons he adduces for justifying independence are conjoined with a defense of the Mexican aristocracy, to which he maintains he belongs because he is descended from a noble family that included among its members a governor and a presiding judge of the Inquisition Tribunal, as well as being—he claims—a descendent of Montezuma on his mother's side. His republicanism is not open to question: the horrible impression made on him as a witness to the excesses of the "Terror" during the French Revolution made him support constitutional order and a certain religious heterodoxy, seeking in the Laws of the Indies, in Sacred Scripture, in oral tradition and in Mexican hieroglyphs age-old principles that could help in achieving the autonomy of New Spain, on the one hand, while on the other not undermining the social privileges of the Creole nobility.

3. This is a sort of nudge in the ribs, a wink on fray Servando's part, because the *gachupines* continued to vaunt the superior powers of their faith in the Spanish Virgen del Pilar as compared to the local faith in the Virgin of Guadalupe. He says as much in another part of his *Memoirs,* directly addressing his compatriots: "Americans, idiots that we are, the Archbishop's Europeans were making fun of us, and far from believing that the Virgin favored you more with [the Virgin of] Guadalupe than she did them with [the Virgin of the] Pillar, [this has been] one of the reasons for their persecuting me." (M 114)

4. Juan de Solórzano Pereira, mentioned several times in this part, was a member of the Council of Castile and of the Council of the Indies. The author of *Política indiana (Policy in the Indies,* 1648), he advocated—among other things—equality of privileges, rights and honors for Creoles and peninsular Spaniards.

5. Count José Moriño y Redondo Floridablanca obtained his title of nobility as a reward for his diplomatic handling of the expulsion of the Jesuits from Spain in 1767 and his negotiations that brought the dissolution of the Society of Jesus through a decision on the part of Rome in 1772. He was Secretary of State under Charles IV, the enlightened despot, between 1776 and 1792, bringing about reforms in vocational schools, giving capital to peasants, and strengthening Spain's industry, agriculture and commerce.

6. On "all the absurdities and stupidities," see the introduction.

7. Showing off his black humor, Mier is alluding here to the confusion caused by the dethronement of King Ferdinand VII and his replacement by Napoleon's brother, Joseph I, in 1808.

CHAPTER VI: ABOUT WHAT HAPPENED TO ME IN MADRID UNTIL I ESCAPED FROM SPAIN TO PORTUGAL TO SAVE MY LIFE

1. Campomanes, the Prosecuting Attorney of the Council of Castile who provided official support and central leadership for the reform, was one of

Charles IV's "enlightened" political figures who did the most to rally the American liberals, along with the Aragonese aristocrat Aranda (Prime Minister after Floridablanca) and Floridablanca himself, a civil conservative (chapter 5, note 5); Meléndez Valdés, Cabarrús and Olavide were regarded as technicians whose knowledge of foreign technology was useful to the Spanish government. Gaspar Melchor de Jovellanos, the Minister of Justice at the end of the century, a liberal whose opposition to the Holy Office cost him his post, formed part of the same group; during his brief eight-month term in office, in 1797, he heard fray Servando's case and granted him an ephemeral rehabilitation (chapter 1, note 1). The funeral referred to by Mier took place in 1802; see the introduction.

2. Another allusion to Mier's aristocratic origins. See the introduction and chapter 5, note 2.

3. Although he was expert at disguises, this was one of the rare times when Mier used another name. However, he was in the habit of always retaining traces of his real identity: in this case, Ramiro de Vendes was "an exact anagram of my name"; another, José Guerra, the pseudonym with which he signed his *Historia de la revolución de Nueva España*, represents the beginning and end of his baptismal name, precisely the two parts of it that, along with his mother's surname, he normally does not use.

4. Mier confesses that he has mistakenly boarded the wrong ship and thus happens to witness the famous battle off Cape Trafalgar, between Cádiz and the Strait of Gibraltar, on October 21, 1805. His count of the number of warships is less than the one recorded in historical documents (one less than thirty-three royal vessels, the sum total of the Franco-Spanish fleet), and for obvious reasons he devotes more attention to the Spanish aspect of the battle. He mentions neither the French, commanded by Admiral Pierre de Villeneuve, nor the twenty-seven ships commanded by Horatio Nelson, whose death, however, he does mention. The encounter was to give England naval primacy for a century, but Mier, being too close to events, regards it merely as part of Bonaparte's strategy for invading Spain; the event itself merits only this one paragraph in his account.

5. Mier could have known of this episode only long after it had happened. In 1815, Napoleon Bonaparte, pressured by the Parliament of France, was forced to abdicate. In Rochefort he tried to board ship and sail to the United States, but a British squadron kept all vessels from leaving port. Napoleon sought the protection of the English government. He boarded the *Bellerophon,* but none of the allied countries wanted to see him land in America, preferring to send him back to France to be tried and executed; the British also refused to allow him into the country and decided to banish him to the island of Saint Helena. It was at that moment that Napoleon uttered his famous phrase "I appeal to history!"

CHAPTER VII: WHAT FOLLOWED THEREUPON IN EUROPE UNTIL MY
RETURN TO MEXICO (FROM THE *Apologetic Manifesto*)

1. Napoleon kept both Charles V and Ferdinand VII in exile to ensure that Joseph Bonaparte remained on the throne of Spain.

2. At the moment when Mier embarked with Javier de Mina in order to fight for independence in what was to be the revolutionary debacle of Soto de la Marina, Mina was already the "famous author of the first history of the Insurgency led by Father Hidalgo, a book that violently attacked the atrocities committed by the royalists, set forth convincing arguments to deny the legitimacy of the Spanish government and once again upheld the thesis of the evangelization of Mexico before the arrival of Cortez." (Brading, *Mito y profecía*, 64)

3. Manuel Mier y Terán, a politician from Chiapas, fought for Mexican independence and the protection of its territories against the expansionist advance of the United States along the border.

4. The antimonarchical revolutions had in fact begun in Spain, forcing Ferdinand VII to adopt, around 1820, the liberal constitution enacted less than a decade before in his name and in his absence. The abolition of the Holy Office was also about to be proclaimed in Mexico.

5. "The lords with the blue cuffs" is a reference to the Inquisition authorities.

6. The allusion to the Venadito (literally, "Little Stag") is ambiguous: at first sight it would appear to be an ironic nickname given the viceroy; but fray Servando finished writing the *Manifesto* very close in time after Javier de Mina's execution in a settlement called Venadito. Since Mier insisted that any accusation against him must be political in nature and not place his religious faith in question, I am of the opinion that the paragraph alludes to his run-ins with Mina and the impossibility of having proof of them at hand at the time of the accusations. Cf. the following paragraph: "Up until the 27th of October [1817], the date on which he was taken prisoner and executed in Venadito, Mina waged a brilliant military campaign, captured San Felipe, threatened León and created great consternation in powerful places, thereby recreating that atmosphere of fear that had accompanied the victories of Morelos a few years before. Mina's defeat did not keep one of Morelos's former lieutenants, Vicente Guerrero, from renewing the struggle in the south of the country, winning a series of victories in 1819." (Cited in Lafaye, *Quetzalcóatl and Guadalupe*, 195).

7. The "green candle" is an allusion to the candles used before the Tribunals of the Inquisition, when, at the time judgment was rendered and the verdict announced, the person accused of heresy made his profession of faith "with a green candle in hand." (See Menéndez Pelayo, *Historia de los heterodoxos españoles*, VI, 229).

8. The "black tribunal" was that of the Church and the "blue tribunal" that of the Inquisition. Fray Servando is here accusing the archbishop and other

such authorities of inculcating fanaticism in believers, etc.; hence I do not believe that he is referring to a civil tribunal. His argument with the tribunal is precisely the fact that he wishes to be treated as a citizen and be judged by a civil or military tribunal according to the provisions of the Constitution. He is doubtless referring to the Constitution adopted in 1812 by the Cortes rebelling against the power of Napoleon in Mexico and in Spain; this Constitution, though annulled by Ferdinand VII, was fully restored in 1820 by the king himself. Mexican independence is in part the product of the restitution of this liberal Constitution. What is most important in this instance is the fact that in this Constitution the clergy was left with no representation in the government—such representation was exactly what Mier was seeking in order to resolve his case.

Bibliography

1. TEXTS BY FRAY SERVANDO TERESA DE MIER

"Sermón predicado en la Colegiata de Nuestra Señora de Guadalupe de México el día 12 de diciembre de 1794." Mexico City, 1794.

Cartas a Juan Bautista Muñoz sobre la tradición guadalupana de México. Burgos, Spain, 1797.

Atala o los amores de dos salvajes en el desierto; escrita en francés por Francisco-Augusto Chateaubriand. Trans. Samuel Robinson. Paris, 1801.

Carta de un americano al Español sobre su número XIX. London, 1811.

Segunda carta de un americano al Español sobre su número XIX. London, 1812.

Historia de la revolución de Nueva España, antiguamente Anáhuac, o verdadero origen y causa de ella, con la relación de sus progresos hasta el presente año de 1813. London, 1813.

Apología y Relación de lo sucedido en Europa hasta octubre de 1805. Mexico City, 1818–19.

Manifesto apologético. Mexico City, 1820.

Carta de despedida a los mexicanos, escrita desde el Castillo de San Juan de Ulúa. Mexico City, 1821.

"Discurso preliminar." In *Breve relación de la destrucción de las Indias Occidentales presentada a Felipe II, siendo príncipe de Asturias,* by Bartolomé de las Casas. Philadelphia, 1821.

Memoria político-instructiva, enviada desde Filadelfia en agosto de 1821, a los jefes independientes del Anáhuac, llamado por los españoles Nueva España. Philadelphia, 1821.

Exposición de la persecución que ha padecido desde el 14 de junio de 1817 hasta el presente de 1822. Mexico City, 1822.

Discursos e intervenciones en el primer y segundo Congreso Constituyentes Mexicanos, 1822–1824. In *Antología del pensamiento político americano: Fray Servando Teresa de Mier.* Ed. Edmundo O'Gorman. Mexico City: Imprenta Universitaria, 1945, 45–192.

Plan de Constitución Política de la Nación Mexicana. Mexico City, 1823.

Discurso del Dr. Servando Teresa de Mier sobre la Encíclica del Papa León XII. Mexico City, 1825.

Vida, aventuras, escritos y viajes del Dr. Servando Teresa de Mier. Ed. Manuel Payno. Mexico City: Imprenta Abadiano, 1856.

Biografía del Benemérito Mexicano D. Servando Teresa de Mier Noriega y Guerra. Comp. José Eleuterio González [1876]. Monterrey: Tipografía del Gobierno, 1895.

Memorias de fray Servando Teresa de Mier. Introduction by Alfonso Reyes. Madrid: Ediciones América, Colección Ayacucho, c. 1917.

El pensamiento del Padre Mier. Ed. Alessio Robles. Mexico City: Biblioteca Enciclopédica Popular, 1944.

Escritos y Memorias. Ed. Edmundo O'Gorman. Mexico City: UNAM, 1945.

Memorias, 2 vols. Ed. Antonio Castro Leal. Mexico City: Porrúa, 1946; reprint, 1988.

Memorias. Oscar Rodríguez Ortiz, ed. Caracas: Ayacucho, 1988.

Causas formadas al doctor fray Servando Teresa de Mier. In *Colección de documentos para la historia de la guerra de independencia de México.* J. E. Hernández y Dávalos, comp. Mexico City: El Sistema Postal, 1879, vol. VI.

Diez Cartas hoy inéditas de fray Servando Teresa de Mier. Monterrey: Impresos Modernos, 1940.

Escritos Inéditos de Fray Servando Teresa de Mier. Ed. J. M. Miguel Vergés and Hugo Díaz-Thomé, introducción, selección y notas. Mexico City: El Colegio de México, 1944.

Idearo político. Ed. Edmundo O'Gorman, Caracas: Biblioteca Ayacucho, 1978.

El heterodoxo guadalupano. Obras completas. Ed. Edmundo O'Gorman. Mexico City: UNAM, 1981.

2. FURTHER READINGS

Arenas, Reinaldo. *El mundo alucinante.* Barcelona: Montesinos, 1981.

Benson, Nettie Lee, ed. *Mexico and the Spanish Cortes, 1810–1822: Eight Essays.* Austin & London: Institute of Latin American Studies, University of Texas Press, 1966.

Bergoend, Bernardo. *La nacionalidad mexicana y la Virgen de la Guadalupe.* Mexico City: Jus, 1968.

Brading, David. *The First America: The Spanish Monarchy, Creole Patriots and the Liberal State, 1492–1867.* Cambridge: Cambridge University Press, 1991.

————. *Miners and Merchants in Bourbon Mexico, 1763–1810*. Cambridge: Cambridge University Press, 1971.

————. *Prophecy and Myth in Mexican History*. Cambridge: Cambridge University Press, 1994. Also published as *Mito y profecía en la historia de México*. Trans. Tomás Segovia. Mexico City: Vuelta, 1988.[?? 327]

Carr, Raymond. *Spain 1808–1939*. London: Oxford University Press, 1966, reprinted 1975.

Cassirer, Ernst. *The Philosophy of the Enlightenment*. Trans. Fritz C. A. Koelln and James P. Pettegrove. Princeton: Princeton University Press, 1951.

Chiaramonte, José Carlos, ed. *Pensamiento de la Illustración: Economía y sociedad iberoamericanas en el siglo XVIII*. Caracas: Biblioteca Ayacucho, 1979.

Chukwudi Eze, Emmanuel, ed. *Race and the Enlightenment: A Reader*. Cambridge: Blackwell, 1997.

Fisher, Lillian Estelle. *The Background of the Revolution for Mexican Independence*. New York: Russell & Russell, 1934.

Gay, Peter. *The Enlightenment: An Interpretation*. 2 vols. New York: Norton, 1969.

Gerbi, Antonello. *La disputa del Nuevo Mundo: Historia de una polémica 1750–1900* [1955].Trans. Antonio Alatorre. Mexico City: Fondo de Cultura Económica, 2d ed., 1982.

Gibson, Charles. *The Aztecs Under Spanish Rule: A History of the Indians of the Valley of Mexico, 1519–1810*. Stanford: Stanford University Press, 1964.

Glendinning, Nigel. *A Literary History of Spain: The Eighteenth Century*. London: Ernest Benn; New York: Barnes & Noble, 1972.

Hargreaves-Mawdesley, W. N. *Eighteenth-Century Spain 1700–1788: A Political, Diplomatic and Institutional History*. London: MacMillan, 1979.

Jara, René, and Nicholas Spadaccini, eds. *1492–1992: Re/Discovering Colonial Writing*. Minneapolis: The Prisma Institute, 1989.

Ladd, Doris M. *The Mexican Nobility at Independence 1780–1825*. Austin: Institute of Latin American Studies, The University of Texas at Austin, 1976.

Lafaye, Jacques. *Quetazalcóatl and Guadalupe: The Formation of Mexican National Consciousness 1531–1813*. Trans. Benjamin Keen, Chicago and London: The University of Chicago Press, 1976.

————. *Mesías, cruzadas, utopías: El judeo-cristianismo en las sociedades ibéricas*. Trans. Juan José Utrilla. Mexico City: Fondo de Cultura, 1984.

Leonard, Irving A. *Los libros del conquistador*. Trans. Mario Monteforte Toledo. Mexico City: Fondo de Cultura Económica, 2d ed., 1979.

Lezama Lima, José. "El romanticismo y el hecho americano." In *La expresión americana*. Madrid: Alianza, 1969, 83–118.

Lombardi, John V. *The Political Ideology of Fray Servando Teresa de Mier, Propagandist for Independence*. Cuernavaca: Sondeos n. 25, 1968.

Lynch, John, ed. *Latin American Revolutions 1808–1826*. Norman and London: University of Oklahoma Press, 1973.

Martínez, Tomás Eloy, ed. Historia de la conquista y Poblacion de Venezuela de José de Oviedo y Baños. Preliminary study by T. E. Martínez and Susana Rotker. Caracas, Biblioteca Ayacucho, 175, 1992, ix–xlvii.

Miranda, José. *Vida colonial y albores de la independencia.* Mexico City: Sep-Setentas, 1972.

Morales, Francisco. *Clero y política en México (1764–1834): Algunas ideas sobre la autoridad, la independencia y la reforma eclesiástica.* Mexico City: Sep–Setentas, 1975.

Menéndez Pelayo, Marcelino. *Historia de los heterodoxos españoles* 7 vols., Buenos Aires: Espasa Calpe, 1951.

Navarro González, B. *Cultura mexicana moderna en el siglo XVIII.* Mexico City: UNAM, 1964.

Reyes, Alfonso. "Fray Servando Teresa de Mier." In *Visión de Anáhuac y otros ensayos.* Mexico City: Fondo de Cultura Económica, 1983.

Ricaurte Soler. *Idea y cuestión nacional latinoamericanas: De la independencia a la emergencia del imperialismo.* Mexico City: Siglo XXI, 1980.

Rink, Paul. *Warrior Priests and Tyrant Kings: The Beginnings of Mexican Independence.* New York: Doubleday, 1976.

Rodríguez Monegal, Emir, ed. *The Borzoi Anthology of Latin American Literature.* Vol. 1. New York: Knopf, 1977.

Rodríguez O., Jaime E., ed. *The Independence of Mexico and the Creation of the New Nation.* Latin American Center Publications, University of California, Los Angeles; Mexico/Chicano Program, University of California, Irvine, 1989.

Romero, José Luis, ed. and Prologue. *Pensamiento político de la emancipación (1790–1825),* 2 vols. Caracas: Biblioteca Ayacucho, 1977.

Ross, Kathleen. "A Natural History of the Old World: the *Memorias* of Fray Servando Teresa de Mier." *Revista de Estudios Hispánicos* XXIII: 3 (October 1989): 87–100.

Saint-Amand, Pierre. *The Laws of Hostility: Politics, Violence, and the Enlightenment.* Foreword by Chantal Mouffe. Trans. Jennifer Curtiss Gage. Minneapolis: University of Minnesota Press, 1996.

Scott, H. M., ed. *Enlightened Absolutism. Reform and Reforms in Later Eighteenth-Century Europe.* Ann Arbor: University of Michigan Press, 1990.

Subirats, Eduardo. *La ilustracion insuficiente.* Madrid: Taurus, 1981.

Tannenbaum, Frank. *Peace by Revolution: An Interpretation of Mexico.* New York: Columbia University Press, 1933.

Tietz, Manfred. "La visión de América y de la conquista en la España del siglo XVIII." In *El precio de la 'invención' de América.* Ed. Reyes Mate and Fridrich Niewöhner. Barcelona: Anthropos, 1992, 219–34.

Todorov, Tzvetan. *La conquista de América: El problema del otro.* Trans. Flora Botton Burlá. Mexico City: Siglo XXI, 3d ed., 1991.

Torre Villar, Ernesto de la and Ramiro Navarro de Anda, comp. *Testimonios históricos guadalupanos.* Mexico City: Fondo de Cultura Económica, 1982.

Whitaker, Arthur Preston. *Latin America and the Enlightenment* [1942]. Ithaca: Cornell University Press, 1967.

Zavala, Silvio. *La filosofía política en la conquista de América.* Mexico City: Fondo de Cultura Económica, 1947.